Thinking Socratically

Sharon Schwarze

Harvey Lape

Prentice Hall
Upper Saddle River, New Jersey 07458

Library of Congress Cataloging-in-Publication Data

Schwarze, Sharon
    Thinking Socratically / by Sharon Schwarze, Harvey Lape.
        p.   cm.
    Includes index.
    ISBN 0-13-438631-0
    1. Critical Thinking. 2. Reasoning. 3. Socrates. I. Lape.
Harvey. II. Title.
BC177.S36 1997
160--dc20

95-26514
CIP

Editorial/production supervision: *Harriet Tellem*
Acquisitions editor: *Angela Stone*
Manufacturing buyer: *Lynn Pearlman*
Cover design: *Bruce Kenselaar*

This book was set in 10/12 Baskerville by *Oakland Publishing Services, Inc.*,
and was printed and bound by *Courier Companies, Inc.* The cover was printed
by *Phoenix Color Corp.*

Grateful acknowledgment is made to the copyright holders on pages xv–xvii
which are hereby made part of this copyright page.

© 1997 by Prentice-Hall Inc.
Simon & Schuster/A Viacom Company
Upper Saddle River, NJ 07458

ISBN 0-13-438631-0

Prentice-Hall International (UK) Limited, *London*
Prentice-Hall of Australia Pty. Limited, *Sydney*
Prentice-Hall Canada Inc., *Toronto*
Prentice-Hall Hispanoamericana, S.A., *Mexico*
Prentice-Hall of India Private Limited, *New Delhi*
Prentice-Hall of Japan, Inc., *Tokyo*
Simon & Schuster Asia Pte. Ltd., *Singapore*
Editora Prentice-Hall do Brasil, Ltda., *Rio de Janeiro*

Dedication

To Betty Flower
Teacher, Friend
Scholar of American Pragmatism.

Contents

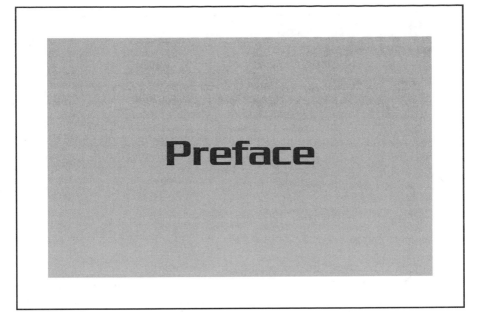

Preface

Two things strike anyone who encounters the ancient Greek philosopher Socrates. First, he is willing to question all assumptions underlying any discussion—even his own. Second, he is determined to make sense of whatever is being discussed. It is this commitment to open rational dialogue which we call **thinking Socratically**. The Socratic critical thinker is someone willing to test her assumptions in open rational discourse, who does not blindly accept the dictates of authority or dismiss ideas as "mere opinions." The Socratic thinker also pays attention to the logic of ideas in context and is interested in more than the acquisition of a few isolated logical tricks. The goal of this text is to supply the skills and contexts likely to foster this kind of Socratic thinking.

Thinking Socratically differs from other critical thinking texts in that it is not simply a book on informal logic or a watered-down version of a formal logic text. It is a book which asks you, the reader, to think critically about specific, "real life" issues which are significant and important in your everyday life. By reading and thinking about these issues, you will gain insight into how to distinguish warranted beliefs from unwarranted beliefs and acquire some specific tools which can be helpful in making this distinction. Our goal is to help you form lifelong habits of critical thinking, not simply to pass on a few course-related skills that are soon forgotten.

We believe a rational person is someone who is committed to rational action and who wants to make the best decisions she can make. The key to making the best decision—on this Socratic model—is to engage in open dialogue which is democratic and pragmatic. This is a dialogue which considers alternative points of view and which is directed toward the end or goal of human well-being and happiness. Our belief in the worth of the open dialogue informs the style of the discussions in each chapter, which are intended as an informal dialogue with you, our reader.

This philosophical approach to critical thinking—which makes *Thinking Socratically* unique—stresses important concepts generally ignored in most critical thinking texts. One of these is the concept of **background knowledge**. Background knowledge plays a very important and increasingly acknowledged role in rational or critical thinking. Most everyday reasoning consists of judgments of the likelihood or probability of what will happen or what did happen. The larger the store of background knowledge one brings to this kind of reasoning, the better decisions one can make. The background knowledge we have forms a web of connected beliefs, some more important than others. This **web of belief** figures prominently in our judgments of whether a statement is warranted or not warranted. *Thinking Socratically* will encourage you to examine your web of belief and to weed out unwarranted assumptions from that web.

The logical techniques helpful to good critical thinking are also included in *Thinking Socratically*, but they are always discussed in context. You will see that these techniques can be very useful, but you will also realize that they have limitations. When all is said and done, you will see that there is no such thing as absolute proof or absolute certainty. Decisions have to be made on less than perfect knowledge. In this sense all decisions are pragmatic.

Another distinctive feature of *Thinking Socratically* is that it treats rational thinking and decision making in a variety of human contexts: the everyday, the scientific, and the moral. The fundamental concepts of rationality—the open-ended dialogue and an expanding store of background knowledge—are shown to characterize all three of these human reasoning contexts. These contexts are presented through an entertaining collection of readings which come from a variety of sources: short stories, newspaper articles, magazine articles, novels, and philosophy. The discussion always follows the readings and develops one or more fundamental themes of critical thinking. The reader develops her own appreciation of the web of belief that informs human reasoning. She begins to see critical thinking as a way of looking at the world and not just a set of techniques to apply in time of doubt or confusion. *Thinking Socratically*, if it is successful, becomes the way of thinking, not a book title or a class on critical thinking.

Acknowledgments

The contributions of several people to this project deserve special recognition. First, thanks go to my husband, Bill, who offered to proofread an early draft and fell asleep after five pages; and to my daughters, Gretchen and Kristen, whose departures for higher education freed up my time as well as a better work space. Thanks also to my friend Joyce Davenport, who persuaded me not to take one more administrative job at Cabrini until this book was finished; to friend and colleague Joe Romano, who is always generous in his support; and thanks especially to my collaborator, peripatetic philosopher Harvey Lape who, like Socrates, is always willing to talk philosophy and whose philosophical insight guides much of this book.

S.S.

We wish to thank the following reviewers: Keith Cooper, Pacific Lutheran University; Dean J. Nelson, Dutchess Community College; Michael Vengrin, Redford University; Kenneth Stern, State University of N.Y. at Albany; C. J. Cassini, Barry University; and James Conroy Doig, Clayton State College.

S.S. and H.L.

Credits

201 Landon to Win (articles). From *The Literacy Digest.* Volume 122. No. 9, August 29, 1936; No. 11, September 12, 1936; No. 19, October 31, 1936.

238 From *Mathematics and the Search for Knowledge* by Morris Kline. Copyright © 1985 by Oxford University Press, Inc. Reprinted by permission.

265 "Fleiss, Freud and Biorhythm" by Martin Gardner. From *Mathematical Carnival.* Copyright © Martin Gardner 1965, 1966, 1967, 1968, 1975. Reprinted by permission.

279 "Love Is A Fallacy" from *THE MANY LOVES OF DOBIE GILLIS* by Max Shulman. Copyright © 1951, © renewed 1979 by Max Shulman. Reprinted by permission of Harold Matson Company, Inc.

288 "The Sleaze Merchants Attack." Copyright © The Suburban and Wayne Times, 1986

304 From *THE BROTHERS KARAMAZOV* (an excerpt) by Fyodor Dostoevsky. A Norton Critical Edition, The Constance Garnett Translation. Revised by Ralph E. Matlaw. Edited by Ralph E. Matlaw. Reprinted by permission of W.W. Norton & Company, Inc. Copyright © 1976 by W.W. Norton & Company, Inc.

320 Immanuel Kant, *GROUNDING FOR THE METAPHYSICS OF MORALS,* (an excerpt) translated by J.W. Ellington, 1993, HACKETT Publishing Co., Inc. © All Rights Reserved.

324 "Existentialism Is a Humanism" (an excerpt) by Jean-Paul Sartre. From *ESSAYS IN EXISTENTIALISM.* Edited by Wade Baskin. Copyright © 1965 by Philosophical Library, Inc. Published by arrangement with Carol Publishing Group.

350 "PRELUDE" Pages 1–12 from *LEST INNOCENT BLOOD BE SHED* by Philip Hallie. Copyright © 1979 by Philip Hallie. Reprinted by permission of HarperCollins Publishers, Inc.

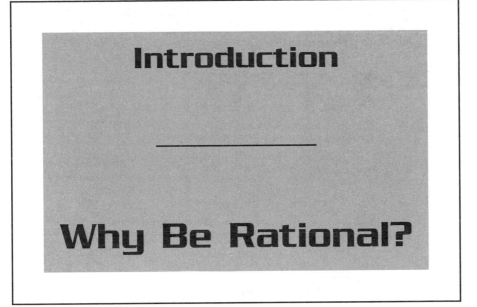

Introduction

Why Be Rational?

Before we talk about the skills that a rational person uses in good critical thinking, we should consider why it is important to be rational and a good critical thinker. Why should a person try to be "logical" or "reasonable"? What about feelings, emotions, affairs of the heart? Isn't it better sometimes just to go with your "gut feelings"? Furthermore, isn't the goal of being rational just a cultural idea, a product of our Western cultural heritage?

These are tough questions. In fact, they get tougher the more you think about them. For example, the more "rational" you try to be, the more conscious you will become of the limits of reason. It seems that we can reason on forever and never come to a conclusion or we can begin reasoning from some claim for which we give no reasons. Neither alternative is very satisfactory. The one is endless and the other is arbitrary. The "Big Bang" theory about the origins of the universe discussed by Lewis Thomas which you will read about in Chapter 1 is a good example of this. If you want to know what there was in the universe before the big bang, scientists admit that they cannot say. The laws of physics as we know them began with the big bang. One is left to wonder: If reason is so limited, then why try so hard to be rational?

This philosophical puzzle led the Danish philosopher Kierkegaard to claim that all choices rest ultimately on "a leap of faith." What Kierkegaard meant by this is that if all reasoning begins from some initial claim, then it would seem that no choice is wholly rational for each choice rests on an initial assumption which is not itself justified. Each choice is, therefore, taken on "faith." Although Kierkegaard concluded from this that people should choose a life of faith, not reason, we disagree. In this introduction we will try to show why we disagree. While Kierkegaard's point about the limits of reason is well taken, it does not follow from these limitations that people should choose a life of faith, not reason. People are still usually better off **trying to be reasonable**.

There are three readings in this introduction. After you have read them, you will be asked to reflect on them. Some, but certainly not all, of the important ideas for critical thinking found in the readings will then be discussed in the dialogue which follows. The format of this Introduction will characterize future chapters as well. You will first be asked to read, think, and reflect–to do your own critical thinking—before there is any discussion of the ideas in the readings.

So let us begin! The first reading of this Introduction is a short story written by the Yiddish story teller Isaac Bashevis Singer. As you read it, notice how Singer captures a complex issue in a very simple story about a boy and his parents. The second reading is a newspaper account of two South American shamans' efforts to save a dying naturalist. A shaman is a tribal wise man or medicine man. This reading will likely raise your curiosity but may raise more questions than answers.

The third reading is a very famous dialogue called *Euthyphro*, written by the fourth century B.C. Athenian philosopher Plato. Socrates and Euthyphro are discussing what they think piety is and who is a pious person. This is a very important question because Socrates is on his way into court where he has been accused of impiety, a charge which will eventually lead to his death. If you think the word *piety* sounds old-fashioned, substitute the word *good* in its place. As you read this dialogue, think about the characters in the dialogue, not just the words. What kind of person is Socrates? What kind of person is Euthyphro? Do you know anybody like Euthyphro?

Why the Geese Shrieked

Isaac Bashevis Singer

In our home there was always talk about spirits of the dead that possess the bodies of the living, souls reincarnated as animals, houses inhabited by hobgoblins, cellars haunted by demons. My father spoke of these things, first of all because he was interested in them, and second because in a big city children so easily go astray. They go everywhere, see everything, read nonreligious books. It is necessary to remind them from time to time that there are still mysterious forces at work in the world.

One day, when I was about eight, he told us a story found in one of the holy books. If I am not mistaken, the author of that book is Rabbi Eliyahu Graidiker, or one of the other Graidiker sages. The story was about a girl possessed by four demons. It was said that they could actually be seen crawling around in her intestines, blowing up her belly, wandering from one part of her body to another, slithering into her legs. The Rabbi of Graidik had exorcised the evil spirits with the blowing of the ram's horn, with incantations, and the incense of magic herbs.

When my brother Joshua questioned these things, my father became very excited. He argued: "Was then the great Rabbi of Graidik, God forbid, a liar? Are all the rabbis, saints, and sages deceivers, while only atheists speak the truth? Woe is us! How can one be so blind?"

Suddenly the door opened, and a woman entered. She was carrying a basket with two geese in it. The woman looked frightened. Her matron's wig was tilted to one side. She smiled nervously.

Father never looked at strange women, because it is forbidden by Jewish law, but Mother and we children saw immediately that something had greatly upset our unexpected visitor.

"What is it?" Father asked, at the same time turning his back so as not to look upon her.

"Rabbi, I have a very unusual problem."

"What is it?"

"It's about these geese."

"What's the matter with them?"

"Dear Rabbi, the geese were slaughtered properly. Then I cut off their heads. I took out the intestines, the livers, all the other organs, but the geese keep shrieking in such a sorrowful voice . . ."

From _A Day of Pleasure_ (1963)

Upon hearing these words, my father turned pale. A dreadful fear befell me, too. But my mother came from a family of rationalists and was by nature a skeptic.

"Slaughtered geese don't shriek," she said.

"You will hear for yourself," replied the woman.

She took one of the geese and placed it on the table. Then she took out the second goose. The geese were headless, disemboweled—in short, ordinary dead geese.

A smile appeared on my mother's lips. "And *these* geese shriek?"

"You will soon hear."

The woman took one goose and hurled it against the other. At once a shriek was heard. It is not easy to describe that sound. It was like the cackling of a goose, but in such a high, eerie pitch, with such groaning and quaking, that my limbs grew cold. I could actually feel the hairs of my earlocks pricking me. I wanted to run from the room. But where would I run? My throat constricted with fear. Then I, too, shrieked and clung to my mother's skirt, like a child of three.

Father forgot that one must avert one's eyes from a woman. He ran to the table. He was no less frightened than I was. His red beard trembled. In his blue eyes could be seen a mixture of fear and vindication. For my father this was a sign that not only to the Rabbi of Graidik, but to him too, omens were sent from heaven. But perhaps this was a sign from the Evil One, from Satan himself?

"What do you say now?" asked the woman.

My mother was no longer smiling. In her eyes there was something like sadness, and also anger.

"I cannot understand what is going on here," she said, with a certain resentment.

"Do you want to hear it again?"

Again the woman threw one goose against the other. And again the dead geese gave forth an uncanny shriek—the shriek of dumb creatures slain by the slaughterer's knife who yet retain a living force; who still have a reckoning to make with the living, an injustice to avenge. A chill crept over me. I felt as though someone had struck me with all his might.

My father's voice became hoarse. It was broken as though by sobs. "Well, can anyone still doubt that there *is* a Creator?" he asked.

"Rabbi, what shall I do and where shall I go?" The woman began to croon in a mournful singsong. "What has befallen me? Woe is me! What shall I do with them? Perhaps I should run to one of the Wonder Rabbis? Perhaps they were not slaughtered properly? I am afraid to take them home. I wanted to prepare them for the Sabbath meal, and now, such a calamity! Holy Rabbi, what shall I do? Must I throw them out? Someone said they must be wrapped in shrouds and buried in a grave. I am a poor woman. Two geese! They cost me a fortune!"

Father did not know what to answer. He glanced at his bookcase. If there was an answer anywhere, it must be there.

Suddenly he looked angrily at my mother. "And what do you say now, eh?"

Mother's face was growing sullen, smaller, sharper. In her eyes could be seen indignation and also something like shame.

"I want to hear it again." Her words were half pleading, half commanding.

The woman hurled the geese against each other for the third time, and for the third time the shrieks were heard. It occurred to me that such must have been the voice of the sacrificial heifer.

"Woe, woe, and still they blaspheme . . . It is written that the wicked do not repent even at the very gates of hell." Father had again begun to speak. "They behold the truth with their own eyes, and they continue to deny their Maker. They are dragged into the bottomless pit and they maintain that all is nature, or accident . . ."

He looked at Mother as if to say: You take after _them_.

For a long time there was silence. Then the woman asked, "Well, did I just imagine it?"

Suddenly my mother laughed. There was something in her laughter that made us all tremble. I knew, by some sixth sense, that Mother was preparing to end the mighty drama being enacted before our eyes.

"Did you remove the windpipes?" my mother asked.

"The windpipes? No . . ."

"Take them out," said my mother, "and the geese will stop shrieking."

My father became angry. "What are you babbling? What has this got to do with windpipes?"

Mother took hold of one of the geese, pushed her slender finger inside the body, and with all her might pulled out the thin tube that led from the neck to the lungs. Then she took the other goose and removed its windpipe also. I stood trembling, aghast at my mother's courage. Her hands had become bloodied. On her face could be seen the wrath of the rationalist whom someone has tried to frighten in broad daylight.

Father's face turned white, calm, a little disappointed. He knew what had happened here: logic, cold logic, was again tearing down faith, mocking it, holding it up to ridicule and scorn.

"Now, if you please, take one goose and hurl it against the other!" commanded my mother.

Everything hung in the balance. If the geese shrieked, Mother would have lost all: her rationalist's daring, her skepticism, which she had inherited from her intellectual father. And I? Although I was afraid, I prayed inwardly that the geese _would_ shriek, shriek so loud that people in the street would hear and come running.

But, alas, the geese were silent, silent as only two dead geese without windpipes can be.

"Bring me a towel!" Mother turned to me.

I ran to get the towel. There were tears in my eyes. Mother wiped her hands on the towel like a surgeon after a difficult operation.

"That's all it was!" she announced victoriously.

"Rabbi, what do you say?" asked the woman.

Father began to cough, to mumble. He fanned himself with his skullcap.

"I have never before heard of such a thing," he said at last.

"Nor have I," echoed the woman.

"Nor have I," said my mother. "But there is always an explanation. Dead geese don't shriek."

"Can I go home now and cook them?" asked the woman.

"Go home and cook them for the Sabbath." Mother pronounced the decision. "Don't be afraid. They won't make a sound in your pot."

"What do you say, Rabbi?"

"Hmm . . . they are kosher," murmured Father. "They can be eaten." He was not really convinced, but now he could not pronounce the geese unclean.

Mother went back to the kitchen. I remained with my father. Suddenly he began to speak to me as though I were an adult. "Your mother takes after your grandfather, the Rabbi of Bilgoray. He is a great scholar, but a cold-blooded rationalist. People warned me before our betrothal . . ."

And then Father threw up his hands, as if to say: It is too late now to call off the wedding.

The Shaman and the Dying Scientist: A Brazilian Tale

ALAN RIDING

The story began with a front-page report Jan. 12 in the Rio de Janeiro daily Jornal do Brasil that carried the headline, "Nature condemns a man who protected her." It recounted how Mr. Ruschi was dying as a result of having touched poisonous Dendrobates toads while carrying out research in the Amapá region of the Amazon in 1975.

New York Times, February 4, 1986

THE POWER OF A POET

Other papers immediately caught onto the story, but it was three days later that President José Sarney was reportedly moved by a newspaper column written by a prominent Brazilian poet, Alfonso Romano de Sant'Anna. The column took its title from a novel by the Colombian Nobel laureate, Gabriel García Márquez, "Chronicle of a Death Foretold."

In it, the poet appealed to the President to order a search for an antidote not only in the United States and the Soviet Union but also among the Indian tribes of the Xingu National Park. "Brazil cannot afford to lose a man of Ruschi's stature just because some shameless toads declared him to be their enemy," Mr. Sant'Anna wrote.

Mr. Sarney immediately told his Interior Minister, Ronaldo Costa Couto, to contact Raoni, the middle-aged cacique, or chief, of the 4,000-strong Txucarramae tribe, who is also recognized as a spokesman for Brazil's 180,000 surviving Indians. And a few days later, an unusual sight in his feathered headdress and with the huge protruding lower lip that members of his tribe develop through wearing a disk, Raoni was received by the President in his office in Brasilia.

Raoni told Mr. Sarney that he had dreamed of Mr. Ruschi struggling with toads and, after looking at photographs of the naturalist, he proclaimed: "He already has the face of a toad. He has become a toad. We have to take the toad from inside or he will soon die."

THE TREATMENT BEGINS

A Brazilian Air Force plane flew to the Xingu, 500 miles northwest of Brasilia, to collect herbs as well as Sapaim, a shaman from the nearby Caimura tribe. And, in the middle of last week, in the presence of newspaper reporters and television crews, Raoni and Sapaim met Mr. Ruschi in Rio de Janeiro.

The naturalist recounted that for more than a year he had suffered intense pain, nausea, fevers and nose bleeding and could rarely sleep for more than two or three hours at a stretch. Further, reporters noted, he was barely able to climb a short stairway and his eyes and mouth looked swollen and red.

The treatment, which was witnessed by a reporter from Jornal do Brasil and by Mr. Ruschi's wife, Marilande, first involved Raoni and Sapaim smoking 10-inch hallucinogenic herbal "cigars" and exhaling over the patient while chanting.

Raoni then massaged Mr. Ruschi's body and appeared to extract a green strong-smelling pasty substance that he identified as the toad poison.

While blowing smoke, the Indian chief rubbed it between his palms and it disappeared, the reporter said. Finally, the naturalist took a herbal bath.

HE IS PRONOUNCED CURED

For three days, with the entire nation's attention focused on the house where the treatment was taking place, the ritual was repeated, with Mr. Ruschi claiming that he was feeling steadily better. By last Saturday, Raoni said all the poison had been removed and Mr. Ruschi was pronounced cured.

Before completing the ritual, though, Raoni indicated that tradition required he be given a present by the person who had called on him—in this case, President Sarney. The present could be a clay pot or, he added more pointedly, land for the Indians. Raoni and Sapaim then went on a shopping spree in Rio de Janeiro and, with Interior Ministry officials paying the bills, acquired $800 worth of beads and trinkets.

The final act will take place in Brasilia when President Sarney presents his gift to Raoni in the presence of Mr. Ruschi, with all three expected to use the occasion to appeal for greater preservation of the natural and native patrimony of this vast land. Then only an epilogue will still have to be written, describing whether Mr. Ruschi was indeed permanently cured.

Not surprisingly, some skepticism has already been heard from physicians. Wallace Magalhães, who treated Mr. Ruschi last year, said his liver was poisoned from excessive self-medication taken to combat chronic malaria. Haity Moustatche, a scientist at the Fundação Oswaldo Cruz medical research center, said, "We have to determine whether, in all the ritual, there was also some treatment."

But, for the moment at least, with patient and shaman as well as public and press delighted with the present happy ending, Mr. Ruschi seemed to offer the best closing words for the fairy tale. He said that, when he died, he wished to be buried in the rain forest near his home. "And I have the hope," he added, "that the hummingbirds will lead me to the Kingdom of God."

Euthyphro

PLATO

CHARACTERS

SOCRATES

EUTHYPHRO

SCENE—The Hall of the King

EUTHYPHRO. What in the world are you doing here in the king's hall,[1] Socrates? Why have you left your haunts in the Lyceum? You surely cannot have a suit before him, as I have.

SOCRATES. The Athenians, Euthyphro, call it an indictment, not a suit.

EUTH. What? Do you mean that someone is prosecuting you? I cannot believe that you are prosecuting anyone yourself.

SOCR. Certainly I am not.

EUTH. Then is someone prosecuting you?

SOCR. Yes.

EUTH. Who is he?

SOCR. I scarcely know him myself, Euthyphro; I think he must be some unknown young man. His name, however, is Meletus, and his district Pitthis, if you can call to mind any Meletus of that district—a hook-nosed man with lanky hair and rather a scanty beard.

EUTH. I don't know him, Socrates. But tell me, what is he prosecuting you for?

SOCR. What for? Not on trivial grounds, I think. It is no small thing for so young a man to have formed an opinion on such an important matter. For he, he says, knows how the young are corrupted, and who are their corrupters. He must be a wise man who, observing my ignorance, is going to accuse me to the state, as his mother, of corrupting his friends. I think that he is the only one who begins at the right point in his political reforms; for his first care is to make the young men as good as possible, just as a good farmer will take care

---

[1]The anachronistic title "king" was retained by the magistrate who had jurisdiction over crimes affecting the state religion–Ed.

of his young plants first, and, after he has done that, of the others. And so Meletus, I suppose, is first clearing us away who, as he says, corrupt the young men growing up; and then, when he has done that, of course he will turn his attention to the older men, and so become a very great public benefactor. Indeed, that is only what you would expect when he goes to work in this way.

EUTH. I hope it may be so, Socrates, but I fear the opposite. It seems to me that in trying to injure you, he is really setting to work by striking a blow at the foundation of the state. But how, tell me, does he say that you corrupt the youth?

SOCR. In a way which sounds absurd at first, my friend. He says that I am a maker of gods; and so he is prosecuting me, he says, for inventing new gods and for not believing in the old ones.

EUTH. I understand, Socrates. It is because you say that you always have a divine guide. So he is prosecuting you for introducing religious reforms; and he is going into court to arouse prejudice against you, knowing that the multitude are easily prejudiced about such matters. Why, they laugh even at me, as if I were out of my mind, when I talk about divine things in the assembly and tell them what is going to happen; and yet I have never foretold anything which has not come true. But they are resentful of all people like us. We must not worry about them; we must meet them boldly.

SOCR. My dear Euthyphro, their ridicule is not a very serious matter. The Athenians, it seems to me, may think a man to be clever without paying him much attention, so long as they do not think that he teaches his wisdom to others. But as soon as they think that he makes other people clever, they get angry, whether it be from resentment, as you say, or for some other reason.

EUTH. I am not very anxious to test their attitude toward me in this matter.

SOCR. No, perhaps they think that you are reserved, and that you are not anxious to teach your wisdom to others. But I fear that they may think that I am; for my love of men makes me talk to everyone whom I meet quite freely and unreservedly, and without payment. Indeed, if I could I would gladly pay people myself to listen to me. If then, as I said just now, they were only going to laugh at me, as you say they do at you, it would not be at all an unpleasant way of spending the day—to spend it in court, joking and laughing. But if they are going to be in earnest, then only prophets like you can tell where the matter will end.

EUTH. Well, Socrates, I dare say that nothing will come of it. Very likely you will be successful in your trial, and I think that I shall be in mine.

SOCR. And what is this suit of yours, Euthyphro? Are you suing, or being sued?

EUTH. I am suing.

SOCR. Whom?

EUTH. A man whom people think I must be mad to prosecute.

SOCR. What? Has he wings to fly away with?

EUTH. He is far enough from flying; he is a very old man

SOCR. Who is he?

EUTH. He is my father.

SOCR. Your father, my good man?

EUTH. He is indeed.

SOCR. What are you prosecuting him for? What is the accusation?

EUTH. Murder, Socrates.

SOCR. Good heavens, Euthyphro! Surely the multitude are ignorant of what is right. I take it that it is not everyone who could rightly do what you are doing; only a man who was already well advanced in wisdom.

EUTH. That is quite true, Socrates.

SOCR. Was the man whom your father killed a relative of yours? But, of course, he was. You would never have prosecuted your father for the murder of a stranger?

EUTH. You amuse me, Socrates. What difference does it make whether the murdered man were a relative or a stranger? The only question that you have to ask is, did the murderer kill justly or not? If justly, you must let him alone; if unjustly, you must indict him for murder, even though he share your hearth and sit at your table. The pollution is the same if you associate with such a man, knowing what he has done, without purifying yourself, and him too, by bringing him to justice. In the present case the murdered man was a poor laborer of mine, who worked for us on our farm in Naxos. While drunk he got angry with one of our slaves and killed him. My father therefore bound the man hand and foot and threw him into a ditch, while he sent to Athens to ask the priest what he should do. While the messenger was gone, he entirely neglected the man, thinking that he was a murderer, and that it would be no great matter, even if he were to die. And that was exactly what happened; hunger and cold and his bonds killed him before the messenger returned. And now my father and the rest of my family are indignant with me because I am prosecuting my father for the murder of this murderer. They assert that he did not kill the man at all; and they say that, even if he had killed him over and over again, the man himself was a murderer, and that I ought not to concern myself about such a person because it is impious for a son to prosecute his father for murder. So little, Socrates, do they know the divine law of piety and impiety.

SOCR. And do you mean to say, Euthyphro, that you think that you understand divine things and piety and impiety so accurately that, in such a case as you have stated, you can bring your father to justice without fear that you yourself may be doing something impious?

EUTH. If I did not understand all these matters accurately, Socrates, I should not be worth much—Euthyphro would not be any better than other men.

SOCR. Then, my dear Euthyphro, I cannot do better than become your pupil and challenge Meletus on this very point before the trial begins. I should say that I had always thought it very important to have knowledge about divine things; and that now, when he says that I offend by speaking carelessly about them, and by introducing reforms, I have become your pupil. And I should say, "Meletus, if you acknowledge Euthyphro to be wise in these matters and to hold the correct belief, then think the same of me and do not put me on trial; but if you do not, then bring a suit, not against me, but against my master, for corrupting his elders—namely, myself whom he corrupts by his teaching, and his own father whom he corrupts by admonishing and punishing him." And if I did not succeed in persuading him to release me from the suit or to indict you in my place, then I could repeat my challenge in court.

EUTH. Yes, by Zeus! Socrates, I think I should find out his weak points if he were to try to indict me. I should have a good deal to say about him in court long before I spoke about myself.

SOCR. Yes, my dear friend, and knowing this I am anxious to become your pupil. I see that Meletus here, and others too, seem not to notice you at all, but he sees through me without difficulty and at once prosecutes me for impiety. Now, therefore, please explain to me what you were so confident just now that you knew. Tell me what are righteousness and sacrilege with respect to murder and everything else. I suppose that piety is the same in all actions, and that impiety is always the opposite of piety, and retains its identity, and that, as impiety, it always has the same character, which will be found in whatever is impious.

EUTH. Certainly, Socrates, I suppose so.

SOCR. Tell me, then, what is piety and what is impiety?

EUTH. Well, then, I say that piety means prosecuting the unjust individual who has committed murder or sacrilege, or any other such crime, as I am doing now, whether he is your father or your mother or whoever he is; and I say that impiety means not prosecuting him. And observe, Socrates, I will give you a clear proof, which I have already given to others, that it is so, and that doing right means not letting off unpunished the sacrilegious man, whosoever he may be.

Men hold Zeus to be the best and the most just of the gods; and they admit that Zeus bound his own father, Cronos, for wrongfully devouring his children; and that Cronos, in his turn, castrated his father for similar reasons. And yet these same men are incensed with me because I proceed against my father for doing wrong. So, you see, they say one thing in the case of the gods and quite another in mine.

SOCR. Is not that why I am being prosecuted, Euthyphro? I mean, because I find it hard to accept such stories people tell about the gods? I expect that I shall be found at fault because I doubt those stories. Now if you who understand all these matters so well agree in holding all those tales true, then I suppose that I must yield to your authority. What could I say when I admit myself that I know nothing about them? But tell me, in the name of friendship, do you really believe that these things have actually happened?

EUTH. Yes, and more amazing things, too, Socrates, which the multitude do not know of.

SOCR. Then you really believe that there is war among the gods, and bitter hatreds, and battles, such as the poets tell of, and which the great painters have depicted in our temples, notably in the pictures which cover the robe that is carried up to the Acropolis at the great Panathenaic festival? Are we to say that these things are true, Euthyphro?

EUTH. Yes, Socrates, and more besides. As I was saying, I will report to you many other stories about divine matters, if you like, which I am sure will astonish you when you hear them.

SOCR. I dare say. You shall report them to me at your leisure another time. At present please try to give a more definite answer to the question which I asked you just now. What I asked you, my friend, was, What is piety? and you have not explained it to me to my satisfaction. You only tell me that what you are doing now, namely, prosecuting your father for murder, is a pious act.

EUTH. Well, that is true, Socrates.

SOCR. Very likely. But many other actions are pious, are they not, Euthyphro?

EUTH. Certainly.

SOCR. Remember, then, I did not ask you to tell me one or two of all the many pious actions that there are; I want to know what is characteristic of piety which makes all pious actions pious. You said, I think, that there is one characteristic which makes all pious actions pious, and another characteristic which makes all impious actions impious. Do you not remember?

EUTH. I do.

SOCR. Well, then, explain to me what is this characteristic, that I may have it to turn to, and to use as a standard whereby to judge your actions and those of other men, and be able to say that whatever action resembles it is pious, and whatever does not, is not pious.

EUTH. Yes, I will tell you that if you wish, Socrates.

SOCR. Certainly I do.

EUTH. Well, then, what is pleasing to the gods is pious, and what is not pleasing to them is impious.

SOCR. Fine, Euthyphro. Now you have given me the answer that I wanted. Whether what you say is true, I do not know yet. But, of course, you will go on to prove that it is true.

EUTH. Certainly.

SOCR. Come, then, let us examine our statement. The things and the men that are pleasing to the gods are pious, and the things and the men that are displeasing to the gods are impious. But piety and impiety are not the same; they are as opposite as possible—was not that what we said?

EUTH. Certainly.

SOCR. And it seems the appropriate statement?

EUTH. Yes, Socrates, certainly.

SOCR. Have we not also said, Euthyphro, that there are quarrels and disagreements and hatreds among the gods?

EUTH. We have.

SOCR. But what kind of disagreement, my friend, causes hatred and anger? Let us look at the matter thus. If you and I were to disagree as to whether one number were more than another, would that make us angry and enemies? Should we not settle such a dispute at once by counting?

EUTH. Of course.

SOCR. And if we were to disagree as to the relative size of two things, we should measure them and put an end to the disagreement at once, should we not?

EUTH. Yes.

SOCR. And should we not settle a question about the relative weight of two things by weighing them?

EUTH. Of course.

SOCR. Then what is the question which would make us angry and enemies if we disagreed about it, and could not come to a settlement? Perhaps you have not an answer ready; but listen to mine. Is it not the question of the just and unjust, of the honorable and the dishonorable, of the good and the bad? Is it not questions about these matters which make you and me and everyone else quarrel, when we do quarrel, if we differ about them and can reach no satisfactory agreement?

EUTH. Yes, Socrates, it is disagreements about these matters.

SOCR. Well, Euthyphro, the gods will quarrel over these things if they quarrel at all, will they not?

EUTH. Necessarily.

SOCR. Then, my good Euthyphro, you say that some of the gods think one thing just, the others another; and that what some of them hold to be honorable or good, others hold to be dishonorable or evil. For there would not have been quarrels among them if they had not disagreed on these points, would there?

EUTH. You are right.

SOCR. And each of them loves what he thinks honorable, and good, and just; and hates the opposite, does he not?

EUTH. Certainly.

SOCR. But you say that the same action is held by some of them to be just, and by others to be unjust; and that then they dispute about it, and so quarrel and fight among themselves. Is it not so?

EUTH. Yes.

SOCR. Then the same thing is hated by the gods and loved by them; and the same thing will be displeasing and pleasing to them.

EUTH. Apparently.

SOCR. Then, according to your account, the same thing will be pious and impious.

EUTH. So it seems.

SOCR. Then, my good friend, you have not answered my question. I did not ask you to tell me what action is both pious and impious; but it seems that whatever is pleasing to the gods is also displeasing to them. And so, Euthyphro, I should not be surprised if what you are doing now in punishing your father is an action well pleasing to Zeus, but hateful to Cronos and Uranus, and acceptable to Hephaestus, but hateful to Hera; and if any of the other gods disagree about it, pleasing to some of them and displeasing to others.

EUTH. But on this point, Socrates, I think that there is no difference of opinion among the gods: they all hold that if one man kills another unjustly, he must be punished.

SOCR. What, Euthyphro? Among mankind, have you never heard disputes whether a man ought to be punished for killing another man unjustly, or for doing some other unjust deed?

EUTH. Indeed, they never cease from these disputes, especially in courts of justice. They do all manner of unjust things; and then there is nothing which they will not do and say to avoid punishment.

SOCR. Do they admit that they have done something unjust, and at the same time deny that they ought to be punished, Euthyphro?

EUTH. No, indeed, that they do not.

SOCR. Then it is not the case that there is nothing which they will not do and say. I take it, they do not dare to say or argue that they must not be punished if they have done something unjust. What they say is that they have not done anything unjust, is it not so?

EUTH. That is true.

SOCR. Then they do not disagree over the question that the unjust individual must be punished. They disagree over the question, who is unjust, and what was done and when, do they not?

EUTH. That is true.

SOCR. Well, is not exactly the same thing true of the gods if they quarrel about justice and injustice, as you say they do? Do not some of them say that the others are doing something unjust, while the others deny it? No one, I suppose, my dear friend, whether god or man, dares to say that a person who has done something unjust must not be punished.

EUTH. No, Socrates, that is true, by and large.

SOCR. I take it, Euthyphro, that the disputants, whether men or gods, if the gods do disagree, disagree over each separate act. When they quarrel about any act, some of them say that it was just, and others that it was unjust. Is it not so?

EUTH. Yes.

SOCR. Come, then, my dear Euthyphro, please enlighten me on this point. What proof have you that all the gods think that a laborer who has been imprisoned for murder by the master of the man whom he has murdered, and who dies from his imprisonment before the master has had time to learn from the religious authorities what he should do, dies unjustly? How do you know that it is just for a son to indict his father and to prosecute him for the murder of such a man? Come, see if you can make it clear to me that the gods necessarily agree in thinking that this action of yours is just; and if you satisfy me, I will never cease singing your praises for wisdom.

EUTH. I could make that clear enough to you, Socrates; but I am afraid that it would be a long business.

SOCR. I see you think that I am duller than the judges. To them, of course, you will make it clear that your father has committed an unjust action, and that all the gods agree in hating such actions.

EUTH. I will indeed, Socrates, if they will only listen to me.

SOCR. They will listen if they think that you are a good speaker. But while you were talking, it occurred to me to ask myself this question: suppose that Euthyphro were to prove to me as clearly as possible that all the gods think such a death unjust, how has he brought me any nearer to understanding what piety and impiety are? This particular act, perhaps, may be displeasing to the gods, but then we have just seen that piety and impiety cannot be defined in that way; for we have seen that what is displeasing to the gods is also pleasing to them. So I will let you off on this point, Euthyphro; and all the gods shall agree in thinking your father's action wrong and in hating it, if you like. But shall we correct our definition and say that whatever all the gods hate is impious, and whatever they all love is pious; while whatever some of them love, and others hate, is either both or neither? Do you wish us now to define piety and impiety in this manner?

EUTH. Why not, Socrates?

SOCR. There is no reason why I should not, Euthyphro. It is for you to consider whether that definition will help you to teach me what you promised.

EUTH. Well, I should say that piety is what all the gods love, and that impiety is what they all hate.

SOCR. Are we to examine this definition, Euthyphro, and see if it is a good one? Or are we to be content to accept the bare statements of other men or of ourselves without asking any questions? Or must we examine the statements?

EUTH. We must examine them. But for my part I think that the definition is right this time.

SOCR. We shall know that better in a little while, my good friend. Now consider this question. Do the gods love piety because it is pious, or is it pious because they love it?

EUTH. I do not understand you, Socrates.

SOCR. I will try to explain myself: we speak of a thing being carried and carrying, and being led and leading, and being seen and seeing; and you understand that all such expressions mean different things, and what the difference is.

EUTH. Yes, I think I understand.

SOCR. And we talk of a thing being loved, of a thing loving, and the two are different?

EUTH. Of course.

SOCR. Now tell me, is a thing which is being carried in a state of being carried because it is carried, or for some other reason?

EUTH. No, because it is carried.

SOCR. And a thing is in a state of being led because it is led, and of being seen because it is seen?

EUTH. Certainly.

SOCR. Then a thing is not seen because it is in a state of being seen: it is in a state of being seen because it is seen; and a thing is not led because it is in a state of being led: it is in a state of being led because it is led; and a thing is not carried because it is in a state of being carried: it is in a state of being carried because it is carried. Is my meaning clear now, Euthyphro? I mean this: if anything becomes or is affected, it does not become because it is in a state of becoming: it is in a state of becoming because it becomes; and it is not affected because it is in a state of being affected: it in a state of being affected because it is affected. Do you not agree?

EUTH. I do.

SOCR. Is not that which is being loved in a state either of becoming or of being affected in some way by something?

EUTH. Certainly.

SOCR. Then the same is true here as in the former cases. A thing is not loved by those who love it because it is in a state of being loved; it is in a state of being loved because they love it.

EUTH. Necessarily.

SOCR. Well, then, Euthyphro, what do we say about piety? Is it not loved by all the gods, according to your definition?

EUTH. Yes.

SOCR. Because it is pious, or for some other reason?

EUTH. No, because it is pious.

SOCR. Then it is loved by the gods because it is pious; it is not pious because it is loved by them?

EUTH. It seems so.

SOCR. But, then, what is pleasing to the gods is pleasing to them, and is in a state of being loved by them, because they love it?

EUTH. Of course.

SOCR. Then piety is not what is pleasing to the gods, and what is pleasing to the gods is not pious, as you say, Euthyphro. They are different things.

EUTH. And why, Socrates?

SOCR. Because we are agreed that the gods love piety because it is pious, and that it is not pious because they love it. Is not this so?

EUTH. Yes.

SOCR. And that what is pleasing to the gods because they love it, is pleasing to them by reason of this same love, and that they do not love it because it is pleasing to them.

EUTH. True.

SOCR. Then, my dear Euthyphro, piety and what is pleasing to the gods are different things. If the gods had loved piety because it is pious, they would also have loved what is pleasing to them because it is pleasing to them; but if what is pleasing to them had been pleasing to them because they loved it, then piety, too, would have been piety because they loved it. But now you see that they are opposite things, and wholly different from each other. For the one is of a sort to be loved because it is loved, while the other is loved because it is of a sort to be loved. My question, Euthyphro, was, What is piety? But it turns out that you have not explained to me the essential character of piety; you have been content to mention an effect which belongs to it—namely, that all the gods love it. You have not yet told me what its essential character is. Do not, if you please, keep from me what piety is; begin again and tell me that. Never mind whether the gods love it, or whether it has other effects: we shall not differ on that point. Do your best to make clear to me what is piety and what is impiety.

EUTH. But, Socrates, I really don't know how to explain to you what is in my mind. Whatever statement we put forward always somehow moves round in a circle, and will not stay where we put it.

SOCR. I think that your statements, Euthyphro, are worthy of my ancestor Daedalus.[2] If they had been mine and I had set them down, I dare say you would have made fun of me, and said that it was the consequence of my descent from Daedalus that the statements which I construct run away, as his statues used to, and will not stay where they are put. But, as it is, the statements are yours, and the joke would have no point. You yourself see that they will not stay still.

EUTH. Nay, Socrates, I think that the joke is very much in point. It is not my fault that the statement moves round in a circle and will not stay still. But you are the Daedalus, I think; as far as I am concerned, my statements would have stayed put.

SOCR. Then, my friend, I must be a more skillful artist than Daedalus; he only used to make his own works move, while I, you see, can make other people's works move, too. And the beauty of it is that I am wise against my will. I would rather that our statements had remained firm and immovable than have all the wisdom of Daedalus and all the riches of Tantalus to boot. But enough of this. I will do my best to help you to explain to me what piety is, for I think that you are lazy. Don't give in yet. Tell me, do you not think that all piety must be just?

EUTH. I do.

SOCR. Well, then, is all justice pious, too? Or, while all piety is just, is a part only of justice pious, and the rest of it something else?

EUTH. I do not follow you, Socrates.

---

[2]Daedalus' statues were reputed to have been so lifelike that they came alive.–Ed.

SOCR. Yet you have the advantage over me in your youth no less than your wisdom. But, as I say, the wealth of your wisdom makes you complacent. Exert yourself, my good friend: I am not asking you a difficult question. I mean the opposite of what the poet[3] said, when he wrote:

"You shall not name Zeus the creator, who made all things: for where there is fear there also is reverence."

Now I disagree with the poet. Shall I tell you why?

EUTH. Yes.

SOCR. I do not think it true to say that where there is fear, there also is reverence. Many people who fear sickness and poverty and other such evils seem to me to have fear, but no reverence for what they fear. Do you not think so?

EUTH. I do.

SOCR. But I think that where there is reverence there also is fear. Does any man feel reverence and a sense of shame about anything, without at the same time dreading and fearing the reputation of wickedness?

EUTH. No, certainly not.

SOCR. Then, though there is fear wherever there is reverence, it is not correct to say that where there is fear there also is reverence. Reverence does not always accompany fear; for fear, I take it, is wider than reverence. It is a part of fear, just as the odd is a part of number, so that where you have the odd you must also have number, though where you have number you do not necessarily have the odd. Now I think you follow me?

EUTH. I do.

SOCR. Well, then, this is what I meant by the question which I asked you. Is there always piety where there is justice? Or, though there is always justice where there is piety, yet there is not always piety where there is justice, because piety is only a part of justice? Shall we say this, or do you differ?

EUTH. No, I agree. I think that you are right.

SOCR. Now observe the next point. If piety is a part of justice, we must find out, I suppose, what part of justice it is? Now, if you had asked me just now, for instance, what part of number is the odd, and what number is an odd number, I should have said that whatever number is not even is an odd number. Is it not so?

EUTH. Yes.

---

[3]Stasinus.

Socr. Then see if you can explain to me what part of justice is piety, that I may tell Meletus that now that I have been adequately instructed by you as to what actions are righteous and pious, and what are not, he must give up prosecuting me unjustly for impiety.

Euth. Well, then, Socrates, I should say that righteousness and piety are that part of justice which has to do with the careful attention which ought to be paid to the gods; and that what has to do with the careful attention which ought to be paid to men is the remaining part of justice.

Socr. And I think that your answer is a good one, Euthyphro. But there is one little point about which I still want to hear more. I do not yet understand what the careful attention is to which you refer. I suppose you do not mean that the attention which we pay to the gods is like the attention which we pay to other things. We say, for instance, do we not, that not everyone knows how to take care of horses, but only the trainer of horses?

Euth. Certainly.

Socr. For I suppose that the skill that is concerned with horses is the art of taking care of horses.

Euth. Yes.

Socr. And not everyone understands the care of dogs, but only the huntsman.

Euth. True.

Socr. For I suppose that the huntsman's skill is in the art of taking care of dogs.

Euth. Yes.

Socr. And the herdsman's skill is the art of taking care of cattle.

Euth. Certainly.

Socr. And you say that piety and righteousness are taking care of the gods, Euthyphro?

Euth. I do.

Socr. Well, then, has not all care the same object? Is it not for the good and benefit of that on which it is bestowed? For instance, you see that horses are benefited and improved when they are cared for by the art which is concerned with them. Is it not so?

Euth. Yes, I think so.

Socr. And dogs are benefited and improved by the huntsman's art, and cattle by the herdsman's, are they not? And the same is always true. Or do you think care is ever meant to harm that which is cared for?

Euth. No, indeed; certainly not.

Socr. But to benefit it?

Euth. Of course.

SOCR. Then is piety, which is our care for the gods, intended to benefit the gods, or to improve them? Should you allow that you make any of the gods better when you do a pious action?

EUTH. No indeed; certainly not.

SOCR. No, I am quite sure that this is not your meaning, Euthyphro. It was for that reason that I asked you what you meant by the careful attention which ought to be paid to the gods. I thought that you did not mean that.

EUTH. You were right, Socrates. I do not mean that.

SOCR. Good. Then what sort of attention to the gods will piety be?

EUTH. The sort of attention, Socrates, slaves pay to their masters.

SOCR. I understand; then it is a kind of service to the gods?

EUTH. Certainly.

SOCR. Can you tell me what result the art which serves a doctor serves to produce? Is it not health?

EUTH. Yes.

SOCR. And what result does the art which serves a shipwright serve to produce?

EUTH. A ship, of course, Socrates.

SOCR. The result of the art which serves a builder is a house, is it not?

EUTH. Yes.

SOCR. Then tell me, my good friend: What result will the art which serves the gods serve to produce? You must know, seeing that you say that you know more about divine things than any other man.

EUTH. Well, that is true, Socrates.

SOCR. Then tell me, I beg you, what is that grand result which the gods use our services to produce?

EUTH. There are many notable results, Socrates.

SOCR. So are those, my friend, which a general produces. Yet it is easy to see that the crowning result of them all is victory in war, is it not?

EUTH. Of course.

SOCR. And, I take it, the farmer produces many notable results; yet the principal result of them all is that he makes the earth produce food.

EUTH. Certainly.

SOCR. Well, then, what is the principal result of the many notable results which the gods produce?

EUTH. I told you just now, Socrates, that accurate knowledge of all these matters is not easily obtained. However, broadly I say this: if any man knows that his words and actions in prayer and sacrifice are acceptable to the gods, that is what is pious; and it preserves the state, as it does private families. But the opposite of what is acceptable to the gods is sacrilegious, and this it is that undermines and destroys everything.

SOCR. Certainly, Euthyphro, if you had wished, you could have answered my main question in far fewer words. But you are evidently not anxious to teach me. Just now, when you were on the very point of telling me what I want to know, you stopped short. If you had gone on then, I should have learned from you clearly enough by this time what piety is. But now I am asking you questions, and must follow wherever you lead me; so tell me, what is it that you mean by piety and impiety? Do you not mean a science of prayer and sacrifice?

EUTH. I do.

SOCR. To sacrifice is to give to the gods, and to pray is to ask of them, is it not?

EUTH. It is, Socrates.

SOCR. Then you say that piety is the science of asking of the gods and giving to them?

EUTH. You understand my meaning exactly, Socrates.

SOCR. Yes, for I am eager to share your wisdom, Euthyphro, and so I am all attention; nothing that you say will fall to the ground. But tell me, what is this service of the gods? You say it is to ask of them, and to give to them?

EUTH. I do.

SOCR. Then, to ask rightly will be to ask of them what we stand in need of from them, will it not?

EUTH. Naturally.

SOCR. And to give rightly will be to give back to them what they stand in need of from us? It would not be very skillful to make a present to a man of something that he has no need of.

EUTH. True, Socrates.

SOCR. Then piety, Euthyphro, will be the art of carrying on business between gods and men?

EUTH. Yes, if you like to call it so.

SOCR. But I like nothing except what is true. But tell me, how are the gods benefited by the gifts which they receive from us? What they give is plain enough. Every good thing that we have is their gift. But how are they benefited by what we give them? Have we the advantage over them in these business transactions to such an extent that we receive from them all the good things we possess, and give them nothing in return?

EUTH. But do you suppose, Socrates, that the gods are benefited by the gifts which they receive from us?

SOCR. But what *are* these gifts, Euthyphro, that we give the gods?

EUTH. What do you think but honor and praise, and, as I have said, what is acceptable to them.

SOCR. Then piety, Euthyphro, is acceptable to the gods, but it is not profitable to them nor loved by them?

EUTH. I think that nothing is more loved by them.

SOCR. Then I see that piety means that which is loved by the gods.

EUTH. Most certainly.

SOCR. After that, shall you be surprised to find that your statements move about instead of staying where you put them? Shall you accuse me of being the Daedalus that makes them move, when you yourself are far more skillful than Daedalus was, and make them go round in a circle? Do you not see that our statement has come round to where it was before? Surely you remember that we have already seen that piety and what is pleasing to the gods are quite different things. Do you not remember?

EUTH. I do.

SOCR. And now do you not see that you say that what the gods love is pious? But does not what the gods love come to the same thing as what is pleasing to the gods?

EUTH. Certainly.

SOCR. Then either our former conclusion was wrong or, if it was right, we are wrong now.

EUTH. So it seems.

SOCR. Then we must begin again and inquire what piety is. I do not mean to give in until I have found out. Do not regard me as unworthy; give your whole mind to the question, and this time tell me the truth. For if anyone knows it, it is you; and you are a Proteus whom I must not let go until you have told me. It cannot be that you would ever have undertaken to prosecute your aged father for the murder of a laboring man unless you had known exactly what piety and impiety are. You would have feared to risk the anger of the gods, in case you should be doing wrong, and you would have been afraid of what men would say. But now I am sure that you think that you know exactly what is pious and what is not; so tell me, my good Euthyphro, and do not conceal from me what you think.

EUTH. Another time, then, Socrates. I am in a hurry now, and it is time for me to be off.

SOCR. What are you doing, my friend! Will you go away and destroy all my hopes of learning from you what is pious and what is not, and so of escaping Meletus? I meant to explain to him that now Euthyphro has made me wise about divine things, and that I no longer in my ignorance speak carelessly about them or introduce reforms. And then I was going to promise him to live a better life for the future.

Reflections on the Readings:

1. Put yourself in the place of the child narrator of Singer's story. With which parent do you identify?

2. What can we learn from the shamans? The article says that after treatment by the shamans Mr. Ruschi felt better. How would you account for his improvement?

3. How would you respond to someone who asked you, "Why be reasonable?"

4. Why is it desirable to have mystery in the world?

5. Who is more pious, Euthyphro or Socrates? Why?

6. Some people believe that an act is good because God wills it. From your reading of _Euthyphro_ do you see any problem with this claim?

Rationality and the Importance of the Open Dialogue

This book is primarily concerned with improving reasoning skills, so a very basic question which cannot be ignored is why people should try to improve their reasoning skills. There seem to be some very good reasons to question the use of reason. For instance, it has already been noted that reason does have its limits. We can only reason from one thing to something else. Our reasoning must begin by assuming something. This might be the axioms of mathematics, a set of scientific laws in physics or chemistry, or the Constitution in United States law. Usually we agree on some set of fundamental assumptions. That is what enables us to talk to each other and that is what enables mathematicians, or scientists, or Americans to talk to each other. Americans, for example, believe that "all [people] . . . are endowed by their Creator with certain unalienable Rights, . . . [namely] Life, Liberty, and the pursuit of Happiness." This assumption then guides further agreements or disagreements they might have.

Sometimes, however, our disagreements are rooted in different ideas about where to start. Two scientists who agree on the "laws of science" might disagree about the existence of God. While one may believe that the world would not exist at all if there was no God to create it, the other may think the assumption of God is unnecessary and unhelpful. What they both, probably, will admit is that the principles of physics (which they both consider to be fundamental to good scientific reasoning) will not settle their disagreement.

Not only is reason limited in its power, but it also seems to ignore a very important aspect of what it means to be a human being, namely, having feelings or emotions. Emotion, not reason, seems to be responsible for the excitement of life, the highs and lows which make our lives richer and more fun. What would life be like without falling in love, shedding tears while watching a sentimental movie, or cheering passionately for your favorite sports team? People who are incapable of having such feelings seem to be missing something in their lives. Mystery, not reason, is exciting. We wait with bated breath while the magician saws the box with the lady in it in two. And most cultures have their "Halloweens" when people pay tribute to spooks and goblins.

Despite these limitations, we find the advantages of being reasonable persuasive. Before we explain this claim, you should notice something rather peculiar going on here. It is hard to make a case for being nonrational without seeming to contradict yourself. Making a case for a position means giving arguments or reasons in support of it. The person arguing against the use of reason is placed in the awkward position of giving reasons for not giving reasons, or of making an argument for not making arguments. Although not contradictory behavior, it is clearly self-defeating behavior. That is, the harder you try to convince me with reasons that I should not pay attention to reasons, and the more successful you are, the more you will fail. It's like a child's trying to convince his parent that he is sufficiently mature to stay up to watch a late-night television show while crying like a baby because the parent says no. Usually when a person asks a question, he wants an answer, not a shower of tears or a sock on the jaw. Although we may be coerced by power, we prefer to be persuaded by argument and evidence. It **makes sense** to us.

By reasonable we do *not* mean someone who acts and responds like a computer or who is so cerebral (like Spock in "Star Trek") that no ordinary person can talk with him. The person who is reasonable in the sense that we intend here is someone like Socrates for whom this book is named and about whom you have just read. Socrates asks many questions. Although you may have found Socrates' repeated questioning somewhat tedious, what is important about his example is that he is always willing to discuss the matter further. The discussion is always open. **We think that this willingness to keep the discussion open is the hallmark of the rational person.** The person who is rational is *not* the person who is always right or the person who never makes a mistake in reasoning. Rather, the person who is rational is always willing to examine his or her beliefs, to entertain alternate possibilities, and to talk with other people about those beliefs and possibilities. As we see it, reasoning is a dialogue and good reasoning means, first and foremost, keeping the dialogue **open. Good reasoning, then, is an open dialogue with our friends.** Friends are people willing to listen and respond. Someone is a friend because he is willing to stay and discuss, not vice versa. That is, the hallmark of a friend is a willingness to engage in rational open dialogue and to keep this dialogue open as long as there is an opportunity for rational resolution.

Sometimes, of course, no friend is available. Then we must carry on the open dialogue with ourselves. This is hard to do. We often fail to question our own beliefs the same way someone else might question them. But it is a very important aspect of being a rational person. To see this consider the matter another way: Thinking is like talking, a kind of talking to ourselves. When the talking stops, the thinking stops. Clearly, there are better and worse ways of thinking. Much of the rest of this book is about telling the difference between the better and the worse. But the most important aspect of being rational is to _do_ the thinking, to carry on the dialogue as far as possible, and not to stop because one is too stubborn or too lazy or even too tired to continue. Socrates always said he was a seeker after wisdom, not a wise person, and, as a seeker, he was always willing to continue the discussion.

Why do rational approaches generally "work better" than nonrational approaches? Philosophers of many schools have offered a wide variety of answers to this question which we cannot recount here.[1] We think the best way to support this claim is to warrant it with statements that most people would accept as factual and which do not require appeal to assumptions (often referred to as metaphysical assumptions) whose warrant many people might question.

First, rational approaches work better than nonrational approaches because human beings are animals with purposes and plans. They live in the present but they have intentions and plans for the future. For these plans to be successful, our expectations about what will happen must be accurate. We use reason and past experience to form our expectations about the future.

---

[1]Two popular views are those of Plato and Thomas Aquinas. Plato claimed that there was a _logos_ or natural logical order in the world that matched the logical order of human reasoning. Thomas Aquinas, on the other hand, claimed that the world was created by a first cause or first mover which itself was rational, namely, God. So, according to both of these views, rational thought works better than irrational thought because it matches the world better. Our Socratic approach tries to avoid claims about the nature of the world and to suggest that the likeliest explanation for the success of rationality is its insistence on giving a hearing to all sides of an issue and to keeping the dialogue going. At the end of the _Euthyphro_, when Euthyphro has tired of trying to give a rationally adequate account of piety, Socrates almost begs him not to abandon the task. We agree with Socrates more than with Plato and Aquinas. Rationality, whatever its shortcomings, is the best game in town.

This rational approach enables us to anticipate what is likely to happen and, therefore, to be successful in fulfilling our intentions.[2]

Singer's story about the shrieking geese is a good illustration of this point. The woman who owns the geese is very upset because her expectation is that properly slaughtered geese do not shriek and her intention is to eat the geese. She is a poor woman and does not want to have to throw out the geese (or bury them in a grave). Since her expectations are reasonable, it is also reasonable to assume that there is an explanation for the fact that the geese are now shrieking. "Dead geese don't shriek." Taking the approach of reason advocated by the mother, and not the approach of awe at the apparent mystery taken by the father, enables her to confirm that her expectations were reasonable and to fulfill her intention to eat the geese.

A second warrant for the claim that rational approaches work better than nonrational ones is that when other people figure in our plans, it works best to include them or bring them along by giving reasons. Obviously, of course, other people are not always persuaded by reason or at least by the reasons we give. This does not mean that there are not other reasons which might be persuasive which we have not given, either because we choose not to give them or we do not know them at the time. Even Socrates was not able to persuade the Athenian jury of his innocence despite his considerable powers of reason.[3] And we can think of times when a sock on the jaw or a veil of tears was persuasive. There are times, moreover, when we are convinced the other side will not listen to reason, as when we are dealing with Nazi fanatics or a thug in the street. Then the reasonable thing to do *may* be to become for the moment unreasonable. Anger and other emotional responses can be successful, *if used with reason!* In general, however, unreasonableness begets further unreasonableness and violence begets violence. Since the collective experience of the human race testifies to this pattern, lapses into unreason should be infrequent.

Keeping the dialogue open not only keeps us from using force but it has the added benefit of keeping us engaged. It means that we must make an **effort**. To continue the dialogue, we must make an effort to find reasons that are persuasive, to understand the other person's point of view, and to

---

[2]Richard Feynman presents a clear example of the need to use reason in his account of the investigations of the *Challenger* disaster in his book, *What Do You Care What Other People Think?* (W. W. Norton & Company, 1988) As a member of the disaster investigation team, Feynman refused to accept NASA safety estimates without also being shown the evidence and the reasoning necessary to support them. NASA estimated the chance of engine failure at one in 100,000, which would lead to the expectation that a shuttle could fly every day for 300 years without failure. Feynman's reexamination of the data revealed the actual probability to be one in 200, which would not make the *Challenger's* failure a surprise.

[3]Plato's account suggests, however, that part of Socrates' failure was due to his unwillingness to offer the kind of "reasons" which were usually persuasive with Athenian juries, namely, to parade his wife and children before them to appeal to their sympathies.

rethink our own point of view. The problem with mystery or with answers from high priests, oracles, and shamans is that they preclude this effort on our part. We have only to accept or follow the voice of authority. We do not have to do any work, either to help our friends and keep them from false beliefs or to weed out our own false beliefs.

This failure of effort makes us powerless with regard to the future. To accept something as a mystery is not to know what will happen in the future or why. We are then at the mercy of whatever happens. We can neither avoid events we would prefer to avoid nor bring about events that make us happy or satisfied. The story which you will read in Chapter 3 of the day-care deaths is a good illustration of this point. The story leaves the reader with the suggestion that both children died of SIDS, which is just to say that their deaths are still a mystery. If we accept this mystery, then we are at a loss as to how to prevent future infant deaths. If we are dissatisfied with this mystery, we will begin a dialogue that may lead to answers which will prevent future infant deaths.

The shaman episode you read about presents us with a similar pattern. The story is fascinating because of its mystery. We do not understand what the two shamans are doing to Mr. Ruschi, but we hope for his sake they succeed. If we just accept the shamans' apparent success as a fortunate but incomprehensible event then we are still at the mercy of future poisonous toad bites. If the cure comes from the mysterious powers of the shaman and not from some naturally existing antidote that the shamans know, then future victims who are not as lucky as Mr. Ruschi will die. The problem with shamans, witch doctors, and others who work in mysterious ways is that the end of the explanation comes too soon. We are stopped by "mystery" from asking precisely the questions which might be helpful in the future. We are precluded from continuing the dialogue long enough to understand how we might affect that future.

Obviously we are not going to be able to anticipate everything that is going to happen. Sometimes, in fact, we would rather not know. Life would be deadly dull if we knew exactly what was about to happen to us. That is why we tend to identify with the narrator in Singer's story. We like the idea of some mystery in the world. On the other hand, we like to avoid pain and suffering when we can. If the geese are ours, we want to be able to eat them, not to bury them uneaten in order to shut them up. Some people, however, have the attitude that reason can resolve every problem. This is not the case. Sometimes there is no right answer and we must make a forced choice between unattractive alternatives. Examples like this are common in the practice of medicine. But the mode of rational inquiry and of open dialogue has the best track record in helping humans to fulfill their plans and goals.

The openness of the dialogue is a critical factor here. Because the dialogue is continuous and never closed, it is always open to revision. If we do

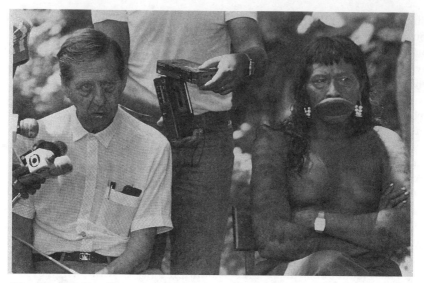

Mr. Ruschi, the ailing naturalist, poses with one of the Brazilian shamans trying to save his life. Reprinted by permission of Bettmann Archive/Bettmann Newsphotos.

not get the results we anticipate, then we revise our expectations. We continue our dialogue with each other and with the world until our expectations match up with our results and we are able to fulfill our purposes. As human beings we are continuously revising our expectations on the basis of the evidence we gather. The shaman, or the believer in mystery, is often not open to revising his beliefs. Since the result is a product of mystery, there are no guidelines for revision. One can only say that the times were not right or that the gods were unwilling. And one can only hope to get the desired result the next time, since it is entirely up to the gods to choose what they wish to do. This view clearly, then, makes us powerless with regard to the future.

Reason and Culture

Some people have argued that this favoring of reason over mystery is simply a result of our Western heritage and that in trying to promote the use of reason we are just promoting Western culture at the expense of cultures which favor mystery. On this view, we do not accept shamanism because it does not fit in with our beliefs and our beliefs are, in part, the product of our culture. People born into a shamanistic culture are comfortable with mystery and find reliance on reason narrow and hard to accept.

Clearly there are cultural differences and it may be that people reared in one culture sometimes do not understand another one or are prejudiced against it only because it is "different." However, it does not follow that our preference for reason over shamanism or mystery is just a prejudice without justification. It may be that our partiality toward rational judgment is a cultural bias, but this bias is warranted by the fact that rational inquiry **works for us**. In our view, it is not the case that the shaman is wrong and reason (or modern medicine) is right. It is just that reason helps us to fulfill *our* purposes.

Rational dialogue, as was pointed out earlier, means keeping the dialogue **open**. That means keeping the dialogue open to other cultures, to other ideas, or to mysteries. It does not mean imposing one culture's values on another. There is room for reason *and* mystery in the world. But keeping the dialogue open does not mean that we must believe or accept the offerings of every cultural alternative. And, indeed, when that alternative avoids open dialogue, then we must resist. The problem with a cultural view that emphasizes mystery is that often it itself is not sufficiently open to rationality.

The Ruschi case presents us with a good illustration of this point. Mr. Ruschi's purpose is to live, and medicine does not seem able to help him. He may fulfill that purpose by taking the shamans' cure even though he does not understand it. It is a mystery, both to him and to Western science. If medicine had been able to help him fulfill his purpose, he would not have turned to the shamans. It is a reasonable thing to try at this point, and he is open to this alternative. Modern medicine, however, has a more successful record to date in meeting the goal of prolonging life than does the medicine of shamans. It is not a question of prejudice or bias. It's a question of purpose. Most of us would not start our cures with shamans because we believe that we have evidence that supports a better cure rate for Western medicine and we want to be cured. A member of a shaman's tribe, however, may seek something different—may have a different purpose—a purpose best met by a visit to the shaman.

The rational open dialogue also has the advantage that it is a good way of persuading others to join us in our plans. It is less likely to have the unpleasant consequences attendant on the use of force, or threats of force, which historically have often been used to persuade others to accept or believe mystery. These uses of force include excommunication from the tribe, burning at the stake, and threats of death by lightning. The rational dialogue invites, but does not force, agreement. It relies solely on the power of evidence. It allows—and even encourages—the other party to think critically and to respond critically to that evidence.

To put the matter another way, the way Socrates would put it: *Rational dialogue is the essence of friendship.* The people we talk to and who talk with us are our friends. When we are friends we are willing to listen; we are willing to change our minds when persuaded; we are willing to go an extra mile to find a common ground. Most people would agree that being a friend means sharing. And what could be more important to share than our thoughts and beliefs. To do this we must talk—together. There is more than irony in Socrates' words when he refers to Euthyphro as his friend each time Euthyphro wants to go away and end the dialogue.

The Limits of Reason

The short story of the shrieking geese illustrates the power of reason to solve problems. The inability of medicine to cure Mr. Ruschi and Socrates' failure to convince Euthyphro to continue the dialogue about the nature of piety betray the limits of reason and of thinking Socratically. Clearly the application of reason does not always solve our problems. Even when we make our best effort, the open dialogue, which is the hallmark of rationality, is not always successful. There are three important limitations to the open dialogue method of rational thinking and you should be aware of them. The first is rather obvious. The open dialogue does not always lead to agreement. Even friends may not agree, not even in the long run! They may begin from different assumptions or fail to have the same goals. The greater the difference in initial assumptions or in goals, the greater the difficulty of coming to agreement. Intercultural dialogues characteristically display this difficulty.

A second limitation on the open dialogue is that we do not always have enough time to resolve differences and find agreement or solve the puzzle or problem. Circumstances may be overwhelming, demanding immediate action. For instance, the imminence of death in Mr. Ruschi's case rules out waiting for medicine to discover a cure for his diseased body. Ruschi must act, not talk. There are certainly situations in life where we cannot delay and still achieve the goals we seek. We must act on the best information available and hope to continue the open dialogue at a later time.

Finally, the open rational dialogue is limited by the values we hold. While we believe that all human beings share the general goals of being able to anticipate and plan for the future and of having friends and pleasant experiences, they do not always place the same value on the same specific experiences as ways of meeting these general goals. Our values act as a constraint on our exercise of reason, directing it to the ends we set. Reason helps us to achieve the ends we value and avoid the ones we do not.

Our claim, then, in behalf of reason is warranted but limited. Reason cannot answer *all* our questions or fulfill *all* our purposes. Sometimes the answers defy human reason and sometimes reason is not persuasive of others. Sometimes our purposes even lie outside the realm of reason as when we choose the sloppy sentimentality of a romantic movie or give ourselves goose bumps by reading a horror story. In general, however, rational thinking and rational behavior are what enable us to meet our goals and expectations. It helps us to have friends who share our outlook on the world. Trying to be rational and to make rational decisions helps us enjoy the pleasant and avoid the unpleasant.

Because the rational dialogue is open, it means that we can learn from our experience and from the experience of others. If we reason well, we get better at fulfilling our goals and purposes. In the following chapters we will give you guidelines for improving your reasoning skills. But in a very important sense, we have already given you the most important tip we can give you, which is always to be **open** to further discussion and to make the **effort** that the open dialogue demands.

Exercises

Intro–I

1. What is the hallmark of the rational person?

2. What are three limitations on human reason?

3. Give two reasons why rational approaches generally work better than nonrational approaches.

Intro–II

1. How would your explanation differ if:
   a. you were explaining to your best friend why your computer was not performing as you expected?
   b. you were explaining to your best friend why you just bought a new Corvette?

2. Find an example in a recent newspaper of an event attributed to mystery.

3. Bring in two different accounts of the same event which are told from very different cultural perspectives.

Intro–III

1. Why do you love your girlfriend/boyfriend? Is this an example of reasonable behavior or an affair of the heart? Explain.

2. Construct a story about an event which could have both a rational and a nonrational cause. Do not, however, just throw in God or the supernatural. Hint: Your story might be about a date, a football game, etc.

3. Do you think there are events for which there are no rational explanations? Why or why not?

chapter 1

Language

Introduction

Do you ever think about how language relates to the world? Most of us don't think about this relationship very often until we just can't quite describe an experience we've had or we're suddenly struck by how much Reginald looks like someone who would be named "Reginald." We connect with our world and with each other in many ways—art, music, body movement—but none of these connections is as important as the language connection. It's how we communicate with ourselves. When we reason, make decisions, offer an explanation, describe our moods and feelings, we use language. Language has its limitations, as we shall see. But it is a tool with an infinite number of uses as well.

We all know how to use language. Otherwise, we couldn't write this and you couldn't be reading it. But we all need to think more about the **connection** between these symbols that we use—words—and the world we live in. For instance, have you heard two people who attended the same event later give two different descriptions of the event? Do you wonder how this happens? Sometimes these differences in description are unimportant, but sometimes they are very important, as when two diplomats are arguing about how many weapons are in a stockpile or when witnesses in court are describing the appearance of the escaping bank robber.

This is our concern here. Not with words themselves or with any particular set of words, but with that **connectedness**. Usually we create strings of words, sentences, to help us make connections. Often, we create a dialogue with another person or even with ourselves. We try to communicate with other people about the world. So there are actually two important ways in which we connect: with the world and with other people. Usually when we try to connect we are successful, but sometimes we fail: We "misinterpret" information and our predictions do not work, or we try hard without success to convince a friend that she ought to vote for a particular candidate but she doesn't. There is always a certain amount of tension involved in making connections. We'll try to see why this should be the case as we proceed.

We will approach **connectedness** through language first by thinking about words. Where do words come from? How do you know when I use a word what it is that I want you to understand by my use of that word? These are tough questions! Philosophers and linguists have wrestled with them for years.

Here are the writings of two different authors who are very concerned with using words to connect. The first reading is from Gertrude Stein, author of *The Autobiography of Alice B. Toklas* and famous for having said, "Rose is a rose is a rose is a rose." (Notice even here her concern about words.) Stein was an American expatriate living in France in the first half of the twentieth century. She was one of the earliest collectors of modern art and her house was a salon where artists and writers such as Picasso, Matisse, Hemingway, and Fitzgerald gathered. You may be rather puzzled or even annoyed by her style in this piece, but ask yourself *why* she has adopted this style. What is she trying to tell us?

The other reading in this chapter is by Lewis Thomas. Thomas was a contemporary "Renaissance man." He was a medical doctor, a biologist, a writer, and an administrator. For many years he was chief executive officer of the Memorial Sloan-Kettering Cancer Center, one of the best specialized hospitals in the United States. As you will see in this reading, he had the ability to use his detailed knowledge of science to muse about the human condition and our place in the cosmos.

The Making of Americans

GERTRUDE STEIN

Sometimes in listening to a conversation which is very important to two men, to two women, to two men and women, sometimes then it is a wonderful thing to see how each one always is repeating everything they are saying and each time in repeating, what each one is saying has more meaning to each one of them and so they go on and on and on and on and on repeating and always to some one listening, repeating is a very wonderful thing. There are many of them who do not live in each repeating each repeating coming out of them but always repeating is interesting. Repeating is what I am loving. Sometimes there is in me a sad feeling for all the repeating no one loving repeating is hearing, it is like any beauty that no one is seeing, it is a lovely thing, always some one should be knowing the meaning in the repeating always coming out of women and of men, the repeating of the being in them. So then.

Every one is a brute in her way or his way to some one, every one has some kind of sensitiveness in them.

Some feel some kinds of things others feel other kinds of things. Mostly every one feels some kinds of things. The way some things touch some and do not touch other ones and kinds in men and women then I will now begin to think a little bit about describing. To begin then.

I am thinking it is very interesting the relation of the kind of things that touch men and women with the kind of bottom nature in them, the kind of being they have in them in every way in them, the way they react to things which may be different from the way they feel them.

I am thinking very much of feeling things in men and women. As I was saying every one is a brute in her way or his way to some one, every one has some kind of sensitiveness in them. Mostly every one has some inner way of feeling in them, almost every one has some way of reacting to stimulus in them. This is not always the same thing. These things have many complications in them.

I am beginning now a little a description of three women, Miss Dounor, Miss Charles and Mrs. Redfern. I am beginning now a little a realisation of the way each one of them is in her way a brute to some one, each one has in her way a kind of sensitiveness in being. This is now some

(an excerpt)

description of each one of the three of them Miss Dounor, Miss Charles and Mrs. Redfern.

In listening to a conversation, as I was saying, repeating of each one and the gradual rising and falling and rising again of realisation is very interesting. This is now some description of the three women and as I was saying of the sensitiveness in each one of them to some things and the insensitiveness to other things and the bottom nature in them and the kinds of repeating in them and the bottom nature and the other natures mixed with the bottom nature in each one of them.

Sensitiveness to something, understanding anything, feeling anything, that is very interesting to understand in each one. How much, when and where and how and when not and where not and how not they are feeling, thinking, understanding. To begin again then with feeling anything.

Mostly every one is a brute in her way or his way to some one, mostly every one has some kind of sensitiveness in them.

Mostly every one can have some kind of feeling in them, very many men and very many women can have some understanding in them of some kind of thing by the kind of being sensitive to some kind of impression that they have in them.

Some kinds of men and women have a way of having sensation from some things and other men and women have it in them to be able to be impressionable to other kinds of things. Some men and some women have very much of sensitive being in them for the kind of thing they can be feeling, they can then be very loving, or very trembly from the abundant delicate fear in them, or very attacking from the intensity of the feeling in them, or very mystic in their absorption of feeling which is then all of them. There are some men and women having in them very much weakness as the bottom in them and watery anxious feeling, and sometimes nervous anxious feeling then in them and sometimes stubborn feeling then in them. There are some who have vague or vacant being as the bottom in them and it is very hard to know with such ones of them what feeling they have ever in them and there are some with almost intermittent being in them and it is very hard to tell with such of them what kind of thing gives to them a feeling, what kind of feeling they ever have really in them. As I was saying mostly every one sometimes feels something, some one, is understanding something, some one, has some kind of sensitiveness in them to something, to some one, mostly every one.

As I was saying some men and some women have very much of sensitive being in them for something that can give to them real feeling. They can then, some of these of them, when they are filled full then of such feeling, they can then be completely loving, completely believing, they can then have a trembling awed being in them, they can have then abundant trembly feeling in them, they can then be so full up then with the feeling in them that they are a full thing and action has no place then in them, they are completely then a feeling, there are then men and women, there are then women and men who have then this finely sensitive completed feeling that is sometime all them and perhaps Cora Dounor was one of such of them. Perhaps she was one of them and was such a one in loving Phillip Redfern. Perhaps that was the whole being she had in her then.

Each one as I am saying has it in them to feel more or less, sometime, something, almost certainly each one sometime has some capacity for more or less feeling something. Some have in them always and very little feeling, some have some feeling and much nervous being always in them, some have as a bottom to them very much weakness and eagerness together then and they have then such of them some sensitiveness in them to things coming to them but often after they are then full up with nervous vibrations and then nothing can really touch them and then they can have in them nervous vibratory movement in them, anxious feeling in them and sometimes stubborn feeling then in them and then nothing can touch them and they are all this being then this nervous vibratory quivering and perhaps Mrs. Redfern was such a one Mrs. Redfern who had been Martha Hersland and was married now to Phillip Redfern and had come to Farnham and had there seen Phillip Redfern come to know Miss Dounor and had been then warned to take care of him by the dean of Farnham Miss Charles. She never knew then, Mrs. Redfern never knew then that she would not ever again have him, have Redfern again. This never could come to be real knowledge in her. She was always then and later always working at something to have him again and that was there always in her to the end of him and of her. There will be a little more description of her written in the history of the ending of the living in her father, in the history of the later living of her brother Alfred Hersland who now just when her trouble was commencing was just then marrying Julia Dehning, in the history of her brother David Hersland her younger brother. More description of her will be part of the history of the ending of the existing of the Hersland family. There will be very much history of this ending of all of them of the Hersland family written later.

The dean Miss Charles was very different from either Miss Dounor or Mrs. Redfern. She had it in her to have her own way of feeling things touching her, mostly there was in her less reactive than self-directive action in her than there was in the two women who were just then concerning her, Miss Dounor and Mrs. Redfern.

It is hard to know it of any one whether they are enjoying anything, whether they are knowing they are giving pain to some one, whether they were planning that thing. It is hard to know such things in any one when they are telling when they are not telling to any one what they know inside them. It is hard telling it of any one whether they are enjoying a thing, whether they know that they are hurting some one, whether they have been planning the acting they have been doing. It is hard telling it of any one whether they are enjoying anything, whether they know that they are hurting any one, whether they have been planning the acting they are doing. It is very hard then to know anything of the being in any one, it is hard then to know the being in many men and in many women, it is hard then to know the being and the feeling in any man or in any woman. It is hard to know it if they tell you all they know of it. It is hard to know it if they do not tell you what they know of it in it. Miss Cora Dounor then could do some planning, could do some hurting with it, that is certain. This is perhaps surprising to some, reading. To begin then with her feeling and her being and her acting.

As I am saying she had it in her to be compounded of beautiful sensitive being, of being able to be in a state of being completely possessed by a wonderful feeling of loving and that was then the whole of the being that was being then in her and then it came to be in her that she could be hurting first Miss Charles and then Mrs. Redfern, then Miss Charles and Mrs. Redfern by planning. This is then the being in her this that I am now with very much complication slowly realising, not yet completely realising, not yet completely ready to be completely describing, beginning now to be describing. The dean Miss Charles was a very different person, she was of the dependent independent kind of them. To understand the being in her there must be now a little realisation of the way beginning is in very many persons having in them a nature that is self growing and a nature that is reacting to stimulation and that have it in them to have these two natures acting in not very great harmony inside them. Mrs. Redfern as I was saying in a long description that has been already written was a very different kind of person from Miss Dounor and Miss Charles. These are then the three of them that were struggling and each of them had in them their own ways of being brutal, hurting some one, had each of them their own way of being sensitive to things and people near them.

Sometimes I am almost despairing. Yes it is very hard, almost impossible I am feeling now in my despairing feeling to have completely a realising of the being in any one, when they are telling it when they are not telling it, it is so very very hard to know it completely in one the being in one. I know the being in Miss Dounor that I am beginning describing, I know the being in Miss Charles that I am soon going to be beginning describing, I know the being in Mrs. Redfern, I have been describing the being in that one. I know the being in each one of these three of them and I am almost despairing for I am doubting if I am knowing it poignantly enough to be really knowing it, to be really knowing the being in any one of the three of them. Always now I am despairing. It is a very melancholy feeling I have in me now I am despairing about really knowing the complete being of any one of each one of these three of them Miss Dounor and Miss Charles and Mrs. Redfern.

Miss Dounor as I was saying was to Redfern the most complete thing of gentleness and intelligence he could think of ever seeing in anybody who was living, Miss Dounor had it to have in her the complete thing of gentleness, of beauty in sensitiveness, in completeness of intelligent sensitiveness in completely loving. She was the complete thing then of gentleness and sensitiveness and intelligence and she had it as a complete thing gentleness and sensitiveness and intelligence in completely loving. It was in her complete in loving, complete in creative loving, it was then completed being, it was then completely in her completely loving Phillip Redfern. And always to the ending of his living in all the other loving and other troubling and the other enjoying of men and women in him he was faithful to the thing she had been, was and would be to him the completed incarnation of gentleness and sensitiveness and intelligence, gentle intelligence and intelligent sensitiveness and all to the point of completely creative loving that was to him the supreme thing in all living. Miss Dounor was then completely what Redfern found her to him, she was of them of the independent dependent kind of them who have sensitive being to the point of creative being, of attacking, of creative loving, creative feeling, of sometimes creative thinking and writing. She was then such a one and completely then this one and she had in her completely sensitive being to the point of attacking. She could have in her a planning of attacking and this came to be in her from the completeness of sensitive creative loving that she had then in her then when she was knowing Phillip Redfern.

Perhaps she was not of this kind of them. Perhaps she was at the bottom, of the resisting kind of them. I think she was of the resisting kind of them and so she needed to own the one she needed for loving, so she could do resisting to planning making an attacking. I am almost despairing, yes a little I am realising the being in Miss Dounor and in Miss Charles and Mrs. Redfern, but I am really almost despairing, I have really in me a very very melancholy feeling, a very melancholy being, I am really then despairing.

Miss Charles was of the kind of men and women that I speak of and have spoken of as the dependent independent kind of them. I will now tell a little about what I mean by self growing activity in such of them and reactive activity in such of them. As I was saying a long time back when I was describing the dependent independent kind of them, reaction is not poignant in them unless it enters into them the stimulation is lost in them and so sets it, the mass, in motion, it is not as in the other kind of them who have it to have a reactive emotion to be as poignant as a sensation as is the case in the independent dependent kind of them. Miss Charles then as I was saying was of the kind of them where reaction to have meaning must be a slow thing, but she had quick reactions as mostly all of them of this kind of them have them and those were her mostly attacking being as is very common in those having in them dependent independent being. . . .

The Corner of the Eye

LEWIS THOMAS

There are some things that human beings can see only out of the corner of the eye. The niftiest examples of this gift, familiar to all children, are small, faint stars. When you look straight at one such star, it vanishes; when you move your eyes to stare into the space nearby, it reappears. If you pick two faint stars, side by side, and focus on one of the pair, it disappears and now you can see the other in the corner of your eye, and you can move your eyes back and forth, turning off the star in the center of your retina and switching the other one on. There is a physiological explanation for the phenomenon: we have more rods, the cells we use for light perception, at the periphery of our retinas, more cones, for perceiving color, at the center.

Something like this happens in music. You cannot really hear certain sequences of notes in a Bach fugue unless at the same time there are other notes being sounded, dominating the field. The real meaning in music comes from tones only audible in the corner of the mind.

I used to worry that computers would become so powerful and sophisticated as to take the place of human minds. The notion of Artificial Intelligence used to scare me half to death. Already, a large enough machine can do all sorts of intelligent things beyond our capacities: calculate in a split second the answers to mathematical problems requiring years for a human brain, draw accurate pictures from memory, even manufacture successions of sounds with a disarming resemblance to real music. Computers can translate textbooks, write dissertations of their own for doctorates, even speak in machine-tooled, inhuman phonemes any words read off from a printed page. They can communicate with one another, holding consultations and committee meetings of their own in networks around the earth.

From *Late Night Thoughts on Listening to Mahler's Ninth Symphony* (1981)

Computers can make errors, of course, and do so all the time in small, irritating ways, but the mistakes can be fixed and nearly always are. In this respect they are fundamentally inhuman, and here is the relaxing thought: computers will not take over the world, they cannot replace us, because they are not designed, as we are, for ambiguity.

Imagine the predicament faced by a computer programmed to make language, not the interesting communication in sounds made by vervets or in symbols by brilliant chimpanzee prodigies, but real human talk. The grammar would not be too difficult, and there would be no problem in constructing a vocabulary of etymons, the original, pure, unambiguous words used to name real things. The impossibility would come in making the necessary mistakes we humans make with words instinctively, intuitively, as we build our kinds of language, changing the meanings to imply quite different things, constructing and elaborating the varieties of ambiguity without which speech can never become human speech.

Look at the record of language if you want to glimpse the special qualities of the human mind that lie beyond the reach of any machine. Take, for example, the metaphors we use in everyday speech to tell ourselves who we are, where we live, and where we come from.

The earth is a good place to begin. The word "earth" is used to name the ground we walk on, the soil in which we grow plants or dig clams, and the planet itself; we also use it to describe all of humanity ("the whole earth responds to the beauty of a child," we say to each other).

The earliest word for earth in our language was the Indo-European root *dhghem*, and look what we did with it. We turned it, by adding suffixes, into *humus* in Latin; today we call the complex polymers that hold fertile soil together "humic" acids, and somehow or other the same root became "humility." With another suffix the word became "human." Did the earth become human, or did the human emerge from the earth? One answer may lie in that nice cognate word "humble." "Humane" was built on, extending the meaning of both the earth and ourselves. In ancient Hebrew, *adamha* was the word for earth, *adam* for man. What computer could run itself through such manipulations as those?

We came at the same system of defining ourselves from the other direction. The word *wiros* was the first root for man; it took us in our vanity on to "virile" and "virtue," but also turned itself into the Germanic word *weraldh*, meaning the life of man, and thence in English to our word "world."

There is a deep hunch in this kind of etymology. The world of man derives from this planet, shares origin with the life of the soil, lives in humility with all the rest of life. I cannot imagine programming a computer to think up an idea like that, not a twentieth-century computer, anyway.

The world began with what it is now the fashion to call the "Big Bang." Characteristically, we have assigned the wrong words for the very beginning of the earth and ourselves, in order to evade another term that would cause this century embarrassment. It could not, of course, have been a bang of any sort, with no atmosphere to conduct the waves of sound, and no ears. It was something else, occurring in the most absolute silence we can imagine. It was the Great Light.

We say it had been chaos before, but it was not the kind of place we use the word "chaos" for today, things tumbling over each other and bumping around. Chaos did not have that meaning in Greek; it simply meant empty.

We took it, in our words, from chaos to cosmos, a word that simply meant order, cosmetic. We perceived the order in surprise, and our cosmologists and physicists continue to find new and astonishing aspects of the order. We made up the word "universe" from the whole affair, meaning literally turning everything into one thing. We used to say it was a miracle, and we still permit ourselves to refer to the whole universe as a marvel, holding in our unconscious minds the original root meaning of these two words, miracle and marvel—from the ancient root word *smei*, signifying a smile. It immensely pleases a human being to see something never seen before, even more to learn something never known before, most of all to think something never thought before. The rings of Saturn are the latest surprise. All my physicist friends are enchanted by this phenomenon, marveling at the small violations of the laws of planetary mechanics, shocked by the unaccountable braids and spokes stuck there among the rings like graffiti. It is nice for physicists to see something new and inexplicable; it means that the laws of nature are once again about to be amended by a new footnote.

The greatest surprise of all lies within our own local, suburban solar system. It is not Mars; Mars was surprising in its way but not flabbergasting; it was a disappointment not to find evidences of life, and there was some sadness in the pictures sent back to earth from the Mars Lander, that lonely long-legged apparatus poking about with its jointed arm, picking up sample after sample of the barren Mars soil, looking for any flicker of life and finding none; the only sign of life on Mars was the Lander itself, an extension of the human mind all the way from earth to Mars, totally alone.

Nor is Saturn the great surprise, nor Jupiter, nor Venus, nor Mercury, nor any of the glimpses of the others.

The overwhelming astonishment, the queerest structure we know about so far in the whole universe, the greatest of all cosmological scientific puzzles, confounding all our efforts to comprehend it, is the earth. We are only now beginning to appreciate how strange and splendid it is, how it catches the breath, the loveliest object afloat around the sun, enclosed in its own blue bubble of atmosphere, manufacturing and breathing its own oxygen, fixing its own nitrogen from the air into its own soil, generating its own weather at the surface of its rain forests, constructing its own carapace from living parts: chalk cliffs, coral reefs, old fossils from earlier forms of life now covered by layers of new life meshed together around the globe, Troy upon Troy.

Seen from the right distance, from the corner of the eye of an extraterrestrial visitor, it must surely seem a single creature, clinging to the round warm stone, turning in the sun.

Reflections on the Readings:

1. Why is the excerpt from Gertrude Stein included in this text?

2. "I may call a chair 'a chair' and someone else may call it 'a bed.' Who can say who is right? We're both right."

   What's wrong with this claim?

   What's right about this claim?

3. In what way does Lewis Thomas share a point of view with Plato?

Language and the World

Why do you believe what you believe? Probably the most common answer to this question is "Because that's the way the world is," implying that it would be foolish to believe otherwise. Sometimes, of course, we are not so sure of our beliefs and we choose other responses like "My mother told me that when I was ten" or "I just can't help being afraid of dogs; I was bitten by a dog when I was six" or "I've never liked the taste of lima beans." That is, we generally think that we have two kinds of beliefs: (1) beliefs which we hold because we think they are accurate pictures of reality and (2) beliefs which are particular to us as individuals, to our upbringing, and to our tastes and preferences. We often refer to the first kind of belief as objective and the second as subjective.

Consider the following two descriptions of nineteenth-century New York City:

> I was much pleased with New York. The new houses are palaces. They are very large and built in a rich . . . ornate style of architecture. The material is brown sandstone which has a fine effect.
>
> Letter quoted by John Maass in _The Victorian Home in America_

> ... the intolerable ugliness of New York ... the narrow houses so lack-
> ing in dignity. ... This little low-studded. ... New York, cursed with its
> universal chocolate-colored coating of the most hideous stone ever
> quarried. ...
>
> Edith Wharton, *A Backward Glance*

How could they differ so much? After all, there could be only one
"objective reality" which is New York. But there are two different authors or
subjects. Perhaps each author has created his or her own "subjective reality."

At this point we might take either of two tacks (and philosophers and
nonphilosophers have a long history of having done this). We could say that
one of the two descriptions is better than the other because it comes closer
to describing the reality which is New York City. That is, the language of the
better one "mirrors" or "corresponds" to the world in ways that the lesser
description does not. We might even go so far as to call the better one "right"
or "true." Or we could say that the two passages describe two realities, realities which are created by the two narrators. On this view reality or the world
is simply a product of our individual subjective experience. No wonder we
disagree so often.

There is a third alternative that we think is preferable, however, to the
objectivist or subjectivist accounts of the relation between language and the
world, and this is our Socratic account. Although there are many good reasons for adopting our Socratic point of view, we will not review them all
here. What you should know is that our Socratic viewpoint enables us to clarify some cloudy issues and to avoid getting bogged down by unsolvable puzzles about the relationship between language and the world.

What is this Socratic account? According to the Socratic account, our
beliefs should be evaluated as parts of larger sets or systems of beliefs. Systems of beliefs either work or don't work in the world. Or perhaps more
accurately, some systems work up to our expectations for them and others
do not. When a set or system of beliefs fails to work up to expectation, we
begin to replace it with a set that works better. These systems of beliefs can
be about the architecture of New York City, the parts of the atom, the nature
of dogs, or the taste of lima beans. All sets of beliefs are evaluated by how
well they work for us as individuals or as members of the larger community.
This means that our belief systems are continuously open. They are continuously being tested by our experience of the world and in our dialogues with
our friends and others. Sometimes we find we have to change or throw out
a belief since it no longer works for us—as, for example, when you become
attached to the big German Shepherd you previously feared. And sometimes
we have to throw out whole sets of beliefs as, for instance, when the Iron
Curtain crumbled across Eastern Europe and the Cold War came to an end.

Or when sixteenth-century astronomers began to doubt that the earth was the center of the universe.

It is our belief that a rational person is a good critical thinker, someone open to this continuous dialogue and who understands why this openness is important. As you seek to improve your reasoning skills, keep your mind open to both of the dialogues which shape our beliefs—the dialogue between ourselves and others and the dialogue between ourselves and the world.

The Uses of Language

Most of the time we simply **use** language without thinking about the **uses** of language. Language can be used to convey information, express feelings, give orders, ask questions, or entertain. In each of these uses our language may be successful or not, and success is usually judged by how much closer we have moved to our various goals. With some oversimplification, our goals usually fall into one of the three following categories:

- **to understand, predict, and control the world around us so that we can survive and prosper,**

- **to maintain and improve our relationships with those around us so that we have more friends, fewer enemies, and can love and be loved,**

- **to have pleasant rather than unpleasant experiences and to enjoy as much of our lives as we possibly can.**[1]

Language which is successful at prediction and control is often considered the most powerful use of language and therefore taken as a model for other language uses. If we stop to think about it, however, it is much more difficult to have "control" over the people around us. Language which is successful in maintaining and improving our relationships with other people is somehow more sophisticated and more complicated than the language of prediction and control of things. We will look at all three of these uses of language, keeping in mind, however, that the language of human relationships is the most important model for our understanding of language and the world.

---

[1] These divisions of human concern have a long and honorable history from Plato to Freud.

Words

Words are the smallest pieces of language. We seldom use them one at a time, although we sometimes do. "Sit," we say sternly to the disobedient dog. "July," we say in response to the question "What month were you born in?" But most of the time our words are strung together into larger pieces of language like statements, questions, orders, and exclamations.

If we do not know what a particular word means, there are ways of finding out. To consider an extreme case, imagine that we're the sole survivors of a shipwreck, washed onto an island where the natives speak a language unknown to us. We notice that the word *gavagai* is frequently uttered. In this case (an example made famous by the philosopher W. V. Quine) we would likely try to determine whether the utterance of the word *gavagai* coincided in any regular way with some obvious feature of the world. Suppose the natives uttered *gavagai* when two or more white rabbits were playing in the morning sunshine. We might then reasonably believe that *gavagai* was the plural form of our word *rabbit* (or perhaps means *white rabbits playing in the sunshine before noon*).

Although few of us will ever be marooned on a strange island needing to build a language from scratch, we all behave somewhat like castaways when we hear or read an unfamiliar word in our own language. In this case, however, we are familiar with most of what was said before or after the unfamiliar word. We have a context to help us define the word. If that does not do the trick, we may fall back on the castaway technique and see if the use of the word coincides with some feature of the world around us.

The process of assigning meanings to words is, of course, called **defining** and there are at least three ways of defining words. In the first and simplest, we define a word by pointing at some part of the world (or at some part of the world in a picture or other representation). This is called an **ostensive definition**. We have already glimpsed ostensive definition in the example of the castaways. As castaways, we hope that the natives' use of *gavagai* will point out some feature of the world for us and thus define *gavagai*.

Another way of defining a word is to survey contemporary users of the word (often a panel of expert users) and ask them what the word means. These **lexical definitions** are then collected into the dictionaries we use to look up unfamiliar words. The notion of lexical definition allows for and assumes change. So, what *horse* meant to our ancestors (say, *the predominant means of transportation, fueled by hay and oats*) it may not mean to us.

Finally a third sort of definition, the **stipulative definition**, attempts to isolate a fixed meaning of a word for particular purposes. For instance, a rocket scientist might define *force* as the product of the mass of a body multiplied by its acceleration, whereas the nonscientist might use _force_ as a synonym for _power_. Often stipulative definitions catch on and become part of our general usage and then show up later in the dictionary as lexical definitions.

Statements

A statement is a group of words which are used to assert something. For example, the statement "This is my book" asserts that this is my book. A statement is not the same thing as a sentence which may contain one statement ("This is my book"), more than one statement ("This is my book and it has a blue cover"), or no statements at all ("Is this my book?"). Except for so-called rhetorical questions, questions do not assert anything at all.

Statements are either **warranted** or **unwarranted**. We warrant our statements by making other statements in support of them. No statement is self-warranting; that is, no statement offers more than trivial support for itself. We are unconvinced by someone who argues "I'm right because I'm right." Although no statement is self-warranting, the process of warranting our statements clearly has practical limits. We usually try to warrant our statements using other statements which though not self-warranting, do not themselves demand further warranting statements. For example, consider what it would take to warrant the statement "That is my book." Suppose, for instance, you notice that the woman with the red hat who has been sitting next to you on the bus picks up your copy of _Thinking Socratically_ and puts it in her handbag and begins to stand up as the bus slows to stop. Your immediate goal is the recovery of your book and to move toward that end you say, "[Excuse me but] that is my book." If the lady then hands you the book saying, "I'm so sorry; I mistook it for a similar-looking one I've been reading," your statement "That is my book" would not need warranting.

If, however, the red-hatted lady clutched the book to her side and said, "I'm sorry but you must be mistaken—this is my copy of _Thinking Socratically_ and I have my receipt from the bookstore to prove it," then your statement would need warranting, since it did not accomplish its goal. It did not get your book back.

If you were still convinced that the book was yours, not hers, you might reply by using the following warranting statements: "But I'm sure that it is _my_ book. I always write my name on the first page of all my books. Let's look at the first page to settle it." The lady agrees and opens the book to the first page where to your great surprise is, written in unfamiliar script, a stranger's name! Now your attempt to warrant seems to need warranting itself and your initial statement "That is my book" seems less warranted than ever. Of course, things might have happened differently. The flyleaf might have revealed your name, enabling you to say "My name is on the flyleaf" and so warranting your set of warranting statements and, retroactively, your first statement—"That is my book."[2]

Factual Statements

Those statements which have been found to be the most warranted— those for which support is seldom asked—we call factual statements. Let us apply this account of factual statements, as those which have been found to be the most warranted, to the saga of the book on the bus. Suppose that even after examination of the flyleaf reveals a stranger's name, you still believe that the book is yours. In desperation you yell, "Driver, stop the bus! Call the police! This woman is trying to steal my book!" The driver stops the bus and calls the police to investigate. The lady—true to her word—pulls a receipt for a copy of *Thinking Socratically* from her handbag and shows the police her name written on the first page. What would be the point of your claiming that it is a **factual statement** that the book is yours if no statement you have made supports that claim? If the statement "That is my book" is ever to be accepted as factual, then it, or some other statement which supports it, must first be warranted.

To emphasize this point: Suppose that despite all your setbacks you persist, and finally one or more of your statements does begin to offer support. For example, suppose that you say, "Microscopic analysis of the hair found between pages 100 and 101 will reveal a match with hair taken from my cat Fred, a member of a breed so rare that he is the sole North American example." And, further suppose that somewhat later a laboratory technician says, "The hair taken from Fred matches perfectly the hair found between pages 100 and 101 of the disputed copy of *Thinking Socratically*." At that moment your initial statement "That is my book" becomes plausible because the statements about Fred's hair warranted it. That is, the statement "That is my book" can only be regarded as a factual statement if those statements which

---

[2]You may be thinking here that calling a statement "warranted" is an awful lot like calling a statement "true." The ordinary notion of truth, however, tends to carry the implication that the individual statements we make can somehow be compared to the real world and then dubbed true or false. But what we actually do is more like this–I look out my window, see a blue sky and think or say, "The sky is blue." Now, the only way I can check the truth of my statement is to look again and see if I am prompted to think or say again, "The sky is blue." What I compare are my two statements, one with the other, not my statement and "the world." Since this comparison between statements and the world cannot be carried out in the way usually intended by users of the word *true*, we prefer to talk about statements as **warranted** or **unwarranted**. If you prefer, you can use the words *plausible* and *implausible*. We will continue to develop the distinction between warranted and unwarranted statements throughout this text.

support it cease to be called into question (perhaps because the results of the microscopic analysis of Fred's hair have become widely known). **Factual statements, after all, are just those statements which for whatever reason are seldom called into question.**

One final note about the warranting of statements. As the above example shows, statements are not warranted individually, but rather as members of a group or set of statements which "lean" on each other for support. Considered as isolated individual statements, none of the group is capable of standing on its own if called into question. Even the laboratory technician's statement that the hair from Fred perfectly matches the hair found in the book does not stand on its own. If called into question it would need to be supported by statements about the accuracy of microscopes, about the identifying features of cat hair, and so on. **Thus, the only way to begin the process of warranting a statement is by making another statement.** Statements are accepted as members of groups of statements, and the relation of a statement to the other statements in the group is what makes it a factual statement.

The selections you read for this chapter make this point very clearly. Probably as you read the selection from Gertrude Stein you were annoyed by the constant repetition of the narrator. One of the reasons people repeat themselves, with slight variation each time, is that they are not sure they have been successful in their communication. They are not sure their statements have worked. Although no statement is self-warranting, we sometimes try to make them self-warranting by repeating them until (we hope) they are no longer questioned. Listen to the people around you. Do you find them

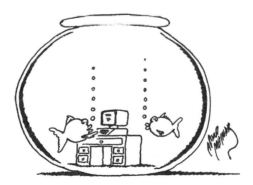

"I FED IN ALL THE AVAILABLE DATA ON THE ORIGIN OF THE UNIVERSE AND THE COMPUTER BEARS OUT MY BIG SPLASH THEORY."

The corner of _whose_ eye also makes a difference! Copyright © Scott Arthur Masear 1993. Reprinted by permission Scott Arthur Masear.

repeating themselves to make sure their statements are accepted or at least understood?

Or consider the essay from Lewis Thomas. Thomas suggests that we may be on the verge of adopting both a new way of looking at the world and a new set of statements to describe and make meaningful what we see. Our planet Earth, according to Thomas, is perhaps most plausibly viewed not "straight on," as a collection of separate interacting life-forms, but rather from "the corner of the eye," as one complex living organism "clinging to the warm stone, turning in the Sun." Such a revolutionary statement as this one, which asks us to rethink our place in the universe, would clearly require a great deal of warranting before it became accepted.

The *Euthyphro* of Plato which you read in the Introduction also raises questions about how we warrant or fail to warrant our statements. Socrates asks Euthyphro to support his claim that he knows what *piety* is. (*Goodness* would be a good modern substitute for the classic term *piety*.) Euthyphro is so sure that he knows enough about piety that he is bringing charges of murder against his own father. But when Socrates questions him, he is unable to supply a single warranting statement. That is, he does not offer any statement which is unlikely to be called into question. The Socratic dialogue form lets us see how we use language in our relationships with others and how difficult it sometimes is to be successful in those relationships. Even though Euthyphro has not been able to provide Socrates with a single warranting statement for his claims, he is still convinced that he knows what piety is and that putting his own father on trial is a pious act. Notice that Euthyphro makes other unwarranted claims, such as his claim that Socrates will win his case. Certainly Euthyphro's claims were not widely accepted among his fellow countrymen, who were soon so convinced of Socrates' impiety that they put him to death. Paradoxically Plato's dialogue called *Euthyphro* and the statements in it made by Socrates have been accepted in the world and have introduced countless numbers of students to philosophy for two thousand years!

Exercises

1–I

1. What three general goals do human beings share?

2. What is a factual statement?

3. Define each of the following: ostensive definition, lexical definition, and stipulative definition.

1–II

1. Words are often used differently in different parts of the country. List ten examples of word usages which depend on geography. The same thing goes for generations. List ten words you and your friends might use whose meanings your parents might find puzzling

2. Words are not neutral. They are often value-loaded. They imply praise or blame, approbation or disapprobation. (Even when used as neutrally as possible, they are sometimes said to be "damning with faint praise.") For each of the words below write a synonym which **changes** the value content of the word.

pretty

large

nice

extrovert

reserved

pale

girl

creative

3. Is "Columbus discovered America in 1492" a warranted statement? Defend your answer.

1–III

1. William James in his book *Pragmatism* describes an argument which like many arguments turns on the meaning of words. Read this well-known passage. Then describe an episode from your own experience which is similar.

> Some years ago, being with a camping party in the mountains, I returned from a solitary ramble to find every one engaged in a ferocious metaphysical dispute. The *corpus* of the dispute was a squirrel—a live squirrel supposed to be clinging to one side of a tree trunk; while over against the tree's opposite side a human being was imagined to stand. This human witness tries to get sight of the squirrel by moving rapidly round the tree, but no matter how fast he goes, the squirrel moves as fast in the opposite direction, and always keeps the tree between himself and the man, so that never a glimpse of him is caught. The resultant metaphysical problem now is this: *Does the man go round the squirrel or not?* He

goes round the tree, sure enough, and the squirrel is on the tree; but does he go round the squirrel? ... Everyone had taken sides, and was obstinate. ... Each side ... appealed to me to make it a majority. ... "Which party is right," I said, "depends on what you *practically mean* by 'going round' the squirrel. If you mean passing from the north of him to the east, then to the south, then to the west, and then to the north of him again, obviously the man does go round him, for he occupies these successive positions. But if on the contrary you mean being first in front of him, then on the right of him, then behind him, then on his left, and finally in front again, it is quite as obvious that the man fails to go round him, for by the compensating movements the squirrel makes, he keeps his belly turned towards the man all the time, and his back turned away. Make the distinction, and there is no occasion for any farther dispute. You are both right and both wrong according as you conceive the verb 'to go round' in one practical fashion or the other."

2. Perceptions are also not neutral. Not only does how we describe our experiences vary, but even the experiences themselves can vary and not just from person to person, but for the same person, from moment to moment. To a larger extent than we usually appreciate, what we see is largely dependent on what we are prepared to see or what we pre-perceive. To see this, consider the following examples.

a.

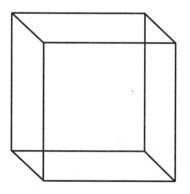

Do you see a cube? In which direction does it protrude? Now look at it again. If you saw it as protruding down toward the right, look at how it protrudes up toward the left. Has the figure changed? How can you account for the difference? Is the figure really a cube—or is it twelve lines on a flat surface?

b.*

Describe the figure in the right foreground. What if someone told you it was an antelope? Are you surprised? Consider the same figure in a different context:

c.*

Now do you see an antelope?

Bring in an example which illustrates how seeing is not neutral.

3. Explain how you would teach a child the definition of *horse*.

---

*From *Patterns of Discovery* by Norwood Russell Hanson. © 1958, 1961. Reprinted with permission of Cambridge University Press.

chapter 2

Knowledge and Certainty

Introduction

Most people would claim that they know quite a lot, especially about themselves, their families, their friends, their neighborhood, and perhaps even about their country. When pressed, however, they usually begin to back off a bit, acknowledging that they certainly cannot prove all the things they would claim to know. While they are pretty sure that their knowledge claims are justified, when they stop to consider, they realize that they could be mistaken about some of the claims they would make. Some of these claims, they would admit, are really belief statements, not knowledge statements.

We usually don't think about whether a statement is a statement of knowledge or a statement of belief unless, of course, we are talking about religious matters where we usually use the vocabulary of belief. If we feel certain, then we say *know*. If we feel somewhat uncertain, then we say *believe*. This distinction in the use of these terms tells our listener something about our ability to warrant our claims and, therefore, how much the listener should believe our claims. These common-sense distinctions are important to good critical thinking. After all, what we would like is to know, not just to believe. To be able to do this, we have to have a clearer idea of the distinction between knowledge statements and belief statements. Philosophers have continually worried about this distinction.

In this chapter we will present our account of what we mean when we say we know something and how that differs from mere belief. We will also look at a traditional attempt to link knowledge with certainty, a famous one by Descartes which is the reading for this chapter. Descartes was a seventeenth-century thinker who was upset because everything he had been taught was being disproved by modern science, which was just in its infancy. He set out to determine what he could know without a shadow of a doubt–that wouldn't shortly be contradicted by science. You probably are already familiar with the answer he gave to his own query. The one thing he found he could not doubt was his own existence. He expressed his proof for his existence in a now famous argument: _cogito, ergo sum._ I think, therefore I am.

Meditations on First Philosophy

RENÉ DESCARTES

MEDITATION ONE: CONCERNING THOSE THINGS THAT CAN BE CALLED INTO DOUBT

Several years have now passed since I first realized how many were the false opinions that in my youth I took to be true, and thus how doubtful were all the things that I subsequently built upon these opinions. From the time I became aware of this, I realized that for once I had to raze everything in my life, down to the very bottom, so as to begin again from the first foundations, if I wanted to establish anything firm and lasting in the sciences.

Yet to this end it will not be necessary that I show that all my opinions are false, which perhaps I could never accomplish anyway. But because reason now persuades me that I should withhold my assent no less carefully from things which are not plainly certain and indubitable than I would to what is patently false, it will be sufficient justification for rejecting them all, if I find a reason for doubting even the least of them. Nor therefore need one survey each opinion one after the other, a task of endless proportion.

(an excerpt)

Rather—because undermining the foundations will cause whatever has been built upon them to fall down of its own accord—I will at once attack those principles which supported everything that I once believed.

Whatever I had admitted until now as most true I took in either from the senses or through the senses; however, I noticed that they sometimes deceived me. And it is a mark of prudence never to trust wholly in those things which have once deceived us.

But perhaps, although the senses sometimes deceive us when it is a question of very small and distant things, still there are many other matters which one certainly cannot doubt, although they are derived from the very same senses: that I am sitting here before the fireplace wearing my dressing gown, that I feel this sheet of paper in my hands, and so on. But how could one deny that these hands and that my whole body exist? Unless perhaps I should compare myself to insane people whose brains are so impaired by a stubborn vapor from a black bile that they continually insist that they are kings when they are in utter poverty, or that they are wearing purple robes when they are naked, or that they have a head made of clay, or that they are gourds, or that they are made of glass. But they are all demented, and I would appear no less demented if I were to take their conduct as a model for myself.

All of this would be well and good, were I not a man who is accustomed to sleeping at night, and to undergoing in my sleep the very same things—or now and then even less likely ones—as do these insane people when they are awake. How often has my evening slumber persuaded me of such customary things as these: that I am here, clothed in my dressing gown, seated at the fireplace, when in fact I am lying undressed between the blankets! But right now I certainly am gazing upon this piece of paper with eyes wide awake. This head which I am moving is not heavy with sleep. I extend this hand consciously and deliberately and I feel it. These things would not be so distinct for one who is asleep. But this all seems as if I do not recall having been deceived by similar thoughts on other occasions in my dreams. As I consider these cases more intently, I see so plainly that there are no definite signs to distinguish being awake from being asleep that I am quite astonished, and this astonishment almost convinces me that I am sleeping.

Reflections on the Reading:

1. Have you ever felt like Descartes, uncertain about everything? Why or why not?

2. How does the fact that you think prove that you exist?

3. Name five things of which you are absolutely certain.

4. Describe a time when you were absolutely certain that you were right about something and later found out that you were mistaken. How did this happen?

Knowledge/Certainty

It has been the dream of philosophers, scientists, and theologians to rule out the possibility of being mistaken. They have sought an account of knowledge which could be regarded as certain or perhaps even infallible. Generally, two different approaches have been taken in pursuit of this dream. The first is that taken by those thinkers called **empiricists** (from the ancient Greek word for knowledge, _empeirei_). Empiricists claim that we can be certain about at least some of the statements we make, because some of them are warranted directly by experience, by the things we see, touch, hear, smell, and taste.

The traditional alternative to empiricism and the second approach to the problem of how knowledge could be certain or infallible is the one used by the French mathematician and philosopher René Descartes. A short excerpt from his _Meditation One_ is the reading for this chapter. Descartes claims that all knowledge has to be either certain or based on something certain. Philosophers usually call approaches of this type **foundational** views of knowledge because of their requirement that each piece of knowledge be based or founded on something certain.

As Descartes himself shows in the reading, however, virtually none of our statements is free from doubt. We cannot even be sure that we are awake and not asleep and only dreaming that we are awake. The only statement which, according to Descartes, meets this high standard of being free from doubt is the statement "I exist" (since in order to doubt I exist, I would need to assume that I exist, for if I didn't exist I couldn't possibly do anything and I certainly could not doubt).

Each of these historical approaches has much to recommend it but each also raises additional questions such as: Can knowledge be warranted by experience alone? Must knowledge be infallible? Rather than ask how knowledge can be certain or infallible, or whether it can be warranted solely by experience, let us see what insight can be gained by looking at an example of a knowledge claim.

Suppose you claim to know that "Koala bears are warm and cuddly." If someone challenged this knowledge claim (or if you had some question about it yourself), you would warrant it by making other statements, either to yourself or others, statements such as "This is a koala bear," "It's brown," "It's cuddly," and so on. That is, you would support your knowledge claim

THE FAR SIDE　　By GARY LARSON

" 'This dangerous viper, known for its peculiar habit of tenaciously hanging from one's nose, is vividly colored.' . . . Oo! Murray! Look! . . . Here's a picture of it!"

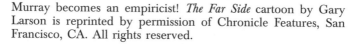

Murray becomes an empiricist! *The Far Side* cartoon by Gary Larson is reprinted by permission of Chronicle Features, San Francisco, CA. All rights reserved.

with other statements. Some of these statements, like the preceding statements, will be about the things you are now experiencing. Others, however, will be about the various things you need to assume in order to make *any* statements about your present experiences. That is, your statement about koala bears *needs* as warrant, not merely other statements like the ones above about your present experience, but also a whole "supporting cast" of other statements, for instance, statements about the general reliability of your memory (e.g., that you didn't call this fuzzy thing in front of you a kangaroo last time around) and about the accuracy of your senses (that this is not an illusion nor are you dreaming or drunk). Most of this supporting cast of statements, of course, remains unuttered except in unusual situations. But it is important to see that the certainty of our knowledge claims and of the statements we make expressing them is supported by whole groups or "webs" of statements which we would use to warrant them should they be called into question by others. Clearly our knowledge, in our everyday world, is made up of those statements which are warranted to the point where we do not call them into question. If asked to warrant them, we warrant them by uttering other statements. Let's look further at this account of knowledge.

The Web of Belief[1]

Knowledge is best thought of as a part of a web–a web we have constructed and continue to construct in order to link together the statements which express our beliefs. We build our webs, not like spiders to catch flies, but rather to have some sort of coherent system, a worldview adequate to guide us through the rest of the day and through the rest of our lives. The center of this web is occupied by our most entrenched belief statements, those it would be hardest to give up. To abandon one of these center-of-the-web belief statements we would have to adjust or even abandon many other belief statements linked to it in the web. The periphery of the web is composed of our belief statements about which we are least sure and which we could give up with minimal readjustment of the web. We warrant our belief statements to ourselves by fitting them into our web. If a statement meshes with none of the other belief statements in our web of belief, then that statement is likely to be rejected. Those statements which mesh with some of the other belief statements in the web remain for the time being "mere" beliefs and are not promoted to the status of knowledge statements. Those statements, however, which fit very well into the web, which mesh with many of the other belief statements in the web–these statements we regard as knowledge. When we say that we *know* something we are not claiming to be infallible. Rather we are indicating that we would be amazed if what we say we *know*, what we have warranted to ourselves, couldn't be warranted to others as well.[2]

For example, the statement "Abraham Lincoln was the author of the Gettysburg Address" will be warranted for you if it fits together with other belief statements from your web such as "The Gettysburg Address was writ-

---

[1] *The Web of Belief* by Quine and Ullian (Random House, 1970) shares many of the same ideas expressed here.

[2] A similar account of what it means to say that we *know* something, as opposed to merely saying that we *believe* it, is offered by the Austrian philosopher Ludwig Wittgenstein (1889–1951). See his *On Certainty* #355, ed. G. E. M. Anscombe and G. H. von Wright, New York: Harper and Row, 1972.

ten by the U.S. President who held office during the Civil War," "Abraham Lincoln was the U.S. President during the Civil War," etc. Hence, you say you know that Lincoln was the author of the Gettysburg Address.

When we wish to warrant one of our statements to some other person, the best way of doing so is to begin an open dialogue with that person. In this dialogue we express those statements from our web which we think offer the greatest amount of support for the statement we wish to warrant. For example, if the statement which you want to warrant is your claim "Abraham Lincoln was the author of the Gettysburg Address" you might begin by uttering the two warranting statements from your web of belief just mentioned.

If the statements which express our knowledge are accepted by almost everyone around us we regard them as **factual**. The statement about Abraham Lincoln is one that you do regard as factual. In the first place, it fits well into your web of belief—so well that you would be amazed if you could not warrant it to others if asked to do so. In the second place, this statement is accepted by virtually everyone around you. From our discussion about the **open dialogue, warranting for ourselves, warranting for others**, and **factual statements** we can describe the goal of critical thinking in the following way: **The critical thinker is someone who makes the effort to warrant as many of his beliefs as is possible, and who attempts to test and share his knowledge with everyone who is willing to participate in an open dialogue.** The result of this goal of critical thinking is something clearly beneficial to all—factual knowledge which has been tested in the arena of open dialogue and found to be warranted. This is clearly preferable to what often passes for factual knowledge, namely, something uncritically accepted on the basis of authority, or prejudice, or some combination of the two.

We can see from this discussion, then, that good critical thinking does not lead to certainty in the traditional sense of infallible knowledge. What it does help us to do is to weed out errors from our own webs of belief and to participate in the shared web of belief of the larger community. This enables us, further, to anticipate and plan for the future, to have friends, and to have pleasant, rather than unpleasant, experiences.

EXERCISES

2-I

1. What is the difference between saying "I believe..." and "I know..."?

2. Suppose Jennifer says, "The grass is green." What additional statements must be assumed for this statement to be warranted?

3. What is the difference between a statement at the center of a web of belief and a statement on the periphery of that web?

2–II

1. Why is it better to know something rather than just believe it?

2. List five belief statements in the center of your web of belief. If you were to take one of these out of your web of belief, what other beliefs would have to be weeded out also?

3. List five belief statements which you find yourself unable to warrant to others but which are sufficiently enmeshed in your web of belief that you believe them anyway.

4. Explain why Descartes's _Meditation_ is a foundational view of knowledge.

2–III

1. Can we ever be certain—in the sense of infallible? Why or why not?

2. Suppose while driving to work you are stopped by the police. The officer examines your license and says, "This license isn't yours." You then look at the license and see that, indeed, it is not your license. What revisions in your web of belief would you make in response?

chapter 3

Arguments and Explanations

Introduction

In the first chapter we looked at words and at groups of words which assert something, namely, statements. In this chapter we will look at groups of statements. The groups of statements we are interested in here are pieces of reasoning called arguments. Arguments try to convince someone else of a particular point of view, predict what is going to happen, or help someone understand why something occurred. Arguments are the primary means of providing warrant for the statements we make.

Arguments are everywhere! We are always trying to convince someone of something: to vote for a particular candidate, to buy a certain product, to give permission to stay out all night after the prom, to accept that we didn't mean it when we insulted them. But, lo and behold, everyone does not vote for the same candidate and Mom is not convinced that we should be allowed to stay out as late as Tom or Mary. Why not? Why don't the claims that we offer convince our listeners of the correctness of *our* point of view? We would all like to be better reasoners so that other people agree with *us!*

Among those people who spend time studying the effectiveness of arguments are philosophers. Philosophers particularly study the differences between good arguments (valid or strong arguments) and poor ones (invalid or weak arguments). Of course, that does not mean that all philosophers' arguments are convincing. Philosophers are known for arguing among themselves and often have trouble convincing one another. But we should expect as much. After all, they are people, too.

We should not take this problem of distinguishing between good and bad arguments too lightly, however. Good reasoning or the lack of good reasoning can make very important practical differences in our lives. The first two readings in this chapter are examples of this. They are from *The Decameron,* which is a famous collection of stories written during the Renaissance by Giovanni Boccaccio. In the first story a young man, Michele Scalza, argues in order to win a bet. To win the bet and claim the prize of a free dinner, Scalza must convince his companions that a certain family—the Baronci—are the oldest and thus the most noble family in the whole world. In the second story Melchizedek, the hero, argues to save his life. If he doesn't convince Saladin of the correctness of his answer, he will die. Saladin's question is a tricky one, too: "Which one of the world's great religions is the true one?"

The third reading here is one you will read with great interest and will puzzle over for a long time because it is about a "real world" mystery. It is a newspaper account of an event that actually happened in Philadelphia in 1982. Two babies in the same day-care center died on the same day. It is a hard story to dismiss as simply an unhappy coincidence.

The Decameron

GIOVANNI BOCCACCIO

Michele Scalza

Michele Scalza proves to certain young men that the Baronci are the most noble family in the whole wide world, and wins a supper.

In our city, not so very long ago, there was a young man called Michele Scalza, who was the most entertaining and agreeable fellow you could ever wish to meet, and he was always coming out with some new-fangled notion or other, so that the young men of Florence loved to have him with them when they were out on the spree together.

Now, one day, he was with some friends of his at Montughi, and they happened to start an argument over which was the most ancient and noble family in Florence. Some maintained it was the Uberti, some the Lamberti, and various other names were tossed into the discussion, more or less at random.

Scalza listened to them for a while, then he started grinning, and said:

'Get along with you, you ignorant fools, you don't know what you're talking about. The most ancient and noble family, not only in Florence but in the whole wide world, is the Baronci. All the philosophers are agreed on this point, and anyone who knows the Baronci as well as I do will say the same thing. But in case you think I'm talking about some other family of that name, I mean the Baronci who live in our own parish of Santa Maria Maggiore.'

His companions, who had been expecting him to say something quite different, poured scorn on this idea, and said:

'You must be joking. We know the Baronci just as well as you do.'

'I'm not joking,' said Scalza. 'On the contrary I'm telling you the gospel truth. And if there's anyone present who would care to wager a supper to be given to the winner and six of his chosen companions, I'll gladly take him up on it. And just to make it easier for you, I'll abide by the decision of any judge you choose to nominate.'

Whereupon one of the young men, who was called Neri Mannini, said:

'I am ready to win this supper.' And having mutually agreed to appoint Piero di Fiorentino, in whose house they were spending the day, as the judge, they went off to find him, being followed by all the others, who were eager to see Scalza lose the wager so that they could pull his leg about it.

They told Piero what the argument was all about, and Piero, who was a sensible young man, listened first to what Neri had to say, after which he turned to Scalza, saying:

'And how do you propose to prove this claim you are making?'

'Prove it?' said Scalza. 'Why, I shall prove it by so conclusive an argument that not only you yourself, but this fellow who denies it, will have to admit that I am right. As you are aware, the older the family, the more noble it is, and everyone agreed just now that this was so. Since the Baronci are older than anyone else, they are *ipso facto* more noble; and if I can prove to you that they really are older than anybody else, I shall have won my case beyond any shadow of a doubt.

'The fact of the matter is that when the Lord God created the Baronci, He was still learning the rudiments of His craft, whereas He created the rest of mankind after He had mastered it. If you don't believe me, picture the Baronci to yourselves and compare them to other people; and you will see that whereas everybody else has a well-designed and correctly proportioned face, the Baronci sometimes have a face that is long and narrow, sometimes wide beyond all measure, some of them have very long noses, others have short ones, and there are one or two with chins that stick out and turn up at the end, and with enormous great jaws like those of an ass; moreover, some have one eye bigger than the other, whilst others have one eye lower than the other, so that taken by and large, their faces are just like the ones that are made by children when they are first learning to draw. Hence, as I've already said, it is quite obvious that the Lord God created them when He was still learning His craft. They are therefore older than anybody else, and so they are more noble.'

When Piero, the judge, and Neri, who had wagered the supper, and all the others, recalling what the Baronci looked like, had heard Scalza's ingenious argument, they all began to laugh and to declare that Scalza was right, that he had won the supper, and that without a doubt the Baronci were the most ancient and noble family, not only in Florence, but in the whole wide world.

And that is why Panfilo, in wanting to prove the ugliness of Messer Forese, aptly maintained that he would have looked loathsome alongside a Baronci.

The Decameron

GIOVANNI BOCCACCIO

Melchizedek

Melchizedek the Jew, with a story about three rings, avoids a most dangerous trap laid for him by Saladin.

Saladin, whose worth was so great that it raised him from humble beginnings to the sultanate of Egypt and brought him many victories over Saracen and Christian kings, had expended the whole of his treasure in various wars and extraordinary acts of munificence, when a certain situation arose for which he required a vast sum of money. Not being able to see any way of obtaining what he needed at such short notice, he happened to recall a rich Jew, Melchizedek by name, who ran a money-lending business in Alexandria, and would certainly, he thought, have enough for his purposes, if only he could be persuaded to part with it. But this Melchizedek was such a miserly fellow that he would never hand it over of his own free will, and the Sultan was not prepared to take it away from him by force. However, as his need became more pressing, having racked his brains to discover some way of compelling the Jew to assist him, he resolved to use force in the guise of reason. So he sent for the Jew, gave him a cordial reception, invited him to sit down beside him, and said:

'O man of excellent worth, many men have told me of your great wisdom and your superior knowledge of the ways of God. Hence I would be glad if you would tell me which of the three laws, whether the Jewish, the Saracen, or the Christian, you deem to be truly authentic.'

The Jew, who was indeed a wise man, realized all too well that Saladin was aiming to trip him up with the intention of picking a quarrel with him, and that if he were to praise any of the three more than the others, the Sultan would achieve his object. He therefore had need of a reply that would save him from falling into the trap, and having sharpened his wits, in no time at all he was ready with his answer.

'My lord,' he said, 'your question is a very good one, and in order to explain my views on the subject, I must ask you to listen to the following little story:

'Unless I am mistaken, I recall having frequently heard that there was once a great and wealthy man who, apart from the other fine jewels contained in his treasury, possessed a most precious and beautiful ring. Because of its value and beauty, he wanted to do it the honour of leaving it in perpetuity to his descendants, and so he announced that he would bequeath the ring to one of his sons, and that whichever of them should be found to have it in his keeping, this man was to be looked upon as his heir, and the others were to honour and respect him as the head of the family.

'The man to whom he left the ring, having made a similar provision regarding his own descendants, followed the example set by his predecessor. To cut a long story short, the ring was handed down through many generations till it finally came to rest in the hands of a man who had three most splendid and virtuous sons who were very obedient to their father, and he loved all three of them equally. Each of the three young men, being aware of the tradition concerning the ring, was eager to take precedence over the others, and they all did their utmost to persuade the father, who was now an old man, to leave them the ring when he died.

'The good man, who loved all three and was unable to decide which of them should inherit the ring, resolved, having promised it to each, to try and please them all. So he secretly commissioned a master-craftsman to make two more rings, which were so like the first that even the man who had made them could barely distinguish them from the original. And when he was dying, he took each of his sons aside in turn, and gave one ring to each.

'After their father's death, they all desired to succeed to his title and estate, and each man denied the claims of the others, producing his ring to prove his case. But finding that the rings were so alike that it was impossible to tell them apart, the question of which of the sons was the true and rightful heir remained in abeyance, and has never been settled.

'And I say to you, my lord, that the same applies to the three laws which God the Father granted to His three peoples, and which formed the subject of your inquiry. Each of them considers itself the legitimate heir to His estate, each believes it possesses His one true law and observes His commandments. But as with the rings, the question as to which of them is right remains in abeyance.'

Saladin perceived that the fellow had ingeniously side-stepped the trap he had set before him, and he therefore decided to make a clean breast of his needs, and see if the Jew would come to his assistance. This he did, freely admitting what he had intended to do, but for the fact that the Jew had answered him so discreetly.

Melchizedek gladly provided the sultan with the money he required. The Sultan later paid him back in full, in addition to which he showered magnificent gifts upon him, made him his lifelong friend, and maintained him at his court in a state of importance and honour.

The Day-Care Deaths:

A Mystery

LINDA HERSKOWITZ

Lisa Hatten and Fran McClendon met each other for the first time on an October afternoon at the day-care center. They didn't know it, but the two had much in common. Each had one child, a baby daughter. Each had nearly miscarried in the fifth month of pregnancy. And each had recovered from the loss of an earlier pregnancy: Lisa had miscarried; Fran had given birth prematurely to twins—one was stillborn, the other died within hours. Both women now used day care because both needed full-time jobs. They were having trouble just getting by.

As the two women exchanged pleasantries, Lisa mentioned that some snowsuits her baby had outgrown would probably fit Fran's baby. Lisa said she'd bring them the next day. That night, she packed a black vinyl Sport-sac with playclothes, Pampers, baby bottles, barrettes, skin ointment, under-shirts, and socks, but no snowsuits. She forgot.

But by the next afternoon, Friday, Oct. 15, 1982, that and everything else that once seemed to matter would not. Both babies would be dead—stricken at the day-care center—with little hope that anyone would ever know why. The parents, as well as the woman who ran the day-care center, would be devastated. The deaths would remain beyond everyone's under-standing and control. Even the investigators—reconciled to the fact that, at times, a single death can defy explanation—would find themselves incredi-bly baffled: how could *two* babies die in the same house on the same day, with no clues as to why?

Fran McClendon, 35, slim and self-possessed, had gone back to work at the Center City insurance company where she had a job before Ashley's birth. She'd learned about Sheila Rolland's day-care service by asking the state welfare department for a list of registered day-care programs nearby. Fran had just started bringing Ashley to day care that week.

The Rolland house in Wynnefield was only a five-minute drive over a bridge from the McClendons' rowhouse on North Wanamaker Street in West Philadelphia. Fran checked the place out and liked what she saw: a white, semi-detached house on Gainor Road, a broad residential street, where neighbors added personal touches like aluminum doors and flower arrange-ments in picture windows. Mrs. Rolland's own living room was done in mus-tard and gold brocade. The house was spotless.

In the finished basement, where she ran the day-care program, there was a large playroom with a tile floor, blackboard, desk chairs, a playpen with a baby chair in it, cots for napping, a toy box, a big chair for Mrs. Rol-land, and a bathroom.

Fran was impressed that Mrs. Rolland taught the kids the alphabet and arithmetic and took them on day trips. And she really took to Mrs. Rolland herself. She was a round-faced, amiable, chatty, heartwarming women of 33, the kind who really loves kids.

Fran's little Ashley, 4 months old, was the first to die.

It was about 11:30 a.m. when the call came. Fran was typing at her desk. It was Mrs. Rolland: "I think you should call the doctor and come and get Ashley. She's not going to bed and she won't eat. Listen to her breathe." Fran could hear the baby being lifted to the phone. Ashley was whimper-ing, as if she were about to cry.

Fran called her pediatrician and talked to the nurse, who asked a few questions and said it sounded like Ashley had a cold. She suggested a drop of Tylenol and nose spray. Then Fran called her mother, who agreed to get a cab and pick up Ashley and tend to her for the rest of the day.

Mrs. Rolland called back before Fran could even tell her. She sounded impatient. *When was Fran coming to get her baby?* Fran explained that her mother would be there within a half-hour.

By now, it was noon. Fran had a lunch date, but she wondered whether she should break it. No, Ashley's condition didn't sound serious. She'd go to lunch, and call to check on her from the restaurant.

Mary Harris, Ashley's 56-year-old grandmother, had a night job, so even though it was after noon, she was still wearing her nightgown when she heard the knocking on her door. She peered through a small window. It was Mrs. Rolland, who had called earlier to tell her to forget the cab, she'd bring Ashley right over. She was holding the baby and seemed flustered and upset. She handed Ashley over, and as Mary Harris looked down at her granddaughter, she was horrified to see the baby's eyes rolled back in her head.

"Oh, my God," she said. "Something is wrong with my baby." She sat down in the armchair near the door, trembling as she cradled the infant. Mary Harris had seen her mother-in-law pass on. She'd been through the deaths of too many people; she knew what death looked like. The baby felt feverish, but she knew Ashley was as good as dead—Ashley, the first new baby in the family in 13 years, the first girl in nearly 20.

Mrs. Rolland, shaking, dialed the rescue squad; Mary Harris called Fran—still at lunch—then ran upstairs to put on some pants. When the rescue squad pulled up, the men yelled, *"Get this baby out of here!"* They took Mary Harris with them. Mrs. Rolland followed in her car. As they ran into street construction on 52d Street, Mrs. Harris was nearly hysterical, crying to the driver to hurry up, find a way around it. Sheila Rolland was praying behind her steering wheel, "Please, God, don't let her die."

At Misericordia Hospital, they rushed Ashley to a room in the back. Mary Harris sat in the waiting area, and Sheila Rolland cried and chanted, "I didn't do it. *I* didn't do it." That irritated Mrs. Harris. "Now wait a minute," she said. "Nobody said nothin' about anybody doin' nothin'."

Then a priest came out. He thrust a piece of paper into Mrs. Harris' pocket and said he was going to read the last rites. "Don't you be giving me no papers. My baby's dead," she said angrily. She didn't want religious words. Then a doctor came out. She looked into his face and whispered, "You know my baby's dead, right?"

It was five minutes to two. "We're sorry," he said.

Darryl Crosby, a 14-year-old, well-mannered boy from the neighborhood who helped Mrs. Rolland after school by changing Pampers and watching the kids, got to her house early, about a quarter to two.

Mrs. Rolland wasn't there. Her husband, Robert, an older man who usually came home for lunch every afternoon, had been minding the kids while his wife had gone to the hospital because one of the babies was sick. Then he went downstairs to check on the workmen who were replacing the back door in the basement.

Darryl went upstairs to check on the kids. Normally they'd be napping on cots in the basement, but today they were upstairs in the rear bedroom because of the workmen. Lisa Hatten's little girl, 10-month-old Lisa, seemed to be the only one asleep. She was lying on top of the covers on one side of the bed, her head turned to one side. Three other kids were scrunched together, giggling, on the other side of the bed. Four more were horsing around on the floor.

Tom Rolland, Darryl's buddy and at 15 the oldest of the three Rolland boys, came home from school at about 2:30. The two boys, Darryl recalled later, decided to go to the Rollands' own bedroom and watch some TV.

Fran got back to her office at 2. A co-worker was waiting with a fist-ful of messages. "You have a family emergency," he said. Get to Misericordia Hospital." She was certain nothing was seriously wrong, but she got there in less than 15 minutes. When she walked through the emergency entrance, someone took her to a small waiting room. Suddenly, there was her family—her mother, two sisters, her brother—and Mrs. Rolland. They looked terrible.

Then her mother said in a choking voice, flat out, "Baby, she's dead."

Fran was still for a moment, then started screaming, "I want to see her!" A nun said, "I'm not going to let you see her until you calm down." *Reprimanded*, Fran thought, like she was disrupting a class. She wanted to hit the nun.

But Fran quieted down, and the nun ushered her into a small room in the back. There was Ashley, lying on a gurney. Her clothes were off; she was wrapped in a hospital gown. She still looked like herself. Fran picked her up; her body was still warm. Suddenly she felt someone watching her and looked up. The door was opened a crack. The eyes of the nun peered through.

"Why don't you leave me alone?" Fran screamed.

"You'll be all right," the nun said. "I have to watch you."

She had no privacy. Fran put Ashley down and stalked past the nun.

A doctor was outside. "We did everything we could," he said. "I'm sorry." She waited for something more, but he was silent. She felt a scream rising in her throat. Then he said, "We think it's a SIDS death." She knew that meant Sudden Infant Death Syndrome, something inexplicable, even to doctors.

"Are you sure?" Fran asked.

"Well, we have to do some tests," he said.

Fran's head was swimming. "If I had gotten here in time, would she have lived?"

The doctor didn't reply. His face was without expression. First the nun, now the doctor.

Fran faced Mrs. Rolland, who chanted pleadingly, almost hysterically, "Please don't blame me, please don't blame me."

What had happened?

"I don't know. I tried. Ashley started having problems breathing. I tried to call emergency, but I was so upset I dialed the number and couldn't make them understand what was wrong. So I grabbed her, got in my car, grabbed my son, and ran her over to your mother's house."

Fran was numb, dazed. She hugged Mrs. Rolland. "I'm sorry," she said. "I know you did everything you could."

She thought of calling her husband, John, at work, but she was so shaken that she couldn't remember his telephone number. Her mother was tugging at her, trying to get her out of the hospital. Mrs. Harris was saying, "We'll call him when we get home."

Fran let herself be led outside to a car.

The men were still working on the back door when they heard Mrs. Rolland's car pull into the driveway. Robert Rolland's car was just pulling away from the curb. It was about 3 o'clock. She trudged through the back door, into the basement, leaned heavily against the wall and said to the workmen, "She's gone."

Then she climbed the back stairs to the kitchen. The boys, still watching television, had heard her come in. She called up to them, "Hurry up, everybody, get the kids down here." Darryl wondered what was wrong. Tom helped him lead the toddling children downstairs, then Darryl went back up for the sleeping Lisa. Leaning over the bed, he noticed that one of her shoes was on the floor. When he bent over to pick it up, he saw dried blood on her face. He carried her downstairs and said to Mrs. Rolland, "What's wrong with this child?"

Sheila Rolland took her, then in a strangled voice, she said, "Oh, my God, she's dead."

Still holding the baby, she dampened a towel in the kitchen, wiped the blood away, then returned to the living room, laying the baby in her lap as she sat down on the sofa. She put her mouth over the baby's nose and mouth, trying to breathe life into it. Then she lifted her head and started screaming.

The workmen downstairs heard the screams, then the steps of someone running to the top of the basement staircase. A teenaged boy yelled down to them, "My mother needs you." As they came upstairs, Darryl heard one of the workmen say to the other, "Yo, Bob, another one's dead."

Darryl thought to himself, *another one?*

At 3:30, Lisa Hatten was practicing on a word processor at the Center for Innovative Training, a secretarial school near 13th and Arch. She was serious about job training and eager to find work because her relationship with Sahib Easley, the father of her child, was rocky after five years. If they went separate ways, she wanted to be able to support herself and the baby.

Lisa heard her name being called on the loudspeaker, *"EMERGENCY CALL."*

Her first thought was *my baby.*

Lisa moved and spoke in a deliberate, thoughtful manner that made her appear older than 23. Even with growing fear and apprehension, she maintained this dignity and reserve as she walked to the school's main office and picked up the phone.

On the other end, Sheila Rolland was crying hysterically, yelling, "Lisa's dead. Lisa's dead."

"What are you talking about? What's wrong with my baby? Where's she at?" Lisa said, her voice rising above its usual deep murmur.

"She's dead, she's dead," Mrs. Rolland said in a nervous staccato. "Another baby died here today. I took the baby to the hospital and when I came back, I checked on her and the baby wouldn't wake up. I was walking around, trying to get her to wake up and she wouldn't wake up."

Lisa was now shaking, overcome by the unreality of what she'd heard. She handed the phone to her friend Susie, the baby's godmother, who worked at the school. But before Susie could finish asking what hospital the baby had been taken to, Mrs. Rolland hung up. Lisa sat in the school office, crying, "This lady keeps telling me my baby is dead."

Susie dialed the Rolland number repeatedly, but it was busy. Finally, she got through, and someone said the baby had been taken to Misericordia. Lisa called her mother, then the grain shipping company where Sahib worked. She left him a message to call the school, and ran out with Susie.

While Susie drove, Lisa sat silently in the car, repeating to herself, *nothing's wrong with my baby. They got the wrong parent. They called the wrong one. This isn't happening.*

They ran into Misericordia's emergency entrance, but were told the baby had been taken to Osteopathic Hospital. They rushed over, and a young doctor ushered them into a small conference room. As they walked in, Lisa saw her mother and sister sitting there, sobbing.

Now she knew something terrible *had* happened. The doctor was talking softly to her, inviting her to sit down. She asked to see the baby, wanting them to say she was all right.

Her mother said, "They did all they could do."

"Everything we did failed," the doctor said softly. The baby had been declared dead at 4:59 p.m.

She sat numbly while the doctor asked questions. All she grasped was this: Had she known that another baby in that house had died that day also?

Her first thoughts were, _something went on that shouldn't have. Something happened. Two babies dying in the same house the same day. It's strange, very strange. She remembered Mrs. Rolland saying something about another baby, but she hadn't comprehended that two babies had died. She thought Mrs. Rolland was talking only about Lisa._

No, she said, she didn't know anything about that.

About a half-hour after the emergency room staff declared Lisa Easley dead, John McClendon turned the key in the front door of his house. He had left work about 3:30, and it took him almost two hours to drive home from the construction site where he worked in Bristol.

When he entered the living room, he was astonished to find it filled with his wife's family. So solemn. Someone was crying. Everyone was there, he thought as he scanned the room, except the two people who belonged there, Fran and Ashley. He knew something was terribly wrong.

No one spoke for a few frozen seconds. Fran's sister was about to say something when Fran herself walked down the stairs. It was she who told him. It went in one ear and out the other. He wanted to say _come on, man, what's the joke?_ All at once, through his fog, someone forced him to pour a shot of vodka down his throat. Everyone was trying to tell him all at once what had happened, but none of it made sense. That's what was driving him crazy.

He was walking with a cane because of a sprained ankle, but he flung the cane away—oblivious to the pain—and ran out the door. Fran's brother and sister ran after him. They caught him a half block away and struggled to keep him from breaking free. All he could see in his mind's eye was Ashley's face as it was the last time he'd seen her, when he'd left for work that morning. She'd been singing.

He was getting angrier and angrier at Fran and her mother. They had left him out. They didn't call him immediately, and had robbed him of the chance to see his daughter in the hospital a last time. They'd acted as if he wasn't central to this.

Back at the house, the 6 o'clock news was on. The anchor was talking about two deaths at a day-care center. _Deaths?_ The people in the McClendon living room were stunned. It was the first they'd heard that another baby had died, too. John exploded, started yelling. Then the doorbell rang. Two homicide detectives walked in.

John told them right off he wanted to see Ashley. John wanted to see her, touch her, check on her, turn her over, look at her closely and make sure she hadn't been beaten or in any way abused. He had heard her *singing* the night before, for God's sake. They told John that she had been taken to the medical examiner's, where an autopsy would be performed the next day.

While they waited, John called the medical examiner's office. It was 7 at night now, and the employee answering the phone said the office was closed. He could come the next morning, on Saturday, at 7. The employee was polite, but abrupt and impersonal. John started yelling at him on the phone. It was all too much. Everyone was shutting him out.

Then the detectives started asking questions. It was like a cross-examination. What had the baby eaten? Was she sick any other time, did she show any signs of respiratory problems, could there be anything the McClendons had done? When detectives heard she'd taken Tylenol, they wanted the bottle.

That night, he would barely sleep.

At 10:30 Friday night, the phone rang in the Fairmount home of Dr. Robert Sharrar, the city's epidemiologist. On the other end was his boss, Dr. Stuart Shapiro, Philadelphia's health commissioner, who told him about the deaths of the two babies. Shapiro wanted to make certain the other kids at the day-care center were all right, that they had not been exposed to something contagious.

Sharrar called Marvin Aronson, the city's chief medical examiner. Aronson said homicide detectives had already made sure that the other kids—there were 10 of them, including three of Mrs. Rolland's own—were examined at hospitals. They all checked out fine.

When Sharrar called Shapiro back, the commissioner told him to attend the autopsies the next morning. That was unusual. Normally, if homicide detectives are looking into a death, the health department leaves the case to the medical examiner. But Shapiro felt that this time, epidemiologists also should be involved.

After he hung up, Sharrar thought about it. Two babies in the same house on the same day. What could it have been?

Bacterial meningitis was the first thing that came to mind. But, he debated with himself, that didn't usually kill within hours. And usually there were more symptoms: fever, stiff neck, sometimes skin rash. And even as lethal as it could be, it wouldn't kill two kids that fast.

Another possibility was homicide—perhaps the children had been abused. But Aronson had told him on the phone that he saw no outward evidence of trauma.

Other possibilities were legion: a malfunctioning heater could have poisoned the kids with carbon monoxide; they could have had a virus or a toxin . . . but so fast?

To a certain extent, Sharrar felt he was on foreign ground. Determining the cause of death was not his job, it was the medical examiner's. Medical examiners investigated the death of anyone who had not been seen by a physician in the previous 24 hours or anyone who might have died of unnatural causes.

Sharrar had almost never been involved in a case where the cause of death was not obvious from the start. His job was to help understand disease by finding what its victims had in common.

When he was in medical school, one of the things he heard repeatedly was that 25 percent of the people got 75 percent of the disease. At the time, he couldn't understand how that could be. He began to understand it, though, when he got interested in epidemiology. The principle underlying epidemiology is that disease does not occur by chance: It is not randomly distributed in the population, and the patterns of distribution say something about how and why it occurs.

That was the professional perspective he brought to this case. Something those babies had in common must have done them in. Whatever it was, however, didn't appear to be an immediate threat to the other kids at the day-care center. So Sharrar felt it was safe to go to bed.

John McClendon woke up early, and was immediately impatient to get to the medical examiner's office. He got there at 6:30 a.m. and had to wait a half-hour before someone would let him in. When he finally saw a representative of the medical examiner, John immediately asked to see his baby. The man said they didn't allow a personal viewing. Then he pulled out a form and said he had some questions. John was disgusted. Everybody wanted something from him. Nobody was interested in giving him anything. Whose baby *was* it, anyway?

The questions were almost identical to the ones the cops had been asking the night before. Sterile, law-type questions. Then the representative left and a doctor came in. John again asked to see Ashley's body. The doctor said they didn't allow it. They hadn't done the autopsies yet, and they didn't want anyone bringing in germs or taking them out, just in case something infectious was involved.

But they would let him see the body on a television monitor; it would help them if he could positively identify her. A small TV was turned on, and there was a black-and-white picture of a naked baby lying on a table. But the camera was too far away for John to tell if there were any signs of abuse. It was just close enough to show that the baby was Ashley. She had a half smile on her face that made him ache. It was the same expression she rewarded him with when he'd pick her up and shake her. Now he was getting really upset, mouthing off at the doctor for the indignity of being shut out from his own baby.

The doctor said it was just policy.

Sharrar got to the medical examiner's building by 9 a.m. He saw the babies lying on the table as soon as he walked into the room. They looked like healthy, well-kept little girls.

Sharrar watched Dr. Robert Segal, an assistant medical examiner, make a half-moon-shaped incision beneath the throat of each body. He peeled back the skin, opened the skull, and took out the brains. They looked perfectly normal. No layer of filmy haze—the sign that white cells had fought against the inflammation of meningitis, which was really what Sharrar had suspected. Nor was the cerebrospinal fluid cloudy. It was clear, showing no signs of infection. So was the middle ear, where infection can spread to the lining of the brain cavity.

They removed the tongue and pharynx for examination, because if they were only slightly inflamed, they could block the throat and cause death. They were normal. They looked at the trachea for signs of infection. One child's trachea was a little congested, and had little streaks of red through it, but that wouldn't cause death. Besides, it was the baby who was said to have had a slight cough that day, and the streaks were consistent with that.

They even got down to checking basic things, like making sure the heart vessels led to the right places. It took about three hours to examine both bodies. Sharrar then took tissue specimens to his office building, where he put them in a special incubator to see if any bacteria or virus would grow.

The next morning, Sunday, Sharrar met the city's lab director to interpret the culture plates. The cerebrospinal fluid showed nothing. The trachea grew some organisms, but only what would be expected. In short, nothing.

Over the next few days, the most plausible explanations were being knocked off, one by one.

When Aronson, the chief medical examiner, first heard about the deaths, he thought the weather had turned suddenly cool and that the daycare center had "turned on the goddamn heater and they got carbon monoxide poisoning." That was disproved when the medical examiner's office sent two investigators to the scene and found it wasn't so.

Neither baby had suffered physical injury. Aronson was convinced that no kind of negligence had contributed to their deaths. And suicide was obviously out. As were barbiturates, opiates, any identifiable poison, or heavy metals. There were no bad reactions to vaccinations, because neither child had been recently vaccinated. The tissues revealed no presence of the types of botulism or viral infections that could kill a baby quickly. The paint and plastering was found free of toxic substances.

Aronson was beginning to consider the impossible—that each baby had been the victim of Sudden Infant Death syndrome, and had just happened to be in the same place at the same time.

SIDS has been around since biblical times, but only recently has it been studied. In the typical case, an apparently healthy baby, usually three weeks to seven months old, is put to bed without the slightest suspicion that anything is wrong. At most, there may be signs of a slight cold. Some time later, the infant is found dead. No one has heard the baby make a sound, and there is no evidence of a struggle. An autopsy reveals, at most, minor inflammation of the upper respiratory tract, but nothing that would kill. Often, the autopsy reveals no evidence of illness.

Individually, Lisa and Ashley were textbook examples of SIDS. But the mathematical odds of two babies being stricken in the same place on the same day were just too unbelievable—one in a billion, maybe one in a trillion, Aronson thought.

He decided it was time to ask for outside help. He conferred with Shapiro, and they agreed to call the Centers for Disease Control (CDC), headquartered in Atlanta. The federal agency had the resources and expertise to perform advanced bacteriological studies.

Hell, Aronson thought, we pay taxes for it, we might as well use it.

Stephen Bowen, the CDC epidemiologist assigned to the New Jersey Health Department, has the look of the outdoors about him. He was, in fact, out in a field in Monmouth County, N.J., collecting ticks suspected of carrying a bacteria that causes arthritis, when his beeper went off. It was Thursday afternoon, Oct. 21, nearly a week after the babies had died.

His boss in Atlanta, the man in charge of about 40 agents assigned to health departments around the country, was calling him to tell him he was on the case. Bowen was pleased; he liked unusual cases.

The next morning he went to see Sharrar, whom he'd known for years. They reviewed the investigation. Practically everything plausible had been ruled out. Except SIDS. The younger baby was well within the common age range, but the 10-month-old was a little old for it. The autopsy findings, they agreed, didn't lean strongly toward or against a SIDS diagnosis.

Then they talked about questioning the principals; maybe someone had forgotten something significant. They decided to begin with Mrs. Rolland.

The week after the deaths had been a nightmare for Sheila Rolland. Television stations camped their lights in her front yard. She repeated the sequence of events to homicide detectives, reporters, inspectors from the state welfare department. The doctors from the health department came three times, once at 7 in the morning, to take throat cultures from everyone in the family.

They all asked her the same questions, and she came to feel they were trying to trip her up. She hadn't done anything wrong. That's why, when friends suggested she get a lawyer, she thought about it, but decided no. What for?

Then the papers printed stories saying that welfare investigators had found some violations of state day-care regulations, although they felt none contributed to the deaths. She had more children than the six allowed for a center of that size. She had no individual files with each child's medical information and back-up telephone numbers. (She *did* have a lot of that information; it just wasn't organized the way they wanted it.) She had no fire extinguisher; she couldn't produce first-aid materials.

As if those things might have made a difference.

It didn't take long before Bowen realized there just weren't many untouched bases. It was becoming increasingly likely that they were heading toward a conclusion that went against the basic tenet of epidemiology: perhaps this *was* that one-in-a-trillion case. If enough cases of anything occur, sooner or later more than one is going to happen in the same place at the same time. It was just a statistical truth. Besides, they had no other explanation.

He knew this was the worst thing to tell the families. They wouldn't accept it. They'd be torn between wanting to blame somebody and feeling guilty that they hadn't done something differently. But there was nothing to say except that these things happen. It's no one's fault.

He concluded his report and sent it off to Atlanta, where it was added to the bulging epidemic assistance file. As often as epidemiologists found the answer, they did not. It would always be that way; new mysteries would come along to replace the solved ones.

Bowen returned to collecting ticks.

EPILOGUE

One night in late November, John McClendon was watching television when a cute little girl came on the screen. He began feeling haunted by Ashley, a feeling that ebbed and flowed. He found Sahib Easley's phone number and dialed it.

McClendon was so anxious to talk, he forgot to introduce himself. "I understand your grief for your child," he began. "Me above all people can understand your plight."

There was silence on the other end. "Who is this?" Easley said gruffly.

McClendon answered softly, "I'm sharing the same kind of grief you have. I'm the father of the other child."

On Thanksgiving, Fran McClendon could hardly get out of bed. Her mother said, "Get yourself together and get over here for dinner." She did, but it was hard to get through the meal. She kept thinking about Thanksgiving the year before, when she was carrying Ashley.

Then, on Christmas, she was plunged into another deep depression. God must know she was strong, Fran thought. He must know she can deal with this. She had to keep telling herself something would happen down the road to make it easier to bear.

Lisa Hatten was resentful. She'd never heard once from Mrs. Rolland, except for a Mailgram she and Sahib received around the time of the funeral. It said, "We are heartily sorry for your loss. May God be with you."

Didn't Mrs. Rolland feel she owed her some personal contact, to help her feel closer to the events of that day—what time she had put the baby to bed, how she had been found, who had been watching her, what had *happened?*

In their two-room basement apartment on the Upper Darby side of Cobbs Creek Park, Lisa and Sahib Easley kept most of their daughter's possessions intact. Baby pictures were all over the living-room wall. A large Pampers box, filled with toys, was in its customary place on the floor next to Sahib's weights.

They kept the crib at the foot of their bed, along with the furry teddy bear mobile that dangled over it. The baby's flannel, ruffled nightgown with blue hearts and flowers, the one that Sahib Easley liked the best because she looked like a little lady in it, rested on his pillow. He still slept with it against his cheek.

Sheila Rolland never dreamed it would end in such a horrible way. She'd started the day-care program six years ago, after the death of her grandmother, who'd raised her and then taken care of her great-grandchildren while Sheila worked.

The day-care program had been a wonderful idea. She had given herself to those kids. They were *her* kids. She had a fragile and intimate relationship with them. Now, she never wanted to work in day care again. She would always wonder whether a child would leave the same way he came in. She explained to the mothers that she was closing down. It wouldn't be fair to the children. She'd always feel hyper. Children are sensitive; they would know.

Some of the mothers called and said their children were upset at being separated from her and wanted to talk to her, just on the phone.

She wouldn't. She told the mothers she had to let go, that the kids would be all right.

She began looking for another job. She wanted something as remote from day care as possible, like bank work. But after several interviews, she came to believe that the publicity over the deaths was hurting her prospects. People recognized her name when she put down "day care" as her previous experience. She still couldn't bring herself to talk to Lisa or Fran; she felt too raw.

But she had to let go of her grief. She asked God when it would be over. The answer came as she awoke one morning. A voice said, "It *is* over. Put it behind you."

She had to return to the world of the living.

On Dec. 14, 1982, Dr. Robert Segal signed the death certificates of Lisa Easley and Ashley McClendon. Segal and Aronson agreed that the deaths of these two babies should not get lost among the thousands of cases of SIDS. They listed the cause of death as "UNDETERMINED." Maybe other babies had died under similar circumstances somewhere else. Maybe it would happen again. Maybe someday someone would figure out why.

Reflections on the Readings:

1. Does Michele Scalza prove his case? How?

2. Why is Melchizedek's argument a good one?

3. Can you think of a time when you (or perhaps your parents) told a story to bring someone (you) around to your (their) point of view? Were you (they) successful?

4. Is SIDS a good explanation in the "Day-Care Deaths" story?

5. How is the investigation in the "Day-Care Deaths" like playing the board game Clue?

Arguments: Premises and Conclusions

As we saw in Chapter 1, statements are what we use to make assertions. A good working definition of statements, then, would be the following:

STATEMENT–A group of words used to assert something.

Our assertions are sometimes accepted, sometimes rejected and sometimes even ignored by those around us. If the statements we assert are accepted we usually move on—to the next statement, the next task, or the next cup of coffee. When our statements are ignored we sometimes repeat or rephrase them hoping they will now be noticed. The excerpt you read from Gertrude Stein in Chapter 1 illustrates this all too human behavior. When our statements are questioned or rejected our usual response is to attempt to support or **warrant** the doubted statement. And, as we have pointed out previously, the only way to warrant a **statement** is by *making other statements* (other assertions)—hoping finally to arrive at a statement or statements for which further support is not requested.

Whenever we attempt to warrant one statement by making others we are offering an **argument**. In an argument, the statement we wish to warrant is called the **conclusion**, while the statement or statements which do the supporting are called the **premise(s)**. Premises and conclusions are often introduced by, or contain, clue words which help you recognize that the speaker or author intends to give an argument and which also help you to distinguish the statement being warranted from the supporting statements being offered. Typical clue words indicating premises are *since, for, being that, because, if.* Clue words indicating conclusions include *therefore, consequently, it follows that, thus.* These words are useful but not infallible guides to recognizing premises and conclusions. Sometimes the author of an argument may misuse them by mistake and sometimes even deliberately as, for instance, when she is trying to make an argument look stronger than it is.

Consider the following example of an argument. Suppose Tom says, "The Beatles were the greatest musical artists of all time." Given the differences we all know exist from person to person with respect to musical taste, we would expect someone somewhere to question Tom's bold pro-Beatles announcement. Suppose that Tom made his "Beatles were the greatest" statement in front of Joan, an avid admirer of classical music in general and of Mozart's music in particular. Joan might well challenge Tom's statement by replying, "Tom, are you nuts? The Beatles greater than Mozart? You'll never convince me of that!"

Now suppose that Tom takes up Joan's challenge and tries to convince her that she ought to accept his "Beatles were the greatest" statement as factual. If you were Tom, how would you attempt to do that? One way might be to show Joan that other statements that she accepts as factual support the statement that "The Beatles were the greatest." Again, when we support statements which have not been accepted as factual by using statements which we expect will be accepted as factual we are giving **arguments**. An argument can be more precisely defined as follows:

ARGUMENT–Two or more statements one of which—the conclusion—is supposed to be supported by the other(s)—the premise(s).

The phrase "is supposed to be supported" indicates that not every argument is successful. That is, sometimes we assume or suppose that our premises support our conclusions when they do not. Premises can support or warrant a conclusion in two ways. They can **logically warrant** the conclusion and they can **factually warrant** the conclusion.

Logical Warranting

One kind of support or warrant which premises can give a conclusion is **logical support or warrant**. **Logical warranting** can be a difficult notion to grasp at first, but a good way to begin to understand it is as connection between statements so that their status as factual is logically linked. This logical linking is such that if the premise statement or statements are considered to be factual then the conclusion statement logically linked to them would, as a result of that linking, have to be regarded as either factual or more likely to be factual. The first kind of logical warranting where the conclusion must be regarded as factual if the premise or premises are regarded as factual is called **reasoning with necessity** (or deductive reasoning). The second kind of logical warranting where the conclusion is only more likely is called **reasoning with probability** (or inductive reasoning). This is different from **factual warranting** where the support is provided not by any linkage between statements but merely by the supporting statement's being factual and/or relevant. Factual warranting will be discussed later.

Reasoning with Necessity

In reasoning with necessity the goal is to give a logically **valid** argument. In a **valid** argument, if you accept the premises as factual then you must also accept the conclusion as factual. The conclusion then is said to follow from or be logically implied by the premises. Logicians call these arguments using reasoning with necessity **deductive arguments**. The key idea here is that the logical relationship between the premises and the conclusion is such that *if* you accept the premises as factual you *also have to* accept the conclusion as factual. The reason the conclusion of a logically valid argument must be accepted as factual has nothing to do with what the premises actually say or assert. The necessity to accept the conclusion is entirely logical—due to the logical structure of the argument. The premises may even be obviously non-factual or nonsensical as in the following example from Lewis Carroll who, in addition to writing such well-known children's stories as _Alice in Wonderland_, was an avid logician.

> All old gorilla keepers are good-tempered people.
>
> All good-tempered people ride bicycles.
>
> Therefore, all old gorilla keepers ride bicycles.

The premises of this argument are likely either nonsense or nonfactual, but the conclusion is necessarily implied by the structure of the argument, which is just to say that _if_ all old gorilla keepers were good-tempered people and _if_ all good-tempered people did ride bicycles _then_ all old gorilla keepers would ride bicycles. This logical relationship between the premises and the conclusion of a valid argument is completely independent of anyone's _actually_ accepting any of them as facts. So, when this logical relationship is present you have to recognize someone's argument as logically **valid** even if you disagree with her premises. And _if_ her argument is valid _and if_ you accept her premises as factual then you _have to_ accept her conclusion as factual also.

Michele Scalza uses a common deductive argument known as _modus ponens_ in the first reading in this chapter. (_Modus ponens_ will be discussed in Chapter 5.) He argues that if the members of a certain family are all very ugly, then this indicates that the family is a very ancient one. And further that if a family is a very ancient one then it must also be a very noble one. Thus, since the Baronci family are the ugliest family in Florence they must also be the most noble family in Florence. In this case logic "pays." Scalza's winning argument buys him a dinner at the expense of his friends. That is, _if_ you accept the claims in his premises about the connection of ugly with ancient, and ancient with noble, then you _must_ accept his conclusion that the Baronci family are the most noble family in Florence. The statements of the premises are logically linked with that of the conclusion so that the factual nature of the premises _necessitates_ the factual nature of the conclusion. The premises logically warrant the conclusion—making this argument a valid argument.

Reasoning with Probability

When the logical linking is such that the statement supported by the linking becomes, as a result of that linking, more likely to be factual—but not _neces-_

sarily factual—we are **reasoning with probability** (also called reasoning inductively). The objective in reasoning with probability is to give a **strong** argument. In a **strong** argument, if the premises are accepted as factual then the conclusion is more likely than not to be factual. With inductive arguments, just as with deductive arguments, the question of **factual warranting** is separate from the **logical warranting**. So in reasoning with probability, as in reasoning with necessity, you may find that the conclusion is logically warranted by the premises even though you *do not* accept those same premises as factual. For example, consider the following strong inductive argument:

The sun has risen in the west for over two thousand years.

Therefore, the sun will rise in the west tomorrow.

Now, the premise of this argument is clearly nonfactual, but let's pretend for a moment that the premise is factual—that it is a fact that the sun has risen in the west for over two thousand years. Then, the conclusion would also have to be regarded as more likely than not to be factual. That is, it would be reasonable to believe *on the basis of the premise offered in support* that it is more likely than not that the sun will rise in the west tomorrow. This, then, is a strong inductive argument, even though we believe that both its premise and its conclusion are nonfactual.

A different type of reasoning with probability with a different kind of logical warranting was used by Melchizedek when he told the story of the three rings in order to save his life. This argument has a well-known form called "argument by analogy." This argument form is very common and very useful, especially when dealing with sensitive issues—like religion or moral behavior. A well-known example of argument by analogy is the story of "The Boy Who Cried Wolf," a story you probably have heard many times.

A person arguing by analogy presents the audience with an argument about a neutral topic in exactly the same form as the argument with the sensitive topic in order to concentrate on the reasoning and to avoid the emotional content of the sensitive material. For example, in this case Melchizedek discusses rings instead of religions so he can avoid the emotional issue of religion. Melchizedek convinces Saladin that there is no answer to the question which of the world's great religions is the true religion, without getting enmeshed in highly charged religious issues. The story of the three rings, which is neutral and analogous to the story of the three great religions, gives Saladin the insight to accept Melchizedek's point of view.

The principle which justifies this form of reasoning is that it is reasonable to assume that if two things share a number of features, they also have additional properties in common. So, if Sue and Sam are both children of Jim and Jane Smith and Sue was allowed to drive the car at age 16, then Sam should be allowed to drive the car at age 16, also.

Surely you have used this argument by analogy form yourself. Consider: "Mom, why can't I stay out all night after the prom? Mary's Mom says she can." Or, "I studied as long as Bob did. Why did he get an 'A' and I only got a 'C'?" Keep this argument form in mind. It can be very useful in discussions when tempers are starting to rise or when very sensitive feelings are aroused.[1]

Factual Warranting

A second way in which premises can support a conclusion is by **factually warranting** it, which is just to say that statements that are widely accepted offer stronger support than do ones that are not widely accepted. Factual warranting can characterize both reasoning with necessity and reasoning with probability. If we can offer factual statements as premises in our arguments, we are factually warranting the conclusions of those arguments. It will be recalled from Chapter 2 that **factual statements** are statements which have themselves been warranted to the point where they are seldom questioned. A factual statement is defined as follows:

FACTUAL STATEMENT–A warranted statement which is seldom questioned.

In using factual warranting we are using statements which have been warranted elsewhere to warrant the statements we now wish to support. We are borrowing warrant from another place and time, however close or recent that place or time was, for the present. We _must_ repeatedly borrow like this. Otherwise we would be condemned to an endless chain of warranting, warranting one statement after another until the end of time. In order for factual warranting to be successful the statement which is supposed to provide the support has to be less likely to be questioned than the statement which is being supported.

In addition, the supporting statement should be **relevant** to the supported statement. One statement is relevant to another when it contains an

---

[1]An excellent example of using argument by analogy to shed light on a very sensitive topic is Judith Jarvis Thomson's article "A Defense of Abortion," _Philosophy and Public Affairs,_ vol. 1, no. 1 (Fall 1971), pp. 47–66, where she draws an analogy between being pregnant and being kidnapped by the Society of Music Lovers who want to use your body for nine months to save the life of a famous unconscious violinist. Her examination of this analogy leads to a better understanding of what it means to say that someone has a "right to life." If you are interested in the issues of analogy or abortion, this article is worth reading.

unequivocal use of one of the terms of that statement. In an argument, for the premises to add support to the conclusion, each premise must be relevant to at least one other premise and at least one premise must be relevant to the conclusion. When irrelevant statements are presented as premises in an argument, they do not weaken the logical or factual warranting of the relevant premises but they do sometimes confuse us, causing us to think that a conclusion is warranted when it is not.[2]

Factual warranting can be better understood by considering the following examples. The first two examples involve reasoning with necessity; the last two involve reasoning with probability.

1. If the sun is rising in the east it must be morning.

   The sun is rising in the east.

   Therefore, it must be morning.

2. If the sun is rising in the west it must be morning.

   The sun is rising in the west.

   Therefore, it must be morning.

3. The sun has risen in the east every morning for over two thousand years.

   Therefore, the sun will rise in the east tomorrow morning.

4. The sun has risen in the west every morning for over two thousand years.

   Therefore, the sun will rise in the west tomorrow morning.

In the first example the first premise, "If the sun is rising in the east it must be morning," is *both factual and relevant.* Both it and the conclusion are about the rising of the sun, and it is a fact that the sun rises in the east in the morning. So if the sun is now rising in the east, as the second premise asserts, then because of both logical and factual warranting, the conclusion will be factual also. It *must* be morning. In the second example the premise, "If the sun is rising in the west it must be morning," is *relevant but not factual.* It is relevant because both it and the conclusion are about the same thing— the rising of the sun. However, since it is not widely accepted that the sun rises in the west, this premise cannot be regarded as factual. Although the

---

[2]Some of these confusions occur so regularly that they have specific names and are often grouped under the heading "fallacies of irrelevance." These will be discussed in Chapter 10.

conclusion of this argument is *logically* supported by its premises, it is not *factually* supported. There are no factual statements in the premises that would make the conclusion factual also. In the third example the premise is both relevant and factual and so lends support to the conclusion. In the fourth example the premise is relevant. Both it and the conclusion are about the sun. But it is not a factual statement that the sun rises in the west, so the premise does not make the conclusion any more likely to be factual.

Notice that the above examples show that what goes on in factual warranting is not exactly the same in reasoning with necessity as in reasoning with probability. In reasoning with probability the factual warranting is closely connected to the logical linking. In reasoning with necessity it is not. A relevant statement *always* adds to the **strength** of an argument when reasoning with probability. When the premises of such an argument are both relevant and factual we call the argument a **cogent** argument. When reasoning with necessity, the statements in the premises must be logically linked to the statement they are supposed to be warranting in order to contribute to the **validity**. To be logically linked they must be relevant but they need not be factual. A valid argument with factual premises is said to be a **sound** argument.

Implicit Premises and Conclusions

Arguments are all around us—in books, in newspaper editorials, in advertisements, and in our discussions with other people. The arguments which surround us, however, are not always clear or complete. Sometimes, in order to avoid repetition or to "trick" the recipient of the argument, the premises or even the conclusion of an argument will be left out. Logicians call such arguments **enthymemes**, and they are more effective for some purposes than are complete arguments. Consider the following enthymeme, which resembles an enthymeme which was part of a very successful advertising campaign:

The bigger the burger, the better the burger.

The burgers are bigger at Burger Heaven.

These two statements, whether or not they are factual (whether or not you or anyone at all agrees with them), are premises which logically imply the following *unstated* conclusion:

The burgers are better at Burger Heaven.

By not stating the conclusion, the writer leads the reader to draw the conclusion for herself, perhaps leaving the impression that the reader *made up her own mind* about the goodness of Burger Heaven's burgers. The writer of the advertisement imagines that you are driving down the boulevard at lunch time and, barely noticed by you, your car radio plays the Burger Heaven jingle. A few minutes later as you approach a Burger Heaven restaurant you hear the implicit conclusion of the jingle/argument playing in your head ("the burgers are better at Burger Heaven") and you turn, zombielike, into the Burger Heaven parking lot.

Explanations

Explanations are a sort of argument but a peculiar sort. We evaluate the typical argument by moving from premises to conclusion—we want to know how well the premises support the conclusion. In the typical explanation the conclusion is already accepted as warranted, and therefore considered to be factual, and what is missing is our understanding of that factual statement. That is, if we are still wondering why *this* factual statement is warranted and not some other statement, then what we need is an **explanation**. Some factual statements we accept without explanation. We don't care or we think the matter is too obvious. For example, if your neighbor's dog is named "Fido" you probably don't care why the dog's name is "Fido." Or you think you know why—Fido is a common dog name and your neighbor is the sort who would choose a common name. But if your neighbor's dog is named "Chewchuck," you might wonder why and ask for an explanation. ("Because he chews it down and chucks it up.")

often you have to know the context to know whether a piece of reasoning is an argument or a member of that special subcategory of argument called explanations. It depends on what is intended by the speaker or writer and on what is "missing"—**what** happened or **why** it happened. In distinguishing explanations from arguments your best judgment about what is intended will usually be correct. Out of context, however, some pieces of reasoning will simply be ambiguous as to whether they are intended to be arguments or explanations.

Explanations have the same forms as arguments. Other than the difference of starting with the conclusion and working "backwards" to the premises, everything is the same. In the typical explanation there is the evidence to support a claim, **the premises**, and the claim itself, **the conclusion**. However, the evidence is not offered to justify belief in the claim but to help us understand **how** or **why** the claimed event occurred. We want to know how or why because we are curious (as in the Chewchuck case) or because we want to be able to predict similar future occurrences (like the weather) or to control possible future occurrences (such as the likelihood of a plane crash).

Explanations use logical and factual warranting and the success of the explanation depends in large part, but not entirely, on the soundness or cogency of the argument implicit in the explanation. We expect the statements in the premises to be both factual and relevant to the conclusion. If the premises of an explanation are frequently questioned and not considered to be factual, then they add little to our understanding of the conclusion. For example, if your car refuses to start in the morning and your friend tells you that it is not starting because you didn't tell it good night the night before, you will reject her explanation as nonfactual and irrelevant. The statement to be explained, "My car won't start," is not factually warranted by the explicit premise, "You didn't say 'Good night' to it the night before" and the implicit premise, "Cars are more likely to start in the morning if you tell them 'Good night' the night before."

A very common form of explanation, especially in science but also in ordinary discourse, is to explain an event by referring to a universal generalization and some factual statement(s) which, together with the generalization, are thought to be sufficient conditions to bring about the event being explained. To take a simple example, suppose you put an ordinary kitchen substance in a glass of water and it dissolves. Your younger brother who is watching wants to know why the substance dissolved in the water. Your response might be, "That was salt I dropped in the water and all salt is soluble in water." If your brother accepts the fact that the substance was salt and trusts your generalization, then he accepts your explanation as having provided conditions sufficient to produce the observed event. The argument form looks like this:

Salt is soluble in water.

This substance in my hand which I put in the glass of water is salt.

Therefore, this substance dissolves in the glass of water.

Of course, if your brother is trying to be a pain, which is likely, he might ask, "But why is salt soluble in water?" Although you have supplied sufficient conditions for the conclusion from a logical point of view, you have not supplied sufficient conditions *for your little brother.* You may then be forced back on your knowledge of the chemical composition of salt crystals and water—which may satisfy your little brother or at least make him go away. The point is that for an explanation to be successful, it must satisfy the listener/reader. If it does not satisfy, then it fails. What this means is that—in addition to being logically and factually warranted—the success of an expla-

Calvin and Hobbes

by Bill Watterson

Explain why Calvin is going to have trouble. CALVIN AND HOBBES © 1988 Watterson. Reprinted with permission of UNIVERSAL PRESS SYNDICATE. All rights reserved.

nation is partly dependent on the nature of the audience. A good explanation for a physical chemist is not necessarily a good explanation for a little brother.[3]

The kind of event being explained is also an important determinant of what kind of explanation will be satisfying. Human actions, for example, can be explained psychologically or physiologically. If Joe suddenly rises from his chair and starts walking toward the door of the classroom, and someone asks, "Why is Joe walking out the door?" we could respond in several ways. We could explain that the muscles of his legs contracted and relaxed in such a way that they pulled on the tendons connected to the bones in his legs in such a way that his body went out the door. We could say that Joe went out the door because class was over. Or we could say that Joe walked out the door because doors are easier to walk out of than walls. Sometimes we may not know the causes or reasons for an event but we usually do understand the context sufficiently to know what kind of explanation is being called for.

You can see from the above examples that for an explanation to be satisfying and successful it has to fit in with other things known or believed, it has to suit the level of the audience, and it has to be appropriate for the context in which it is given. A satisfactory explanation can be long or short. Four-year-olds often demand explanations that run on forever. Exasperated parents often have a very short explanation, "Because I said so," which, because of the tone of voice, is usually accepted!

---

[3]One of the most interesting examples of what constitutes a satisfactory explanation occurred in the government's investigation of the *Challenger* disaster mentioned in footnote 2 of the Introduction. The physicist Richard Feynman refused to accept NASA scientists' assertions about the safety of the *Challenger* and its rocketry even when every other member of the investigation team was satisfied. Feynman's persistent questioning of NASA's explanations finally led to reexamination of the safety of the *Challenger* spaceflights and eventually to safer missions. You may want to read his humorous account of his experiences in his book *What Do **You** Care What Other People Think?*

An explanation is not acceptable to anyone if it is circular. That is one of the features that is bothersome about the day-care mystery in the readings for this chapter. To say that a child died of Sudden Infant Death Syndrome is to say that the child died suddenly in the absence of any apparent symptoms. In effect, it is like saying we don't know why the child died. No known causes can be found. "The child's death is a mystery." "The child died of SIDS." They say the same thing. Two children dying of SIDS on the same day, in the same day-care center, is more than a mystery. It's bizarre. It does not fit in with other things we believe about the likelihood of such an event taking place. Consequently, we do not feel satisfied.

EXERCISES

3–I

1. What is the conclusion of an argument?

2. What is an implicit premise?

3. What is a valid argument?

3–II

1. Bring in examples of arguments from newspapers, magazines, or books. Find one of each of the following types of arguments:

   a. An argument with clearly stated premises and a conclusion.

   b. An argument with an implicit premise.

   c. An argument with an implicit conclusion.

   d. An argument with an implicit premise and an implicit conclusion.

   e. An argument where the conclusion is clearly intended to follow with necessity from the premises.

   f. An argument where the conclusion is not intended to follow with necessity from the premises.

   g. An argument intended to be an explanation which you judge to be satisfying.

   h. An argument intended to be an explanation which you judge to be unsatisfying, which fails to explain.

2. Explanations can take the same forms as arguments. One argument form we talked about is the argument by analogy. Can you think of

any examples of explanations in that form, that is, an explanation that uses an analogy to aid our understanding?

3. Rewrite the following arguments, putting the premises first and the conclusion last. If there is an implicit premise, add it and circle it. If there is an implicit conclusion, add it and circle it.

   a. Also, what is simple cannot be separated from itself. The soul is simple; therefore, it cannot be separated from itself.

   b. Pure Schwalmbach's Baby Powder helps you feel good about yourself by keeping you feeling soft and smelling clean. It helps you come across to other people, too, because it helps bring out your best. Your skin looks soft and feels silky. And you smell so clean and natural. Now that you're older, haven't you got your own reasons for Schwalmbach's Baby Powder?

   c. "How do you feel about the metric system?" he asked.

   "I'm opposed to it," I said. "Inalterably opposed to it."

   "But why?"

   "Because," I said, "I'm sick and tired of people fooling around with my habits. Why should I, at my advanced stage of life, have to learn to measure all over again in some strange, new system?"

   d. Why, then, did it all end in the Great Depression of the 1930s? The answer is that changes that imparted thrust to capitalism at the end of the nineteenth century slowly lost their vitality and relevance during the first quarter of the twentieth century. The trusts and monopolies, for instance, temporarily lessened but could not eliminate competition so that as time went on the great giants watched the unruly forces of the market once again invade their precincts.

   e. It is peculiar that we put such great emphasis on debating. As Richard Nixon found out, the mechanism whereby the candidates are asked by a panel of questioners to respond in turn to softball inquiries doesn't amount to debating at all. Candidates can simply memorize harmless answers and if something unexpected comes up, politely beg off and give a speech.

   f. He'll drive recklessly only if he's upset and he's not upset.

   g. Why are there not enough data? One reason is that the academics and international functionaries have too seldom gone into the field to collect them. The voluntary agencies in direct contact with local populations have made the ethical choice to devote their limited energies to relieving suffering, not collecting data.

h. Economically, women are substantially worse off than men. They do not receive any pay for the work that is done in the home. As members of the labor force their wages are significantly lower than those paid to men, even when they are engaged in similar work and have similar education backgrounds.

i. Previously, the pope had said that women may not be ordained because Christ, faced with the possibility of choosing women to be priests, did not do so and the practice of the church today must model that of its founder.

4. Consider the following arguments and decide whether you think the author of the argument intends it to be reasoning with probability or reasoning with necessity.

a. Janet must have gone south for her vacation. She has a beautiful tan.

b. Although I couldn't have an abortion myself, I support that right for other women. The quality of life is important, and what kind of life do many unwanted children end up having?

c. Source critics found that most of Mark is reproduced in Matthew or Luke. They also found that where one departs from the order of events in Mark, the other usually retains the Markan order. Therefore, they concluded that Matthew and Luke each used Mark as a source when composing his own gospel.

d. If John had asked me to the dance, then I would have gone. Since you didn't see me there, you know he didn't ask me.

e. The murder had to have been done by Mrs. White, Miss Scarlet, or Colonel Mustard. It wasn't Mrs. White or Colonel Mustard, so Miss Scarlet had to be the murderer.

f. Forty-five percent of the people surveyed are not happy with the job President Clinton is doing. Thus, 45 percent of the American public is down on Clinton.

3–III

1. Distinguish logical warranting from factual warranting.

2. Explain why in our daily lives reasoning with probability is more common than reasoning with necessity.

3. Suppose you just bought a brand new Excaliber sports car. Today you go out to start it and it will not start. You call the dealership and their mechanic comes over and checks out the car. She tells you,

"There's nothing wrong with the car. It's perfect. It just won't start. The warranty covers every mechanical and electrical defect, but there are none. Some of the Excalibers are like that. So there is nothing we can do for you. It just doesn't start." How would you react to this explanation?

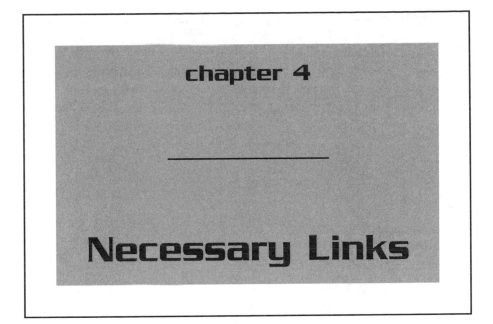

chapter 4

Necessary Links

Introduction

Generally we are happier when other people agree with the statements we make. When we think our audience might not agree with one of our statements or claims, we often try to support that claim by giving an argument. We could use arguments which involve either reasoning with necessity or reasoning with probability to support our claim. You might think that reasoning with necessity is always preferable to reasoning with probability since the link between the premises and the conclusion of such an argument is a necessary one. We will see, however, that reasoning with necessity has some limitations. While it can be useful to give a valid argument to support a statement, if the premises of the argument are not accepted as factual, then the audience does not have to accept the conclusion as factual–despite its being linked with necessity to the premises.

Reasoning with necessity is very common in mathematics. You are probably familiar with some version of Euclid's plane geometry which is an excellent example of reasoning with necessity. In plane geometry we begin by *agreeing* to accept certain statements as factual (axioms or definitions) and we determine through reasoning with necessity the postulates and theorems that follow logically from those accepted statements. Later we may empiri-cally check our reasoning with a protractor and a ruler to confirm the pos-tulates we proved.

Probably the most prevalent contemporary example of reasoning with necessity is the computer. Computers "reason with necessity" as they carry out the myriad of commands we give them. They are not nearly as well suited to reasoning with probability as the typical person, however, which is one of the reasons why the artificial intelligence experts have found it much harder to mimic the human mind than they first thought it would be.

The logical linking that occurs in reasoning with necessity was briefly explained in Chapter 3. In this chapter it is explored in greater detail and with different kinds of examples so you can become more familiar with the fundamental concepts of validity and logical implication and their relation-ship to factual warranting. These concepts make "good sense" to us because they are so logical! At the same time they sometimes give us trouble because, since they are so much like common sense, there is a tendency to shrug them off as obvious and not pay enough attention to them. Reasoning with neces-sity, however, is like arithmetic. When we use it, it is either right or wrong. So we must take care.

The reading in this chapter is an excerpt from the dissenting opinion of Justice Thurgood Marshall. The case is *Gregg v. Georgia*, a 1976 case. In 1972 the Supreme Court held in *Furman v. Georgia* that the death penalty was unconstitutional because it was being applied in a capricious and discrimi-natory manner. Between 1972 and 1976 the state of Georgia established rules to guard against the discriminatory imposition of this sentence, so the Court was asked to reconsider the death penalty. The Court's decision was 7–2 that the death penalty is not inherently cruel and unusual punishment and is, therefore, not prohibited by the Constitution. Justices Marshall and Brennan dissented. The significance of the issue in this reading makes clear how important reasoning with necessity is in helping us to consider and decide important issues through warranting our statements with arguments.

Dissenting Opinion in Gregg v. Georgia

THURGOOD MARSHALL

The two purposes that sustain the death penalty as nonexcessive in the Court's view are general deterrence and retribution. In *Furman*, I canvassed the relevant data on the deterrent effect of capital punishment. The state of knowledge at that point, after literally centuries of debate, was summarized as follows by a United Nations Committee:

> "It is generally agreed between the retentionists and abolitionists, whatever their opinions about the validity of comparative studies of deterrence, that the data which now exist show no correlation between the existence of capital punishment and lower rates of capital crime."

The available evidence, I concluded in *Furman*, was convincing that "capital punishment is not necessary as a deterrent to crime in our society." . . .

. . . The evidence reviewed in *Furman* remains convincing, in my view, that "capital punishment is not necessary as a deterrent to crime in our society." The justification for the death penalty must be found elsewhere.

The other principal purpose said to be served by the death penalty is retribution. The notion that retribution can serve as a moral justification for the sanction of death finds credence in the opinion of my Brothers STEWART, POWELL, and STEVENS. . . . It is this notion that I find to be the most disturbing aspect of today's unfortunate [decision].

The concept of retribution is a multifaceted one, and any discussion of its role in the criminal law must be undertaken with caution. On one level, it can be said that the notion of retribution or reprobation is the basis of our insistence that only those who have broken the law be punished, and in this sense the notion is quite obviously central to a just system of criminal sanctions. But our recognition that retribution plays a crucial role in determining who may be punished by no means requires approval of retribution as a general justification for punishment. It is the question whether retribution can provide a moral justification for punishment—in particular, capital punishment—that we must consider.

My Brothers STEWART, POWELL, and STEVENS offer the following explanation of the retributive justification for capital punishment:

(an excerpt)

The instinct for retribution is part of the nature of man, and channeling that instinct in the administration of criminal justice serves an important purpose in promoting the stability of a society governed by law. When people begin to believe that organized society is unwilling or unable to impose upon criminal offenders the punishment they "deserve," then there are sown the seeds of anarchy—of self-help, vigilante justice, and lynch law.

This statement is wholly inadequate to justify the death penalty. As my Brother BRENNAN stated in *Furman,* "[t]here is no evidence whatever that utilization of imprisonment rather than death encourages private blood feuds and other disorders." It simply defies belief to suggest that the death penalty is necessary to prevent the American people from taking the law into their own hands.

In a related vein, it may be suggested that the expression of moral outrage through the imposition of the death penalty serves to reinforce basic moral values—that it marks some crimes as particularly offensive and therefore to be avoided. The argument is akin to a deterrence argument, but differs in that it contemplates the individual's shrinking from antisocial conduct, not because he fears punishment, but because he has been told in the strongest possible way that the conduct is wrong. This contention, like the previous one, provides no support for the death penalty. It is inconceivable that any individual concerned about conforming his conduct to what society says is "right" would fail to realize that murder is "wrong" if the penalty were simply life imprisonment.

The foregoing contentions—that society's expression of moral outrage through the imposition of the death penalty pre-empts the citizenry from taking the law into its own hands and reinforces moral values—are not retributive in the purest sense. They are essentially utilitarian in that they portray the death penalty as valuable because of its beneficial results. These justifications for the death penalty are inadequate because the penalty is, quite clearly I think, not necessary to the accomplishment of those results.

There remains for consideration, however, what might be termed the purely retributive justification for the death penalty—that the death penalty is appropriate, not because of its beneficial effect on society, but because the taking of the murderer's life is itself morally good. Some of the language of the opinion of my Brothers STEWART, POWELL, and STEVENS . . . appears positively to embrace this notion of retribution for its own sake as a justification for capital punishment. They state:

[T]he decision that capital punishment may be the appropriate sanction in extreme cases is an expression of the community's belief that certain crimes are themselves so grievous an affront to humanity that the only adequate response may be the penalty of death.

They then quote with approval from Lord Justice Denning's remarks before the British Royal Commission on Capital Punishment:

> The truth is that some crimes are so outrageous that society insists on adequate punishment, because the wrong-doer deserves it, irrespective of whether it is a deterrent or not.

Of course, it may be that these statements are intended as no more than observations as to the popular demands that it is thought must be responded to in order to prevent anarchy. But the implication of the statements appears to me to be quite different—namely, that society's judgment that the murderer "deserves" death must be respected not simply because the preservation of order requires it, but because it is appropriate that society make the judgment and carry it out. It is this latter notion, in particular, that I consider to be fundamentally at odds with the Eighth Amendment. The mere fact that the community demands the murderer's life in return for the evil he has done cannot sustain the death penalty, for as JUSTICES STEWART, POWELL, and STEVENS remind us, "the Eighth Amendment demands more than that a challenged punishment be acceptable to contemporary society." To be sustained under the Eighth Amendment, the death penalty must "compor[t] with the basic concept of human dignity at the core of the Amendment;" the objective in imposing it must be "[consistent] with our respect for the dignity of [other] men." Under these standards, the taking of life "because the wrongdoer deserves it" surely must fail, for such a punishment has as its very basis the total denial of the wrongdoer's dignity and worth.

The death penalty, unnecessary to promote the goal of deterrence or to further any legitimate notion of retribution, is an excessive penalty forbidden by the Eighth and Fourteenth Amendments. I respectfully dissent from the Court's judgment upholding the [sentence] of death imposed upon the [petitioner in this case].

Reflections on the Reading:

1. Outline Marshall's argument. What are his premises and how do they link to his conclusion?

2. Do you agree or disagree with Marshall that the death penalty ought to be considered unconstitutional? Write a valid argument of your own to support your answer.

3. What do you think is most questionable in Marshall's argument? Why do you think that a majority of the justices did not agree with Marshall?

Validity and Logical Implication

The objective in reasoning with necessity, it will be recalled, is to give a valid argument. A logically valid argument is one where if the premises are regarded as factual, the conclusion must also be regarded as factual because of the logical linking present. Another way of saying this is to say that the premises **logically imply** the conclusion. A logically valid argument, then, is defined as follows:

VALID ARGUMENT–An argument where if the premises are regarded as factual the conclusion must also be regarded as factual. In a logically valid argument the premises logically imply the conclusion.

To return to our "Beatles were the greatest" example from Chapter 3, let us suppose that Tom intends to reason with necessity and wants to present a **valid** argument. What Tom needs is an argument with premises which Joan accepts as factual and which necessarily supports his conclusion that the Beatles were the greatest musical artists of all time. What might such premises be? Tom might try, for example, the following argument:

If a musical artist (or group) had the largest amount of commercial success (air play, record sales, earnings, etc.) then that person or group was the greatest musical artist of all time.

The Beatles have had the largest amount of commercial success.

Therefore, the Beatles were the greatest musical artists of all time.

Now if Joan regards Tom's premises as factual, then logically she must regard his conclusion as factual also, because that conclusion is logically warranted by those premises. In this case, Tom's conclusion is **logically implied** by his premises, which means that *if* his premises are factual then his conclusion *must* be factual also. The notion of **logical implication** may seem at first to be mysterious. "How," it might be asked, "can one statement cause another statement to be factual?" The answer to this question is that logical implication relies on the meanings of ordinary connecting words used in specific patterns to link statements together logically so that their factual nature is also linked. To see this consider the next example that Tom might offer to Joan:

Either the Beatles *or* Mozart is the greatest musical artist of all time.

Since Mozart was not commercially successful, he is not the greatest musical artist of all time.

Therefore, the Beatles are the greatest musical artists of all time.

We can see that if we regard Tom's premises as factual, we must regard Tom's conclusion as factual also. The premises logically imply the conclusion. It is also clear that Tom's argument relies on the meaning of the ordinary English words "either" and "or" used in a certain pattern. When we say "either A or B" and then say "and not A," this logically implies "B." There is really nothing very mysterious about this. Suppose I tell you that I will either be in my office or in Room 2 at 4:00 P.M. on Tuesday, and later I tell you that I will not be in my office at all on Tuesday. My statements about my whereabouts on Tuesday together logically imply that at 4:00 P.M. on Tuesday I will be in Room 2. This is just the way the words I uttered, "either" and "or," work when they occur in the patterns I used. The traditional name of arguments in this pattern is disjunctive argument.

All languages contain words which are logically significant when used in certain recognized patterns. We use these logically significant words and patterns when we want to establish very strong links between statements, logical implication being the strongest possible link. Obviously, the person who has mastered the use of these logical links has a big advantage when it comes to expressing his ideas clearly and forcefully.

Notice again that the question of **logical warranting** is separate from the question of **factual warranting**. Tom's conclusion is logically warranted by his premises even if we do not accept his premises as factual. If we reject any of Tom's premises as nonfactual, however, we need not accept his conclusion as factual, even though it is logically implied by his premises.

Aristotle called this kind of dilemma the law of the excluded middle. DOONES-BURY © 1984 Gary Trudeau. Reprinted with permission of UNIVERSAL PRESS SYNDICATE. All rights reserved.

Now let us return to Joan and Tom. Suppose that Joan rejects Tom's conclusion because she doesn't accept one of the premises which supports it, say premise one, which claims a direct connection between commercial success and musical greatness. Perhaps in Joan's view, musical greatness depends on how long a time an artist has been a major influence on other musicians. If Joan were to offer a logical counterargument, it could be the following:

> If an artist has been a major influence on other musicians for the longest period of time, then that artist is the greatest musical artist of all time.
>
> Mozart has been a major influence on other musicians for the longest period of time.
>
> Therefore, Mozart is the greatest musical artist of all time.

Just as Joan should accept Tom's conclusion *if* she accepts his premises, so now Tom should accept Joan's conclusion *if* he accepts her premises. This is because Joan has also come up with an argument the conclusion of which is logically implied by its premises. So if Joan's premises are factual then her conclusion is factual also.

Joan's argument is an example of a conditional argument. Conditional arguments always contain at least one conditional statement. Conditional statements are our main language tool for describing and establishing conditional relationships. Conditional relationships exist whenever one thing is either necessary (required) or sufficient (enough) for another. In Joan's argument the conditional premise, "If an artist has been a major influence on other musicians for the longest period of time, then that artist is the greatest musical artist of all time," says that being a major influence on other musicians for the longest period of time is a sufficient condition (is enough) for being the greatest musical artist of all time. So if we accept this statement as factual and if we also accept as factual that Mozart has been a major influence on other musicians for the longest period of time, then we would also have to accept as factual Joan's conclusion that Mozart was the greatest musical artist of all time.

Joan, like Tom, has presented us with a logical implication and a valid argument to support her belief that Mozart is the greatest musical artist of all time. Since *both* Tom's and Joan's conclusions are logically implied by their premises, *both* would have to be regarded as factual if their premises are factual. We can see that it is unlikely that Joan and Tom are going to resolve their difference of opinion about music—unless they first come to some agreement about the various factual claims made in the premises of their arguments.

One way they might try to come to an agreement about the facts is to offer further arguments, either necessary or probable, in support of the factual claims in their premises. "But," it might be objected, "if the arguments which are supposed to establish or warrant our factual claims themselves depend on further factual claims, won't we need to warrant those factual claims with even more arguments which will require further factual claims, which will require more arguments, which will require further factual claims, and so on and so forth for ever and ever?" In reality, our attempts to establish statements as factual usually end when we arrive at statements which for whatever reason are not called into question. In the music dispute between Tom and Joan, a stalemate can likely be averted only if they can first agree that some statement in one of their arguments is warranted and should be considered factual.

In this chapter's reading from Supreme Court Justice Thurgood Marshall, Justice Marshall gives a valid argument to support his claim that the death penalty is unconstitutional. The intended form of Marshall's argument can be seen more clearly when summarized as follows:

If the death penalty is to be considered constitutional, it must either serve the purpose of deterrence (i.e., must make it less likely that others will commit the crime punished by death) or it must serve the purpose of retribution (i.e., must satisfy society's demand that offenders get the punishment they deserve).

The death penalty is not necessary for deterrence, since it has little proven deterrent effect nor is it necessary for retribution since no living human being deserves to be a dead human being.

Thus, the death penalty is unconstitutional.

Marshall's argument, like Joan's Mozart argument, is a conditional argument which claims that in order for the death penalty to be justified it must be necessary either to deter others from committing the same crime or for retribution. Because, argues Marshall, the death penalty is necessary for neither, it cannot be considered to be constitutional. This is a typical example of logical implication used in an important, everyday context. Since Marshall's opinion is a dissenting opinion, we know that not all of Marshall's fellow justices agreed with that conclusion, even though Marshall's premises logically imply his conclusion. This means they must have rejected at least one of his premises as not factual.

The notions of valid argument, logical implication, and arguing with necessity can be further understood by considering an example about Tony. Suppose Tony is a tiger. Which of the following statements are logically implied by that supposition (premise)?

1. Tony does not like carrots.

2. It is not the case that Tony is not a tiger.

3. Tony is either a tiger or a mouse.

Although you might think that "Tony does not like carrots" follows from the claim that Tony is a tiger, it is not **logically implied** by it. For us to regard "Tony does not like carrots" as logically implied we would need an additional statement, "Tigers do not like carrots," which we do not have. Statement 2 is logically implied by "Tony is a tiger" because it is the denial of the denial of "Tony is a tiger," which is just to say that Tony is a tiger. It may surprise you but Statement 3 is also logically implied by "Tony is a tiger" because, although we know Tony is not a mouse, all that is required for Statement 3 to be factual is that either Tony be a tiger or Tony be a mouse. Both are not required. And since "Tony is a tiger" is a factual statement (our original supposition), "Tony is either a tiger or a mouse" must be factual.

Exercises

4–I

1. What do we call an argument when the premises logically imply the conclusion?

2. What is the simplest statement that is logically implied by "Tony is a tiger"?

3. Give three examples of English words that are logically significant.

4–II

1. Who, in your opinion, is the greatest musical artist of all time? Write an argument to support your claim in which the premises logically imply the conclusion.

2. Suppose someone questions the premises you used in your argument in Exercise 1. Now write arguments to support those premises. Tell whether your arguments are necessary or probable.

3. Suppose, as probably happened, that the other Supreme Court justices questioned Justice Marshall's second premise about the deterrent effect of the death penalty and his claim that no human being

deserves to be put to death. How would you help Justice Marshall defend his premise? Write at least two arguments which use logical implication to support premise two.

4–III

1. We saw that from "Tony is a tiger" it logically follows that Tony is either a tiger or a mouse. How many possible conclusions, then, are logically implied by "Tony is a tiger" (or any other claim)?

2. What limitations do you see to reasoning with necessity?

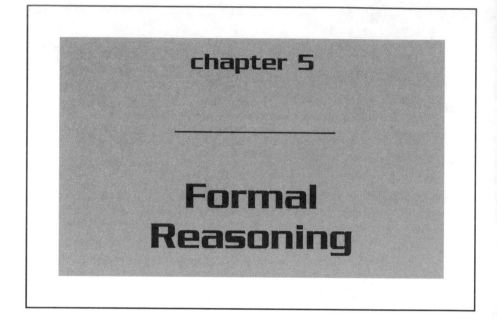

chapter 5

Formal Reasoning

Introduction

Formal reasoning skills, which we use when we reason with necessity, are part of our natural reasoning processes. We use these skills in our everyday reasoning without even thinking about them. They are an important aspect of good critical thinking, but they are only a small part of it. Most of our everyday reasoning is reasoning with probability rather than reasoning with necessity. When we do use reasoning with necessity, it is often intermixed with reasoning with probability. Mathematics and computer programming, as mentioned earlier, however, are examples of reasoning which more exclusively involve reasoning with necessity. Since we sometimes make mistakes in reasoning with necessity, it is helpful to learn some common valid arguments in order to avoid these mistakes and to avoid being misled by the mistakes of others.

Formal reasoning is often called **logic, formal logic**, or **deductive logic.** *Logic* comes from the Greek word *logos* or *word*. You could say that logic refers to the use of patterns of words, namely, patterns of words that are considered to be valid arguments—where the linkages between the premises and the conclusions are necessary. If symbols are used instead of words, then the patterns are referred to as symbolic logic. Symbols are help-ful because they allow us to avoid the confusions of language that we talked about in Chapter 1. We will use some simple symbols in this chapter to avoid these confusions and to make the patterns of the valid arguments clearer and easier to recall.

The reading in this chapter is a version of a very famous argument by St. Anselm, who is trying to convince others to accept as factual the belief that God exists. The argument is so famous that it has a name, Anselm's Ontological Argument. (*Ontological* comes from the Greek word *ontos* which means *to be*.) This is an argument about the being or existence of God but it is different from most other arguments about God's being or existence (or the existence of any other being) because it does not use any premises which are about experience. It uses premises which are about the meanings of words, in particular, the word *God*. What Anselm is saying, in effect, is if you accept his definition of God, then you must also accept his conclusion that God necessarily exists because of the necessary links between the premises and the conclusion. This particular version of Anselm's argument comes from a discussion of the argument by the American philosopher Norman Malcolm. The argument is very short but you will probably want to read it several times.

"Anselm's Ontological Argument"

NORMAN MALCOLM

1. Let me summarize the proof. If God, a being greater than which cannot be conceived, does not exist then He cannot *come* into existence. For if He did He would either have been *caused* to come into existence or have *happened* to come into existence, and in either case He would be a limited being, which by our conception of Him He is not. Since He cannot come into existence, if He does not exist His existence is impossible. If He does exist He cannot come into existence (for the reasons given), nor can He cease to exist, for nothing could cause Him to cease to exist nor could it just happen that He ceased to exist. So if God exists His existence is nec-essary. Thus God's existence is either impossible or necessary. It can be the

(an excerpt) From Norman Malcolm, "Anselm's Ontological Arguments," *Philosophical Review*, 69 (1960), 49–50.

former only if the concept of such a thing is self-contradictory or in some way logically absurd. Assuming that this is not so, it follows that He necessarily exists.

Reflections on the Reading:

1. What is the first premise of Anselm's argument? How does Anselm justify this premise?

2. What is the conclusion?

3. Do you think Anselm's argument is successful? Why or why not?

4. Do you see any patterns of reasoning which are familiar to you in the argument?

Some Common Valid Arguments

Formal reasoning consists of following argument patterns which have long been accepted by philosophers and logicians as valid, so that if the premises are considered factual the conclusion must also be considered factual. There are two fundamental assumptions in formal reasoning. The first is that any argument that has the same pattern as one of the accepted valid arguments is also valid. And the second is that valid argument patterns may be combined into larger arguments which are then also valid.

Systems of formal reasoning vary in their definitions of these valid argument patterns and, hence, they vary somewhat in the number of argument patterns they contain. Consequently, all logic textbooks are not alike. Some logic textbooks will even contain more than one system of formal reasoning. All of these systems of formal reasoning, however, try to capture the same fundamental patterns we use when we reason with necessity in our ordinary rational discourse and to make them clearer by making them more explicit.

We are going to look at the definitions of five valid formal reasoning patterns, all of which will be somewhat familiar to you. It is helpful to know and to be able to recognize these valid patterns so you can check your own reasoning (or someone else's reasoning) when you are in doubt about the validity of an argument as when, for example, you find you accept the premises of an argument as factual, the linkage between the premises and the conclusion seems to be necessary, yet you find yourself unable to accept the conclusion as factual. Since **a valid argument cannot have all factual premises and a nonfactual conclusion,** then in such a case either one or more of the premises is not factual or the linkage between the premises and the conclusion is not a necessary one. Knowing the definitions of valid argument forms will enable you to check the necessity of that linkage.

One group of valid argument patterns involves conditional statements, statements in English that express or establish conditional relations between things. One conditional relation is that of being a **sufficient condition.** If P is sufficient condition for Q, then if you have P, then you have Q. That is what being a sufficient condition means. Thus, to say "If P, then Q" is to say that P is a sufficient condition for Q, which is to say that having P is adequate for having Q also. The valid argument pattern which depends on this relation of sufficient condition is called **modus ponens**. This name may be unfamiliar to you but it is a very familiar pattern. Modus ponens is defined:

If P, then Q

P

Therefore, Q

P and Q each stand for a description of an event or set of circumstances. It does not matter what these circumstances are, as long as P is sufficient for Q, if you have P, then you have Q. For example, suppose Mary says, "If Paul invites me to the dance, then I'll go." Paul does invite Mary to the dance. You would expect, then, to see Mary at the dance. Paul's invitation is a sufficient condition for Mary's going and he has invited her. This pattern makes sense to us. We use it all the time. All arguments in this pattern are valid arguments: If P then Q, P, therefore Q. That is what being a sufficient condition means.

The other important conditional relation is **necessary condition**. To say that Q is a necessary condition of P is to say that you cannot have P without Q. Two ways of expressing this relation in English are "P only if Q" and "Not P unless Q." Both of these English sentences say that Q is a necessary condition for P. Without Q, there can be no P. Q is necessary for P. It is important to realize that every time we establish one of these two conditional relations, necessary or sufficient, we actually establish both of them. That is, **if P is a sufficient condition for Q, then Q is a necessary condition for P**. You can see this clearly by looking at the Paul and Mary example again. If Paul's inviting Mary to the dance is a sufficient condition for Mary's going with him, then when he asks her, she will say "Yes." So P cannot happen without Q's happening. Mary's going to the dance is, therefore, a necessary condition for Paul's asking her. If Mary does not go with Paul, we know that Paul did not ask her. This brings us to our second valid argument pattern which is called **modus tollens**. The definition of modus tollens is: If P is a sufficient condition for Q and Q does not occur, then P does not occur. Or

> If P, then Q
> Not Q
> Therefore, not P

That is, if P is a sufficient condition for Q, Q is a necessary condition for P. So if we do not have Q, we cannot have P because a necessary condition for having P is missing.

We have seen that if P is a sufficient condition for Q then Q must be a necessary condition for P. This means that there are several ways we can express this conditional relationship in English:

> If P, then Q
> P implies Q
> P only if Q
> Not P unless Q

All of these English sentences express the assertions "P is a sufficient condition for Q" or "Q is a necessary condition for P." The best way to master the definitions of modus ponens, modus tollens, and these variations of expression of the relationships of necessary and sufficient conditions (and the other definitions of valid arguments which follow) is to think through the meanings of these English sentences until it is clear to you that they all express the same logical relationship. Then memorize them, being careful to get the P's and the Q's in the right places, so you do not have to reason them through each time you encounter them. (Perhaps this is where the expression "Mind your P's and Q's" comes from!) In general, memorization is the opposite of good critical thinking, but here memorization is a convenient shorthand. It makes the reasoning go faster and helps to avoid mistakes—just as memorizing mathematical formulas does.

Suppose, again, that Mary says, "If Paul asks me, I will go to the dance." And suppose Mary does go to the dance but not with Paul. Did Mary tell a lie? Not necessarily. The only case where Mary would have told a lie is if Paul asked her and she did not go. Paul may not have asked Mary to go to the dance so she decided to go with Ron. P (Paul's asking) is a sufficient condition for Q (Mary's going to the dance) but it is not a necessary condition. She could go with someone else if Paul does not ask her. Q, however, is a necessary condition for P, as we have seen. So if Q does not happen, P does not happen.

Is Calvin lying? CALVIN AND HOBBES © 1994 Watterson. Reprinted with permission of UNIVERSAL PRESS SYNDICATE. All rights reserved.

Let's look at some more examples of reasoning which involve sufficient and necessary conditions to practice using these valid argument patterns.

EXAMPLE 1   If the Eagles win the Super Bowl, then the Cardinals don't.

The Cardinals do win the Super Bowl.

What about the Eagles?

EXAMPLE 2   If the Eagles win the Super Bowl, then the Cardinals don't.

The Cardinals don't win the Super Bowl.

What about the Eagles?

EXAMPLE 3   If the Eagles win the Super Bowl, then the Cardinals don't.

The Eagles don't win the Super Bowl.

What about the Cardinals?

EXAMPLE 4   If the Eagles win the Super Bowl, then the Cardinals don't.

The Eagles do win the Super Bowl.

What about the Cardinals?

The answer to the question at the end of each is easily answered if we pay attention to the valid arguments, modus ponens and modus tollens, which are the primary patterns of conditional arguments or arguments that contain "if ... then ..." statements. If you look carefully at Example 1, you will notice that the second premise is a denial of the Q statement or, as logicians say, the **consequent** of the conditional. (If "Q" is "the Cardinals do not win the Super Bowl," then "Not Q" is "the Cardinals do win the Super Bowl.") The two premises, then, are in the form of modus tollens and, consequently, we know that P cannot occur. The Eagles do not win the Super Bowl.

The second example looks similar but be careful. It is not the same. In the second example the second premise is simply Q. "If P, then Q" and "Q" is *not* one of our valid argument patterns. Consequently, we cannot say anything about whether the Eagles win the Super Bowl. Maybe they do, maybe they don't. Maybe the 49ers win or the Redskins. There is no **necessary** link between the two premises and the fate of the Eagles. The third example is like the second. The form looks a little like modus ponens but it is not modus ponens because the second premise asserts "Not P" instead of "P." (Logicians call "P" the **antecedent**.) We cannot know the fate of the Cardinals. The Eagles' winning is a sufficient condition for the Cardinals' not winning but not a necessary condition. The Cardinals may win the Super Bowl or they may not. We do not have sufficient information to say.

There is no necessary link between the two premises of this argument and its conclusion.

The fourth example is obviously in the pattern of modus ponens. The Eagles' winning is sufficient for the Cardinals' not winning and the Eagles do win, so the Cardinals do not. The pattern seems so much a part of our common sense that we do not think about it when we are using it. But every now and then we are not sure about our own or another's reasoning. By knowing these patterns we can check our common sense and make sure that we are reasoning correctly.

Another very common pattern of formal reasoning using conditionals is the **pure hypothetical argument** (sometimes referred to as _hypothetical syllogism_). For example, suppose Mary says, "If Paul asks me to the dance, then I'll go with him. If I go with Paul, then I won't go with Ron. So if Paul asks me, then I won't go with Ron." In the pure hypothetical argument all the premises are hypothetical or conditional statements and so is the conclusion. We define pure hypothetical argument as having the pattern:

If P, then Q

If Q, then R

Therefore, If P, then R

Pure hypothetical arguments can have a longer chain of premises than two and will be valid as long as this pattern is continued. You probably have heard this pattern being used by politicians: "If my opponent is elected, then . . . ," until some horrible consequent is claimed to follow.

The **disjunctive argument** is another common valid argument. We often use it, especially when we are trying to make a decision. Mary says to herself, for instance, " I don't know with whom to go to the dance, Paul or Ron. They have both asked me. Which will it be? I don't think I really want to go with Ron. So I guess I'll go with Paul." The definition of disjunctive argument is

P or Q

Not Q

Therefore, P

Like the pure hypothetical argument, the disjunctive argument can be longer and give the appearance of being more complicated but the definition of the logical linkage is still the same. The detective trying to solve a murder may use disjunctive argument, for instance. If she has five murder suspects, then she will try to eliminate possible suspects until she has only one who is presumed to be the murderer. If you ever played the board game Clue, you did this yourself: If the murder was done by either A or B or C or D or E (Colonel Mustard, Miss Scarlet, Mr. Green, etc.) and it wasn't A or B or C or D, then it has to have been done by E. The necessary link between the premises of the disjunctive argument and its conclusion is quite obvious to us. Where we sometimes make mistakes in our disjunctive reasoning is when we think we have considered all the possibilities and have not. With Clue we know how many possible suspects there are, but the professional detective, of course, does not.

The final formal reasoning pattern that we will define here is as familiar as the others. It is called the **categorical argument**. The most well known categorical argument is probably "All men are mortal, Socrates is a man, therefore, Socrates is mortal," which everyone has heard is a valid argument. The definition of the categorical argument, however, looks a bit different from this well-known example. It is defined as

All A's are B's

All B's are C's

Therefore, all A's are C's

The argument about Socrates can be seen to be a categorical argument if we think of "Socrates" as standing for "all things identical with Socrates," which is how logicians have traditionally thought of it. The necessary linkage between the premises and the conclusion of this argument is easily seen. Where we get confused when reasoning with categorical arguments and may draw invalid conclusions is when we are sloppy about the application of the definition and don't get our A's, B's, and C's in the right places.

These simple valid arguments we have defined are part of our everyday reasoning. We use them frequently. They give us more power in reasoning than may be apparent from their simplicity because they can be combined to create more complicated valid arguments. For example, we can combine modus ponens and disjunctive argument to form a more complicated pattern which actually has a name of its own, **constructive dilemma**. Here is the definition of constructive dilemma; look at it closely to see that it is a combination of the two arguments we have already introduced:

A or B

If A, then C

If B, then D

Therefore, C or D

Debaters are fond of using this valid argument to set the stage for leading you out of the dilemma they have created for you! We could also have a **destructive dilemma**:

Not A or not B

If C, then A

If D, then B

Therefore, not C or not D

Formal reasoning or logic is a basic component of good critical reasoning. In many ways it is the easiest component because the conclusions either follow necessarily from the premises or they do not. We only have to follow the definitions carefully and we will not make reasoning mistakes about the links between the premises and the conclusions. The definitions of the valid arguments are not very complex but we can make very complex arguments by combining them or by stringing them together in long chains of reasoning. Formal reasoning is fun and useful, and sometimes it can be put to use resolving major issues which many human beings have pondered— like whether God exists.

Anselm's Ontological Argument

Anselm's ontological argument is the most famous argument that tries to prove God's existence only from the definition of God, without reference to experience. There are other arguments which also try to do this, but none has generated as much interest as Anselm's. The philosophical questions it raises have intrigued philosophers since Anselm first formulated it in the eleventh century. The version of it that you read, for example, comes from an article on the argument by the twentieth-century philosopher Norman Malcolm. Our focus here is only on the logical structure of the argument, but you may want to think about the force of the argument in general and whether one can prove the existence of God—or any other thing—simply by reasoning about its definition.

To look at the logical structure we will set out the reasoning explicitly from the first premise through to the conclusion. Keep in mind as you read this that you are reading our version of Malcolm's version of Anselm's argument. You may see other accounts of Anselm's argument that are somewhat different in structure. All of these accounts, however, are trying to clarify a very interesting but challenging argument about a question which many people ask, whether the belief that God exists is warranted.

The Argument:

1. If God, a being so great that no greater being can be thought, does not exist, he cannot come into existence.
   Argument for premise 1: If he did come into existence, he would be caused or he would just have happened (by chance) and then he would be limited. But God, by definition, is not limited. [If God were caused, then he would be dependent on that which caused him. If he happened by chance, then he would be just an accident, a bit of luck.]

2. Therefore, if God does not exist, his existence is impossible. (Since he cannot come into existence or have ceased.)

3. And if God exists, his existence is necessary.

4. God either does or does not exist.

5. Therefore, God's existence is either impossible or necessary.

6. God's existence is not impossible since the concept of God is not inconsistent.

7. Therefore, God's existence is necessary.

Now we will look at the structure still more explicitly, looking for the valid argument patterns we have defined previously. The purpose of the first premise is to rule out the possibility that God's existence is contingent, like the existence of other things in the world. That is, most things in the world do not have to exist or happen. They could have not existed or they could have not happened. They exist or happen because the right set of causal circumstances came together, but those circumstances could have not occurred. Your existence, for example, is contingent. If your parents had never met, then you would not exist. To be contingent is to be dependent on those causal circumstances coming together.

Anselm assumes but does not explicitly state, as can be seen from the rest of his argument, that existence is either necessary, impossible, or contingent, because he goes on to reason that if God's existence is not contingent, then it must be either necessary or impossible. We can symbolize this implicit argument:

Either N or I or C

Not C

Therefore, N or I

This is clearly an example of **disjunctive argument**. Now we will look more closely at this argument for "Not C." If God's existence is contingent, then

God would be dependent on the right causal circumstances coming together. But then God would be limited and God would not be that "being greater than which cannot be conceived" because we could then conceive of a being like God but without this dependence and limitation. But God is God. That is, we assume that God is that being greater than which cannot be conceived. Let's look at a simplified version of the structure of this argument in support of Premise 1:

> If C, then not G. (If God's existence is contingent, then God is not God.)
>
> G [Not not G] (But God is God, that being greater than which cannot be conceived.)
>
> Therefore, not C. (God's existence is not contingent.)

You can now see this argument is an example of **modus tollens**.

Let's look at the structure of the argument as a whole:

1. If G and not E (E = God exists), then not C.
   1a.   If C, then not G.
   1b.   G
   1c.   Therefore, not C.
   1d.   Either N or I or C.
   1e.   Not C.
   1f.   Therefore, either N or I.

2. If not E, then I. (If God does not exist, then his existence is impossible.)

3. If E, then N. (If God does exist, then his existence is necessary.)

4. Either E or not E. (God exists or he does not exist. There are no other alternatives.)

5. Therefore, either I or N. (God's existence is either impossible or necessary.)

6. Not I. (God's existence is not impossible, since the concept is consistent and not self-contradictory.)

7. Therefore, N. (God's existence is necessary.)

By symbolizing the argument in this way, we can see that Premises 2–5 form a **constructive dilemma**. Lines 5–7 are a **disjunctive argument**. Notice that one line of argument (in this case Line 5) can be a conclusion of one valid argument and a premise of another. That way we can create long, significant pieces of formal reasoning. By combining these arguments into one longer argument, Anselm has argued that *if* we assume that God is a being so great that no greater being can be thought of (Premise 1) and that this concept or definition of God is not inconsistent (Premise 6), God exists and he exists necessarily. We can see from this example that simple valid arguments can be used to prove very interesting conclusions. That is, if the premises are regarded as factual (i.e., we accept the assumption or initial premises) and the links between each set of premises and their respective conclusions are necessary, then the final conclusion should also be regarded as factual.

We do not use formal reasoning so explicitly very often in our everyday lives. When we do use it, we usually use it without even thinking about it. We use modus ponens and disjunctive argument, and even constructive dilemma. It is helpful to know these valid arguments so when we are not sure of our reasoning or of someone else's reasoning, we can check it by explicitly formalizing it to make sure that it uses only valid arguments. This is particularly the case when we accept the assumptions or premises as factual but we do not think the conclusion which is claimed to follow from them is factual. Then we want to look closely at the links between the premises and the conclusions to see if they are necessary as claimed. This is why Anselm's argument has generated so much attention. Many people find it not hard to accept his assumptions or his reasoning but then balk at accepting his conclusion. As a consequence, his argument has been the subject of much discussion and analysis through many centuries!

Review of Common Valid Arguments

Modus Ponens　　**Modus Tollens**

If P, then Q　　　　If P, then Q

P　　　　　　　　Not Q

Therefore, Q　　　Therefore, not P

Logically equivalent English expressions of "If P, then Q":

P implies Q

P only if Q

Not P unless Q

Pure Hypothetical Argument　　**Disjunctive Argument**

If P, then Q　　　　　　　　　P or Q

If Q, then R　　　　　　　　　Not Q

Therefore, if P, then R　　　　Therefore, P

Constructive Dilemma	**Destructive Dilemma**
A or B	Not A or not B
If A, then C	If C, then A
If B, then D	If D, then B
Therefore, C or D	Therefore, not C or not D

Categorical Argument

All A's are B's

All B's are C's

Therefore, all A's are C's

EXERCISES

5-1

1. Which of the following arguments are valid?

   a. All women are nuns.
   Madonna is a woman.

   Therefore, Madonna is a nun.

   b. All nuns are women.
   Sr. Theresa is a nun.

   Therefore, Sr. Theresa is a woman.

   c. Some women are nuns.
   Sr. Theresa is a woman.

   Therefore, Sr. Theresa is a nun.

   d. Some women are nuns.
   Madonna is a woman.

   Therefore, Madonna is a nun.

   e. All cats have four legs.
   All dogs have four legs.

   Therefore, all cats are dogs.

   f. All cats have four legs.
   All four-legged animals are dogs.

   Therefore, all cats are dogs.

   g. All widgets are gidgets.
   All gidgets are smidgets.

   Therefore, all widgets are smidgets.

   h. All smidgets are gidgets.
   All smidgets are widgets.

   Therefore, all gidgets are widgets.

2. The validity of the following arguments is less obvious. Which of the following arguments are valid?

a. He'll drive recklessly only if he's upset.

He's not upset.

Therefore, he won't drive recklessly.

b. If he's upset, he'll drive recklessly.

He's not upset.

Therefore, he won't drive recklessly.

c. He'll drive recklessly if he's upset.

He is driving recklessly.

Therefore, he is upset.

d. He won't drive recklessly unless he's upset.

He is driving recklessly.

Therefore, he is upset.

e. If he's upset, he'll drive recklessly.

He is not driving recklessly.

Therefore, he's not upset.

f. If he's upset, he'll drive recklessly.

He is driving recklessly.

Therefore, he is upset.

3. Give the names of the arguments that are valid arguments in Exercise 2.

5–11

1. If Jones is having tea, then if he is eating crumpets, he is not in London.

If Jones is not in Africa, he is not in Tanzania.

If he is not in Tanzania, he does not smell the odor of spices.

If he does not smell the odor of spices, he is in London.

Jones is having tea.

He is not in Africa.

Is Jones eating crumpets? What valid arguments did you use to help you determine the right answer?

2. PAUL: "What are you going to do tonight?"

JOE: "I don't know. There's a good movie at the Cinema 3. But I have a paper due tomorrow. I also heard there's a fraternity party. What are you going to do?"

PAUL: "I heard no one is going to the party. They've got a lousy D.J. coming. And my brother saw that movie. He hated it."

JOE: "I guess I'll work on my paper, then–and wait for something to happen."

What valid argument is Joe using in determining what to do?

3. Many everyday situations involve multiple sufficient or necessary conditions.

   a. Suppose your television broke and you are shopping for a new television. List as many sufficient conditions as you can think of that would enable you to leave the store with a new television.

   b. Suppose you are obtaining a driver's license. What are the necessary conditions for obtaining a driver's license?

5–III

1. Describe three recent instances when you used a valid argument to make a decision, persuade someone, prove a point, etc.

2. Why do we not need to know anything about football and the organization of professional teams into leagues to be able to answer or not answer the questions about the Eagles and the Cardinals in this chapter?

3. What are the assumptions Anselm uses to construct his ontological argument? Do you find any of these unacceptable?

chapter 6

Supporting Our Claims

Introduction

There are many things we believe of which we are absolutely certain. It would take a lot of work for someone to convince us to give up one of these beliefs. These beliefs range from common ordinary everyday kinds of beliefs such as "my name is Hildegaard Higgenbottom" to more complicated kinds of beliefs such as "the United States is the most powerful country in the world." We realize when pressed, of course, that we cannot be **absolutely** certain about these beliefs. There is always a chance that we might be mistaken. (A famous puzzle about this kind of certainty was raised by the philosopher Bertrand Russell who pointed out that we cannot prove that the world was not created yesterday—just as it is, with all its books and fossil evidence and records of the past!)

For instance, you now believe that when you are finished reading this book that you will put it down, stand up, and walk across the room. You believe that the floor will feel firm under your feet, that your legs will move as they have in the past. In fact, you won't even think about it. You will just do it. Although you are quite justified in this belief, there is always the possibility that something will be amiss—that the floor will collapse under your feet, for example, or that your knee will suddenly give and send you sprawling on the floor. But these possibilities are not sufficient to cause you any worry. You do *not* get up slowly, tentatively putting one foot before the other, testing the floor or your knee. In fact, people would think you very neurotic if you did! Common sense tells you not to worry. Common sense is the name usually given to good reasoning of a particular kind, namely, reasoning with probability. You believe it is highly **improbable** that the floor will collapse under your feet since it looks to be made of wood (or concrete), was firm a few minutes ago, and has not suffered any damage in the meantime. Consequently, you act with assurance when you finish your reading despite the remote chance that your expectations could be wrong.

But remember the time someone pulled that chair out from under you just as you sat down? Or the time you were going down the stairs in the dark and thought you were at the bottom and almost fell down that last step? The point is sometimes we mistake the probabilities and our common sense lets us down—literally. And sometimes the unexpected is just plain unforeseeable, even though we have used good common sense, as when your friend decides to become a practical joker. In this section we will examine common sense, or reasoning with probability, in order to improve the skills we all already possess. Although these skills generally get us safely through the day without anxiety, we do sometimes make some mistakes and mistakes can be quite serious. (Remember the *Challenger.*) Also, sometimes we are uncertain. We are not sure whether to buy a Buick or a Ford, or whether the price of computers will go down or up in the future, or whether the latest crisis in the Middle East can be solved by diplomacy alone. When we make decisions about the future, we are relying on reasoning with probability. Improving our skills can help make those choices easier. The readings in Chapters 6–8 display various types of reasoning with probability. You will find most of them very familiar kinds of examples. You may be surprised, however, to find scientific reasoning included in reasoning with probability. You may think of science as giving us laws about what must be the case. We will see, however, that science uses the same kind of reasoning with probability we all do every day.

When someone asks us why we believe a certain claim to be true or why we have made the assertion we have just made, he is usually asking us for **evidence** for that claim or assertion. He wants to know whether the claim is credible, that is, worth believing himself. "I just think so" or "That's what my mother always said" does not (except in rare cases) make a statement credible. The questioner wants to know why *he* should believe the claim, not hear our psychological history.

Evidence, however, is not a simple matter. What constitutes evidence for one person may not be evidence for another. Daily newspapers almost always contain some story of a trial where the two parties do not agree about the nature of the evidence. They may disagree about what happened or they may agree about what happened but disagree about what it is evidence of or for. Consider a soft-drink bottle found on the beach. To a contemporary American the bottle appears as someone's trash, left over from a beach party or washed ashore from a boat. To a person unfamiliar with such bottles, the soft-drink bottle may appear to be a treasure, washed ashore or unearthed by the tide. (The film *The Gods Must Be Crazy* presents a highly amusing example of this situation.)

The readings in this chapter raise many problems of evidence. The first reading is a classic Sherlock Holmes mystery story—only you have to supply the ending. If you use your reasoning skills and think hard about the possibilities from your own storehouse of knowledge, you may be able to come up with Holmes's answer. As you read the story, pay careful attention to the reasoning skills Holmes uses in solving the mystery. The other readings are about a murder case that happened in the early 1980s. Two books and a made-for-television movie have dramatized this case so you may already be familiar with it. Put yourself in the place of a jury member. Would you vote to convict William Bradfield of conspiracy to commit murder?

The Adventure of the Blanched Soldier

Sir Arthur Conan Doyle

The ideas of my friend Watson, though limited, are exceedingly pertinacious. For a long time he has worried me to write an experience of my own. Perhaps I have rather invited this persecution, since I have often had occasion to point out to him how superficial are his own accounts and to accuse him of pandering to popular taste instead of confining himself rigidly to facts and figures. "Try it yourself, Holmes!" he has retorted, and I am compelled to admit that, having taken my pen in my hand, I do begin to realize that the matter must be presented in such a way as may interest the reader. The following case can hardly fail to do so, as it is among the strangest happenings in my collection, though it chanced that Watson had no note of it in his collection. Speaking of my old friend and biographer, I would take this opportunity to remark that if I burden myself with a com-

---

From: *The Casebook of Sherlock Holmes* by Sir Arthur Conan Doyle (incomplete)

panion in? my various little inquiries it is not done out of sentiment or caprice, but it is that Watson has some remarkable characteristics of his own to which in his modesty he has given small attention amid his exaggerated estimates of my own performances. A confederate who foresees your conclusions and course of action is always dangerous, but one to whom each development comes as a perpetual surprise, and to whom the future is always a closed book, is indeed an ideal helpmate.

I find from my notebook that it was in January, 1903, just after the conclusion of the Boer War, that I had my visit from Mr. James M. Dodd, a big, fresh, sunburned, upstanding Briton. The good Watson had at that time deserted me for a wife, the only selfish action which I can recall in our association. I was alone.

It is my habit to sit with my back to the window and to place my visitors in the opposite chair, where the light falls full upon them. Mr. James M. Dodd seemed somewhat at a loss how to begin the interview. I did not attempt to help him, for his silence gave me more time for observation. I have found it wise to impress clients with a sense of power, and so I gave him some of my conclusions.

"From South Africa, sir, I perceive."

"Yes, sir," he answered, with some surprise.

"Imperial Yeomanry, I fancy."

"Exactly."

"Middlesex Corps, no doubt."

"That is so. Mr. Holmes, you are a wizard."

I smiled at his bewildered expression.

"When a gentleman of virile appearance enters my room with such tan upon his face as an English sun could never give, and with his handkerchief in his sleeve instead of in his pocket, it is not difficult to place him. You wear a short beard, which shows that you were not a regular. You have the cut of a riding-man. As to Middlesex, your card has already shown me that you are a stockbroker from Throgmorton Street. What other regiment would you join?"

"You see everything."

"I see no more than you, but I have trained myself to notice what I see. However, Mr. Dodd, it was not to discuss the science of observation that you called upon me this morning. What has been happening at Tuxbury Old Park?"

"Mr. Holmes——!"

"My dear sir, there is no mystery. Your letter came with that heading, and as you fixed this appointment in very pressing terms it was clear that something sudden and important had occurred."

"Yes, indeed. But the letter was written in the afternoon, and a good deal has happened since then. If Colonel Emsworth had not kicked me out——"

"Kicked you out!"

"Well, that was what it amounted to. He is a hard nail, is Colonel Emsworth. The greatest martinet in the Army in his day, and it was a day of rough language, too. I couldn't have stuck the colonel if it had not been for Godfrey's sake."

I lit my pipe and leaned back in my chair.

"Perhaps you will explain what you are talking about."

My client grinned mischievously.

"I had got into the way of supposing that you knew everything without being told," said he. "But I will give you the facts, and I hope to God that you will be able to tell me what they mean. I've been awake all night puzzling my brain, and the more I think the more incredible does it become.

"When I joined up in January, 1901—just two years ago—young Godfrey Emsworth had joined the same squadron. He was Colonel Emsworth's only son—Emsworth, the Crimean V. C.—and he had the fighting blood in him, so it is no wonder he volunteered. There was not a finer lad in the regiment. We formed a friendship—the sort of friendship which can only be made when one lives the same life and shares the same joys and sorrows. He was my mate—and that means a good deal in the Army. We took the rough and the smooth together for a year of hard fighting. Then he was hit with a bullet from an elephant gun in the action near Diamond Hill outside Pretoria. I got one letter from the hospital at Cape Town and one from Southampton. Since then not a word—not one word, Mr. Holmes, for six months and more, and he my closest pal.

"Well, when the war was over, and we all got back, I wrote to his father and asked where Godfrey was. No answer. I waited a bit and then I wrote again. This time I had a reply, short and gruff. Godfrey had gone on a voyage round the world, and it was not likely that he would be back for a year. That was all.

"I wasn't satisfied, Mr. Holmes. The whole thing seemed to me so damned unnatural. He was a good lad, and he would not drop a pal like that. It was not like him. Then, again, I happened to know that he was heir to a lot of money, and also that his father and he did not always hit it off too well. The old man was sometimes a bully, and young Godfrey had too much spirit to stand it. No, I wasn't satisfied, and I determined that I would get to the root of the matter. It happened, however, that my own affairs needed a lot of straightening out, after two years' absence, and so it is only this week that I have been able to take up Godfrey's case again. But since I have taken it up I mean to drop everything in order to see it through."

Mr. James M. Dodd appeared to be the sort of person whom it would be better to have as a friend than as an enemy. His blue eyes were stern and his square jaw had set hard as he spoke.

"Well, what have you done?" I asked.

"My first move was to get down to his home, Tuxbury Old Park, near Bedford, and to see for myself how the ground lay. I wrote to the mother, therefore—I had had quite enough of the curmudgeon of a father—and I made a clean frontal attack: Godfrey was my chum, I had a great deal of interest which I might tell her of our common experiences, I should be in the neighbourhood, would there be any objection, et cetera? In reply I had quite an amiable answer from her and an offer to put me up for the night. That was what took me down on Monday.

"Tuxbury Old Hall is inaccessible—five miles from anywhere. There was no trap at the station, so I had to walk, carrying my suitcase, and it was nearly dark before I arrived. It is a great wandering house, standing in a considerable park. I should judge it was of all sorts of ages and styles, starting on a half-timbered Elizabethan foundation and ending in a Victorian portico. Inside it was all panelling and tapestry and half-effaced old pictures, a house of shadows and mystery. There was a butler, old Ralph, who seemed about the same age as the house, and there was his wife, who might have been older. She had been Godfrey's nurse, and I had heard him speak of her as second only to his mother in his affections, so I was drawn to her in spite of her queer appearance. The mother I liked also—a gentle little white mouse of a woman. It was only the colonel himself whom I barred.

"We had a bit of barney right away, and I should have walked back to the station if I had not felt that it might be playing his game for me to do so. I was shown straight into his study, and there I found him, a huge, bow-backed man with a smoky skin and a straggling gray beard, seated behind his littered desk. A red-veined nose jutted out like a vulture's beak, and two fierce gray eyes glared at me from under tufted brows. I could understand now why Godfrey seldom spoke of his father.

" 'Well, sir,' said he in a rasping voice, 'I should be interested to know the real reasons for this visit.'

"I answered that I had explained them in my letter to his wife.

" 'Yes, yes, you said that you had known Godfrey in Africa. We have, of course, only your word for that.'

" 'I have his letters to me in my pocket.'

" 'Kindly let me see them.'

"He glanced at the two which I handed him, and then he tossed them back.

" 'Well, what then?' he asked.

" 'I was fond of your son Godfrey, sir. Many ties and memories united us. Is it not natural that I should wonder at his sudden silence and should wish to know what has become of him?'

" 'I have some recollections, sir, that I had already corresponded with you and had told you what had become of him. He has gone upon a voyage round the world. His health was in a poor way after his African experiences, and both his mother and I were of opinion that complete rest and change were needed. Kindly pass that explanation on to any other friends who may be interested in the matter.'

" 'Certainly,' I answered. 'But perhaps you would have the goodness to let me have the name of the steamer and of the line by which he sailed, together with the date. I have no doubt that I should be able to get a letter through to him.'

"My request seemed both to puzzle and to irritate my host. His great eyebrows came down over his eyes, and he tapped his fingers impatiently on the table. He looked up at last with the expression of one who has seen his adversary make a dangerous move at chess, and has decided how to meet it.

" 'Many people, Mr. Dodd,' said he, 'would take offence at your infernal pertinacity and would think that this insistence had reached the point of damned impertinence.'

" 'You must put it down, sir, to my real love for your son.'

" 'Exactly. I have already made every allowance upon that score. I must ask you, however, to drop these inquiries. Every family has its own inner knowledge and its own motives, which cannot always be made clear to outsiders, however well-intentioned. My wife is anxious to hear something of Godfrey's past which you are in a position to tell her, but I would ask you to let the present and the future alone. Such inquiries serve no useful purpose, sir, and place us in a delicate and difficult position.'

"So I came to a dead end, Mr. Holmes. There was no getting past it. I could only pretend to accept the situation and register a vow inwardly that I would never rest until my friend's fate had been cleared up. It was a dull evening. We dined quietly, the three of us, in a gloomy, faded old room. The lady questioned me eagerly about her son, but the old man seemed morose and depressed. I was so bored by the whole proceeding that I made an excuse as soon as I decently could and retired to my bedroom. It was a large, bare room on the ground floor, as gloomy as the rest of the house, but after a year of sleeping upon the veldt, Mr. Holmes, one is not too particular about one's quarters. I opened the curtains and looked out into the garden, remarking that it was a fine night with a bright half-moon. Then I sat down by the roaring fire with the lamp on a table beside me, and endeavoured to distract my mind with a novel. I was interrupted, however, by Ralph, the old butler, who came in with a fresh supply of coals.

" 'I thought you might run short in the night-time, sir. It is bitter weather and these rooms are cold.'

"He hesitated before leaving the room, and when I looked round he was standing facing me with a wistful look upon his wrinkled face.

" 'Beg your pardon, sir, but I could not help hearing what you said of young Master Godfrey at dinner. You know, sir, that my wife nursed him, and so I may say I am his foster-father. It's natural we should take an interest. And you say he carried himself well, sir?'

" 'There was no braver man in the regiment. He pulled me out once from under the rifles of the Boers, or maybe I should not be here.'

"The old butler rubbed his skinny hands.

"Yes, sir, yes, that is Master Godfrey all over. He was always courageous. There's not a tree in the park, sir, that he has not climbed. Nothing would stop him. He was a fine boy—and oh, sir, he was a fine man.'

"I sprang to my feet.

" 'Look here!' I cried. 'You say he _was_. You speak as if he were dead. What is all this mystery? What has become of Godfrey Emsworth?'

"I gripped the old man by the shoulder, but he shrank away.

" 'I don't know what you mean, sir. Ask the master about Master Godfrey. He knows. It is not for me to interfere.'

"He was leaving the room, but I held his arm.

" 'Listen,' I said. 'You are going to answer one question before you leave if I have to hold you all night. Is Godfrey dead?'

"He could not face my eyes. He was like a man hypnotized. The answer was dragged from his lips. It was a terrible and unexpected one.

" 'I wish to God he was!' he cried, and, tearing himself free, he dashed from the room.

"You will think, Mr. Holmes, that I returned to my chair in no very happy state of mind. The old man's words seemed to me to bear only one interpretation. Clearly my poor friend had become involved in some criminal or, at the least, disreputable transaction which touched the family honour. That stern old man had sent his son away and hidden him from the world lest some scandal should come to light. Godfrey was a reckless fellow. He was easily influenced by those around him. No doubt he had fallen into bad hands and been misled to his ruin. It was a piteous business, if it was indeed so, but even now it was my duty to hunt him out and see if I could aid him. I was anxiously pondering the matter when I looked up, and there was Godfrey Emsworth standing before me."

My client had paused as one in deep emotion.

"Pray continue," I said. "Your problem presents some very unusual features."

"He was outside the window, Mr. Holmes, with his face pressed against the glass. I have told you that I looked out at the night. When I did so I left the curtains partly open. His figure was framed in this gap. The window came down to the ground and I could see the whole length of it, but it was his face which held my gaze. He was deadly pale—never have I seen a man so white. I reckon ghosts may look like that; but his eyes met mine, and they were the eyes of a living man. He sprang back when he saw that I was looking at him, and he vanished into the darkness.

"There was something shocking about the man, Mr. Holmes. It wasn't merely that ghastly face glimmering as white as cheese in the darkness. It was more subtle than that—something slinking, something furtive, something guilty—something very unlike the frank, manly lad that I had known. It left a feeling of horror in my mind.

"But when a man has been soldiering for a year or two with brother Boer as a playmate, he keeps his nerve and acts quickly. Godfrey had hardly vanished before I was at the window. There was an awkward catch, and I was some little time before I could throw it up. Then I nipped through and ran down the garden path in the direction that I thought he might have taken.

"It was a long path and the light was not very good, but it seemed to me something was moving ahead of me. I ran on and called his name, but it was no use. When I got to the end of the path there were several others branching in different directions to various outhouses. I stood hesitating, and as I did so I heard distinctly the sound of a closing door. It was not behind me in the house, but ahead of me, somewhere in the darkness. That was enough, Mr. Holmes, to assure me that what I had seen was not a vision. Godfrey had run away from me, and he had shut a door behind him. Of that I was certain.

"There was nothing more I could do, and I spent an uneasy night turning the matter over in my mind and trying to find some theory which would cover the facts. Next day I found the colonel rather more conciliatory, and as his wife remarked that there were some places of interest in the neighbourhood, it gave me an opening to ask whether my presence for one more night would incommode them. A somewhat grudging acquiescence from the old man gave me a clear day in which to make my observations. I was already perfectly convinced that Godfrey was in hiding somewhere near, but where and why remained to be solved.

"The house was so large and so rambling that a regiment might be hid away in it and no one the wiser. If the secret lay there it was difficult for me to penetrate it. But the door which I had heard close was certainly not in the house. I must explore the garden and see what I could find. There was no difficulty in the way, for the old people were busy in their own fashion and left me to my own devices.

"There were several small outhouses, but at the end of the garden there was a detached building of some size—large enough for a gardener's or a gamekeeper's residence. Could this be the place whence the sound of that shutting door had come? I approached it in a careless fashion as though I were strolling aimlessly round the grounds. As I did so, a small, brisk, bearded man in a black coat and bowler hat—not at all the gardener type— came out of the door. To my surprise, he locked it after him and put the key in his pocket. Then he looked at me with some surprise on his face.

" 'Are you a visitor here?' he asked.

"I explained that I was and that I was a friend of Godfrey's.

" 'What a pity that he should be away on his travels, for he would have so liked to see me,' I continued.

" 'Quite so. Exactly,' said he with a rather guilty air. 'No doubt you will renew your visit at some more propitious time.' He passed on, but when I turned I observed that he was standing watching me, half-concealed by the laurels at the far end of the garden.

"I had a good look at the little house as I passed it, but the windows were heavily curtained, and, so far as one could see, it was empty. I might spoil my own game and even be ordered off the premises if I were too audacious, for I was still conscious that I was being watched. Therefore, I strolled back to the house and waited for night before I went on with my inquiry. When all was dark and quiet I slipped out of my window and made my way as silently as possible to the mysterious lodge.

"I have said that it was heavily curtained, but now I found that the windows were shuttered as well. Some light, however, was breaking through one of them, so I concentrated my attention upon this. I was in luck, for the curtain had not been quite closed, and there was a crack in the shutter, so that I could see the inside of the room. It was a cheery place enough, a bright lamp and a blazing fire. Opposite to me was seated the little man whom I had seen in the morning. He was smoking a pipe and reading a paper."

"What paper?" I asked.

My client seemed annoyed at the interruption of his narrative.

"Can it matter?" he asked.

"It is most essential."

"I really took no notice."

"Possibly you observed whether it was a broad-leafed paper or of that smaller type which one associates with weeklies."

"Now that you mention it, it was not large. It might have been the *Spectator*. However, I had little thought to spare upon such details, for a second man was seated with his back to the window, and I could swear that this second man was Godfrey. I could not see his face, but I knew the familiar slope of his shoulders. He was leaning upon his elbow in an attitude of great melancholy, his body turned towards the fire. I was hesitating as to what I should do when there was a sharp tap on my shoulder, and there was Colonel Emsworth beside me.

" 'This way, sir!' said he in a low voice. He walked in silence to the house, and I followed him into my own bedroom. He had picked up a time-table in the hall.

" 'There is a train to London at 8:30,' he said. 'The trap will be at the door at eight.'

"He was white with rage, and, indeed, I felt myself in so difficult a position that I could only stammer out a few incoherent apologies in which I tried to excuse myself by urging my anxiety for my friend.

" 'The matter will not bear discussion,' said he abruptly. 'You have made a most damnable intrusion into the privacy of our family. You were here as a guest and you have become a spy. I have nothing more to say, sir, save that I have no wish ever to see you again.'

"At this I lost my temper, Mr. Holmes, and I spoke with some warmth.

" 'I have seen your son, and I am convinced that for some reason of your own you are concealing him from the world. I have no idea what your motives are in cutting him off in this fashion, but I am sure that he is no longer a free agent. I warn you, Colonel Emsworth, that until I am assured as to the safety and well-being of my friend I shall never desist in my efforts to get to the bottom of the mystery, and I shall certainly not allow myself to be intimidated by anything which you may say or do.'

"The old fellow looked diabolical, and I really thought he was about to attack me. I have said that he was a gaunt, fierce old giant, and though I am no weakling I might have been hard put to it to hold my own against him. However, after a long glare of rage he turned upon his heel and walked out of the room. For my part, I took the appointed train in the morning, with the full intention of coming straight to you and asking for your advice and assistance at the appointment for which I had already written."

Such was the problem which my visitor laid before me. It presented, as the astute reader will have already perceived, few difficulties in its solution, for a very limited choice of alternatives must get to the root of the matter. Still, elementary as it was, there were points of interest and novelty about it which may excuse my placing it upon record. I now proceeded, using my familiar method of logical analysis, to narrow down the possible solutions.

"The servants," I asked; "how many were in the house?"

"To the best of my belief there were only the old butler and his wife. They seemed to live in the simplest fashion."

"There was no servant, then, in the detached house?"

"None, unless the little man with the beard acted as such. He seemed, however, to be quite a superior person."

"That seems very suggestive. Had you any indication that food was conveyed from the one house to the other?"

"Now that you mention it, I did see old Ralph carrying a basket down the garden walk and going in the direction of this house. The idea of food did not occur to me at the moment."

"Did you make any local inquiries?"

"Yes, I did. I spoke to the station-master and also to the innkeeper in the village. I simply asked if they knew anything of my old comrade, Godfrey Emsworth. Both of them assured me that he had gone for a voyage round the world. He had come home and then had almost at once started off again. The story was evidently universally accepted."

"You said nothing of your suspicions?"

"Nothing."

"That was very wise. The matter should certainly be inquired into. I will go back with you to Tuxbury Old Park."

"To-day?"

It happened that at the moment I was clearing up the case which my friend Watson has described as that of the Abbey School, in which the Duke of Greyminster was so deeply involved. I had also a commission from the Sultan of Turkey which called for immediate action, as political consequences of the gravest kind might arise from its neglect. Therefore it was not until the beginning of the next week, as my diary records, that I was able to start forth on my mission to Bedfordshire in company with Mr. James M. Dodd. As we drove to Euston we picked up a grave and taciturn gentleman of iron-gray aspect, with whom I had made the necessary arrangements.

"This is an old friend," said I to Dodd. "It is possible that his presence may be entirely unnecessary, and, on the other hand, it may be essential. It is not necessary at the present stage to go further into the matter."

The narratives of Watson have accustomed the reader, no doubt, to the fact that I do not waste words or disclose my thoughts while a case is actually under consideration. Dodd seemed surprised, but nothing more was said, and the three of us continued our journey together. In the train I asked Dodd one more question which I wished our companion to hear.

"You say that you saw your friend's face quite clearly at the window, so clearly that you are sure of his identity?"

"I have no doubt about it whatever. His nose was pressed against the glass. The lamplight shone full upon him."

"It could not have been someone resembling him?"

"No, no, it was he."

"But you say he was changed?"

"Only in colour. His face was—how shall I describe it?—it was of a fish-belly whiteness. It was bleached."

"Was it equally pale all over?"

"I think not. It was his brow which I saw so clearly as it was pressed against the window."

"Did you call to him?"

"I was too startled and horrified for the moment. Then I pursued him, as I have told you, but without result."

My case was practically complete, and there was only one small incident needed to round it off. When, after a considerable drive, we arrived at the strange old rambling house which my client had described, it was Ralph, the elderly butler, who opened the door. I had requisitioned the carriage for the day and had asked my elderly friend to remain within it unless we should summon him. Ralph, a little wrinkled old fellow, was in the conventional costume of black coat and pepper-and-salt trousers, with only one curious variant. He wore brown leather gloves, which at sight of us he instantly shuffled off, laying them down on the hall-table as we passed in. I have, as my friend Watson may have remarked, an abnormally acute set of senses, and a faint but incisive scent was apparent. It seemed to centre on the hall-table. I turned, placed my hat there, knocked it off, stooped to pick it up, and contrived to bring my nose within a foot of the gloves. Yes, it was undoubtedly from them that the curious tarry odour was oozing. I passed on into the study with my case complete. Alas, that I should have to show my hand so when I tell my own story! It was by concealing such links in the chain that Watson was enabled to produce his meretricious finales.

Colonel Emsworth was not in his room, but he came quickly enough on receipt of Ralph's message. We heard his quick, heavy step in the passage. The door was flung open and he rushed in with bristling beard and twisted features, as terrible an old man as ever I have seen. He held our cards in his hand, and he tore them up and stamped on the fragments.

"Have I not told you, you infernal busybody, that you are warned off the premises? Never dare to show your damned face here again. If you enter again without my leave I shall be within my rights if I use violence. I'll shoot you, sir! By God, I will! As to you, sir," turning upon me, "I extend the same warning to you. I am familiar with your ignoble profession, but you must take your reputed talents to some other field. There is no opening for them here."

"I cannot leave here," said my client firmly, "until I hear from Godfrey's own lips that he is under no restraint."

Our involuntary host rang the bell.

"Ralph," he said, "telephone down to the county police and ask the inspector to send up two constables. Tell him there are burglars in the house."

"One moment," said I. "You must be aware, Mr. Dodd, that Colonel Emsworth is within his rights and that we have no legal status within his house. On the other hand, he should recognize that your action is prompted entirely by solicitude for his son. I venture to hope that if I were allowed to have five minutes' conversation with Colonel Emsworth I could certainly alter his view of the matter."

"I am not so easily altered," said the old soldier. "Ralph, do what I have told you. What the devil are you waiting for? Ring up the police!"

"Nothing of the sort," I said, putting my back to the door. "Any police interference would bring about the very catastrophe which you dread." I took out my notebook and scribbled one word upon a loose sheet. "That," said I as I handed it to Colonel Emsworth, "is what has brought us here."

Murder on the Main Line

MIKE MALLOWE

Soon it will be two years since Susan Reinert's death.

Her children are still missing.

Her estate is still unsettled.

Whoever killed her is still at large.

The mystery of her life and the tragedy of her death remain unexplained.

There is no statute of limitations on murder, but there is a limit to patience.

The people who loved Susan Reinert and her children, the friends and relatives who cared deeply about her, the fellow professionals who taught with her at Upper Merion High School, and the neighbors who befriended her on Woodcrest Avenue in Ardmore—these are the people who are running out of hope.

Soon it will be two years since the stubborn riddle of Susan Reinert's death began and still the enigma persists.

Who killed her and why? And where are the children?

At some point later this month, Assistant U.S. Attorney Peter Schenck, the intense, young prosecutor in charge of the continuing investigation into Susan Reinert's murder and the disappearance and presumed kidnap-murder of her two young children, will be forced to stand before a grim, black-robed judge in the Federal Building at 6th and Market Streets and put up or shut up.

Schenck is preoccupied with that appearance already. He sounds testy when he discusses it; worried, afraid to say anything that might jeopardize the thin leads the government has been pursuing. When asked about the progress of the Reinert investigation, Schenck will reply sharply only, "It is not a closed shop. We are working on it and we hope to solve the thing."

Schenck's choice won't be an easy one this month when he stands before the bar.

He will either announce that the government of the United States is prepared to seek indictments against one or more individuals in the murder of Susan Reinert and the disappearance of her children; or he will find himself pressured into arguing in his most lawyerly fashion for one more continuance, one last shot at closing the 21-month-old investigation—an investigation that most of the men who have worked on, who have become

obsessed with, become consumed by, would agree should have been concluded long ago.

It was the kind of murder that *should* have been wrapped up in a couple of weeks.

The police found her body stuffed into the tire well of a red Plymouth
hatchback. At that point she was simply an unidentified female Caucasian
in her mid-30s. She was naked and there were deep bruises on her face and
arms.

She'd been bound in the fetal position, according to the coroner's
report, and traces of a denim-like substance, probably fabric, had been
imbedded into coarse thigh wounds. The indications of a struggle were
clear.

At first, they thought she'd been raped; but the medical experts soon
discounted that theory. She was very small, petite in fact, with short, brown
hair and it wouldn't have been difficult to overpower her.

Her right eye was blackened and the tissues around it were visibly
raised and fissured. It was impossible to determine the time of death just
then, but an autopsy would later reveal that she could have been dead for
as long as 24 hours before her body was discovered.

The most striking abrasion on the corpse was a long, thin line of shallow puncture marks that ran along the woman's back and buttocks. They
looked like they could have been made by spurs, and this gave rise to speculation that she had been the victim of some sort of ritual killing. But that
idea was soon discarded, as well, in favor of the less lurid but more likely
explanation that at some point she had been bound, perhaps by a bicycle
chain, and dragged for some distance.

In the beginning they would also assume that the victim had been suf-
focated, and her death would be listed as "homicide by asphyxiation."

That was all they had to go on when the body was discovered and the
investigation opened. But back then, it seemed like more than enough—a
nuts-and-bolts murder, they kept telling themselves.

* * *

It was still dark when the cops first approached the car. The call had
come in at 5 a.m. on a Monday and they responded almost immediately.
The parking lot was nearly empty and the little Plymouth Horizon was off
by itself.

The heat that singes central Pennsylvania in midsummer was still bot-
tled up behind the mountains, and the predawn darkness made it seem
cooler than it really was.

The night dispatcher in the old courthouse in Harrisburg, the state
capital, had taken the call and quickly turned it over to his supervisor,

Kevin Molloy. After dark, every police call in Dauphin County, Pennsylvania, had to be routed through their switchboard, along with civil defense emergencies and act-of-God disasters, and technically speaking, the dispatcher and Molloy constituted Dauphin County's entire Office of Emergency Preparedness and Communications, as well as the nighttime police radio network.

No one, including the civil defense officers themselves, had ever taken any of that very seriously until three months before when, on the blustery evening of March 28th, 1979, the massive nuclear reactor at Three Mile Island, just outside Harrisburg, had begun heading toward a meltdown. Since then, the night dispatcher has been taking his job very seriously.

A man who seemed to speak with a slight accent phoned the police to say, "There's a sick woman in a car out at the Host motel." He claimed to be calling from a phone booth on U.S. Route 22, about five miles north of Harrisburg. That was the last the police would ever hear from the anonymous caller.

The Host Inn was in rural Swatara Township, about three miles from the Pennsylvania Turnpike, and it was to Swatara's police department that the courthouse call was routed. Actually, the township cops had noticed the red Plymouth, parked all by itself, more than four hours earlier, first spotting it just after midnight, but no one had seen any reason to investigate. Now, there was a reason.

The Host Inn was a colorful, comfortable, family-oriented place that catered to sedate business meetings and seminars, as well as to the turnpike politicians from Philadelphia and southeastern Pennsylvania who had overnight business near the capital.

The inn had never caused the local cops any trouble, and the report of a sick woman in the parking lot seemed routine enough. They approached the car as an ordinary assist-motorist call.

But there *was* something unusual. The car's hatchback had been left conspicuously open, almost inviting notice in the deserted parking lot. When they looked inside, they saw the tiny, broken body jammed into the tire well.

Three Mile Island's nuclear problems notwithstanding, homicide was a little out of the township cops' normal range of activity. Their customary procedure, in rare cases like this, was to contact the Pennsylvania State Police Barracks out of Troop H, near Harrisburg, and let it handle things.

That's exactly what they did. But somewhere between the initial discovery of the body and the commencement of the homicide probe, mistakes—costly, frustrating mistakes, with ultimately irrevocable consequences —would be made that would still haunt law enforcement nearly two years later.

But back then, back during the early morning hours of June 25th, 1979 in the fresh coolness of the Pennsylvania dawn, the battered body in the Host Inn parking lot would still look like a nuts-and-bolts case.

In big cities, like Philadelphia or Pittsburgh, the body in the parking lot would have been assigned routinely to whichever detective was on duty, or "up" in the homicide squad. In Philadelphia, at homicide headquarters downtown, the detective would actually pluck the case from a "spinning wheel" file that seems to be in perpetual motion, since, in a good year, close to 400 Philadelphians could be counted on to assassinate each other in a bewildering variety of ways.

But even before the big-city homicide cop got the case, he could be reasonably certain that the crime scene and any physical evidence was preserved, that any witnesses were on call, and that the expert pathologists in the crime lab were busily at work identifying and tagging the grisly artifacts of medical jurisprudence.

That's the way it's done where homicide is as common as a domestic disturbance. But out in gorgeous, summer-green Dauphin County, an unidentified white female's naked corpse is something of an event.

While the state troopers and Swatara cops were still examining the car for clues, checking on the identity of the victim and questioning the Host Inn people for leads, the body itself was already en route to Community General Osteopathic Hospital in Harrisburg.

When it arrived, a routine autopsy would be performed by Dr. Robert Bear, a clinical pathologist, and the autopsy would ultimately be certified by Dr. William Bush, the veteran coroner of Dauphin County.

Bear would determine what circumstances or trauma within the body had caused the victim's mechanisms to shut down, with the resultant death. It was not his job to decide what the specific physical cause of death had been. Still, after this preliminary autopsy, "homicide by asphyxiation" would be mistakenly entered on the official report. Six months later, a minute sample of frozen tissue taken at that preliminary autopsy would reveal belatedly the real cause of death.

As far as a good homicide cop is concerned, medical information like that obtained by Dr. Bear might be interesting, but irrelevant. What *is* vitally important is the evidence unearthed, not by a clinical but by a forensic pathologist, whose specialty it is to describe the probable cause of death— the *reason* for the clinical shutdown of the body.

In most cases, that would be the first and only way that the cops would know exactly what kind of doer they were dealing with—a shooter, a stabber, a poisoner, a junkie, etc.

Without the information supplied by a forensic pathologist, it would be practically impossible for a homicide investigation to proceed quickly and professionally.

Yet, within a matter of hours, these were precisely the circumstances in which the police would find themselves on that lovely summer day in central Pennsylvania. No sooner had their investigation begun than their corpse disappeared.

County Coroner Bush insists that nothing improper took place. So does the spokesman for Community General Hospital. Charges were never filed, and they are probably right. It's just that, as the investigation into the body in the parking lot continued, very little would turn out to be as it had originally appeared.

The first break for the police came when they realized that the victim had actually been dumped into her own car—a 1978 Plymouth Horizon, registered to Susan Reinert, 37, of 662 Woodcrest Avenue, Ardmore, a small suburb on Philadelphia's exclusive Main Line.

What Susan Reinert had been doing in Swatara Township, near Harrisburg, in a motel parking lot more than 100 miles from her home, was anyone's guess.

Reinert's family was immediately contacted, including an ex-husband, Kenneth Reinert, who lived near her home outside Philadelphia; and a brother, W. Patrick Gallagher, a chemist, who worked in Pittsburgh.

While the police were just beginning to ask themselves who and what Susan Reinert was, and how and why she had turned up lifeless and naked in the tire well of her own car, her family was making arrangements to claim her remains.

In fact, her brother had immediately contacted an undertaker who was already in the process of removing her body from Community General in Harrisburg. The family had decided on cremation, and he was there later that morning to carry out their wishes. All of this was happening only hours after the body had been discovered.

Once the preliminary autopsy was completed, Coroner Bush ordered her body released to the family. He did this before the police had even begun their medical detective work.

In the meantime, before noon, the state police had taken over the investigation and Sergeant Joseph Van Nort of the Criminal Investigation Unit in Harrisburg was on the phone to Coroner Bush. Hold on to the body, he told him, so that the lab could fingerprint it and conduct a more thorough examination.

After Van Nort's call, the coroner immediately notified the hospital and told them to keep the undertaker waiting. But by early afternoon the corpse had been fingerprinted and the undertaker was again requesting the remains.

No forensic pathologist had shown up yet and the hospital was under a standing order, as well as a Pennsylvania state law, _not_ to release any body without the coroner's specific permission. But the undertaker was getting impatient.

By this time Coroner Bush had both okayed the removal of the body and rescinded that order after the state police intervened, but somewhere along the line somebody misunderstood—and no sooner had the corpse been fingerprinted than the undertaker was permitted to leave with the remains of Susan Reinert. He cremated her at once.

Later that afternoon, when the men from the Criminal Investigation Unit came looking for the body, the stunned personnel at Community General could only stammer, "What body?"

By the early evening of June 25th, 1979, most of the people closest to Susan Reinert were aware of what happened. Her ex-husband, Kenneth, an Employee Benefits administrator with Fidelity Bank in Philadelphia, who had been called to Harrisburg to identify the body, telephoned his parents in upstate Pennsylvania and told them that Susan, with whom they had remained very close despite the divorce, had been injured in a serious automobile accident. It wasn't until hours later that he could bring himself to tell them what had really happened.

As stunned and distraught as they were over Susan's death, both her ex-husband and his parents were even more concerned about the whereabouts and safety of the young Reinert children, Michael, 11, and Karen, 12.

By that evening, the Pennsylvania State Police, too, realized that they were confronting not simply the murder of Susan Reinert, but also the disappearance, virtually certain kidnapping, and probable demise of her children, as well.

Suddenly, the unidentified female Caucasian discovered in the parking lot at the Host Inn had all the markings of a triple murder. It was quickly dawning on them that the nuts-and-bolts case they had anticipated that morning had escalated into something far more complicated.

Governor Thornburgh's recently appointed commandant of the Pennsylvania State Police was Daniel Dunn, a former FBI special agent-in-charge from the Pittsburgh bureau, where Thornburgh himself had served for many years as western Pennsylvania's relentless United States attorney. He and Dunn understood each other quite well, and Dunn's response to the Reinert murder was instant and predictable.

He wanted his old colleagues from the bureau in on this one at once. They didn't need any jurisdictional approval to offer their assistance and lab facilities to Troop H at Harrisburg—they had done so often in the past. The mere fact that Reinert's two kids were missing was enough to raise the federal kidnapping issue. Besides, the way this case was shaping up, Dunn knew that Troop H could use all the help it could get.

One of the first FBI agents to be assigned to the Reinert investigation was Michael Wald, then 35, a nine-year veteran of the Harrisburg office and one of the most experienced agents anywhere in the bureau. The day they discovered Susan Reinert's body, Wald was vacationing in Florida.

He had no idea who Susan Reinert was or why she had been killed or what had happened to her children. In fact, when her body was discovered, a tough homicide case was the last thing on his mind. Within weeks, however, all that would change dramatically.

The last time the neighbors recall seeing Susan Reinert and her children alive was on Friday evening, June 22nd, 1979, three days before her body was discovered.

That was at approximately 9:15 p.m. Her children, Michael and Karen, were outside their home playing. There had been a sudden, savage, summer cloudburst and the kids were picking up hailstones that had pelted the quiet, family street in Ardmore.

About 15 minutes later, the neighbors claim, just after they'd heard the Reinert phone ring, Reinert and the kids rushed out of the house rather quickly, the car doors slammed, and Reinert's small Plymouth was backing out of her driveway. Some of the hailstones crunched under the tires as the car left Woodcrest Avenue.

No one knows who called Susan Reinert or why, or if, in fact, anyone did really call. If the police have any theories on this point, they aren't disclosing them. Somehow, probably by that phone call, Reinert and her kids were lured away from the safety of their home. Whoever served as the bait, most investigators agree, will one day figure prominently when and if indictments are ever handed down.

Earlier that evening Reinert's son, Michael, had spoken on the phone with his father, Kenneth, and explained that he was going away for the weekend to visit his paternal grandparents near Phoenixville. Otherwise, he would have spent much of the weekend with his father. Ever since their separation and divorce about three years before, Kenneth Reinert had managed to see the kids practically every weekend. Both he and Susan were devoted to them, and divorce or not they were determined to maintain the children's lives as normally as possible.

Susan Reinert had also been on the phone during the early evening that Friday calling John and Florence Reinert, her ex-in-laws, around 5 p.m. to check with John about whether or not a single tank of gas would get her back and forth to Allentown that weekend. Before she left Woodcrest Avenue that night, the neighbors also remember her asking other people on the street if they thought a tank of gas would do it.

The gas shortage had been gripping Pennsylvania and Governor Thornburgh had instituted the odd/even license plate rationing plan only days before. Gas lines and empty fuel tanks were common and Susan Reinert was understandably nervous about risking a long trip. Still, ever since her divorce she had gotten used to doing things on her own, and appeared to have every intention of hitting the turnpike the next day.

Reinert, an English teacher at Upper Merion High School and a very popular organizer on the faculty, had also become active recently in Parents Without Partners, a self-help group for widowed, divorced or separated parents.

The next day she was supposed to help conduct a workshop in Allentown for the group. Following the seminar, Michael was to be dropped off at his grandparents' house where he would begin a week's visit. Susan Reinert and her daughter, Karen, were then going to attend a gym clinic, since Karen was an enthusiastic gymnast. Later that week Reinert was planning to visit Valley Forge Music Fair, as well as Washington Memorial Chapel in Valley Forge with her kids. Susan and Michael's grandmother were making plans for Michael to be baptized there.

When Susan and Michael failed to show up at the elder Reinerts' home, they knew something was wrong.

In her own quiet, reserved, well-bred way, Susan Reinert had been looking—searching desperately, in fact—for Mr. Goodbar.

Privately, many investigators are convinced it could have been that very search that led to her death. Almost no one disputes the fact that ever since her divorce, the pixieish Reinert, with her big, dark eyes set behind large, round glasses and her short, bouncy brown hair, had been consumed by a sense of loneliness. She was a woman who needed a man—a woman struggling to make it with two children whom she adored and who, she hoped, would bear no lingering scars from the divorce that had shattered her life.

Over the last few years the English teacher had worked long and hard at broadening her circle of friends, at trying to meet the kind of men who measured up to her emotional and intellectual standards, and at anchoring her career on the fast-track faculty of Upper Merion High School.

She had met her ex-husband, Kenneth, when both were students at a small college in upstate Pennsylvania, then later married him and spent the first few years of that marriage traveling with him from one air base to another while he was in the Air Force. In the early 1970s they had settled down in another small Main Line suburb, just outside Philadelphia.

She rarely spoke about the divorce, and her husband, who has since remarried, routinely declines comment except through his attorney, who is deeply involved in the Susan Reinert saga even now.

Somewhere along the line, she and her husband had grown apart, had wearied of each other's temperaments and dispositions and had conceded reluctantly that the marriage just wasn't making it. Many of her friends would later claim that when the divorce finally became a reality, Susan Reinert at first embraced it as a sort of deliverance. Later, however, she would succumb, almost visibly and physically at times, to the vacuum and the loneliness that it had created.

One of the very first things the investigators did following that gruesome discovery in the parking lot of the Host Inn was to begin questioning her friends and relatives and neighbors about her boyfriends. The name that kept cropping up was William S. Bradfield, 47, now on a recovery-of-health sabbatical from the faculty of Upper Merion High School; but then, a fellow teacher of Susan Reinert's and the most charismatic figure by far, in the cliquish, pseudo-intellectual faculty community of Upper Merion High.

While other investigators were running down leads, especially about Bradfield and several other teachers at the high school, the FBI's Michael Wald was establishing a kind of beachhead for the murder probe in Philadelphia.

By early August, Wald and his partner of several years, Don Redden, now the bureau's agent-in-charge in their office in Covington, Kentucky, were working full-time on the Reinert investigation. Eventually, dozens of state troopers and more than 16 FBI agents in four separate states would attack the case. But back in August 1979, Wald was attempting to coordinate things pretty much on his own.

He'd spent the last few years on cases like official corruption in Harrisburg; a bloodthirsty ring of black Muslim bank robbers in central Pennsylvania, and interstate vice as it affected the state capital. A homicide was a distinct change of pace, and at first a not-altogether unpleasant one.

Wald's family was from the Shenandoah Valley coal country in upstate Pennsylvania, but the agent had grown up in New York. He still retained his heavy Bronx accent and didn't look anything like the prototypical FBI farmboy-turned-agent. Where they were tall, Wald was stocky; where they were light and blond, Wald was swarthy with kinky black hair and a thick, full mustache. In fact, he looked a good deal more like somebody the FBI would arrest.

In the past, this had often served Wald to good advantage as one of the bureau's top undercover men. In that capacity he had helped infiltrate and close down a cigarette-smuggling operation in North Carolina; before that, he had been involved in one of the bureau's pioneer offensives against videocassette and eight-track-tape pirates on the East Coast. As an undercover man, Wald was typecast—he always played a fast-talking hustler from New York.

That summer a Reinert command post was set up in the Pennsylvania State Police's Belmont Barracks on Belmont Avenue in West Philadelphia. The agents, like Wald, who had been dragooned in from outlying bureau offices like Harrisburg, were put up at the nearby Marriott on City Line.

Wald had actually put in for a transfer to Philadelphia before Reinert's body had been discovered. The agent-in-charge in Philadelphia, Edgar Best, had been Wald's boss or "control" on two of his previous clandestine assignments, and the two men were looking forward to working together again. The Reinert murder, however, wasn't exactly what they had in mind, and when Wald started on the case, neither he nor any of the other investigators dreamed that they would practically be making a career of it.

One of the first things that Michael Wald did was to visit the Reinert house at 662 Woodcrest Avenue in Ardmore. "It was a very child-oriented house, if you know what I mean," Wald would remember nearly two years later, still prepared to describe the interior of the home and the feelings that welled up around him there, with a vivid, detailed, almost total recall. Like most of the other state troopers and agents in on the Reinert murder, Wald had kids of his own.

"There were toys and games all over the place . . . posters up on the walls and schoolpapers that they'd brought home had been hung up—that sort of thing. The little boy, Michael, had a race car set up upstairs, and the little girl, Karen, had her suitcases and overnight bag all packed. . . . It was a nice environment for a kid to grow up in. . . . From what we could determine, they were really nice kids, too; well-behaved. . . . I don't have to tell you what it felt like whenever we went there.

"It's hard to imagine how much more difficult those kids made the case. They were always there in the back of your mind. . . . You *wanted* to find them—it was your *job* to find them; but if you found them buried somewhere . . . in a grave in somebody's backyard or out in the woods, you couldn't tell how you'd react to that, either. . . . It was just so *damn* hard . . . one of the worst things I ever had to go through.

"It really affected everybody. Joe Van Nort, the state trooper in charge of this thing—you can't imagine what it's done to him. . . . This is his *life* now.

"When the weekend would come, when it would be Friday night and I'd hit that turnpike for Harrisburg and know that I was going home, I'd be so glad. I'd just feel the weight lifting off. Then, come Monday morning I'd hit the road again; the pressure would start building up for an hour before I even got to Philadelphia. . . . But I guess we made the same mistake that everybody else did in the beginning. We never expected that it would take this long—we started out by looking at it as a nuts-and-bolts thing."

About two months before her death, Susan Reinert purchased several hundred thousand dollars worth of life insurance which she added to an already sizable estate. Her mother had died the year before, in October 1978, leaving her approximately $30,000 in cash and about $200,000 in property near Ridgeway, Pennsylvania, in upstate Elk County. About a month after her mother died, Susan Reinert drew [up a] will naming her brother, W. Patrick Gallagher, executor, and her children, Michael and Karen, sole beneficiaries.

But those plans changed radically just seven weeks before her death. Besides purchasing a half-million-dollar life insurance policy (which included a $200,000 accidental death rider) from the United States Automobile Association of San Antonio, Texas, she also obtained a $160,000 policy from New York Life. The Great-West Assurance Company, a Canadian firm, had also written a substantial policy on her life.

At that point, in the spring of 1979, Susan Reinert's estate amounted to a little over $1.1 million.

She had amazed her friends and stunned her family by suddenly revising her will in early May, eliminating her brother as executor and also writing out her children as beneficiaries. In their place she substituted William S. Bradfield, her fellow teacher at Upper Merion High School, as both the new executor and the sole beneficiary.

A significant phrase in the revised will identified Bradfield as "my future husband."

Today, through his lawyers, big, bearded Bill Bradfield insists that that's news to him.

During his only court appearance in connection with the Reinert investigation, Bradfield stared through what one observer called "stony blue eyes" and contended that he and Susan Reinert had been merely very good friends. "She didn't take my advice very often. . . . She asked me about who she should date. She dated people I thought she ought not to, went places I thought she ought not to, lived a lifestyle I thought was not. . . ."

Bradfield was wisely interrupted at that point as he testified before Judge Francis Catania in the County Courthouse in Media, Delaware County, by his attorney, John Paul Curran.

The man questioning Bradfield then, on June 10th, 1980—almost a full year after Susan Reinert's body had been found—was Deputy District Attorney John A. Reilly of Delaware County, the court-appointed administrator of the embattled Reinert estate. Reilly would charge that all along Bradfield had been "leading her down the primrose path with a promise of marriage."

Without ever putting it in so many words, Bradfield and his defenders refuted this accusation by implying that Susan Reinert had actually been an unhappy and desperately lonely woman, perhaps neurotic, and that she had wistfully manufactured an imaginary romance with Bradfield, capped in her own mind by her naming him in her will.

However, friends of the victim, her former psychologist, police investigators speaking off the record, and a horde of aggressive reporters would eventually come up with a much different version of events.

According to that unofficial consensus, Reinert and Bradfield had been casual lovers for approximately six years, despite the fact that Bradfield had been living with another teacher at Upper Merion, Susan Myers, for much of that time. (Bradfield was also previously married.)

Just prior to her death, Susan Reinert had told friends of plans to move to England with Bradfield, along with the children, and marry him. And neighbors on Woodcrest Avenue in Ardmore told investigators that Bradfield had been a frequent visitor at Susan Reinert's house, going on trips with the murder victim, playing with her kids, and occasionally staying all night.

Bradfield, who had recently been elected head of the teachers' union at Upper Merion, claimed that this was nonsense, that he had no intention of leaving for England, and that he was looking forward to negotiating the school district's new contract.

Naturally, the police investigating Susan Reinert's murder were spellbound by all this, especially by the fact that Bradfield profited so handsomely and directly as a result of Susan Reinert's death.

Today, John Paul Curran, a top-notch, Jesuit-educated defense lawyer in center city Philadelphia, scoffs at this speculation.

"William Bradfield has never been charged with anything and has not done anything. He has become as much as victim of all this as Susan Reinert. It has ruined his health and jeopardized his career.

"The people trying to link him to this must subscribe to the 'butler always did it theory'. . . . Well, this time the butler *didn't* do it."

On the advice of Curran and his other attorneys, Bradfield has declined all comment on the case. His only public statement on it was a brief written denial of any involvement in the murder and a wish for its speedy solution, which he issued when he abruptly stepped aside as the head of the Upper Merion teacher's union. He has, according to investigators, declined to cooperate with the FBI or the state police.

Bradfield had been teaching at Upper Merion since 1963 with certifications in English and Latin. A native of Colorado, he graduated from Haverford College in 1955 and has spent much of the rest of his life either taking or giving courses.

Most considered him the premier figure at Upper Merion, academically as well as politically. Students fought to get into his classes and female teachers, like Susan Reinert, apparently melted under the gaze of those "stony blue eyes." Stories—never really substantiated—circulated around the Upper Merion campus that in his younger days, Bradfield had fought with Castro in Cuba and lived the dashing life of a romantic scholar. While the Bradfield legend was almost certainly more fascinating than the real thing, the fact remained that among the catty, warring cliques within the faculty, Bradfield's was the predominant. In fact, the only educator in the township with as much clout as Bradfield was Upper Merion's veteran principal, Jay C. Smith. It appeared to many that together, the two actually ran the school. Bradfield has always adamantly maintained though, that because of his union activities and because he was faculty rather than administration, their relationship was adversarial.

Outside the school, Bradfield was the part owner of a craft shop in the Montgomeryville Mall, and also the holder of some choice real estate in Chester County. He was bright, charming and mesmerizing. Sometimes Bradfield's admirers couldn't help but wonder what he was doing in the English department of a high school. As one of them expressed it, "He is what a teacher should be. When you think of somebody poring over the Great Books, when you think of your typical Ivy League professor, the image that pops into your mind immediately is a guy like Bill Bradfield. It's not hard to see why a little English teacher like Susan Reinert went nuts over him."

The police, meanwhile, were singularly unimpressed with Bradfield's credentials and personality. *He* was the one who would get the money after Reinert's death, and that was good enough for them.

Bradfield's whereabouts on the night Reinert disappeared have never been confirmed by the police. However, that early summer weekend of the slaying, he and three fellow teachers from Upper Merion checked into a boarding house in Cape May, New Jersey, where they remained until Monday, the day that Susan Reinert's body was found. On that day, June 25th, 1979, Bradfield and another teacher took a night flight to Santa Fe, New Mexico, where they would spend the summer taking graduate courses. In fact, Bradfield was still in New Mexico when he contacted John Paul Curran of Curran, Mylotte, David & Fitzpatrick.

Long after Bradfield had become a central figure in the investigation— though one who, to this day, has never been charged with anything—the police determined that Susan Reinert had been killed sometime between 12:15 and 6:15 a.m. on Sunday, June 24th, 1979.

Eventually, Bradfield; his ex-roommate, Susan Myers; and Christopher Pappas, all teachers at Upper Merion, would hire Guardsman Security Systems Inc. to give them polygraph tests to determine if they were telling the truth about being in Cape May that weekend (where witnesses had seen them, anyway). A fourth teacher, Vincent Valaitis, who was also there, declined to participate, and instead, chose to cooperate with investigators. According to a spokesman for the polygraph firm, there were "no signs of any deception at all" in Bradfield's and the others' replies to questions about Susan Reinert's murder or their own whereabouts at that time.

Nearly one year after Susan Reinert's death, in June 1980, Bradfield, through his attorneys, finally moved to probate Susan Reinert's will and collect the $1.1 million estate.

Almost immediately, Reinert's brother, W. Patrick Gallagher, and her ex-husband, Kenneth Reinert, sought to block that probate. Both claimed to be acting in behalf of the missing children. According to the objection filed by Patrick Gallagher, there had been "undue influence exerted by William Bradfield, who was in a confidential relationship" with Susan Reinert, Gallagher's sister.

While a monumental will contest over the Reinert estate was taking shape—"the kind of an estate fight that comes along only about once every ten years in the entire United States," according to the fiery John Paul Curran—the cops were still searching for a murderer—and two missing kids.

After the episode of Susan Reinert's cremation before a proper forensic examination could take place, the FBI and the state police figured that things couldn't get any worse. But that was before they decided to reexamine the tape recording of the anonymous caller who had first informed the courthouse dispatcher that a sick woman was in a car in the Host Inn parking lot.

Susan Reinert's circle of friends was huge, and the FBI agents and state cops would eventually wind up interviewing hundreds of people—then double-checking their stories, their movements, their backgrounds and, in several cases, their alibis.

Originally, they had hoped to use electronic wizardry to test the voice of the anonymous phone caller against the voices of several of Susan Reinert's male friends and then check for similarities. All they needed to do that was the original tape. Courthouse employees had been instructed to keep the tapes for 30 days, just in case official police business ever required them.

But just as the hospital had greeted the investigators with, "What body?" people at Dauphin County Courthouse would shriek, "What tape?"

Like the corpse, the tape had also vanished. Employees in the courthouse claimed that they must have run short of tapes at some point because of the volume of incoming calls over the recent Three Mile Island scare, and accidentally reused the tape, thereby erasing one of the earliest and most promising leads.

After that, the investigators reluctantly headed back to Belmont Barracks. But by that time they were attempting to get a fix on Upper Merion High School or "Peyton Place South," as the students and an increasing number of their parents were beginning to label it—even before Susan Reinert's murder and her children's disappearance.

One Philadelphia *Daily News* headline read "Sex, Drugs Trouble Upper Merion High." Others called it "a school in trouble" or one "bedeviled" by reports of satanism, black masses and freewheeling sex. Even before the Reinert case, Upper Merion High School and especially its principal, Jay C. Smith, constituted one of the best tabloid stories in town.

Geographically, Upper Merion formed the northern tier of the newer sections of the traditional Main Line. The foremost town in the area was King of Prussia, a classy, pre-Revolutionary War neighborhood, only a short drive from the national historical park at Valley Forge.

The area was very upper-middle-class, bordering on the affluent. Though not as chic and wealthy as Lower Merion Township in Montgomery

County, close to where Susan Reinert lived, Upper Merion had already come into its own. In fact, residents there joked, only half-kiddingly and with more than a passing nouveau-riche gleam in their eyes, that of all the moneyed suburbs around Philadelphia, Upper Merion had been selected as the site for a new Bloomingdale's.

The 1,300-student high school itself was one of the finest physical plants in the state, with more labs, more library volumes, bigger and better playing fields, more sophisticated audiovisual aids, better gym facilities, more functionally designed classrooms and a grander cafeteria than the vast majority of the private colleges in the Philadelphia area. It was, without the slightest doubt, the state of the art in rich, upscale, snobby, suburban high schools.

Susan Reinert had been an excellent English teacher and a valued addition to the Upper Merion faculty. Her pet project was filmmaking and she had become _the_ audiovisual lady at Upper Merion. The kids thought she was great; the administration felt fortunate to have her, and her fellow professionals held her in high esteem.

The principal at Upper Merion, Jay C. Smith, whom Bill Bradfield had characterized as his adversary, was born and bred in Chester, Pennsylvania, and had been the undisputed boss of the school for the last dozen years. Personally, according to published accounts of the situation at Upper Merion, his life was becoming a shambles, with an estranged wife dying of cancer and a daughter and son-in-law who were both beset with problems of their own. However, for most of his tenure at Upper Merion, the outside world knew Smith as a spit-and-polish colonel in the Army Reserve and a thoroughly competent administrator in a demanding school district. In the beginning the school had flourished under Smith and had attracted dedicated educators like Susan Reinert. But all that began to change for Smith and Upper Merion High about two years before the English teacher's murder.

Today, Jay C. Smith, now 52, is serving hard time at the State Correctional Institution in Dallas, Pennsylvania, one of the toughest prisons in the East.

Since May 1979, Smith has been convicted of or has pled no contest to a whole series of crimes. It all began when he was accused of trying to steal $158,000 from a Sears store in St. Davids in December 1977. Since then he has pled no contest to a weapons offense, disorderly conduct, and possession of instruments of crime. Juries found him guilty of theft by deception, attempted theft by deception, possession of marijuana, and receiving stolen property. All told he could spend the next 4 to 12 years behind bars.

His last sentencing in June 1980, before a Dauphin County judge, saw Smith plead unsuccessfully for leniency. He had, he told the judge, "made a mess" of his life over the last two years. Today, homicide investigators are still trying to determine whether that mess could possibly shed any light on the fate of Susan Reinert as well.

In the months immediately following her murder and the revelations about Smith's "secret life," as the principal himself termed it in rambling open letters to the faculty written from prison, the Upper Merion community erupted.

Allegations of everything from teen orgies to satanic cults to sex between students and teachers ripped through the neighborhood like an outbreak of herpes—and Smith's name was linked to all of it by stop-the-presses newspaper coverage. Smith was portrayed, while still principal, as having amassed a huge porno collection; as having dabbled in swingers' sex clubs, where he was known as Colonel Jay; and as having sometimes donned a devil's costume during his escapades. *Today's Post*, a local paper, published excerpts of a journal allegedly kept by Smith's estranged wife, which provided more details.

These allegations were and are vehemently contested by Jay Smith. He reacted to the massive tabloid coverage with the "open letters" to the faculty at Upper Merion and filing suits for libel against several publications, including *Today's Post*, the *Daily News* and the Philadelphia *Inquirer*. Those lawsuits are presently pending and the truth of the allegations is still in dispute, but these rumors did little to calm the parents at Upper Merion and only created more leads for the investigators of Susan Reinert's murder to track down.

Even after Smith had been arrested and removed in 1978, Upper Merion parents screamed at one public protest meeting after another that they were still afraid to send their children to school. Reinert's murder coming on top of all this less than 12 months later left them absolutely hysterical.

On top of everything else, the police soon learned that Smith's daughter and son-in-law had not been seen near their Montgomery County home for almost a year-and-a-half.

Counting the Reinert kids, that made four missing persons the police had to deal with, plus one cremated corpse.

Investigators looking hard for any possible parallels between the Smith and Reinert cases soon found one in the person of William S. Bradfield.

In May 1979, the month before Reinert's murder, Bradfield had provided Smith's alibi at the principal's trial for the attempted theft of the Sears in St. Davids in 1977. Bradfield told the court that on the day of the incident he had actually run into Smith in Ocean City, New Jersey; spent time with him there looking for a mutual friend, and even shared a meal with him.

Bradfield's alibi for Smith obviously wasn't sufficient. Smith was convicted on May 31st. His sentencing date, when he was to appear before a state judge in Harrisburg, Pennsylvania, was Monday, June 25th, 1979—the day Susan Reinert's body was discovered in the parking lot of the Host Inn in Swatara Township about eight miles from Harrisburg.

According to published reports and stories later circulated by her friends at Upper Merion, Susan Reinert was very upset over Bradfield's testimony. The psychologist who had been treating her since 1973 would say later in an interview that: "Sue Reinert had serious and deep concerns that Bradfield may have committed perjury for Smith at his trial. When she confronted him about a month before her death, he acted high and mighty, Sue said. She said he became very indignant that she would dare question his honesty."

The problem was, Reinert confided to some of her friends, that she had been with Bradfield that day in Ocean City and couldn't recall Bradfield even seeing Smith, much less spending any time with him.

Over the next few weeks, just before her death, her relationship with Bradfield became strained. Neighbors even recall seeing her start to run after him, crying, as Bradfield left her house one day. For his part, Bradfield started hinting to friends that Sue Reinert had gone off the deep end.

This wasn't the first time their relationship had been troubled. A few years before, Sue Myers, Bradfield's roommate, and Reinert had argued and even come to blows over Bradfield one day at the high school. However, her friends were very concerned about the split that was developing because Sue Reinert still insisted that she and Bradfield were to be married in England that fall.

Michael Wald was still working the Reinert case in September, 1979, when the daily papers' sizzling inquest-by-headline into the murder reached what he would later term an "outrageous climax."

While Wald and other FBI agents were attempting to round up Norristown, Pennsylvania, prostitutes, who supposedly had some leads on the Smith/Reinert riddle, the pot continued to boil in Upper Merion. There were unsubstantiated claims recounted by the *Daily News* and soon picked up by other papers, as well, that janitors at the high school had sometimes come upon Smith sitting naked behind his principal's desk, late at night, dazed and incoherent. Students and teachers also came forward saying in print that Smith had sometimes used the school intercom system to deliver long, rambling dissertations on matters that didn't even affect them. Suddenly, people were popping out of the woodwork eager to embellish the scare stories about Upper Merion.

Yet none of these things seemed at all related to the matronly Main Line existence of Sue Reinert and the quiet scholarship of her career. But there *were* some tantalizing links—most of them in the form of evidence found at the crime scene that the police had been keeping secret—as well as a still-developing theory on the real cause of Susan Reinert's death.

As the investigation dragged on, growing from days to weeks to months, and as additional state troopers and FBI agents checked out leads and anonymous tips, practically every detail of the case became public knowledge and fodder for the kind of classic textbook case study in sensational journalism that only the grinning ghost of William Randolph Hearst could appreciate.

Some of the reporters who covered the story became as haunted by the mystery as the cops themselves—even to the point of digging for shallow, child-size graves on their own time in the dense woods of Chester County. Occasionally on weekends or late at night, the off-duty reporters would run into off-duty state troopers or FBI agents doing exactly the same thing. They all realized that their nuts-and-bolts homicide had gotten out of hand.

Other investigators and reporters close to the case practically went berserk in print in their frenzy to make all the pieces fit.

When word leaked out that in addition to an umbrella, a matchbook cover, an empty Coke container and several fast-food wrappers, found in Reinert's abandoned car, the police had also retrieved a rubber phallus, or male sex organ, from the springs underneath the front seat, the tabloids went crazy.

Suddenly, stories began to appear, first hatched in Philadelphia and eventually made national by Rupert Murdock's *New York Post*, claiming that the FBI was actively pursuing the possibility that Reinert's death had been carried out by some sort of satanic cult, centered in Upper Merion, as part of a black-mass ritual—that the murder had then been recorded as an underground snuff film and actually circulated commercially. FBI agents were supposed to be combing the Times Square area for prints.

Someone had ingeniously put together the disputed press accounts about Jay C. Smith and his Satan costume, the stories about swingers, the rubber phallus, the nude body of Susan Reinert and Reinert's fascination with filmmaking and had come up with the devil cult theory.

Investigators disowned the stories at once. Besides, they were already pursuing what appeared to be a much stronger lead.

There had been one more piece of evidence found in the Reinert car— a small, blue, plastic comb with the inscription "79th USARCOM." That happened to be the same Army Reserve unit where Jay C. Smith was a colonel.

New developments on the botched autopsy were also giving investigators like Wald still more to go on. Over five months after the body had been found, a forensic pathologist in Philadelphia, working his way backwards and using those tiny samples of frozen tissue taken at the preliminary autopsy, determined that Susan Reinert had not died of asphyxiation, as originally certified, but from an overdose of morphine. Because they no longer had the body, it was impossible to double-check it for needle marks, but the pathologist was certain that the drug overdose had been induced from the outside.

The police also attempted to determine whether fibers found in Reinert's hair could match those found in a rug in Jay C. Smith's home. Further legwork revealed that when Smith had been arrested at the Gateway Shopping Center in Devon in 1978 while allegedly attempting a holdup, the police had confiscated a hypodermic syringe —the kind that could have possibly been used to induce a morphine overdose.

Also, the police could place Jay C. Smith in Harrisburg the day Reinert's body was found. He had shown up in a judge's chamber for sentencing that day, several hours late, explaining that he had been caught in a gas line—the same kind of gas line that Susan Reinert had worried about.

The FBI and the state police spent the rest of 1979 trying to put the whole thing together. They looked for meetings between Bradfield and Smith, sought to interview Jo Ann Aitkens—a former student who had driven Bradfield's car to New Mexico—and checked phone records to determine who had called Sue Reinert the night she disappeared. Subpoenas were issued and a grand jury began investigating the case, as well.

The police were especially curious about Bradfield's and Smith's movements on the night Reinert and her children disappeared.

Bradfield claimed that he had been visiting his ex-wife, miles from the Reinert neighborhood. He had waited for her but she had never shown up. Smith declared that he, too, had been visiting his wife in Bryn Mawr Hospital, but the staff there didn't recall seeing him.

Every lead seemed promising, every new clue significant, every shift in the case hopeful—but still, no arrests were made and no one could supply any new information on the fate of the children.

When Michael Wald left the case near the end of October, he felt confident that something would break.

Wald was leaving to take part in a supersecret undercover assignment with his old friend, Edgar Best, the chief of the Philadelphia FBI office. Wald would be playing the central role in it as a character named Michael Cohen—a fast-talking hustler from New York who was supposed to be a financial front-man for some phony Arabs (FBI agents, too) who wanted to buy a casino in Atlantic City.

Wald wasn't clear about all the details himself yet, but the persona of Michael Cohen would be a real challenge since Wald knew little or nothing about big-time, financial wheeling-and-dealing. Besides, he would be glad to forget the Susan Reinert murder for a while.

On February 2nd, 1980, the world would come to know that clandestine operation as Abscam.

For the next eight months, the Reinert case festered. Gradually, the state police cut their full-time manpower on the investigation back to three, still headed by Sergeant Joseph Van Nort; and the FBI removed 14 of the original 16 agents who had been assigned to the case. But that small five-man team would remain in business, still headquartered at Belmont Barracks.

Psychics occasionally intervened, claiming that they could locate the bodies of the children, but they always failed. By then, everyone was certain that the children had been killed.

In the spring of 1980, following a six-month probe of the investigation by a private detective hired by Susan Reinert's brother, a missing persons bulletin was suddenly issued for the children, based on new information that they might still be alive, being held in a commune. There was even speculation that the Reinert kids and the missing daughter and son-in-law of Jay C. Smith might be together. But nothing ever came of that, either. As time went by, the case became one of the most written-about and discussed unsolved murders in Philadelphia history.

Joseph Wambaugh, the ex-cop-turned-[bestselling-author], was even rumored to be considering Reinert as a possible movie or book.

Still, after all those months, after all the time and energy and manpower, after one of the most extensive state police/FBI investigations in memory, nothing happened.

No one was arrested, indicted, or charged with anything. Jay C. Smith went off to jail and William S. Bradfield vowed to return, vindicated, to Upper Merion High, after a sabbatical to restore his health following a bout with hypertension brought on by the investigation.

A tough new principal and a realistic disciplinary code slowly brought the traumatized Upper Merion High School back to health.

Critics questioned the lack of arrests and the apparent stagnation of the investigation, but the men still working the Reinert murder insisted that progress was being made.

In June 1980, when William S. Bradfield quietly moved to probate the will and collect on the insurance policies that named him as executor and sole beneficiary of Susan Reinert's $1.1 million estate, interest in the case revived again.

It was later that month that Delaware County [Deputy] District Attorney John Reilly would accuse Bradfield of leading Susan Reinert down the primrose path to marriage.

That took place in Orphans Court where Reilly, as [administrator] of the estate, had forced Bradfield to take the stand to answer an accusation that shortly before her death he had taken $25,000 of Susan Reinert's money, as well as a diamond ring, to invest in some financial scheme involving a $100,000 certificate of deposit, of which Susan Reinert would have been a part owner. Now, Reilly said, the money and ring were missing and unaccounted for, and therefore owed to the estate.

What Assistant DA John Reilly really was doing was forcing *someone* to testify in open court about the Reinert case for the first time in over a year. William Bradfield denied any knowledge of the money or the ring. From law enforcement's point of view, that hearing in Orphans Court proved little, but at least it was a start—maybe even the beginning of the end.

On July 26th, 1980, William Bradfield's lawyers, who were still trying to probate the Reinert will, responded to the efforts by the dead woman's ex-husband and brother to contest it.

Running behind a legal blocking line comprised of defense attorney John Paul Curran, Charles A. Fitzpatrick, III, an expert in estate law, and Walter ReDavid, the former register of wills in Delaware County, Bradfield dramatically put the opposition on the defensive by demanding that the investigators' notes and files on the case be turned over to him to facilitate the probate. Once and for all, Bradfield had to know if he was a suspect or not. That was the only way, his lawyers insisted, that his name could be cleared, his life be put back together again and the charge that he had exerted "undue influence" on Susan Reinert be thrown out once and for all.

By now, another renowned expert in estate law, Robert Costigan, the former register of wills for Philadelphia, had also entered the case as the attorney for Kenneth Reinert. If nothing else, it seemed certain that the will fight would make judicial history with one of the most able casts of courtroom heavyweights ever assembled in the arcane field of estate law.

In the meantime, the several insurance companies involved were going to court themselves, and balking at paying anything to anybody who might conceivably be considered a suspect in Reinert's murder.

Somehow, the mystery of the Reinert children had to be cleared up, too. So much—from a legal standpoint—hinged on them:

If the will was validated as it stood, then William Bradfield could collect as the sole beneficiary and return to Upper Merion High School in triumph.

But if the will were thrown out, as Susan Reinert's brother and ex-husband wanted, then the fate of Michael and Karen Reinert, Susan's missing children, would be crucial.

If the children were somehow found alive, they would be entitled to the estate.

If the kids really were dead and the police could demonstrate that they had died prior to their mother, then Susan Reinert's brother, W. Patrick Gallagher, would stand to benefit. However, if there was proof that the children had died after Susan Reinert, then her ex-husband, Kenneth, would probably be entitled to some of the money, as party-of-interest through the estates of the children.

Then, of course, there was always the possibility that there could have been prior wills that the investigators hadn't even discovered yet. At stake was over $1 million in property and insurance.

In the event of any criminal prosecutions for the murder of Susan Reinert, then the Pennsylvania Slayer's Act would come into effect. By statute, that prevents anyone from profiting by their own misdeed.

Since the case was an ongoing investigation, the Justice Department responded to Bradfield by refusing to turn anything over to him. All along, investigators had been incensed over his refusal to cooperate on the case. At this point, they had no intention of turning over their findings to him. Instead, the feds pleaded for—and eventually all parties agreed to—six months, continuance on the request.

Sources close to the investigation claim that the work is almost completed and the case nearly closed. The identity of the murderer is known, they hint. Every detail of the investigation, however, is being checked and double-checked and made as air-tight as possible. This is being done because of the double-jeopardy rule in a murder trial. The prosecution will only have one crack at whoever they name. After that, even new evidence won't make much difference.

Very discreetly, prosecutors—in Dauphin County were the body was found, in Delaware County where Susan Reinert lived, and in other undisclosed locations that also figure in the investigation—are being contacted right now in an effort to determine who will bring charges and where—as well as when and if.

"The FBI can't charge anybody in a homicide," says one attorney close to the case. "It's not a federal thing. So they'll have to go through the state courts to push for Murder One. That's risky. Reinert will be a very big one to try; and a very big one to win. It will also be a very big one to lose. Nobody wants that.

"Right now, I see the FBI trying to come up with someone who's brave enough or ambitious enough—or just plain dumb enough—to take this thing into court.

"From a prosecutorial viewpoint," he went on, "the fact that they've been playing around with this case for nearly two years trying to solve it doesn't look good. On the other hand, I can't see them dropping it—not after all this."

In the next few weeks, six months' continuance will expire. At that point the judge is expecting to hear the government ask for indictments or declare the case closed—or bite the bullet once again and plead for one more extension.

That's when Assistant U.S. Attorney Peter Schenck, the prosecutor for the five-man team still investigating the case, will have to put up or shut up.

According to lawyers for both sides in the bitter estate fight, their respective clients are prepared to proceed with the will contest immediately thereafter.

The FBI's Michael Wald is back on the scene too, following his Abscam assignment. Since his cover has been temporarily blown as a clandestine operative, he has been reassigned as the bureau's press officer in Philadelphia—and has spent a good deal of his time answering questions about the Reinert murder.

"This thing isn't just a murder anymore," Wald says. "This is a movie script, but the arrests still have to be made. It's the kind of a movie that has to end up in the courtroom when that last reel is unwound. But in _this_ movie, the last 20 minutes are missing."

Until then, until that final reel is played, Susan Reinert will remain little more than that sad, naked female Caucasian found stuffed in the tire well of her own car.

Until then, her children, too, will still be missing. Her estate will remain unsettled. The people who loved her and who loved the children will still be wondering. And her killer or killers will still be at large.

Coded Bradfield note: 'My Danger Conspiracy'

FBI expert decodes message

EMILIE LOUNSBERRY

HARRISBURG, October 25, 1983 — In a dramatic conclusion to the state's case against William S. Bradfield Jr., the prosecution yesterday produced a cryptic note in Bradfield's handwriting that an expert witness said was topped with the coded message: "Immunity improbable. My danger conspiracy."

Jacqueline Taschner, who analyzes codes for the FBI, said the note was deciphered by comparing it to a code listed on pages of a book owned by Bradfield, a former Upper Merion High School teacher who is charged in the June 1979 slayings of fellow teacher Susan Reinert and her two children.

The book, titled _The Works of Confucius_ by Ezra Pound, and the note were obtained by police from Susan J. Myers, who lived with Bradfield until April 1980.

The note was taken from Ms. Myers' apartment in February 1981, according to testimony, and Ms. Myers gave the book to authorities this month or last.

The note and an enlarged copy viewed by the jury were the last two of 63 exhibits admitted into evidence before the prosecution rested its case against Bradfield, 50. The trial began Oct. 15.

Bradfield is charged with conspiring with at least one unnamed accomplice to plan the Reinert slayings.

The note concluded the prosecution's efforts to construct a web of circumstantial evidence showing that Bradfield had plotted the killings to inherit $900,000 in life-insurance and estate benefits.

The Dauphin County trial is expected to resume at 9 a.m. today with the defense beginning its case. Defense attorney Joshua D. Lock said yesterday that he would call Bradfield to the stand as the first witness.

In her testimony concerning the coded message, Ms. Taschner said the note also contained references to a typewriter.

The text included the following: "Does FBI have typewriter," "Does FBI know V has it" and "FBI must not get it."

A red IBM typewriter of Bradfield's has been mentioned during the testimony of several previous witnesses.

One of those witnesses, Jeffrey Olsen, 26, a former friend and student of Bradfield's, testified yesterday that Bradfield had asked him to keep the typewriter.

Bradfield, Olsen testified, said the typewriter "had produced letters to Mrs. Reinert that could be made out to be important."

Olsen, who now lives in Kansas City, Mo., testified that the conversation had occurred after the Reinert slayings, while he and Bradfield were attending summer school at St. John's College in Santa Fe, N.M.

Olsen said that during that summer, Bradfield burned a handful of documents in Olsen's fireplace in Santa Fe. He said Bradfield stirred the ashes and "made sure everything was destroyed." Olsen said that Bradfield told him, "they were just school papers of Mrs. Reinert's."

Another witness, Christopher Pappas, a former substitute teacher at Upper Merion, testified yesterday that Bradfield had discussed destroying the ball of the typewriter because he was afraid it would link him to the killings.

Joanne Aitken, an architect who said she is still romantically involved with Bradfield, testified Friday that she now has the typewriter.

Outside the courtroom, the prosecutor, Deputy Attorney General Richard L. Guida, declined to say to what, or to whom, "V" might refer in the message, except to suggest that Bradfield might have been referring to anyone who had possession of the typewriter after Mrs. Reinert's body was found on June 25, 1979.

The testimony by Ms. Taschner also suggested that "V" may have referred simply to "you."

The coded message, Ms. Taschner said, consisted largely of numbers but also contained some translations of those numbers into letters.

The words "immunity improbable, my danger conspiracy," however, were not already translated, she said.

Ms. Myers testified earlier that the code was based on numbering of lines in Bradfield's book by fives, up to 100 on several pages. Another teacher at Upper Merion High, Vincent Valaitis, testified that he, Bradfield and others had used the book in a code system to communicate.

The coded message was the second document containing cryptic notations to be introduced into evidence during the trial. On Friday, Pappas testified that he had obtained a list in 1980 that included the notation "lured and killed kids, taped her" in Bradfield's handwriting.

The jury heard conflicting testimony yesterday about Bradfield's plans for $730,000 in life-insurance benefits from three policies in which Mrs. Reinert named Bradfield as beneficiary.

Olsen quoted Bradfield as saying, shortly after Mrs. Reinert's killing, "I don't want that goddamn money."

"He said it would be put up as a trust for the children, but he'd never keep it himself," Olsen said.

Later, representatives of two insurance companies told the jury that Bradfield had attempted to claim the $730,000 by filing lawsuits against the companies in 1980.

In each case, both witnesses said, Bradfield agreed to drop the suit in exchange for a $100 settlement.

In other testimony, Olsen said that shortly after Mrs. Reinert's death, the defendant said former Upper Merion High School principal Jay C. Smith probably had committed the killing. Olsen said Bradfield had discussed his feelings about Mrs. Reinert's death and said "how awful it was that Smith got her."

Olsen testified that Bradfield had first discussed Mrs. Reinert and Smith with him when he visited Bradfield at Upper Merion High during Christmastime 1978. At that time, he said, Bradfield appeared preoccupied and depressed.

When he coaxed Bradfield into discussing what was wrong, Olsen said, Bradfield told him that he was troubled by what he had learned about Smith, who recently had been arrested for theft, attempted theft, drug possession and weapons charges.

Smith, 55, is serving a prison term at Dallas State Prison in Wilkes-Barre as a result of his 1978 arrests.

Bradfield said Smith "was a crook, and not just a petty crook," Olsen told the court. "Smith was under suspicion for several crimes, and Bill Bradfield said they were small potatoes compared to the real truth."

Bradfield said Smith was a murderer, was trafficking in drugs and may have been involved in prostitution, Olsen said.

He said Bradfield also disclosed that he thought Smith was going to kill Mrs. Reinert.

Olsen said Bradfield had told him that "Mrs. Reinert had been Smith's mistress, and therefore she might have some of the same kind of information about Smith that Bradfield claimed to have. And therefore, Smith would have to kill her to silence her potential testimony."

After Guida rested his case yesterday, defense attorney Lock moved for the dismissal of the murder charges against Bradfield.

WHAT DECODER FOUND

The following is the text of a message written in a numerical code and deciphered by Jacqueline Taschner, a cryptanalyst for the FBI. The prosecution and the defense agreed that the numbers in the message were in Bradfield's handwriting. Ms. Taschner said she had been able to decode the message by assigning letters to the numbers based on a numerical code found on pages of a book belonging to Bradfield.

Ms. Taschner said her analysis showed that the full message said:

Immunity probable

My danger conspiracy

Does FBI have typewriter

Does FBI know V has it

Have V remove ball or destroy it, or better claim it was stolen

Did I sell it to you

Then get rid of it

FBI must not get it

Does FBI know you mailed it

Can you think of substitute—same weight—until V claims it stolen

Lock contended that the state had not produced evidence that Bradfield had planned the deaths of Mrs. Reinert's two children, Karen, 11, and Michael, 10, and that the evidence suggests that Bradfield was in Cape May, N.J., when Mrs. Reinert was killed.

The children, who were last seen alive on June 22, 1979, while leaving their Ardmore home with their mother, never have been found. The statewide grand jury that recommended Bradfield's arrest concluded that they, too, had been slain.

The only evidence that placed Bradfield at the slayings, Lock told the judge, was testimony by former prison inmate Proctor Nowell, who said Bradfield had confided that he had been present when "they" were killed but that he did not kill them.

Lock said that the evidence shows that Mrs. Reinert died no earlier than around noon on Sunday, June 24, 1979, and that Bradfield had spent that weekend in Cape May, N.J.

Guida countered that Bradfield's alleged admission that he had been present when "they" were killed could have referred to the children.

Nowell testified that Bradfield had said, " 'None of this was meant for the kids, only Susan, but you can't leave a stone unturned. You have to tie up all the loose ends.' "

Perhaps, Guida suggested yesterday, the children were killed because "they saw what happened to their mother."

Guida further argued that the law states that murder can be established "by complicity in the actual act."

"Whoever planned the killing is as guilty of first-degree murder under the law as the person who actually committed it," Guida said.

Lock's request to dismiss the charges was denied by Bucks County President Judge Isaac S. Garb, who was specially appointed by the state Supreme Court to preside over the trial.

The jury: Convinced or confused?

EMILIE LOUNSBERRY AND HENRY GOLDMAN

HARRISBURG, October 25, 1983 — Unanswered questions in the mysterious murders of Susan Reinert and her two children could end up weighing more heavily on the minds of the jurors than the web of circumstantial evidence tying William S. Bradfield Jr. to the crimes.

Despite eight days of testimony from more than 60 witnesses, the prosecution rested its case yesterday without producing a "smoking gun." And that may pose problems in proving Bradfield's guilt beyond a reasonable doubt.

The most compelling aspect of the prosecution's case is the totality of testimony that portrays Bradfield as a manipulator capable of committing such crimes.

Witnesses testified that he was so successful in getting others to do his bidding that a friend built a gun silencer for him, others helped destroy evidence at his request, two people stored money in a safety deposit box for him, and others agreed to lie or otherwise obstruct a police investigation that Bradfield allegedly feared would center on him as the suspect.

But the question remains whether a jury will be confused by the hours of detailed, sometimes contradictory, testimony, in which subtle, seemingly unimportant facts must be woven together to support a theory of guilt.

What is the jury to make of the red IBM typewriter, for example, which was often spoken of by witnesses and was the subject of a coded message introduced yesterday in which Bradfield said: "FBI must not get it."

All they know is that the typewriter was given to Susan J. Myers, with whom Bradfield was living, as a birthday present, that it became the source of concern for Bradfield in the weeks and months after Mrs. Reinert's murder.

Bradfield tried to exchange the machine's typing ball with a friend, the jury has been told. He said "important documents" had been typed on it.

But the jurors don't know what those documents are. Even the typewriter, now in the possession of Joanne Aitken, who described herself as still romantically involved with Bradfield, has not been introduced as evidence.

The jury may also have difficulty determining guilt because of the prosecution's presentation of Bradfield's whereabouts on June 22, 1979, the night Mrs. Reinert was last seen alive.

Deputy District Attorney Richard L. Guida has tried to establish that Bradfield cannot account for his whereabouts between 8:30 and 11:30 that night.

Autopsy results concluded that Mrs. Reinert died sometime after noon on Sunday, June 24. Her body was discovered at 5 a.m. Monday, June 25, and three witnesses testified that they accompanied Bradfield to Cape May, N.J., that weekend, leaving for the shore about 11:30 p.m. Friday and returning after 4 p.m. Monday.

That time sequence would appear to make it physically impossible for Bradfield to have been present when Mrs. Reinert was killed—regardless of his whereabouts during the unexplained two hours on that Friday.

What Guida did succeed in demonstrating to the jury was a possible motive for the murders: Bradfield had been named the beneficiary of more than $900,000 in life insurance and estate benefits shortly after Mrs. Reinert's death.

The most dramatic, and perhaps the most damning, evidence in Guida's case came in the last few days, when he introduced several notes in Bradfield's handwriting that appeared to show the defendant trying to hide his complicity in the crime.

In testimony yesterday, Guida introduced a coded message, in Bradfield's handwriting, found by police on Feb. 18, 1981, in the apartment he once shared with Ms. Myers.

An FBI cryptanalyst testified that she decoded the message, and that it says, in part: "My danger conspiracy."

And on Friday, Guida introduced into evidence two lists in Bradfield's handwriting. One contained cryptic notations including "lured and killed kids, taped her."

The prosecution has presented expert testimony that said Mrs. Reinert's body showed signs of having been taped, chained and beaten.

The other list contained questions that a witness said Bradfield had compiled to coach him in answering police questions about Mrs. Reinert's death.

Among the other problems the prosecution faced in presenting its case:

- Police could not conclude with certainty where the killings took place.

- The bodies of Mrs. Reinert's children, who are presumed dead, have never been found.

- No physical evidence links Bradfield to the body or Mrs. Reinert's hatchback car, in which her body was found on June 25, 1979, in the parking lot of a motel near Harrisburg.

- Because of a bungled autopsy, officials did not learn until five months after her death that blood samples showed Mrs. Reinert had died of an overdose of morphine. The autopsy, performed by an osteopathic pathologist who was not a specialist in forensic medicine, had concluded that that cause of death was suffocation. And because Mrs. Reinert's body was cremated soon after her death, it could not be reexamined for evidence.

- Much of the testimony depicting Bradfield as obsessed with the impending death of Mrs. Reinert and with ensuring himself of an alibi came from witnesses who testified only after receiving grants of immunity from the prosecution.

- The only witness to connect Bradfield to the murders of the children is Procter Nowell, a convicted felon who faces criminal charges of his own and who may have agreed to testify because of promises of leniency.

- The prosecution has sought to establish that Bradfield conspired to commit the murder—which carries the same penalty as actually committing the murder—but no other co-conspirators have been named.

As Guida pointed out yesterday while successfully arguing against a defense motion to dismiss the case, "The murder of Mrs. Reinert can be established by an actual act or complicity in an actual act. Whoever planned it is as guilty as whoever did it."

Guida pointed out that under Pennsylvania law, the prosecution need not produce other conspirators to prove a case of conspiracy.

And, it is on the hunch that he can prove conspiracy that Guida has hung his case.

Defense attorney Joshua D. Lock, relying on the remaining mysteries, will take his shot at the jury beginning today. He has said he will present plausible explanations for testimony that appeared to incriminate Bradfield.

Whether the mysteries that still surround the case are enough to create a reasonable doubt as to Bradfield's guilt is a question only the jury can answer.

Lawyers on both sides say they expect an answer to that question by early next week.

Bradfield, on stand, denies any role

EMILIE LOUNSBERRY

HARRISBURG, October 26, 1983 — Testifying in his own defense, former Upper Merion High School teacher William S. Bradfield Jr. yesterday denied killing—or planning to kill—fellow teacher Susan Reinert and her two children.

He denied that he had intended to marry Mrs. Reinert, denied that he had had an affair with her and denied that he had influenced her to name him as beneficiary of $730,000 in life-insurance benefits.

"I never hurt Mrs. Reinert or her children in any way," Bradfield, 50, told a packed courtroom in Dauphin County.

Under questioning by his defense attorney, Joshua D. Lock, Bradfield insisted that he had played no role in the June 1979 deaths.

"Did you kill Susan Reinert?" Lock asked.

"No," Bradfield replied.

"Did you kill the children?"

"No."

"Did you plan to kill them?"

"I did not."

Under cross-examination by Deputy Attorney General Richard L. Guida, Bradfield said he did not know who had killed the Reinerts. But he suggested that former Upper Merion principal Jay C. Smith—or any of several men Mrs. Reinert had been dating—might have committed the slayings.

Smith, 55, who is imprisoned in Dallas State Prison near Wilkes-Barre on charges including theft, drug possession and weapons offenses, was subpoenaed yesterday by the defense to testify, according to documents filed in Dauphin County Court. Lock has contended that Smith, not Bradfield, should be on trial for the Reinert slayings.

Bradfield's daylong testimony opened the defense portion of the case yesterday, the ninth day of the trial. He testified in a soft, even voice that at times was barely audible. He gave such expansive and detailed testimony that prosecutor Guida made numerous objections.

Spectators, many from the Philadelphia area, waited in line for seats in the courtroom throughout the lunchtime recess and lined up an hour early before the start of the evening session. Once inside, the spectators remained silent, straining to hear Bradfield's explanation of the months before and after the killings.

Bradfield named several men who he said Mrs. Reinert had been dating and who he thought might have killed her and her children.

One of those, he suggested, was a man named Alex who lived near Harrisburg. He also mentioned Jay, Ted and Grant.

Bradfield said Mrs. Reinert had told him that "they were into group sex and were advocates of bondage."

Earlier, Bradfield testified that he had grown concerned that Smith was going to kill Mrs. Reinert months before her death. Her body was found on June 25, 1979, stuffed in the rear of her hatchback car outside a suburban Harrisburg motel.

Bradfield testified that Smith had said a number of people "did not deserve to live." Smith's "hit list," Bradfield said, included the Upper Merion School District superintendent, the deputy superintendent and Mrs. Reinert.

Bradfield testified that he had become concerned about Mrs. Reinert's safety shortly after he began helping Smith to defend himself against the various charges he faced, all of which were unrelated to the Reinert case.

"His arrest and charges had become the gossip of the school. I had really been shocked and saddened," Bradfield said in explanation of why he offered to assist Smith.

But soon after he began meeting with the principal, Bradfield testified, Smith began telling him that he had ties with "figures of the underworld."

When Smith informed him that Mrs. Reinert was among those who did not deserve to live, Bradfield said he "expressed surprise."

"He said I didn't know Susan Reinert as well as I thought I did," Bradfield testified.

Bradfield said he discussed with friends whether Smith's threats might be real and decided "we didn't know the answer so the best thing was to keep an eye on Dr. Smith."

Bradfield said that although Smith continued to make the threats, he decided to avoid going to the authorities because "we just couldn't get ourselves to believe it was true. It was just too bizarre."

Later, when asked if he believed that he should have called the police, Bradfield replied, "Looking back, I wish at this point it was done."

He said he approached Mrs. Reinert "indirectly" [regarding the] threats, questioning her about whether she had been involved with Smith. Mrs. Reinert, he said, denied any involvement, so he continued his efforts to control Smith, whom he called an "unguided missile."

By the end of 1978, Bradfield said, he had become physically exhausted from "keeping an eye" on Smith and trying to protect Mrs. Reinert.

"I was at the point of being so concerned about Susan Reinert that I checked on her almost constantly," he said.

He said he continued to meet with Smith so he could monitor the former principal's plans. Smith continued to imply that he was going to harm someone, Bradfield testified.

At one point, Bradfield said, Smith gave him guns, chains, tape and hydrochloric acid, which Smith claimed to have used on victims.

The bottle of acid, Bradfield said Smith had told him, "was the kind of thing to remove identification marks from bodies. I recall he said the tape was useful in disarming someone."

Bradfield said that as soon as he obtained any "objects or intelligence" from Smith, he showed the items to a friend and former student, Christopher Pappas.

Bradfield said that although he and Pappas had continued to discuss approaching authorities with the information, they decided "the danger was too great to do that."

Smith, he said, had claimed to have connections with several police officers.

Bradfield further explained that he was perplexed by Smith's inferences.

"Smith spoke in a very circumspect way," Bradfield said. "Dr. Smith never said, 'I have killed somebody.' Dr. Smith never said, 'I'm going to kill somebody.'

He said, 'I've been involved in things I wish I hadn't been.'" Bradfield said Smith had claimed to have been involved as a "screen of eliminations."

"We concluded from what Dr. Smith had told me what it meant," Bradfield said. "None of us knew what screen of eliminations meant. But when used in connection with [talk about] assassinations, it sounds like he meant hit man.

"We never really knew whether to take Smith that seriously or whether he was deranged," Bradfield said.

"We became more afraid to do anything. We were prisoners of our own fear."

Under cross-examination by Guida, Bradfield testified that he and Pappas had become so terrified of Smith that they discussed killing him.

Bradfield and women

Henry Goldman

HARRISBURG, October 26, 1983 — Two say they still care for him. One says she parted amicably from him years ago. One, 27 years younger than he, says she was engaged to marry him. And one of them is dead.

They were the women in the life of William S. Bradfield Jr. during the days and nights in 1978 and 1979, when the prosecution contends that Bradfield plotted the killing of fellow Upper Merion teacher Susan Reinert.

In the past five days, four women who have been involved with Bradfield, 50, have taken the stand at his Dauphin County trial for the June 1979 slaying of Mrs. Reinert and her two children. In their testimony, they revealed—sometimes reluctantly—intimate details about their lives and relationships with Bradfield, 50, a handsome and imposing man.

When it was Bradfield's turn to testify yesterday, the jury heard a story that sometimes differed remarkably from what the women had said.

"Susan Myers offered me the one really comfortable home base I had had since leaving home," Bradfield testified of his relationship with the teacher who shared an apartment with him from 1973 to 1980.

"We had a warm, close relationship. I cared for her very much. I think we loved each other, but we were no longer lovers after we returned from Europe in 1973. We were not intimate."

To Ms. Myers, 40, the apartment she shared with Bradfield was anything but a "comfortable home base." She testified that Bradfield's relationships with other women, and his frequent absences from home, had taken an emotional toll on her. She said she had been forced to rely on an assortment of mind-altering drugs, including Librium, to treat her depression.

"I became unhappy when we returned from Europe, and he became involved with Susan Reinert, Wendy Zeigler and Joanne Aitken," she recalled. She said she had been about to leave Bradfield at one point in 1976 when he "begged me to stay." She did, she said, "because I loved him."

Ms. Myers testified with some sarcasm that when she asked Bradfield about his relationships with other women, he told her he was conducting "poetry research."

When Bradfield asked her in late 1978 to sign a cohabitation agreement dividing their assets in the event that they split up, she refused.

In the fall of 1980, after the Reinert killings, she changed the locks of the apartment she shared with Bradfield and refused to let him in. She said she even refused to return his high school photographs and pictures of his parents.

"I would tell him to have his attorney call my attorney, but he never did," Ms. Myers testified.

In February 1981, Ms. Myers turned over to the FBI several notes that the prosecution has introduced as evidence in an attempt to show that Bradfield was concerned about possible circumstantial evidence that might tie him to the killings.

Yet, Ms. Myers ended her testimony by saying, "I still have feelings for him."

There were others that felt, or feel, the same way.

Wendy Zeigler, 23, testified last week that she and Bradfield had become engaged in 1978 and planned to marry when she graduated from college.

Ms. Zeigler, 23, a slender woman with clear blue eyes, a creamy complexion and long brown hair, was a student of Bradfield's at Upper Merion. During his testimony, Bradfield described her as one of "my favorite students" in his English, Latin and Greek classes.

According to Bradfield, the two had "discussed marriage but never made any plans." In testimony, they both described how they would go to motels and talk intimately but never engage in sex.

Their relationship was close enough for Bradfield to entrust her with a safety deposit box in which he placed $28,500 in cash and what she said he described as "important documents."

While Bradfield discussed marriage with Ms. Zeigler, he was involved with Joanne Aitken, a Harvard graduate student in architecture now living in Philadelphia.

When Ms. Aitken, 32, testified last week, she wore no makeup, and her long brown hair was wound tightly in a bun. She smiled faintly at Brad field as she told the court that she remained "romantically involved" with the man on trial for Susan Reinert's killing.

As Bradfield explained it yesterday, his relationship with Ms. Zeigler had been based on "mutual admiration," while his involvement with Ms. Aitken had grown since 1974, when she was director of admissions at St. John's College in Annapolis, Md.

"Ms. Aitken was a very liberated person. Certainly we had a sexual relationship, but that was not the central relationship between us," he testified. "It [sex] didn't have the importance that it might have with Wendy Zeigler, for example."

As for Mrs. Reinert, who had named Bradfield the beneficiary of about $900,000 in life-insurance and estate benefits, Bradfield adamantly denied that he had ever asked her to marry him.

"She had told me about her past, her family," he said. "It was honest on her part; it was not so honest on my part. It would have been more honest if I had told her the burden [she] was on me."

Instead, Bradfield testified, he endured several years during which Mrs. Reinert sent him love notes, sometimes in view of his students and other teachers.

Bradfield testified that in the months up to Mrs. Reinert's killing, he had established what amounted to a death watch. He said he visited her home as often as three times a week, kept one of his cars parked at her house and called her when he could not be with her. All of this, he said, was done in an effort to protect her.

Bradfield said he told his friends that Mrs. Reinert had become "increasingly insistent since 1976 or so that I could solve her personal problems as a husband and father to her children. I told them she was . . . morbidly concerned with her own death—from cancer—particularly after her mother died."

Bradfield also told his friends that Mrs. Reinert had been dating a man named Alex, who Bradfield said was interested in "bondage and discipline" and "urination during sex."

What attracted Bradfield to these women?

"Physical appearance has never been important to me," he testified yesterday. "You can see that by some of the women I've been involved with. My poor wife, Muriel, was certainly not a bathing beauty—nor did it bother me," he said.

Muriel Bradfield testified last week that Bradfield left her in 1967 and that she had obtained an "amicable" divorce from him in March 1979. They were married in 1963.

Reflections on the Readings:

1. What are some possible explanations for the strange behavior of Godfrey Emsworth? What clues might help you to choose one of these possibilities over the others?

2. What do you think is the difference between evidence and proof?

3. What is the strongest evidence in the case against William Bradfield?

4. Do you think Bradfield is guilty of conspiracy to commit murder? Beyond a shadow of a doubt? Beyond a reasonable doubt?

Traces and Background Knowledge

When a statement makes "good common sense," we think we are justified in holding it as a belief. It is sensible to believe it. The evidence warrants it. This warrant, however, can be strong or weak. That is, sometimes we have very little doubt that our belief is correct; in fact, we are apt to say that we are certain—even though we know that nothing (except death and taxes) is certain. Sometimes, however, we believe a statement only because it has more warrant than any of the alternatives we can think of. We say that it is plausible or likely and, therefore, we are justified in believing it—given the evidence at hand.

When we reason this way, we are **reasoning with probability**. Philosophers call this type of reasoning **inductive reasoning**. Reasoning with probability is something we do *all* the time, from the time we get up in the morning to the time we go to bed at night. We do it unconsciously most of the time. Reason leads us to *expect* certain patterns and we act in accordance with those patterns. For example, when you brush your teeth in the morning, you do so expecting not to get cavities, to have better smelling breath, to not feel fuzz on your teeth, and to have a peppermint (or some other flavor) taste in your mouth. If you use the same brand of toothpaste today as you did yesterday, you expect to have the same taste in your mouth as yesterday morning. It is highly probable that you will.

This kind of reasoning with probability in which we are constantly engaged is rather informal. We never articulate "rules" to ourselves. Yet we do surprisingly well. Our expectations are upset only infrequently, as when we miss that last step of the cellar stairs. It is not our purpose here to set up rules for this most common kind of reasoning. (This is the work of scientists, statisticians, and philosophers in the field of artificial intelligence.) These ordinary skills, however, can be improved by recognizing the lessons to be learned from Sherlock Holmes, which are clearly demonstrated in the story you have just read about him. In later chapters you will learn some guidelines which can be articulated for reasoning with probability.

It is important to clear up a confusion, for which Holmes himself is responsible, before examining what he actually does. We have said Holmes's reasoning is reasoning with probability (or inductive reasoning), while he himself is most famous for having said on many occasions, "Brilliant deduction, my dear Watson." Who is right, Holmes or we? Here we have to say that the great detective is not as great a logician. Holmes's reasoning (or Watson's) can only be deductive—or reasoning with certainty—_if_ real life were like the board game Clue. In Clue the murder can only have been done by so many possible murderers. (Miss Scarlet, Mrs. White, Professor Plum, Colonel Mustard, etc. Remember?) If one has eliminated all but one of the possibilities, then one can reason with certainty that the one remaining character is the murderer. This form of reasoning is called disjunctive argument and was discussed in the previous chapter. In the real world, however, we cannot be sure that we have thought of all the possibilities. It can happen, even if it is very unlikely, that we have missed a possibility and, therefore, our reasoning is probable, not certain. Holmes is an outstanding example of **reasoning with probability**. Let's examine why.

The first thing a detective does on beginning a case is to gather evidence. This means looking for **traces**. Traces are everywhere. Those footsteps in the sand. These fingerprints on the wall. The candy wrapper blowing by in the wind. The list is endless. Traces indicate that something has happened. But what? Most traces go unnoticed by us. As we pointed out in the very first chapter, we tend to see what we are prepared to see. If we are not looking for evidence or clues, we ignore the traces. Holmes is very good at noticing traces. Is this because he is just more observant? Yes and no.

Holmes sees more than ordinary observers do for two reasons. First, Holmes finds more traces because he sees more of his perceptions _as_ traces. He does this because of a very important second characteristic: He has a very large storehouse of **background knowledge** that he brings to his experience. This storehouse of background knowledge is most important to "good common sense" and is too often ignored in discussions of good reasoning. Holmes seems to know a lot about everything. He is a better observer because he sees patterns where others do not. As a consequence, little escapes his attention because everything has meaning for him. Consider his initial characterization of James M. Dodd. Holmes's observation of Dodd relies on his knowledge of

history, geography, and military life. If he did not have this background information, it is highly unlikely that he would have noticed the traces which the
person of James M. Dodd presented and been able to categorize him with
such surprising accuracy. Background knowledge continues to be the key to
Holmes's success throughout the story—and other Sherlock Holmes stories as
well. In fact, **background knowledge is the key to success in reasoning
with probability and to "good common sense."**

Let's see what this means by considering another example. Suppose
you were traveling through the woods with a guide who is a noted woods-
man and tracker. Along the trail there are many traces left by the animals
who normally inhabit those woods. You, however, see few of them. The
guide, however, sees traces everywhere. A broken twig. A footprint in the
mud. A scent in the air. A rustle of the leaves. He then announces that you
are about to come upon a herd of deer, which you shortly do. The guide has
observed things you have not because he sees **traces** where you have not.
He sees traces because he sees **patterns**. That is, he notices the broken twig
because he knows that broken twigs go together with certain animal behav-
iors. He knows that pattern from his background knowledge of animal habits.
The guide **sees** something to be a trace because he **sees it as** a sign of something else.

Before returning to Holmes, let's take a look at one more example
which you may find familiar. The basketball player Larry Bird is considered
to be one of the best players in recent history. Yet Bird was not particularly
fast, nor did he jump particularly high. But Bird had an uncanny ability to
know where the court was open and thereby to set up the winning play. He
saw things that other players didn't see. This is because he saw the opponent's behavior as a trace of a particular mode of attack or defense and then
played off that pattern. He saw patterns where other players did not! In basketball, at least, Bird had excellent skills in reasoning with probability.

The guide's background knowledge about the ways of animals, the kind
of animals which might be found in that particular woods, the nature of the
pattern in the mud, all contribute to drawing the best conclusion about what
lies ahead. Same for Larry Bird. His knowledge of passing patterns, of body
language, and of a particular player's talent contribute to his gamesmanship.
And Holmes's wide range of background information enables him to see
traces in patterns which are familiar to him, when they are not to us.

We are all familiar with the role of the detective. His role is not only
to discover evidence but also to "solve" the mystery. This usually means
determining "whodunit," but it also means being able to explain why and
how. We would be very angry at a mystery writer if he just gave us the name
of the culprit without the evidence which explains why and how. And we
think a mystery writer who leaves a lot of loose ends (traces) that do not fit
into the explanation a pretty poor one, indeed. Not only does background

THE FAR SIDE   By GARY LARSON

Smart deer searches his background knowledge for a pattern!
The Far Side cartoon by Gary Larson is reprinted by permission
of Chronicle Features, San Francisco, CA. All rights reserved.

knowledge help Holmes see traces where others do not, it also helps him
reach his solution and to explain why and how. His solution rests on a **story**
that weaves the traces into an even larger **pattern** so the traces become **evidence** for that story.

To put the matter another way, Holmes's solution is really the conclusion of a long argument from probability which explains the traces, or what happened. Holmes's wealth of background information is his most important strength in making this argument. Because he is so knowledgeable, he can see patterns in the traces which, in turn, give them the power of evidence for a story. For example, James M. Dodd's tan is a trace of his recent past. Holmes's knowledge that Englishmen rarely have tans except if they go abroad and that English soldiers had recently been fighting in South Africa where it is invariably sunny turns that trace into evidence, the evidence that Dodd has recently been abroad. It is a common pattern. Well, maybe not too common. But the handkerchief in the sleeve and the short-trimmed beard add to the evidence to make the pattern more likely. They complete the story. And Holmes solves the problem of the whereabouts of Godfrey Emsworth the same way. He sees a pattern in the traces he collects so that the traces become evidence for the story which explains the recent behavior of Godfrey Emsworth.

It should also be noted that in addition to the traces he notices, Holmes creates evidence as well. He asks questions and performs actions which turn out either to support or not support his story. That is, Holmes starts looking in his storehouse of knowledge for a pattern that will fit all the traces he has noticed. When he has determined a likely pattern, he tests that pattern or hypothesis by asking further questions or looking for additional traces. If he gets the response he expects, his hypothesis has warrant and he will continue to pursue the same story line. If he does not, he will have to retest and possibly reformulate his hypothesis. In each step of the process it is his wealth of **background knowledge** that is the key to his success. He knows people like these. He knows situations like this. He knows smells like these. Knowledge of these patterns become the basis for his story that will weave all the traces into a coherent whole of what has happened.

Evidence, then, is just a collection of relevant traces–made relevant by our background knowledge and the story we tell which organizes the traces into an ordered whole. Evidence exists as a consequence of our reports and is not independent of those reports. A trace is evidence for what has gone before because of the story we tell. As we tell this story, we must be careful not to overlook other traces and other possible stories. Like Holmes, we must continually look for additional traces which support our story and confirm the absence of traces which would refute our story.

Confirmation and Proof

The situation of a criminal prosecutor is not that different from that of Holmes. The prosecutor charges someone with a crime and then sets out to prove to the jury that this is the right choice by weaving a **story** around the evidence that has been gathered. The prosecutor's job is to make the pieces fit together in a way that is believable to the jury. He does this by bringing witnesses who testify to the existence of certain traces which, if the jury accepts them, become evidence for the prosecutor's story. Each bit of evidence that fits into the story makes the story more credible. Notice that no piece of evidence "proves" the story. Eyewitness accounts are often wrong and even confessions of guilt are sometimes lies (for example, to protect a loved one or to bargain for an easier sentence). Rather, each piece adds to the total picture that the prosecutor presents. Each piece helps to **confirm** or disconfirm the picture or story. The jury decides to accept or reject that picture.

You are familiar enough with the behavior of juries to know that, although all members of the jury have heard the same evidence, they sometimes do not all agree about the verdict. This is because the story that they hear must not only fit the traces together well but it must also fit in with background knowledge that each juror has. That is, it must fit the patterns with which he or she is familiar. Since they each have different stores of background knowledge, they will have different reactions to the prosecutor's (or the defense attorney's) story. We can see, then, why some juries are prejudiced for or against particular defendants even though they might not be openly hostile or even bigoted. No two of us have the same set of background knowledge, so the fit will vary. That is why it is thought important in the United States for a person to be tried by a jury of his peers.

All of this boils down to what one might call the **limits of evidence**. Evidence can confirm a hypothesis or a story but it cannot prove it. A story can be highly confirmed or only more than likely, but it cannot be proven like a proof in mathematics or logical reasoning.

A hypothesis which rests on reasoning with probability can be credible even "beyond a shadow of a doubt" without such proof, however. You believe now—without a shadow of a doubt—that you will wake up tomorrow (sometime, anyway), even though the evidence only confirms and does not prove this belief. This simple belief is actually part of a very complex story supported by a large storehouse of background knowledge. Other beliefs are not so credible and we often have to make decisions and judgments based on less evidence than we would like. Whether the strawberry ice cream cone will taste better than the vanilla one is not so important to us over time, so we may not demand much in the way of evidence for making a decision. (But, then again, you may ask for a lick.) But we hope in our courts—and many other "high places"—that decisions are based on a pattern of evidence that fits in with the broadest collection of background knowledge.

When we reason with probability, then, we can confirm conclusions, not prove them. What we are looking for when we seek to confirm them is a good fit, a good fit among the traces we have selected as evidence and a good fit of the story as a whole with the background knowledge we bring to it. The story must make sense to us and it must make sense with the rest of the world around us. Our background knowledge is what enables us to judge whether or not that is so. What this means is that we must always be open to that world. We need to be curious. We need to learn as much as we can about it. Pity the poor student who says, "I don't know why I have to take chemistry. I'll never have to know chemistry." You can rest assured Holmes never said a thing like that!

EXERCISES

6–I

1. What is a trace?

2. What is background knowledge and why is it important?

3. Why is Sherlock Holmes a good detective?

4. What is evidence?

6–II

1. The car in front of you suddenly flashes its brake lights. Your foot automatically moves from the accelerator to the brake. Explain the reasoning with probability involved in this act based on common sense.

2. Your boyfriend (girlfriend, significant other) forgot your birthday. What is your reaction? What is this trace evidence for? Why?

3. Give an example where common sense came to your rescue in a tense situation. What background knowledge was important in your success?

4. Describe a belief you hold which you know is based on little evidence. How would you go about seeking confirmation of it?

6–III

1. You know the subject matter of the course as well as your roommate but your roommate consistently gets better grades than you do. How could background knowledge explain this difference?

2. You and your father disagree about which candidate to vote for in the coming election. How might background information play a role in this disagreement? Can you prove who is the better candidate? Why or why not?

3. Describe a belief you hold for which you have proof. Write out your proof. How has your response to this exercise been influenced by the material in this chapter?

4. What is the difference between beyond "the shadow of a doubt" and beyond "a reasonable doubt"?

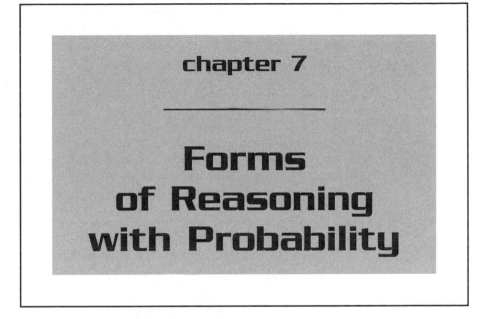

chapter 7

Forms
of Reasoning
with Probability

Introduction

We reason with probability constantly in our ordinary everyday lives. We also use this kind of reasoning in more formal situations: to formulate scientific laws, to predict the outcome of elections, to diagnose an illness and its treatment, and so on. Common forms of reasoning with probability are "All X's are Y's," "If this is an X, it is (or probably is) a Y," and "X causes Y." The underlying pattern of reasoning we are using when we reason with probability is "X percent of **observed** cases have the property Y, so X percent of **all** cases have the property Y." We reason from the observed to the unobserved and often unobservable cases (such as those in the future).

There are three very useful patterns of reasoning with probability that we use all the time but which *never* give us answers which follow necessarily from the evidence provided. These three patterns of reasoning are **generalizations**, **analogies**, and **causal claims**. All three of these patterns make claims that "stretch" beyond the evidence available to us. Thus there is plenty of room to make mistakes, and we need guidelines to avoid potential errors.

Since we cannot examine all the X's to see if they are Y's, reasoning with probability presents many reasoning puzzles. Consider generalizations, for example. "All circles are round" is clearly a warranted generalization. So is "All humans need food to live." But we are not so certain about some generalizations, such as "All humans have ten toes" or "Small-town librarians lead boring lives." It would be nice, indeed, to have a rule which told us when to generalize and when not to generalize. Our expectations for the future would be more accurate and we would be disappointed less often. Unfortunately, it is difficult to develop such a rule and there are some interesting reasons why. What is equally interesting, however, is despite the absence of any such rule we actually do fairly well with our generalizations so that most of us feel confident enough to fly in airplanes, brush our teeth to prevent tooth decay, and regularly watch our favorite shows on television without disappointment.

In this chapter we will suggest some guidelines (but not a rule or rules) for making warranted generalizations and for distinguishing warranted generalizations from unwarranted ones. We will also look at the other two major types of reasoning with probability, namely reasoning by analogy and causal reasoning. Since there are so many variations on the process of reasoning with probability, we will begin with four different readings showing how such reasoning works–and sometimes doesn't work.

The first reading comes from the field of medicine and gives several examples of the reasoning doctors go through when trying to determine how to treat their patients. Medical reasoning is a good example of reasoning with probability (or inductive reasoning) since, as you have heard many times, "medicine is not an exact science." The second reading is about health, but is not exactly about medical reasoning. It is a good example of the problems of causal reasoning. In this case, the effort is to determine the cause of the tragic fact that for a period of time, more members of the San Francisco 49ers football team were afflicted with Lou Gehrig's disease, or ALS, than one would expect. It is a good example of expectations not being realized, thus suggesting a need for a correction and, perhaps, a causal explanation. The third reading is a collection of articles about whether a newly "discovered" poem is really a lost poem of Shakespeare. This example shows how historians and critics use reasoning by analogy in their work. The last set of readings comes from an American magazine which was very popular in the 1930s, *The Literary Digest*. It shows another very important use of generalization: predicting the victors in elections or at least trying to predict the victor. As you read this classic election poll *faux pas,* look for reasons why *The Digest's* prediction that Alf Landon would win the 1936 presidential election over Franklin Roosevelt was not a good generalization to make! Today, of course, pollsters do a better job than *The Literary Digest* did. We can, however, learn a lot from looking at its mistakes.

Doctors as Detectives

Cynthia Clendenin

They have all the qualities of good detectives: alert minds and sound training, the tendency to welcome challenge, and a certain stick-to-it-ive-ness—even when hard work leads to dead ends.

There are a lot of such medical "detectives" around MCP [Medical College of Pennsylvania]. They're in the halls and laboratories; they walk in and out of patients' rooms, often wearing lab coats with name tags pinned on.

Wherever they are—at work in the Hospital or their own office, relaxing at home, even stuck in a line of traffic on their way to MCP—chances are these superb diagnosticians are thinking about some medical mystery they are trying to solve.

The range of possible culprits, or hidden diseases, is broad. Everything from overlooked allergies to hormonal deficiencies can provide a puzzling picture, and sometimes the cooperation of a number of specialists is required to solve a difficult case.

SORTING THE CLUES

For MCP patients with puzzling conditions, faculty and staff follow a series of logical steps and use their best judgement to sort the clues and select the treatments that are most likely to be effective. They also judge when to initiate treatment and when, in certain cases, to refrain from using it.

Matthew E. Levison, M.D., Professor of Medicine and Chief of the Infectious Diseases Division, explains: "It is important that the doctor make a 'differential diagnosis,' or a list of possible diseases that could explain the patient's illness."

Once this list has been established, an investigation using various diagnostic tests can proceed systematically to rule in or out the various, potential disorders.

The diagnostic tests proceed from the least risky to those which pose the most risk to the patient. This diagnostic process is called the "work-up." The rapidity of a work-up, and whether shortcuts are taken, depends upon the general state of the patient's health, and upon how rapidly the illness is developing.

"The physician should first investigate any clues in the patient's history or physical examination," notes Dr. Levison. Physicians must also observe the course of the disease for the development of new clues—avoiding, where possible, procedures or medications that might confuse the clinical picture by altering the symptoms.

The case of Steve K. illustrates this point. A man in his early thirties, Mr. K. was admitted to another hospital with fever that had persisted for several months. There were few clues to be found in his history or physical examination, but Mr. K.'s doctor, suspecting bacterial endocarditis (infection of the heart valves), obtained a blood culture and began treatment with antibiotics. Since this did not prove effective, a laparotomy (exploratory incision into the abdominal cavity), was performed. When examination of the tissues removed at surgery proved unrevealing, and the patient's fever persisted, Mr. K. was referred to MCP.

The MCP physicians began with a differential diagnosis, trying systematically to rule in and out various possible diagnoses. All the while, they observed the course of the disease for new clues. They were also careful not to prescribe any therapy that might alter the course of Mr. K.'s illness.

During the second week of his hospitalization, Mr. K. developed a peculiar rash. He also developed joint pain and for the first time evidence of joint inflammation—redness, heat and swelling of his wrists and knees.

Ultimately, through continued observation and progressive ruling out of certain diseases, the MCP team was able to narrow the possibilities to one: juvenile rheumatoid arthritis, a rarity in adults of Mr. K.'s age. Treatment for this illness was begun, then Mr. K. was released to the care of his personal physician. Today he is doing well. He has returned to work but still requires low doses of aspirin and corticosteroids to suppress the inflammation.

ASKING THE RIGHT QUESTIONS

"In making a diagnosis you need to keep asking questions," says Harry Gottlieb, M.D., Clinical Professor of Medicine, Head of the Section of Endocrinology and Diabetes. "Ask questions of yourself and ask them of the record—what does it show? Most of all, ask them of the patients, who may not recognize the significance of some detail of the experiences leading up to their illnesses. What did they eat, and when? How much, and how frequently? What did they do next? Sooner or later you're going to be able to establish a pattern, and that may lead to your diagnosis."

Dr. Gottlieb tells the story of Mr. J., a 74-year-old businessman who went to a 5 p.m. movie with his wife one Saturday evening and was startled to realize that he couldn't make any sense at all out of the credits show-ing on the screen. His confusion persisted into the evening, and he became alarmed that he might be having a stroke. He couldn't speak clearly, his mind refused to concentrate, and his vision was distorted. Nevertheless, he did manage to eat supper, and as the evening progressed, his symptoms dis-appeared as strangely as they had begun. Within a short time after eating he felt perfectly normal, as though nothing had happened.

The next afternoon the same sort of symptoms recurred. This time, his walking was also affected. Fortunately Mr. J. and his wife were at home this time, but they were very much worried nonetheless. However, once again they decided not to bother their doctor over the weekend.

Without knowing why it seemed like a good idea, they decided to eat supper, and once again Mr. J. began to lose the alarming symptoms. He was feeling fine on Monday morning when he telephoned Dr. Gottlieb to describe the frightening events of the past weekend.

"I began asking a lot of questions," Dr. Gottlieb notes. "Did he do anything differently? Did he take any pills or unusual food? How long had it been since he had eaten? I had to draw out this information because Mr. J. did not associate any connection between eating and feeling better. But when he said that the first incidence of trouble occurred about four-and-one-half hours after lunch, I began to suspect a problem with low blood sugar."

Dr. Gottlieb arranged for Mr. J. to come to his office immediately. Although Mr. J. was feeling fine, blood studies revealed that he did indeed have low blood sugar.

To confirm the diagnosis, Dr. Gottlieb admitted Mr. J. to the MCP Hos-pital for further tests. These included fasting under close supervision, with the blood sugar checked hourly. After seven hours of fasting, Mr. J.'s symp-toms recurred. A test performed immediately confirmed the low blood sugar level.

Now even more diagnostic tests became necessary. "What we were looking for, given the sudden onset of low blood sugar, and his high insulin levels, was some form of insulin-producing tumor of the pancreas," explains Dr. Gottlieb. "Often these tumors are benign, but they cause a lot of trou-ble by upsetting the chemical balance."

When a CAT scan and other tests failed to show a definite tumor (as often occurs), Mr. J. did not want to undergo surgical exploration and pan-creatic resection. So Dr. Gottlieb explained that a drug could be used to control Mr. J.'s blood sugar.

Today, five years after the frightening episode at the movie, Mr. J. is doing well. With medication, blood glucose monitoring at home, and care-ful attention to regular, more frequent meals, he leads a normal and active life.

WHEN PATIENTS ARE FAILING FAST

Intuitive thinking is often required when patients are deteriorating rapidly. Nelson M. Wolf, M.D., Professor of Medicine and Director of the Cardiac Catheterization Laboratory, remembers a 50-year-old man, Mr. R., who suffered an electrical shock at work. The accident threw him across the room and against a wall, knocking him unconscious. When he awoke, he felt bruised but otherwise reasonably well, and a check-up at the local hospital revealed nothing amiss.

Over the next few weeks, however, Mr. R. began to experience unexplainable fatigue. When his symptoms increased, his wife, a nurse, checked his blood pressure. Finding it unusually low, she urged her husband to see their doctor.

When a medical examination revealed a heart murmur, Mr. R. was referred back to his local hospital in New Jersey for tests. Because that hospital had limited facilities, Mr. R. was sent by ambulance to MCP for ultrasound studies. These completed, he was preparing to return to New Jersey when an MCP fellow who was reading the results showed the ultrasound image to the attending physician.

The image reminded the diagnosticians of a problem which occurs occasionally in automobile accidents, in which the sudden impact causes the outer layer of the aorta of the heart to be peeled from the inner layer. Reflecting upon the circumstances of Mr. R.'s accident, the physicians realized that the conditions of thrust and impact were similar.

They promptly ordered further tests which confirmed their analysis: the layers of the aorta were attached only by small areas of connective tissue. Immediate surgery was ordered to save Mr. R.'s life.

MANY "DETECTIVES" ARE SOMETIMES NEEDED TO SOLVE A CASE

Lee W. Greenspon, M.D., Assistant Professor of Medicine and Chief of Pulmonary Medicine, credits the Radiology, Surgery, and Pathology Departments with helping to solve the case of 45-year-old Mrs. W., who had persistent shortness of breath and a cough which did not improve with two months of care by her family doctor. She was admitted to MCP for a complete work-up, including blood tests, breathing tests, chest x-rays, and CAT scans. The test results, however, were inconclusive, so the doctors weighed the potential risks and benefits of more aggressive investigation.

"Symptoms that are increasing in extent or severity motivate us to be as specific as possible early in the diagnosis so that we can give appropriate therapy promptly," comments Dr. Greenspon. "Sometimes, as in Mrs.

W.'s case, the evaluation may require one of the more risky procedures, such as a surgical biopsy of the lung."

From the results of the surgical biopsy, the pathologists determined that Mrs. W. was suffering from a rare form of lung disease called bronchiolitis obliterans (inflammation of the small airways in the lung). She was placed on a regimen of corticosteroids which brought total relief of her symptoms.

THE IMPORTANCE OF DOUBLE CHECKING

"One of the most difficult problems in making a diagnosis is knowing when to get excited," relates Rosaline R. Joseph, M.D., '53, Professor of Medicine and Chief of Hematology and Oncology. "At any point along the way, if a test turns out unexpectedly, it's important to check again and to consider the total picture."

Dr. Joseph cites the case of an 81-year-old woman who was supposedly healthy. As part of a routine examination by her family doctor, this woman was given a number of tests. One test seemed to reveal a mild form of chronic lymphocytic leukemia. When the test was repeated, it continued to show a slight elevation in white blood cells and the patient's lymphocyte count. At this point, the physician advised the woman to seek a second opinion at MCP.

When she arrived at the Hospital, the woman was obviously worried about the possibility of having cancer. The tests were run once again, and the results were judged to be so close to normal that they posed no problem. The woman's regular doctor was congratulated for his care in seeking a second opinion, the patient was reassured that her health was not threatened, and a very relieved octogenarian was able to enjoy life once more.

ANOTHER MYSTERY IS SOLVED

Anna K., a woman of 38, was referred to the Rheumatology Division with a history of neck pain. At the time of her evaluation, Mrs. K. described a history of aching which dated back to her early twenties. She said she slept poorly and awoke very stiff in the morning. Stress and changes in the weather seemed to exacerbate the symptoms. Examinations at other institutions had shown minimal degenerative changes in her cervical spine, and she had failed to respond to a variety of anti-inflammatory agents.

The results of Mrs. K.'s examination were normal, except for multiple tender areas on her neck, back, chest, and knees. Laboratory studies, including blood tests and x-rays were normal. These findings helped the rheumatologists rule out rheumatoid arthritis or systemic lupus. At the same time,

the diagnosticians took note of her fatigue and insomnia, and her acknowl-
edgement that she worried a lot about her job—all factors known to exag-
gerate the symptoms of fibrositis.

"Aching, stiffness, and tenderness, rather than inflammation, typically
characterize this illness," explains Bruce I. Hoffman, M.D., Clinical Associate Professor of Medicine and Chief of Rheumatology. In Mrs. K.'s case, ten
painful "trigger points" led to the correct diagnosis.

Once the physicians had reached their conclusion, they set about reas-
suring Mrs. K. and encouraging her to begin changing her way of dealing
with stress. An antidepressant agent was prescribed, to improve sleep patterns. As she began to feel less achy, Mrs. K. took an interest in a graded
exercise program. With very little medication, her self-confidence was reinforced, and the pain which brought her for help greatly diminished.

So the mysteries go on, and there are no easy answers. In all ways,
physician-detectives must keep the total picture in mind. As Sherlock
Holmes would have said, "That's elementary, my dear Watson!"

1964's Football 49ers Face Grim Puzzle

Lou Gehrig's disease has hit three teammates—why?

MIKE ANTONUCCI

The rough-and-tumble men who played football for the San Francisco
49ers 23 years ago have not spent much time recently swapping lies or reliv-
ing moments in the sun.

Instead, they have held grim conversations about a mysterious disease
that killed two 1964 teammates and is draining life from a third. They have
filled out questionnaires about their health while wondering if toxic time
bombs are hiding in their nerve cells and muscles.

Day after day, they have scrounged through untrustworthy memories,
trying to figure out how three members of one team could develop an incur-
able and fatal illness that strikes only one or two in 100,000 Americans
annually.

The illness is amyotrophic lateral sclerosis (ALS), a muscle-destroying
affliction more commonly known as Lou Gehrig's disease. Former running

back Gary Lewis died from it in December at age 44, less than a month after being diagnosed. Former linebacker Matt Hazeltine died in January at age 53 after six years with the disease.

The survivor—for now—is former quarterback Bobby Waters, 48.

DIAGNOSED 2 YEARS AGO

The football coach at Western Carolina University in Cullowhee, N.C., Waters has lost virtually all use of his arms and hands since being diagnosed a little more than two years ago. His wife and children bathe him, dress him, feed him and protect him from such simple dangers as having his limp fingers nipped by the family's retriever puppy.

But Waters is determined to be more of an aggressor than a victim. By opening his office, home and emotions to anyone who expresses an interest, he has turned his plight and the disease's extraordinary link to the 1964 49ers into symbols of the desperate search for more information about ALS.

"I need," Waters said calmly, "to get to the disease before it gets to me."

Waters' best hope is the hypothesis that a statistical aberration such as a three-teammate ALS "cluster" is not a coincidence. Somewhere in the shared experiences of ex-49ers may be a clue that would end a decades-long search for the cause of ALS.

Former teammates are eager to help, but some admit that it is more than a bit unsettling in middle age to be asking themselves if something deadly could have been in the air they breathed, the ground they practiced on or, perhaps most frighteningly, the medicine they took.

"My initial reaction," former linebacker Mike Dowdle said, "was that we've been hearing about the AIDS virus for two years now. I understand there are five years' incubation on AIDS. Is there a 20-year incubation on ALS?"

BRAIN UNAFFECTED

The disease does not affect mental faculties, so victims languish until they are minds trapped within bodies that become totally paralyzed in stages. When swallowing and breathing are affected, death usually follows because of nutritional and respiratory complications.

The ALS Association quotes an unidentified patient as saying, "It's like having a ringside seat to your own demise."

Waters has crusaded for an investigation of the 49ers' ALS cluster, sending questionnaires to former players to survey them about their health.

Waters' physician, Stanley Appel at the Baylor College of Medicine in Houston, said no questionnaires have been returned revealing any additional ex-players who have been diagnosed with ALS.

The most conspicuous result of Waters' campaign has been a furor over fertilizer.

A couple of 1964 players said they had strong memories of the practice fields in Redwood City being strangely affected by a fertilizer. Charlie Krueger, a former defensive tackle, described the turf as bubbling with garbage as condoms and bits of glass sometimes emerged from the soil.

The man in charge of maintaining the fields at that time, former Redwood City Parks Superintendent Pasco Balzarini, said he had used a fertilizer called Milorganite, a processed sludge that contains heavy metals and is made by the Milwaukee Metropolitan Sewerage District.

STUDY URGED

That led a Wisconsin ALS researcher, Dr. Benjamin Brooks, to call in early February for a study of the product after he was told by three of his patients that they had used the fertilizer.

Since then, the executive director of the Milwaukee sewerage district, Patrick Marchese, has labeled the idea of a link between Milorganite and ALS as "patently absurd." Brooks also came under strident public attack from other scientists who contended there was no merit in singling out Milorganite for suspicion.

Brooks, however, is refusing to back off. After an expert in biostatistics derided Brooks' concern, Brooks responded that he was reminded of a quote about medical statistics being "like a bikini. They're startling in what they reveal but even more startling in what they conceal, which is vital."

Although Brooks stressed that he never said there is evidence of a causal connection between Milorganite and ALS, he argued that questions raised by patients about possible risks to the nervous system from sludge fertilizers are more than enough reason for a scientifically controlled study.

Forbes Norris Jr., the doctor for Hazeltine and Lewis, characterized the information on Milorganite as "a red-hot clue." But he added that "whether it's going to fizzle out like so many other clues remains to be seen."

Most of the 1964 49ers are at a loss for other suggestions to offer Waters.

Almost all remember widespread use of DMSO ointment (dimethyl sulfoxide), which was considered to be a nearly miraculous treatment for bruises and soreness. But few believe it could be involved in causing ALS, even though they remember Hazeltine as being a fan of the unpleasant-smelling stuff.

Waters and Appel also have raised the subject of what medications were given to players 20-plus years ago. The 49ers' management has been unable to locate any pertinent records about Waters, even though current team doctor James Klint was persistent enough to track down and question 1964 physician Lloyd Milburn in South America (his most recent location on a round-the-world sailboat cruise).

One of Waters' concerns is the possible ramifications of anabolic-steroid samples he recalls being given by Milburn.

Klint said Milburn made a general comment that anabolic steroids were not used at the time. Waters, who had problems keeping his weight up, said he believes he was the one 49er to receive such drugs.

A Lost Poem By Shakespeare?
Selected Newspaper Articles

A Scholar's Find: Shakespearean Lyric

JOSEPH LELYVELD

OXFORD, England, Nov. 23—A 32-year-old American from Topeka, Kan., has discovered a previously unknown nine-stanza love lyric that is attributed in the manuscript copy to William Shakespeare. It appears to be the first addition to the Shakespeare canon since the 17th century.

The untitled poem, unusual for its intricate scheme of internal rhymes in short, six-syllable lines, had been sitting in the Bodleian Library at Oxford University in a bound folio of poems that the library has had in its archives for 230 years. The volume itself, transcribed in a calligraphic style known as upright English secretary hand, appears to date from the 1630's.

In printed catalogues of the Bodleian's vast manuscript collection, it has twice been noted—in 1895 and again in 1969—that the volume contained a poem attributed to Shakespeare. Until Friday afternoon at about 3 o'clock, when the collection was placed in the library's vault, any scholar could have walked into the Bodleian and called it up for examination.

From _The New York Times_, Sunday, November 24, 1985

NEW COLLECTION OF WORKS

But, as far as anyone can tell, no one ever did this with an eye to examining the poem attributed to Shakespeare until Gary Taylor did it last week. Mr. Taylor has been working for seven and a half years as an editor of a new one-volume collection of Shakespeare's works that Oxford University Press is to publish next year, and he was making a final check of manuscript sources as a matter of scholarly "duty and thoroughness."

The 1969 Bodleian catalogue had listed the first lines of poems in manuscript form in the library, including a line ("Shall I die? Shall I fly") that the young American did not recognize. It was a loose end that needed checking, so Mr. Taylor, who began work on a doctorate 10 years ago at Cambridge University but never completed it, left a call-up slip overnight at the Bodleian so the volume would be available for his examination the next day.

He did not allow himself, he said today, to consider the possibility that he was about to make a major literary discovery. The next morning, Nov. 15, he even did some office chores at the university press's Shakespeare department before heading to the Bodleian to peruse the manuscript.

"I tried not to think about it," he said. "The chances of actually finding something like this are so grotesquely small that you don't want to get excited. You can easily talk yourself into these things if you start to get excited."

The volume actually contained two poems attributed to Shakespeare. One was a brief epitaph already familiar to scholars. The longer poem, a lustful reverie in the standard genre of Elizabethan love lyrics, was entirely unknown to Mr. Taylor.

After a close examination of the folio, a search of other manuscript sources in major libraries and close reading of the poem itself, he and Dr. Stanley Wells, a leading authority who heads the university press's Shakespeare department, are planning to include the poem in the new edition they are jointly editing.

Internal evidence in the poem—the choice of words and images—strongly indicates to them that Shakespeare must have written it between 1593 and 1595, the period in which the youthful playwright—just turning 30—wrote "A Midsummer's Night Dream," "Love's Labour's Lost" and "Romeo and Juliet."

For instance, there is a pairing of images in the sixth stanza of the poem that Shakespeare may have recycled in Romeo's speech under the balcony to Juliet. The lyric tells how the beloved lady's "star-like eyes win love's prize/when they twinkle."

It then speaks of her cheeks displaying "beauty's banner." Romeo finds "two of the fairest stars in all the heaven" in Juliet's eyes. They "twinkle in their spheres till they return . . . the brightness of her cheeks."

Later, Romeo speaks of "beauty's ensign in her cheeks."

"It's not Hamlet," Mr. Taylor observed when he was asked to assess the significance of his find. "It's a kind of virtuoso piece, a kind of early Mozart piece."

This kind of critical weighing-up and comparing only came later. When he first looked at the poem in the Bodleian, his immediate task was to study the manuscript itself for evidence that it might be misattributed or a literary hoax.

EXAMINING THE PENMANSHIP

The first thing he did was to examine the penmanship in which the name William Shakespeare was written at the end of the poem by the unknown scribe who copied it, maybe for his own enjoyment or on commission for some nobleman. The name was written in the same black ink and upright hand as the poem itself; it did not seem possible that it could have been added later.

Moreover, the poem began in the middle of one page and ended in the middle of another, on which there were flourishes and decorative curlicues in red ink, as there are throughout the volume. This appeared to show that it could not have been inserted at a later date.

Deciphering the dense script, Mr. Taylor then transcribed the poem so he could type it out, show it to his colleagues and map a strategy for further testing to disprove the attribution to Shakespeare.

Then he returned to the Bodleian and looked closely at the 50 other poems attributed in the collection to poets such as John Donne, Robert Herrick and Ben Jonson. None of these attributions were demonstrably wrong, which amounted to a vote of confidence in the compiler.

The history of the collection itself—it had been bequeathed to the Bodleian by a bibliophile named Richard Rawlinson who died in 1755—was another positive sign: this was not some unknown manuscript suddenly appearing out of nowhere.

Having checked over the collection, the scholar now came to what he calls the "forensic" stage in his literary sleuthing: he studied the body of the poem, relying on various scholarly tools, including a computerized concordance to all Shakespeare's work that tells scholars exactly how often and in what context Shakepeare used every word he ever wrote.

There were clusters of language that seemed to fit in tidily with Mr. Taylor's tentative dating of the poem. But even more persuasive than these parallels, which might conceivably have been equaled, was evidence of the seemingly inimitable Shakespearean facility to do new things with the English language.

"Everything he wrote contained words he didn't use anywhere else," Mr. Taylor said. "Paradoxically the appearance in the poem of words that don't appear anywhere else in Shakespeare is good evidence that the poem could be by Shakespeare."

Thus, in the newly discovered poem there are two words that, if Mr. Taylor's dating is correct, were used here earlier than the first recorded use discovered in each case by the compilers of the Oxford English Dictionary. The words were "admiring" as a noun—in the witty suggestion in stanza six that "admiring desiring/Breeds"—and the word "scanty."

The scholarly testing of the poem continued with growing intensity throughout the week. The search extended to the British Library in London, the Folger Library in Washington, the Rosenbach Library in Philadelphia, the Huntington collection in California, to Harvard and to Yale, to see if anyone could find a trace of this poem, attributed to Shakespeare, to anyone else, or unattributed. The responses all came back negative.

Finally, on Friday afternoon Oxford University Press was prepared to claim the discovery. Early reactions from scholars at Oxford have ranged from enthusiastic to cautious.

"It looks bloody good to me," said John Pitcher of St. John's College. "It's important. There may be more. It's not the best verse he ever wrote but, nonetheless, it's very exciting."

John Carey, the Merton Professor of English Literature, was less inclined to commit himself. Professor Carey said that although he had great respect for Mr. Taylor's scholarship he regarded the case as unproven.

Mr. Taylor and Dr. Wells believe the burden of proof is now on anyone who wants to cast doubt on the attribution.

"Someone can come along tomorrow and find something that proves that 'Hamlet' was not written by Shakespeare," Mr. Taylor said. "All the evidence says this poem belongs to Shakespeare's canon and, unless somebody can dislodge it, it will stay there."

Untitled: The Long Lost Lines

1

Shall I die? Shall I fly
Lovers' baits and deceits, sorrow breeding?
Shall I fend? Shall I send?
Shall I shew, and not rue my proceeding?
In all duty her beauty
Binds me her servant for ever.
If she scorn, I mourn,
I retire to despair, joying never.

2

Yet I must vent my lust
And explain inward pain by my love breeding.
If she smiles, she exiles
All my moan; if she frown, all my hopes deceiving—
Suspicious doubt, O keep out,
For thou art my tormentor.
Fly away, pack away;
I will love, for hope bids me venter.

3

'Twere abuse to accuse
My fair love, ere I prove her affection.
Therefore try! Her reply
Gives thee joy—or annoy, or affliction
Yet howe'er, I will bear
Her pleasure with patience, for beauty
Sure [will] not seem to blot
Her deserts, wronging him doth her duty.

4

In a dream it did seem —
But alas, dreams do pass as do shadows—
I did walk, I did talk
With my love, with my dove, through fair meadows.
Still we passed till at last
We sat to repose us for our pleasure.
Being set, lips met,
Arms twined, and did bind my heart's treasure.

5

Gentle wind sport did find
Wantonly to make fly her gold tresses,
As they shook I did look,
But her fair did impair all my senses.
As amazed, I gazed
On more than a mortal complexion.

[Them] that love can prove
Such force in beauty's inflection.

6

Next her hair, forehead fair,
Smooth and high; next doth lie, without wrinkle,
Her fair brows; under those,
Star-like eyes win love's prize when they twinkle.
In her cheeks who seeks
Shall find there displayed beauty's banner;
Oh admiring desiring
Breeds, as I look still upon her.

7

Thin lips red, fancy's fed
With all sweets when he meets, and is granted
There to trade, and is made
Happy, sure, to endure still undaunted.
Pretty chin doth win
Of all [the world] commendations;
Fairest neck, no speck;
All her parts merit high admirations.

8

A pretty bare, past compare,
Parts those plots which besots still asunder.
It is meet naught but sweet
Should come near that so rare 'tis a wonder.
No mishap, no scape
Inferior to nature's perfection;
No blot, no spot:
She's beauty's queen in election.

9

Whilst I dreamt, I, exempt
[From] all care, seems to share pleasures in plenty,

But awake, care take—
For I find to my mind pleasures scanty.
Therefore I will try
To compass my heart's chief contenting.
To delay, some say,
In such a case causeth repenting.

WILLIAM SHAKESPEARE

EDITORS' NOTE

The text of a poem attributed to William Shakespeare that accompanied an article yesterday on the poem's discovery in the Bodleian Library at Oxford University included five words in brackets.

The words in brackets were inserted by Gary L. Taylor, who found the poem, to replace words in the manuscript copy that he considered small textual mistakes made by the person who copied the original manuscript in the 1630's.

Line 29 of the manuscript copy included the word "wit," which Mr. Taylor said did not make sense in the context. He said he changed it to "will" because that word was often spelled with one "l" in Elizabethan times and he felt that the copier had inadvertently substituted the word "wit."

Line 49 included the word "then," which for similar reasons, Mr. Taylor said, he changed to "Them."

Line 68 had the words "thats cald," which Mr. Taylor changed to "the world."

Line 82 included the word "for," which Mr. Taylor changed to "From," with an uppercase "F."

It is standard practice for textual editors to call attention to such alterations. Such an explanation, which had been provided by Mr. Taylor, should have accompanied the text of the poem that appeared in The Times.

In addition, the third word of the fourth line should have been "tend," not "fend." Mr. Taylor's late correction of the word failed to reach The Times in time for publication.

* * * * *

Of the Bard

Gary Lynn Taylor

OXFORD, England, Nov. 23—"I didn't actually plan to discover this poem when I started looking for work," said Gary Taylor. But only days after making his discovery—a nine-stanza love lyric that appears to be the first addition to Shakespeare's canon since the 17th century—he already knows he will always be identified with it, and it with him.

"I imagine," he said, "I will be expected to teach it for the rest of my life."

Gary Lynn Taylor was born in Topeka, Kan., on Sept. 2, 1953, the son of an Air Force sergeant. He received his early education near Air Force bases in Oklahoma, South Carolina, Texas and Delaware.

After his parents divorced, he moved with his mother back to Topeka. Bookish from the time he could read, he nurtured an interest in the theater as a student at Topeka High.

WORKED AT ODD JOBS

He went to the University of Kansas in Lawrence, 30 miles from home, where he majored in classics and English, married his high school sweetheart, and worked at odd jobs to supplement his scholarships.

His love for Greek drama almost carried him to Yale to study classics. But he went instead to England to study English literature at Cambridge, mainly because he and his wife were eager to see the world.

Seven and a half years ago, Mr. Taylor left Cambridge without finishing his doctoral work and took a junior editorial position with the Oxford University Press. The press was laying the groundwork for its first general edition of Shakespeare's works in nearly a century.

Eventually Mr. Taylor became a joint editor with Dr. Stanley Wells, who is an authority on Shakespeare and editor of The Shakespeare Survey, a leading journal for scholars. It was to Dr. Wells that Mr. Taylor carried the first evidence of his Shakespearean discovery last week.

Mr. Taylor has published various scholarly articles and also edited "Henry V" for the Oxford Shakespeare series.

Special to The New York Times

He is the co-editor of a volume called "The Division of the Kingdoms," which seeks to disentangle the two distinct texts of "King Lear" that scholars have tended to run together. And a book of his own has just been published by University of Delaware Press with the title "To Analyze Delight: A Hedonist's Criticism of Shakespeare."

MAY RETURN TO U.S.

Mr. Taylor retains an American accent and intonation but chooses and articulates his words in a way that sounds more British. Slight of build and self-effacing in manner, he wears an earring in his left ear.

With the Oxford Shakespeare project drawing to a close, he and his wife, Rebecca Germonprez, say they are thinking about returning to the United States with their two sons, Isaac, 8, and Joshua, 5, both of whom were born in England.

Since he came upon the Shakespearean lyric last week, Mr. Taylor has been involved in an effort to test and confirm his discovery, and he has not yet had a chance to celebrate.

"I will probably celebrate tomorrow."

* * * * *

Is It Really Shakespeare?

_____

ANTHONY BURGESS

Gary Taylor, an Oxford scholar at 32, who as an American has a stronger claim to be taken seriously as a Shakespeare scholar than any of his British colleagues, has just discovered what he believes to be a previously unknown poem by the great and enigmatic Will. I am not being ironic when I relate his nationality to his presumed scholarship, since America has the time and the money to spend on Shakespeare studies, while we in Britain have good-humoredly relinquished them to American brains and American computers. If Gary Taylor asserts that the poem in question—which has turned up in the Bodleian Library at Oxford in a volume dated 1630—is by Shakespeare, then we are inclined to take seriously his American instinct, poetic ear and background of Shakespearean know-how. Nevertheless, I do not think that the poem (published in full in last Sunday's Book Review, with an essay by Mr. Taylor) is by Shakespeare.

There are several works in the Shakespeare canon that we know are not by Shakespeare. The age of Elizabethan drama was an age of collaboration, and we know that Shakespeare, especially in his later days, when he had grown tired of the London theater and was concentrating on being a landowning gentleman in Stratford retirement, was very willing to hand over part of the burden of writing a new play to a colleague—usually either Francis Beaumont or John Fletcher, sometimes both. His historical play "All Is True," which we know as "Henry VIII," has undoubtedly great chunks of either Beaumont or Fletcher (or both) in it. The rhythm seems to tell us when we are not listening to Shakespeare. There is a characteristic melody that is unique to Shakespeare's lines, as well as a concentrated knottiness, a deliberate desire to be difficult.

It is always difficult to prove, as in a mathematical problem, that a particular play, or passage of a play, is not by Shakespeare. One has to rely on instinct, on the subtle testimony of the ear. The same kind of instinct informs us that we are listening to Mozart, not Salieri; to Beethoven, not to Weber. Mr. Taylor's poetic discovery does not sound like Shakespeare. It sounds like the work of an Elizabethan songwriter, a man who has either devised a lyric to be set to music or, with no such intention, is nevertheless haunted by the sound of song. Listen to the opening lines:

> Shall I die? Shall I fly,
> Lovers' baits and deceits,
> Sorrow breeding?
> Shall I tend? Shall I send?
> Shall I sue, and not rue
> My proceeding?

Note the internal rhymes, one of the properties of the Broadway songs of Cole Porter, who was learned in poetry and knew the Elizabethans. They are also a property of a far greater composer of popular stage lyrics, Lorenz Hart, who was descended from and devoted to Heinrich Heine. The internal rhyme is very useful in song. The repetition of a musical phrase is matched by a rhyme pattern. The above passage has more rhymes in it than are apparent to the modern ear, since the pronunciation of English has changed since Shakespeare's time. "Baits" rhymes with "deceits." The following shows a near-total conformity of Elizabethan pronunciation to modern:

> In a dream it did seem
> But alas, dreams do pass
> As do shadows.
> I did walk, I did talk

With my love, with my dove,
Through fair meadows.

This is, as I say, the work of a songwriter. Shakespeare wrote songs for his plays, but they are not the best songs in the world. Shakespeare was too impatient to carve and cut and polish his lyrics. A far better songwriter was his friend and rival Ben Jonson, whose song "Drink to me only with thine eyes" was once much sung towards closing time in British pubs, while Shakespeare songs like "Sigh no more, ladies" and "Hark, hark the lark" have never had a large public (though Schubert set many of them for concert singers).

It is recognized that Shakespeare lacked two things in his songs—sincerity and a concern with careful craftsmanship. The newly discovered lyric is too ingenious to be sincere, but its ingenuity makes it cry out for a musical setting.

When, outside his plays, Shakespeare writes about love, there can be no doubt of his sincerity. He writes about love in his sonnets, both homoerotic (to the Earl of Southampton, his young and handsome patron) and heterosexual (to the "Dark Lady"). There can be no doubt of the sincerity of the amorous complexity in these poems. When, disgusted by his own lust, he writes the sonnet beginning "The expense of spirit in a waste of shame," he brings emotional fury and steely intellectuality to a universal experience.

If he wanted to write, as he never apparently did, an ingenious song—as opposed to a passionate declaration—to a loved lady, he would never have dreamed of playing with internal rhymes. He would have employed rhymes but, being used to the blank verse of his plays, he would have been impatient with them. He would have kept the craft of rhyme to the minimum. The poem Mr. Taylor has unearthed is clearly a clever exercise in the lyric mode, probably intended for music, but it is conventional in content and as insincere as all such songs were in that singing age.

Clever, I say, but sometimes the rhyme scheme breaks down. The poet rhymes "tresses" with "senses" and "breeding" with "deceiving"—solecisms Shakespeare would never permit. Knowing that the use of so complicated a rhyme scheme might lead him to such ineptitude would be a good enough reason for not attempting the form. And if he did not write the poem to express genuine personal emotion, he could have only one other reason for writing it—a commercial one. Yet there is nowhere any evidence in his career that he tried to make money out of writing songs. He was committed to the theater. He wrote two long narrative poems—"Venus and Adonis" and "The Rape of Lucrece"—in order to secure the patronage of the Earl of Southampton, to whom he dedicated them. He wrote the Sonnets first as a commission from the Earl's mother—the Dowager Countess of Southampton, who wanted her son to marry and believed he might be persuaded to do so through poetic arguments—and later as a kind of personal diary of amorous desire and frustrations. His songs were hastily com-

---

Who's Sorry Now?

GARY TAYLOR

Anthony Burgess wittily proposes that my being born in Kansas makes me especially qualified to arbitrate on English poetry. Unfortunately for his paradox, all my research on Shakespeare for the last 10 years has been supported by British money, in a British institution, using British computers.

Mr. Burgess astutely recognizes that the untitled poem is "a song." But this need not mean, in Shakespeare's case any more than Donne's, that he intended or expected it to be set to music. The 676 pages of the standard anthology of "English Madrigal Verse 1588–1632" (Oxford, 1967) do not contain a single lute lyric or madrigal of this length. The poem is therefore probably a literary song, presumably written to impress a patron, or a woman, or a woman patron—or simply as a technical exercise.

Mr. Burgess wants to absolve Shakespeare of rhyming "tresses" with "senses." But he fathered equally illegitimate rhymes elsewhere: *broken/ open* ("Venus and Adonis," lines 47–8), temp'ring/ vent'ring (544–6), *downs/hounds* (677–8), etc. As for the rhyme *breeding/ deceiving,* I too suspect that Shakespeare did not write it—because I suspect that "breeding" (which repeats the word in the identical position of the previous stanza) is textually corrupt. But in first offering up the poem to public scrutiny it seemed wise to make only the simplest, most obvious emendations to its text.

Is there nothing "new and surprising" in the phrase "beauty's inflection"? It describes the curvature of the face, the twisting of hair in the wind, the conventionally admired arch of eyebrows, the modest bowing of the head, but also paradoxically defines "bending" (usually a sign of weakness) as a source of power, so that "inflection" suggests the more conventional image of beauty as an "infection" that is "more than mortal." That sounds to me like Shakespeare. Sorry, Mr. Burgess.

posed interludes for his plays, and he probably considered that they had no extradramatic value.

If Shakespeare did not write Mr. Taylor's discovery, who did? If you examine John Donne's "Songs and Sonnets" (among which there are no sonnets) you will find an ingenuity of internal rhyme that suggests the song text, but you will also find the same kind of wit and intellectual rigor that mark Shakespeare's known poetry. Donne was, in effect, raising to high art the ingeniously rhymed song form and, in raising it, lifting it above the possibility of the musical setting. If Shakespeare had wanted to do the same thing, he would have written rather like Donne—with a kind of intellectual irritability, a verbal vigor that produced new and surprising images, not conventional ones like "Star-like eyes win love's prize/When they twinkle." I think you have to discount totally authorship by a poet of the stature of Shakespeare or Donne or Ben Jonson. There were plenty of songwriters about in Elizabethan London, and they had talent, but no genius. Genius was reserved to the music. Most of these songwriters were modest enough not to wish to disclose their names. Take any big fat book of Elizabethan song lyrics, and you will find that the bulk of the work is attributed to a writer called "Anonymous." Anonymous wrote much. He wrote this poem, which is, I believe, mistakenly attributed to the one man who would never have dreamed of writing it. Sorry, Mr. Taylor.

"Digest" Poll Machinery Speeding Up

First Figures in Presidential Test to Be Published Next Week

Swinging into higher speed, THE LITERARY DIGEST's great Presidential Poll machinery of 1936 is now settling into the steady, certain, increasingly-swifter pace that will carry it to a country-shaking climax just before Election Day.

Who will win—Roosevelt or Landon? Will the country repudiate the New Deal or give its leader a new, four-year mandate? To-day, nobody knows. But THE DIGEST is seeking the answer—in the same way that has enabled it, time after time, to tell the country exactly what was going to happen when the voters went to the polls.

The Literary Digest, New York, August 29, 1936

Hints of what the voters will do this year began trickling into DIGEST Poll Headquarters last week. This week the volume increased. Next week— and in next week's issue the first figures to be tabulated will be published— the volume of returning votes will be even larger. Thereafter it will rise steadily to avalanche proportions, with scores of thousands of ballots weekly.

FIGURES

Finally, the last of the more than 10,000,000 secret ballots which now are being broadcast to every State, county, city, town and hamlet will be in the mails; the last of the voted ballots will have been returned, checked and tallied.

In that great mass of post-card votes, representing the opinions of every section, class, age and occupation, will be found the answer as to the political fate of Franklin D. Roosevelt, Alfred M. Landon, William Lemke, Earl Browder, Norman Thomas.

In election after election, as the public so well knows, THE LITERARY DIGEST has forecast the result long before Election Day. For this journalistic feat and public service it has received thousands of tributes during many years. To-day the praise is continuing. For instance, Percy B. Scott, Editor, writes in the September issue of *The American Press*, "a magazine for makers of newspapers":

> "With the advent of the Presidential election campaign comes THE LITERARY DIGEST Poll—that oracle, which, since 1920, has foretold with almost uncanny accuracy the choice of the nation's voters. . . .

> "Nothing which could be construed as bias has ever been permitted to crop into the stories or operation of the Poll. No matter what the returns may have indicated, those indications must be given to the public without qualification or color.

> "Political leaders have praised and damned the Poll—depending upon whether or not it coincided with their hopes and prayers—but, like the brook, it has gone merrily on its way, confounding its critics and accurately forecasting the hitherto unpredictable."

TEMPERS LOST

That is correct. There never has been a DIGEST Poll that was not sharply criticized. Frequently there have been charges that it had "sold out" to this, that or the other interest. Such criticism may be expected again, as the campaign grows hotter and this or that faction, seeing the tide running against them, find themselves losing their tempers.

But THE DIGEST would like to mention in advance that such criticism will be as unfounded in 1936 as it was in every other poll. Most of our readers know that it costs a "king's ransom" to conduct a Poll. But THE DIGEST believes that it is rendering a great public service—and when such a service can be rendered no price is too high.

In 1924 the first large Presidential Poll was launched. Coolidge, Davis and La Follette were the candidates. That poll predicted the Electoral College result within three votes—more than 99 per cent. right—and the popular vote for Coolidge within 1 per cent.—99 per cent. correct.

This extraordinary performance attracted the attention of the press of the world. To many papers it was "amazing." "Here," said the Cincinnati *Post*, "is the way to economy and comfort in elections." But its very accuracy made the Poll machinery a target for political sharpshooters. Ever since, each poll has been watched meticulously to guard against the slightest chance of error.

It was in 1928 that THE DIGEST Poll met perhaps its greatest test. When the returns began to pour in, some Poll observers began to suffer a slight case of jitters. It was not so astonishing that the Hoover Republicans should be shown carrying such States as Kentucky, Tennessee and West Virginia, for they were considered border States. But when the voters began to indicate firmly that Alfred E. Smith would not carry such States of the "Solid South" as Virginia, Texas, North Carolina and Florida—would not even carry his own State, New York—the experts began to wonder about the accuracy of the Poll.

But the election showed that the Poll had forecast the popular vote with an error of only 4.4 per cent. and had predicted the first break-up of the "Solid South" since the War between the States.

During earlier Presidential Polls, the Democrats had consistently hammered at them because they predicted Republican victories. In 1932 the tables were turned. Republicans became critical. The Poll that year indicated that Roosevelt would win by pretty much of a landslide; it was over 99 per cent. correct.

By the spring of 1934 there appeared to be a sharp division of opinion on the New Deal. THE DIGEST asked the voters what they thought, on the whole, of Roosevelt's acts and policies. The response showed about 61 per cent. for the New Deal.

Again, in the fall of 1935, when rumblings of criticism of the New Deal became louder, THE DIGEST, using virtually the same list, sent out 10,000,000 ballots to find out what the country then thought. As many readers will remember, that Poll showed more than 63 per cent. of the total vote registered against the Administration's acts and policies.

To the casual observer, this might mean that a Republican landslide is due this fall. But it must be remembered that that Poll was taken on policies and not on personalities.

And so the great question remains: Who will win the election next November? To repeat: To-day, nobody knows. But THE DIGEST is seeking the answer—in the same way that has enabled it, time after time, to tell the country exactly what was going to happen when the voters went to the polls.

* * * * *

"Digest's" First Hundred Thousand

Ballots Quadrupled by Early Returns From Five More States

Landon, 61,190; Roosevelt, 33,423; Lemke, 4,169.

That is the score, as THE LITERARY DIGEST's Presidential Poll of more than 10,000,000 voters swings into its third week.

It shows the original handful of 24,000-odd ballots quadrupled to 99,734. It shows preliminary returns in scattered sections of five new States, as the tabulators dip below the Mason and Dixon Line to size up two States nominally heavily Democratic—Texas and Oklahoma. It shows Governor Landon leading in three Midwestern farm States—Ohio, Minnesota and Indiana—on early returns. And it shows President Roosevelt whittling his opponent's first-return margin of more than two to one in three of the original four States—New York, New Jersey, Pennsylvania and Maine—to slightly under two to one.

Will the New Deal leader continue to close the gap, as tens of thousands of secret post-card ballots swell the flood of incoming returns, this week and every week until November? Will the man in the White House reach and pass the man in Topeka, Kansas, at the half-million-mark—the million-mark?

SEVERAL SHIFTS

Only the final results can tell, but here is what happened in Maine's column from the first week to the second: From a lead of 1,831 to 522 (more than three to one), the Landon margin dropped from 4,826 to 2,179 (only a little more than two to one). That change in political fortune amply illustrates what THE DIGEST means by its warning to the public: These are only the scattering early returns; the leadership may shift again and again during the progress of the Poll.

Interesting, too, is the first showing for Minnesota. Here is a predominantly farming State whose eleven electoral votes may well be a vital factor in the ultimate outcome. The Boston _Globe_ thinks the home of the Farmer-Labor Party "may be a key-State."

Until a fortnight ago, political experts appeared to be agreed that Minnesota would wind up in the Roosevelt column. Reason: Gov. Floyd B. Olson, head of the Farmer-Labor Party, was a vigorous supporter of the New Deal. Then Governor Olson died. Result: The whole political picture in Minnesota has been thrown into confusion.

ONE EXPLANATION

As its St. Paul Correspondent writes in the New York _Times:_

"Democratic tactics in Minnesota for three and a half years have been predicated on the assumption that President Roosevelt would have the powerful support of Governor Olson in the 1936 campaign.

"In return for this expected support, the dominant wing of the Democratic Party practically abdicated in favor of Farmer-Labor State, Congressional and Senatorial candidates. The Democrats now are in the predicament of having an extremely weak ticket in deference to Farmer-Labor desires, and getting nothing in return. With the death of Mr. Olson has largely expired the ability of the Farmer-Labor Party to be of service to President Roosevelt. . . ."

First returns from Minnesota give Landon 8,620; Roosevelt 5,939. Does that mean that Minnesota will go Republican? Not necessarily, for it must be remembered that these returns are far from final. And there is another factor: Lemke.

Governor Olson had been slated to run for the United States Senate. A few days after his death, the Farmer-Labor Party's State Central Committee picked Representative Ernest Lundeen to run for the Senate. Without giving Lemke outright indorsement, Representative Lundeen nevertheless has been openly sympathetic toward the Union Party candidate. The State gives Lemke 1,544 in first returns—the largest vote he had received in any State, by far. And 1,137 of those 1,544 had voted for Roosevelt in 1932; only 207 for Hoover. Will the Lemke vote be a sufficient factor to defeat the Democrats in Minnesota?

* * * * *

Landon Holds Lead in "Digest" Poll

Kansan Ahead in 21 States, Roosevelt in 10, Lemke in None

Landon holds his lead. As the candidates round the far turn in this exciting Presidential race, the Kansas Governor is still in front.

But Roosevelt is inching up, and Lemke, the amazing "dark horse," refuses to quit, tho far behind.

In this, the fifth report of THE LITERARY DIGEST 1936 Presidential Poll, the Republican's total has been whittled from last week's 58.38 per cent. to 57.95 per cent. The score stands: Landon, 438,601; Roosevelt, 282,524; Lemke, 29,083.

ELECTORAL LINE-UP

In terms of Electoral votes, Landon has 290 from twenty-one States; Roosevelt 111 from ten states; Lemke none.

But the Poll has four weeks to run, and much can happen in four weeks. Roosevelt has been moving up steadily, may break into a breath-taking sprint in these remaining weeks, when the big city vote makes its full force felt.

DEMOCRATIC HOPE

For the Democrats maintain that the President's chief strength lies in these urban centers.

This week, the total of ballots tabulated is swelled to 756,807. These include supplementary returns from twenty-one States listed last week, and ten States reporting for the first time.

And what a realm of conjecture and debate in the campaign some of those ten new States open up!

UNCERTAIN ILLINOIS

Take Illinois: With twenty-nine Electoral votes, the State that sent Abraham Lincoln to the White House may well be a determining factor in the final outcome.

Its shift one way or another would represent a difference of fifty-eight votes, with only 266 needed for victory in the Electoral College.

And shifts are nothing new in Illinois. In 1928, the State gave Hoover a 454,324 plurality over Smith; in 1932, it piled up a 449,548 plurality for Roosevelt—a million-vote shift. Another factor which makes Illinois significant is that it is one of the "half-and-half" States—half city-industrial, half rural-agricultural.

The Republicans, counting heavily this year on the downstate farmer vote, point to the recent Democratic intraparty rift between Gov. Henry Horner and the Chicago machine headed by Mayor Edward Kelly and Boss Pat Nash. The G.O.P. says Nash fought Horner's renomination because the latter sponsored an Honest Elections Bill, and quotes the Cook County Elections boss as wailing that the measure "would cost the organization 250,000 votes in Chicago."

SHOWING IN PRIMARY

The Democrats, on the other hand, insist that National Chairman James A. Farley patched up that quarrel, and that Cook County will erase any Republican edge that can be rolled up downstate. And they point gleefully to the April primaries, when the President, running unopposed, piled up 1,300,000 votes, whereas Republican aspirants Borah and Knox, in a neck-and-neck race, were able to get a combined total of only 915,780.

Where will Illinois' twenty-nine Electoral votes go?

This week, in first returns, they go to Landon, with 12,409 ballots to 5,484 for Roosevelt, only 459 for Lemke.

MICHIGAN PROBLEM

No less an "if" quantity than Illinois' twenty-nine are Michigan's nineteen.

First returns from this State give Landon 7,784 to Roosevelt's 3,704, with a meager 575 for the Union Party candidate.

Michigan, too, did some shifting in 1932. Traditionally Republican, the State went for the President by a majority of nearly 132,000. It elected a Democratic Governor and ten Democratic Representatives out of seventeen. But it developed that the 1932 shift was not to be the last.

Two years later, the Republicans recaptured the Governorship and elected eleven Representatives. Will that swing back to the G.O.P. be accelerated in November?

No one knows for certain, but Republicans are heartened by a spring primary vote that outnumbered the Democratic total by about three to two.

In the face of this apparent trend back to normal Republicanism, a number of polls other than THE DIGEST's still show the State leaning toward the president. Which points the right way?

AN EDITORIAL VIEW

In an effort to find out, and at the same time explain the apparent discrepancy, the Detroit *Free Press* recently took "a straw vote of straw votes," and announced:

"We have not been able to find any resident of Michigan who has ever been mailed a ballot by any of these (other) services or who has been approached or asked an opinion.

"On the other hand, we do find at least one out of every twenty, in all walks of life, who have received their LITERARY DIGEST ballots.

"This does not mean that *The Free Press* vouches for the absolute accuracy of THE DIGEST Poll—but we do know that one is being taken."

* * * * *

Landon, 1,293,669; Roosevelt, 972,897

Final Returns in The Digest's Poll of Ten Million Voters

Well, the great battle of the ballots in the Poll of ten million voters, scattered throughout the forty-eight States of the Union, is now finished, and in the table below* we record the figures received up to the hour of going to press.

These figures are exactly as received from more than one in every five voters polled in our country—they are neither weighted, adjusted nor interpreted.

Never before in an experience covering more than a quarter of a century in taking polls have we received so many different varieties of criticism—praise from many; condemnation from many others—and yet it has been just of the same type that has come to us every time a Poll has been taken in all these years.

The Literary Digest, New York, October 31, 1936

*An abbreviated version of this table is included following this reading.–Ed.

A telegram from a newspaper in California asks: "Is it true that Mr. Hearst has purchased THE LITERARY DIGEST?" A telephone message only the day before these lines were written: "Has the Republican National Committee purchased THE LITERARY DIGEST?" And all types and varieties, including: "Have the Jews purchased THE LITERARY DIGEST?" "Is the Pope of Rome a stockholder of THE LITERARY DIGEST? And so it goes—all equally absurd and amusing. We could add more to this list, and yet all of these questions in recent days are but repetitions of what we have been experiencing all down the years from the very first Poll.

PROBLEM

Now, are the figures in this Poll correct? In answer to this question we will simply refer to a telegram we sent to a young man in Massachusetts the other day in answer to his challenge to us to wager $100,000 on the accuracy of our Poll. We wired him as follows:

"For nearly a quarter century, we have been taking Polls of the voters in the forty-eight States, and especially in Presidential years, and we have always merely mailed the ballots, counted and recorded those returned and let the people of the Nation draw their conclusions as to our accuracy. So far, we have been right in every Poll. Will we be right in the current Poll? That, as Mrs. Roosevelt said concerning the President's reelection, is in the 'lap of the gods.'

"We never make any claims before election but we respectfully refer you to the opinion of one of the most quoted citizens to-day, the Hon. James A. Farley, Chairman of the Democratic National Committee. This is what Mr. Farley said October 14, 1932:

" 'Any sane person can not escape the implication of such a gigantic sampling of popular opinion as is embraced in THE LITERARY DIGEST straw vote. I consider this conclusive evidence as to the desire of the people of this country for a change in the National Government. THE LITERARY DIGEST poll is an achievement of no little magnitude. It is a Poll fairly and correctly conducted.' "

In studying the table of the voters from all of the States printed below, please remember that we make no claims at this time for their absolute accuracy. On a similar occasion we felt it important to say:

> "In a wild year like this, however, many sagacious observers will refuse to bank upon appearances, however convincing. As for THE DIGEST, it draws no conclusions from the results of its vast distribution of twenty million ballots. True to its historic non-partisan [sic] policy—or 'omni-partizan,' [sic] as some editor described it in 1928—we supply our readers with the facts to the best of our ability, and leave them to draw their own conclusions.

"We make no claim to infallibility. We did not coin the phrase 'uncanny accuracy' which has been so freely applied to our Polls. We know only too well the limitations of every straw vote, however enormous the sample gathered, however scientific the method. It would be a miracle if every State of the forty-eight behaved on Election day exactly as forecast by the Poll."

We say now about Rhode Island and Massachusetts that our figures indicate in our own judgment too large a percentage for Mr. Landon and too small a percentage for Mr. Roosevelt, and altho in 1932 the figures in these two States indicated Mr. Hoover's carrying both, we announced:

"A study of the returns convinces us that in those States our ballots have somehow failed to come back in adequate quantity from large bodies of Democratic voters."

Our own opinion was that they would be found in the Roosevelt column, and they were. We will not do the same this year; we feel that both States will be found in the Landon column, and we are reaching this conclusion by the same process that led to the reverse conclusion in 1932.

Pennsylvania is another State which requires special mention. Four years ago, our figures gave the State to Mr. Roosevelt, and Mr. Hoover carried it on Election day. In comparing our ballot this year with that of 1932, we find that in many cities in Pennsylvania our figures showed a much higher trend toward Mr. Roosevelt than was justified by the election figures on Election day in 1932. In examining the very same cities now we discover the reverse trend, and in cities that in 1932 indicated an approximately 60–40 per cent. relationship between Roosevelt and Hoover, we now find 60 per cent. for Landon and 40 per cent. for Roosevelt.

That's the plain language of it. Many people wonder at these great changes in a State like Pennsylvania, and we confess to wonderment ourselves.

On the Pacific Coast, we find California, Oregon and Washington all vote for Mr. Landon in our Poll, and yet we are told that the Pacific Coast is "aflame" for Mr. Roosevelt.

A State like California is always a difficult State to get an accurate opinion from by the polling method, and we may be far astray, yet every one should remember that in the Gubernatorial campaign a few years ago, we took a Poll of California when it was believed by most of California citizens that Mr. Upton Sinclair would be elected Governor, and the result of our Poll showed that Mr. Sinclair would *not* be elected Governor and the Poll was correct.

The State of Washington seems to be more favorable to Mr. Landon than either Oregon or California. We can not in our Poll detect anything that would indicate a reason for this difference.

SEATTLE

Right here we wish to say that in 1932 our Poll in Seattle gave Mr. Roosevelt 65.43 per cent. of the vote, and he carried that city by 61.58 per cent. of the vote. In the current Poll, 1936, Seattle gives Mr. Landon 58.52 per cent. and Mr. Roosevelt 40.46 per cent. Our readers will notice we over-estimated Mr. Roosevelt in 1932—are we overestimating Mr. Landon now? We see no reason for supposing so. And the three Pacific Coast States which now show for Mr. Landon and which millions believe will vote for Mr. Roosevelt (they may be right) in 1924, 1928 and 1932 were correctly forecast in THE LITERARY DIGEST Polls.

In the great Empire State, New York, the figures for so large a State are what might be called very close. After looking at the figures for New York in the column at the left, remember that in 1932 we gave Mr. Roosevelt 46.1 per cent. and Mr. Hoover 43.9 per cent., even closer than it is to-day. And yet we correctly forecast that Mr. Roosevelt would carry the State.

And so we might go on with many States that are very close, and some not so close, but in which local conditions have much to do with results, not in polls such as our Poll, but on Election day.

The Poll represents the most extensive straw ballot in the field—the most experienced in view of its twenty-five years of perfecting—the most unbiased in view of its prestige—a Poll that has always previously been correct.

Even its critics admit its value as an index of popular sentiment. As one of these critics, _The Nation_, observes:

"Because it indicates both the 1932 and 1936 vote, it offers the raw material for as careful a prognostication as it is possible to make at this time."

Final Report "Literary Digest" 1936 Presidential Poll (Abbreviated by Schwarze and Lape)

	Landon 1936 Total	How Same Voters voted in 1932 Election						Roosevelt 1936 Total	How Same Voters voted in 1932 Election						Lemke 1936 Total	How Same Voters voted in 1932 Election					
		Rep.	Dem.	Soc.	Other	Did Not Vote	Vote Not Indicated		Rep.	Dem.	Soc.	Other	Did Not Vote	Vote Not Indicated		Rep.	Dem.	Soc.	Other	Did Not Vote	Vote Not Indicated
CA	89516	65360	16200	315	53	3519	4069	77245	15165	53520	1816	63	3578	3103	4977	1620	2560	117	25	163	492
MA	87449	70576	10105	330	31	3213	3203	25965	5141	17499	744	16	1635	930	5415	1002	3670	133	3	236	371
NY	162260	114574	53052	805	45	7125	6659	139277	18241	99938	4101	141	10604	6252	14656	2106	10414	303	20	670	1143
OR	11747	8593	2014	72	6	521	541	10951	1966	7666	298	7	567	447	655	196	313	46	7	30	63
PA	119086	86433	20097	543	115	6461	5437	81114	14502	56082	1340	55	5733	3402	7507	1121	5089	187	11	467	632
RI	10401	8165	1269	32	5	511	419	3489	600	2470	90	–	208	121	794	148	545	12	3	31	55
WA	21370	14841	4800	67	30	806	826	15300	2281	11423	278	53	709	556	683	170	374	28	27	31	53
US Total	1293669	920225	250059	5629	825	61323	55608	972897	142942	714194	18420	772	57310	39309	83610	14845	55757	2333	223	3679	6773

❉ ❉ ❅ ❊ ❊

What Went Wrong with the Polls?

None of Straw Votes Got Exactly the Right Answer—Why?

In 1920, 1924, 1928 and 1932, THE LITERARY DIGEST Polls were right. Not only right in the sense that they showed the winner; they forecast the _actual popular vote_ with such a small percentage of error (less than 1 per cent. in 1932) that newspapers and individuals everywhere heaped such phrases as "uncannily accurate" and "amazingly right" upon us.

Four years ago, when the Poll was running his way, our very good friend Jim Farley was saying that "no sane person could escape the implication" of a sampling "so fairly and correctly conducted."

Well, this year we used precisely the same method that had scored four bull's-eyes in four previous tries. And we were far from correct. Why? We ask that question in all sincerity, because _we want to know._

"REASONS"

Oh, we've been flooded with "reasons." Hosts of people who feel they have learned more about polling in a few months than we have learned in more than a score of years have told us just where we were off. Hundreds of astute "second-guessers" have assured us, by telephone, by letter, in the newspapers, that the reasons for our error were "obvious." Were they?

Suppose we review a few of these "obvious reasons."

The one most often heard runs something like this: "This election was different. Party lines were obliterated. For the first time in more than a century, _all_ the 'have-nots' were on one side. THE DIGEST, polling names from telephone books and lists of automobile owners, simply did not reach the lower strata." And so on. . . .

"HAVE-NOTS"

Well, in the first place, the "have-nots" did not reelect Mr. Roosevelt. That they contributed to his astonishing plurality, no one can doubt. But the fact remains that a majority of farmers, doctors, grocers and candlestick-mak-

The Literary Digest, New York, November 14, 1936

ers *also* voted for the President. As Dorothy Thompson remarked in the New York *Herald Tribune*, you could eliminate the straight labor vote, the relief vote and the Negro vote, and *still* Mr. Roosevelt would have a majority.

So that "reason" does not appear to hold much water. Besides—

We *did* reach these so-called "have-not" strata. In the city of Chicago, for example, we polled *every third registered voter*. In the city of Scranton, Pennsylvania, we polled every *other* registered voter. And in Allentown, Pennsylvania, likewise other cities, we polled *every* registered voter.

Is that so? chorus the critics, a little abashed, no doubt. Well, they come back, you must have got the right answer in *those* towns, anyway.

Well, we didn't. The fact is that we were as badly off there as we were on the national total.

CITIES

In Allentown, for example, 10,753 out of the 30,811 who voted returned ballots to us showing a division of 53.32 per cent. to 44.67 per cent. in favor of Mr. Landon. What was the actual result? It was 56.93 per cent. for Mr. Roosevelt, 41.17 per cent. for the Kansan.

In Chicago, the 100,929 voters who returned ballots to us showed a division of 48.63 per cent. to 47.56 per cent. in favor of Mr. Landon. The 1,672,175 who voted in the actual election gave the President 65.24 per cent., to 32.26 per cent. for the Republican candidate.

What happened? Why did only one in five voters in Chicago to whom THE DIGEST sent ballots take the trouble to reply? And why was there a preponderance of Republicans in the one-fifth that did reply? Your guess is as good as ours. We'll go into it a little more later. The important thing in all the above is that all this conjecture about our "not reaching certain strata" simply will not hold water.

HOOVER VOTERS

Now for another "explanation" dinned into our ears: "You got too many Hoover voters in your sample."

Well, the fact is that we've *always* got too big a sampling of Republican voters. That was true in 1920, in 1924, in 1928, and even in 1932, when we *over*estimated the Roosevelt popular vote by three-quarters of 1 per cent.

In 1928 in Chicago, we underestimated the Democratic vote by a little more than 5 per cent., overestimated the Republican vote by the same margin.

We wondered then, as we had wondered before and have wondered since, why we were getting better cooperation in what we have always regarded as a public service from Republicans than we were getting from Democrats. Do Republicans live nearer mail-boxes? Do Democrats generally disapprove of straw polls?

We don't know that answer. All we know is that in 1932, when the tide seemed to be running away from Hoover, we were perturbed about the disproportion of Republican voters in our sampling. Republican and Demo-cratic chieftains from all points in the country were at the telephones day after day for reports of what the Democrats called our "correctly conducted" system. And then the result came along, and it was so right, we were inclined to agree that we had been concerned without reason, and this year, when it seemed logical to suppose that the President's vote would be lighter, even if he won (hadn't that been the rule on reelections for more than a hundred years?) we decided not to worry.

FIGURES

So the statisticians did our worrying for us on that score, applying what they called the "compensating-ratio" in some cases, and the "switch-factor" in others. Either way, for some of the figure experts, it didn't matter; inter-pret our figures for 2,376,523 voters as they would, the answer was still Lan-don. Then other statisticians took our figures and so weighted, compensated, balanced, adjusted and interpreted them that they showed Roosevelt.

We did not attempt to interpret the figures, because we had no stake in the result other than the wish to preserve our well-earned reputation for scrupulous bookkeeping. So we sent out more than ten million ballots, exactly as we had sent them out before. We don't know what proportion went to persons who had voted for Roosevelt in 1932 or what proportion went to persons who had voted for Hoover, because our polls are secret always, and the ballots come back with no signatures, no identifying char-acteristics of any sort except the post-marks.

BASIS

However, since the basis of the 1936 mailing-list was the 1932 mail-ing-list, and since the overwhelming majority of those who responded to our Poll in 1932 voted for Mr. Roosevelt, it seems altogether reasonable to assume that the majority of our ballots this year went to people who had voted for Mr. Roosevelt in 1932. There simply was no way by which THE DIGEST could assure itself or the public that the marked ballots would come back in the same proportion. We couldn't very well send duplicate ballots to indifferent Democrats, or personal letters prodding them into action, because we didn't know which were Democrats and which were Republicans, let alone which would vote for Roosevelt and which for Landon.

If any of the hundreds who have so kindly offered their suggestions and criticism can tell us how we could get voters to respond proportionately, and still keep the poll secret, as we believe it ought always to be, then we wish these critics would step up and do so. And with arguments more convincing than the familiar ones about our not reaching the "lower strata" and "sampling too many Republicans." Because those two theories explain nothing; they only add to the multiplicity and confusion of words—words—words.

TOO MANY

And there's another "explanation" that doesn't seem to hold much water, when you examine it closely. That's the one that argues that we polled too many voters, that cites the experience of another poll that sent out less than a fourth as many ballots and came closer to being right. The answer here is that the Baltimore *Sunpapers* polled more persons per square mile in Maryland than we did anywhere except in the cities—and the *Sunpapers* were a lot nearer right than this "model poll" for Maryland. Also, the man who came nearer the right answer than all the polls put together was Jim Farley, and Jim based his prediction on reports from tens of thousands of precinct leaders in every city, town and hamlet in the country.

So—what?

So we were wrong, altho we did everything we knew to assure ourselves of being right.

We conducted our Poll as we had always done, reported what we found, and have no alibis. We drew no special satisfaction from our figures, and we drew no conclusions from them. The result was disappointing only in the sense that it threw our figures out the window, and left us without even the satisfaction of knowing why.

FUTURE

As for the immediate future, THE DIGEST feels that in truth "the Nation has spoken." THE DIGEST hails a magnificent President against whom it never uttered one word of partizan [sic] criticism. THE DIGEST can not support him, in the sense that newspapers support a President editorially, because THE DIGEST does not editorialize. But it can obtain genuine satisfaction from the knowledge that its several Editors, as American citizens, and its millions of readers, as American citizens, will stand behind the First Citizen.

Speaking of the President, there is a spot of comfort for us in the knowledge that he himself was pretty badly off on his Electoral total, and that he "laughed it off" in his genial way. His last guess was 360 votes to Mr. Landon's 171. (On June 5 he had estimated his margin at 315 to 216.)

As for the more distant future, the questions have been asked: Will THE DIGEST conduct another Poll? Will it change its methods?

The answer to the first question we phrase in others: Should the Democratic Party have quit in 1924, when it reached a modern low-ebb in power and confidence, instead of going on to the greatest triumph in its history? Should the Republican Party have quit in 1912, when it carried only two States? Should the University of Minnesota, with the greatest record in modern football, give up the sport because it finally lost one game, after a string of twenty-one victories?

The answer to the second question is: We'll cross that bridge when we come to it.

Reflections on the Readings:

1. As a patient, which would you prefer your doctor to have, assuming you have a choice, a warm bedside manner or sound critical thinking skills? Why?

2. How can the illness of former San Francisco 49er Bobby Waters be seen as illustrating a generalization that failed?

3. Describe a health puzzle similar to the San Francisco 49ers puzzle which has sent health officials looking for possible causes.

4. What are the most compelling reasons for thinking that the untitled poem "Shall I die? . . ." was written by Shakespeare? What are the best reasons for thinking that its author was someone other than Shakespeare? What does this argument reveal about the nature of evidence?

5. In 1936 Americans were shocked to wake up the day after the presidential election to find that Roosevelt, not Landon, had won. Why should they not have been so surprised? What suggestions would you make to *The Literary Digest* for its future predictions of elections?

6. *The Literary Digest* had a very large number of responses in its informal poll, many more than current pollsters use to predict election

results. Why wasn't that sufficient to avoid its embarrassing mispre-diction of the election results? Be specific in your answer.

Generalizations

When we make generalizations we are observing at least one or more spe-cific cases and then projecting the **pattern** we have observed onto future cases. The key word here is *pattern*. We must first observe a pattern, rather than randomness. Then we must decide if it makes sense to expect that pat-tern always, frequently, or sometimes in the future, given what we know. We discussed patterns in the previous chapter where we pointed out that many patterns of traces frequently go unnoticed by us. We begin to see patterns, however, when we have some interest that motivates us or when the pattern has been repeated so often that we cannot avoid recognizing it. An example of the former is the 49ers example in the readings. No one saw any pattern or any connection between fertilizer and ALS until someone realized that there was a cluster of victims of the disease and began to look for an expla-nation for the cluster by looking for patterns. The typical American high school with its daily class schedule marked by the ringing of bells would be a good example of the latter, a repeated pattern imposed on students with such regularity that they cannot help but notice it.

The patterns we are talking about can be very complex like weather patterns or the behavior of nations at war, or they can be rather simple like ice cubes melting in warm cola. The importance to us of these patterns and our ability to generalize these patterns into the future cannot be exaggerated. They help us to know what to **expect** and to a certain extent how to **con-trol** what happens to us in the future.

Let's take an example of a generalization to see how generalizations work. Consider, for instance, "Small-town librarians lead boring lives." Some-one might make that generalization on the basis of observing the lives of sev-eral librarians living in small towns. Or someone might have conducted a survey of librarians in small towns, asking them if they found their lives bor-ing. Or someone might have made this generalization solely on the basis of her own beliefs about the lives of librarians and her beliefs about life in a small town. The generalization also has something to do with what the speaker may find boring or not boring. The point is that not every librarian in a small town has been observed. Even if one tried to observe or survey every such librarian, one could never be sure one had and certainly there are future librarians in small towns that one cannot now survey. So the claim is broader than the evidence for it and projects a presently observed pattern onto the future or onto cases not yet observed. Moreover, it suggests a cer-tain expectation. That is, if you should happen to observe the life of a small-town librarian in the future, you should not expect it to be a life of excitement. It also suggests that if you are considering becoming a librarian in a small town, you should not expect the excitement and glamour of sailing to Monte Carlo on a luxury liner.

Now the question we are concerned with here is when should we project our observations of patterns onto the future and when should we avoid projecting them. Are we warranted in saying—and believing—"Small-town librarians lead boring lives," given that we have only visited a limited number of small-town libraries? The answer is: Maybe. In fact, you might wonder if we are justified in projecting a past pattern onto the future at all. That is, we seem to be assuming that the future will be like the past. But what evidence do we have for that assumption? Only that in the past the future was often like the past! This evidence, of course, is no evidence at all. It is just a restatement of the very point for which it is supposed to be evidence. It's like asking your friend who is always eating yellow gumdrops, "Why do you like the taste of yellow gumdrops?" and your friend's replying, "I like yellow gumdrops because they have a good flavor." It's an answer that's a nonanswer. This puzzle, which philosophers call **the problem of induction**, does not have a solution. It's an assumption that we humans make (and perhaps animals do, too) which we cannot prove but which we must make to have order and stability in our lives. Thus, we need to keep in mind that when we generalize, our reasoning rests on an unprovable assumption about the likelihood of resemblance between past and future; therefore, one guideline for making warranted generalizations is that we should proceed with caution.

It should be noted that this reasoning puzzle cannot be avoided by changing our "all" statement to a "some" statement about a certain percentage of cases. That is, you might think that maybe we can't prove that all librarians in small towns lead boring lives but surely we are warranted in believing that some of them do. Indeed we may be. But our warrant does not mean that we can be certain that the cases we have not observed will be like the ones we have. If 40 percent of the lives of small-town librarians we have observed are boring we may be warranted in believing that 40 percent of _all_ librarians in small towns lead boring lives, if we have followed the guidelines suggested here. But our projection still rests on the unprovable assumption that the future will be like the past.

Some generalizations do not rest on this unprovable assumption. They are really quasi generalizations, not based on past experience at all but rather on the meanings of the words used in the generalization. The example given earlier, "All circles are round," is a quasi generalization. Such quasi generalizations are definitions and not pieces of reasoning.

But consider the generalization "A whale is a mammal." If we found a whalelike creature that was not a mammal would we then say, "This creature is not a whale" or would we be more willing to say, "This creature is a whale that is not a mammal"? (The contemporary philosopher Hilary Putnam has made the ambiguity of statements like these famous in philosophical circles.) There is no right answer to this question. We can imagine circumstances in which both responses might be warranted. Usually we defer to the scientific community, or the community of language speakers closest to the context, and the common usage within that community.

Notice, however, for the statement "a whale is a mammal" to be a statement **about the world**, it must be about some possible experience. Our observations of the world cannot be irrelevant to its being a warranted or an unwarranted claim. To put the matter another way, if the statement "a whale is a mammal" is about *whales* and not about the definition of the term *whale*, then our whalelike creature must at least have the possibility of being a whale even though it is not a mammal, if it is sufficiently whalelike. What this means is that all generalizations about the world must allow the possibility of counter examples. They cannot be immune to new information gained from experience. This is one of the meanings of the old adage, "The exception proves the rule." The possibility of an exception proves that the generalization is about the world and not about words and their definitions. This possibility suggests another important guideline to keep in mind when making warranted generalizations, which is that we must always to be ready to revise our generalizations in the light of new information. We will have more to say about this later.

Let's go back to our small-town librarian and our fundamental assumption, the future will be like the past. The problem is: Which future will be like which past? Failure to give the right answer to this question leads to bigotry, phobias, and thwarted expectations! The question is both more simple and more complex than it might seem. On the one hand, as human beings we are always projecting into the future. We have expectations. We make plans. We don't even think about it. We get up, we get dressed, we eat, expecting today to be like yesterday. Most of our daily life is based on these simple projections of the past onto the future. If it were not, we would have trouble surviving. We would be worn out deciding what to do and how to do it. (This is what happens to us when we are put in a new environment and must think about how to accomplish the most basic tasks. Travelers in a foreign country and first-year college students are people who feel this kind of fatigue.)

On the other hand, some of our projections onto the future are very complex. Realizing this, we worry about what to expect, what to choose, whom to believe, and we make mistakes. There are too many variables, too many uncertainties, too little time. While we want to focus on these problems here and to suggest guidelines for meeting them, **we should not forget or underestimate how well we actually anticipate the future or how adept human beings are at drawing warranted generalizations.**

First, let us talk about "which past." This is a much more complicated problem than is often acknowledged. Usually something motivates us to pick out a particular pattern, or to collect data on a particular issue, whose worth is considered obvious. For example, we collect data on voter preferences because we want to help a candidate get elected. We look for patterns of authoritarian behavior in ordinary people because we want to understand why German soldiers could obey such inhumane orders during World War II. We look for patterns in the biological responses of rats to a particular chemical compound because we want to know if the compound will be helpful in the treatment of some disease in humans.

This goes back to the point made in the previous chapter about **traces**. Traces abound. We notice those that have interest for us. One could say (as some philosophers have said) that we place **value** on them. Similarly, we notice **patterns** of traces because we place value on them. We generalize a **pattern of traces** and project it into the future when it has value for us or when we think it has value for us. To put the matter another way, data are not there in our experience to be collected by us. We create data by valuing them or by collecting them. Our experience is one big cauldron of patterns of traces, or data, which we sort out according to our interest. This is why, despite what historians say, there are no lessons in history. Because there is every lesson in history! For every battle that was followed by X, there was some battle, virtually identical, which was followed by the opposite of X. History, then, is a story that people tell to understand the traces they have picked out or placed value on. When people value things differently, they tell different stories. They have different histories.

If, to go back to our example, we are talking about small-town librarians, we will have to make some decisions about which patterns to generalize. We will have to decide how small is a small town, for example. We will also have to consider who is a librarian. Are we considering only those who are librarians by occupation or anyone who works in a library? Perhaps we should limit our pattern to only librarians with blond hair or only bald, six-feet-tall librarians who speak with a Russian accent. How do we decide whether hair, height, weight, and all the many other features librarians could have are relevant to our generalization or to some other pattern worth generalizing? For example, maybe our focus should be the lives of bald librarians living in big cities. Why pick out only the feature of living in a small town? Which past, it becomes clear, is determined by us, by our interest, by what we value—and by the background knowledge which we bring to these experiences. Our background knowledge tells us, for example, that hair color or height has little to do with the amount of excitement in one's life, whereas living in a small town often precludes certain activities which might make life more interesting and exciting. We cannot emphasize too much the importance of background information in helping us to decide "which past" to generalize.

Background knowledge is the key here but there are some very specific ways to use our background knowledge in determining when and what to generalize. When we make a generalization we are projecting features of a sample population, or a certain number of observed cases, to a larger population. This sample population needs to meet certain criteria for our projections to be warranted. First, it needs to be random or representative. Second, it must be of sufficient magnitude.

To say that a sample population needs to be **random** means that, strictly speaking, any member of the **target population** could have been among our sample, the target population being simply the group that we are interested in in the future, such as all small-town librarians or, simply, whales. For instance, if you gave every thing or person or event in the target population a name and put all the names in a hat and then drew names from the hat, the sample of the target population would be a random sample. Of course, this is often not possible or would be very time consuming so we make compromises such as choosing every tenth name on a list (like a telephone book or a class roster).

Truly random samples are hard to come by and so we often opt for a **representative sample**. A representative sample is a selection of the target population that contains individuals (things or people or events) with a range of particular features similar to the range of particular features in the target population and in the same proportion. Which particular features are picked out to make a representative sample, again, depends on background information. If our target population is small-town librarians in the United States, then our sample population must be representative of the United States as a whole. It cannot just include librarians from Vermont or from the outskirts of Las Vegas. The proper selection of representatives is what allows presidential pollsters to predict national elections on samples as small as 1,500 responses!

This last comment brings up the issue of the magnitude of the sample. A sample of 1,500 doesn't seem like a sample of enough voters to predict a national presidential election. But pollsters know on the basis of their background knowledge, namely, their past successes and failures, how large their representative sample must be. Generally, the larger the sample, the more warranted we are in projecting into the future. Too often we can cite instances where a generalization or a prediction was not warranted because the sample was too small with respect to the target group. (For example, "I don't like people who go to State University. I met someone from there once and he was extremely stuck up.")

The Literary Digest's prediction of Alf Landon's victory in the presidential election of 1936 is a classic violation of these guidelines. *The Digest* obviously sent out a lot of ballots relative to the size of the target population. They also had a good track record using their method of presidential voter sampling. But *The Digest*, among other things, had to rely on the ballot recipients to return their ballots. Thus, its sample was not random but rather self-selected by the respondents themselves. (Surveys of sexual habits sent out by popular magazines have this same bias.) Clearly, more Republicans returned ballots than Democrats. Although *The Literary Digest* may not have had a bias toward either candidate, its straw polling procedure did!

We can see from *The Digest* example that the magnitude of the sample is only part of the story. In fact, there are times when **one** instance is enough for us to be warranted in drawing a generalization and there are times when after any number of instances we would not be willing to project the pattern into the future.[1] **In general, the better the resulting generalization fits in with other beliefs we consider warranted, the smaller the sample necessary to warrant making that generalization, and vice versa, that is, the poorer the fit between a generalization and other beliefs we hold, the larger the sample we should seek before considering it warranted.**

In the reading "Doctors as Detectives," there are several good examples of how background knowledge influences the number of instances necessary for generalizing. In the second case, for example, about Mr. J. who has bouts of incoherence over the weekend, his physician, Dr. Gottlieb, begins to suspect a connection between Mr. J.'s having not eaten for a long while and his loss of coherence. Although he has had only a few episodes of this pattern, Gottlieb suspects this pattern is generally the case. That is, every time Mr. J. has not eaten for four or five hours, he will suffer from loss of coherence and inability to concentrate. Gottlieb's background knowledge as a physician trained in the area of insulin and sugar balance warrants him in making this generalization despite the small number of times it has occurred. Of course, he will go on to confirm this generalization with other tests. The next to last case in that reading exemplifies the opposite type of situation. In this case an eighty-one-year-old woman is suspected of having a mild form of leukemia because of the results of several tests. The general good health of the woman leads her physician, Dr. Joseph, to suspect that those results were false positives; and repeated testing shows that the woman, indeed, does not have leukemia. Again, Dr. Joseph's background knowledge of the symptoms of chronic lymphocytic leukemia and the results of her clinical examination of the patient warrant her refusal to generalize the results of the previous blood tests of her patient.

From the discussion above and the examples we have looked at it is clear that background knowledge plays a big role in how successful we are at

---

[1]This point was recognized by David Hume, the philosopher who has most influenced our understanding of reasoning with probability. See, for example, his *Treatise of Human Nature*, Book I, Part III, Section VIII.

reasoning with probability. Not only does background knowledge help us to see traces and patterns of traces, as we discussed in Chapter 6, but it also helps us in judging whether to project these patterns into the future and in determining what guidelines to use in the process of generalizing or projecting.

Note: Our generalization can be warranted, that is, we can be justified in projecting from our sample of observed cases to future unobserved cases, but there is no guarantee that the outcome will be as predicted. When we project into the future we are always reasoning with probability, not with necessity.

There is something we can do, however, that can help us to avoid disappointments and unpleasant surprises and which is fundamental to our making warranted generalizations. That is, **we must always revise our store of background knowledge in light of new information.** Our store of background knowledge is not fixed. Each new case goes into our collection of observed cases and changes the warrant for making future projections. The person who is a good critical thinker is the person who is open to the increasing number of relevant cases and who does not become fixed on a certain set of background knowledge which she refuses to change.

Our background knowledge is constantly growing. When we are children, it is growing exponentially. As we grow older its growth rate slows down. Sometimes as we get old, we get stubborn and then it may grow so little that we deteriorate as critical thinkers and, consequently, as movers and shakers in the world. There is no guaranteed protection from warranted generalizations that disappoint us in the future. What we can do is protect ourselves from being disappointed by that *same* future projection. We do this by continually revising our background knowledge and, consequently, the patterns of traces that we project.

Let's look at an example of how this pattern of continual revision works. The high incidence of Lou Gehrig's disease among 1964 San Francisco 49ers can illustrate this point. In 1964 it would have been warranted to believe that members of the 49ers team ran the same risk as everyone else of developing Lou Gehrig's disease, that is, about a one in 100,000 chance. With three members of this team having developed the disease, however, one would be warranted in thinking that members of the 1964 team have a better than average chance of being stricken. Hence, scientists have been looking for some causal agent which could have brought about this statistical anomaly. Of course, this cluster of cases could be simply an unhappy coincidence; but given the gravity of the matter, one is certainly justified in looking for a causal agent to avoid possible future cases.

We perform these revisions in the patterns we note all the time. After being bitten by a dog, we are more careful the next time we encounter an unfamiliar canine. If we find ourselves underprepared for Dr. Smith's exam, we study harder for the next exam. If Joe is a practical joker who likes to pull the chair out from under people when they sit down, we sit down slowly when Joe is around. But sometimes we become lazy or even stubborn and refuse or fail to revise our generalizations in the light of new experiences. Again, in the story about the 49ers, we see Patrick Marchese unwilling even to consider a link between his product, Milorganite, and ALS. He calls a link "patently absurd." His failure to be open to the **possibility** of a linkage could have had dire consequences, just as cigarette smokers' (and the tobacco industry's) previous refusal to acknowledge a link between cigarette smoking and lung cancer had dire consequences for many individuals, including some nonsmokers. We are fortunate that our background knowledge is continually growing. As critical thinkers we must grow and adjust our thinking accordingly.

Before looking at some alternative forms of reasoning with probability, let's review the guidelines mentioned in this section which can help us to reason well. These guidelines are very general and apply to all forms of reasoning with probability. Statistics and probability theory are sources of more specific applications of this kind of reasoning and are useful to physical scientists and social scientists.

Guidelines for good reasoning with probability:

1. Proceed with caution. Remember, there are no guarantees that the future will be like the past.

2. Be open to the world around you. Look for traces and patterns of traces. The storehouse of background knowledge you bring to the reasoning process is crucial to the success of your projections.

3. Base your projections on an appropriate sample. Generally, this means that the sample must be either random or representative and it must be of sufficient magnitude relative to the size of the target group.

4. Continually revise your projections (generalizations) in light of your increasing storehouse of background knowledge.

Analogies

Analogies are an important form of reasoning with probability. Since no two things in the world are identical, for every analogy (or similarity) we see in the world, there is always a disanalogy (or dissimilarity). That is, no matter how much alike two (or more) individuals (things) are, there is always some way in which they are not alike. Consider, for example, identical twins. No matter how much alike they are, people who know them well can usually find something that can be used to distinguish them. Or consider two identical automobiles just off the assembly line. If they have no other difference, they at least have the difference of occupying different spaces. Hence, our reasoning using analogies is always probable, never certain. We talked about argument by analogy in Chapter 3. The underlying principle is the same here. The principle is that it is reasonable to assume that if two things share a number of features, they also have additional properties in common. You can see that this is another type of projection of a **pattern** because we are projecting from a set of observed cases possessing a certain **pattern** of properties to some additional cases where the whole pattern has yet to be observed.

"Doctors as Detectives" presents us with a good example of reasoning by analogy in the case of Mr. R., who suffered a severe electrical shock at work. Because his doctors were able to see the ultrasound images of his heart as having the same properties that ultrasound images of hearts damaged in automobile accidents have, they were able to make a diagnosis that saved Mr. R.'s life. The pattern of reasoning looks like this:

Case A has the properties P_1, P_2, P_3, P_4, P_5.

Case B has the properties P_1, P_2, P_3, P_4, so Case B probably also has the property P_5.

This is a very common form of reasoning. Here we see it used in medicine but it is just as fundamental to law (treating like cases alike); to grading tests, papers, or products; or to testing the effectiveness of new drugs, where we reason from the effectiveness in rats to the effectiveness in humans. There is also a well-known theological argument which uses reasoning from analogy to support the claim that God exists. William Paley proposed a version of this argument in 1805 in his book *Natural Theology*. There he argues that the universe is like a great big watch, filled with careful design and order. Just as the watch must be made by a watchmaker, so the universe must be made by a super watchmaker, namely God.[2]

Reasoning by analogy presents us with some of the same reasoning puzzles as generalizations. We have already talked about patterns and how some people see patterns that others do not. This raises the problem when dealing with analogies of whether to focus on the analogous features or the disanalogous. The example of testing drugs (and other products) on rats to see if the drugs are safe for humans illustrates this problem. How meaning-

---

[2]For another view of the analogy between the universe and a watch look at the philosopher David Hume's (mentioned in Footnote 1) reply to Paley. This can be found in his *Dialogues Concerning Natural Religion*, Parts II, V, and VII.

ful such a test is depends on whether rats are sufficiently analogous to humans physically so that it makes sense to say rats and humans will have analogous reactions to the same product.[3]

Whether we focus on similarities or dissimilarities depends on our interest or what we value at the time. It's like the situation with twins. Sometimes you focus on the ways they are alike. Other times you note, or try to figure out for purposes of identification, how they are different. Neither focus is better all the time. Again, background knowledge is important. Background knowledge tells us which features to focus on, given our interest. This can be clearly seen in the medical cases in the readings. In the case of Mr. R., the doctors realized that the electrical shock Mr. R. suffered could be similar in thrust and impact to the thrust and impact of an automobile accident. In the first case of that same reading, the case of Mr. K., the doctors used their background knowledge to recognize the similarity of the joint pain and joint inflammation Mr. K. was suffering to the symptoms of juvenile rheumatoid arthritis, even though Mr. K. was in his early thirties.

The readings which most clearly demonstrate reasoning by analogy are the ones concerned with the authorship of the poem "Shall I die? . . ." These readings show both the usefulness and the weaknesses of reasoning by analogy. Analogy is the main form of reasoning used by both sides in this argument. The poem has many properties commonly found in poems by Shakespeare. Therefore, argues Gary Taylor, it has the further unobservable property of having been authored by Shakespeare. No, says Anthony Burgess, the poem is a song, a very good song, and Shakespeare was just not that careful about his songs. Burgess himself says that it's "instinct" which tells the Shakespearean scholar whether this poem is from the bard himself. What he means by instinct is background knowledge. One must listen to the poem, he says, and compare that sound with the sounds of other poems in one's background knowledge. Burgess even goes so far as to impugn the background knowledge of Taylor because Taylor is from Kansas!

This dispute over a possible lost poem of Shakespeare shows that reasoning by analogy is not conclusive. But it is still a very useful form of reasoning with probability which we use frequently in our daily lives. Like reasoning with generalizations, we need to keep in mind guidelines to avoid disappointment and too much surprise in our lives.

---

[3]A well-known controversial case here was a study that showed that laboratory rats exposed to large amounts of saccharin developed cancer in significant numbers. Some people argued that the amount of saccharin consumed by the rats was so great that the results had little relevance for humans who would be consuming only small amounts in diet sodas or other products. That is, they argued that the two situations were not sufficiently analogous for the test results to be taken seriously for humans. What must be kept in mind in this particular case, however, is that it is not the amount of a substance that makes it carcinogenic.

Guidelines for good reasoning using analogies:

1. Keep in mind that reasoning by analogy is always probable, never certain.

2. Remember that your reasoning by analogy depends on background knowledge and how well the reasoning fits in with that background knowledge.

3. Realize that the reasoning becomes more warranted with increasing numbers of cases.

4. Constantly revise the conclusions you draw on the basis of analogy as you encounter more and more cases and add them to your storehouse of background knowledge.

Causal Claims

One of the **patterns** we observe and then use to our advantage is the pattern of correlation. Correlations occur between events or properties which happen together frequently or even constantly. Some correlations are coincidental. Others, we say, are causal in nature. The events or properties are so correlated with one another as to be conjoined. This is because the first **causes** the second. They *have* to happen that way. These are the correlations of interest to us since they help us to expect and control future events in our lives. As with warranted and unwarranted generalizations, we are usually very good at distinguishing coincidental correlations from causal connections. However, we have the same problem of having no rule for drawing a firm distinction between coincidental correlations and causal connections. Rather, we can have only guidelines for making warranted causal claims.

Consider the well-known example of the correlation between cigarette smoking and the incidence of lung cancer. The two are said to be significantly correlated. This means that a much greater percentage of people who smoke cigarettes end up with lung cancer than in the general population or in the population of nonsmokers. Is this just a coincidence? Have smokers just had bad luck? Have they tended to live in environments with other pollutants which cause lung cancer? Or does the correlation indicate a causal relation? After all, not all smokers develop lung cancer. As you know, many smokers refuse to acknowledge that this higher than expected correlation indicates a causal connection.

Let's consider two cases of correlations about which there is little disagreement. If you let go of your pencil in midair, it falls to the ground. Every time you let go of it, it falls to the ground. Letting go of it and its falling to the ground are so highly correlated that you certainly believe a causal rela-tion is involved. It *has to* fall to the ground. On the other hand, suppose every time you reach in your pocket for a coin, the coin you come up with is a penny. Even if this happened time after time, you would never believe that if a coin is in your pocket it has to be a penny. You observe constant conjunction but refuse to attribute a causal connection! This is the puzzle of causal reasoning: How do we distinguish between causation and mere cor-relation if all we have to go on is our experience of the world, namely, our experience of constant conjunction?

The philosopher Hume noted that when it comes to causation there is a gap between what we experience and what we believe on the basis of that experience. What we experience is constant conjunction. The pencil's being let go is constantly conjoined with the pencil's falling to the floor. Lightning is always followed by thunder. Salt dropped in water always dissolves. This constant conjoining of events leads us to **expect** that in the future if the first event occurs it will be followed by the second event; in fact, it leads us to say that the second *has* to happen. The connection between the events is a necessary one because the first event is **causing** the second. Notice that this necessary connection is *not* something we observe (What would it look like?) but rather is something we attribute to our experience. **There is always a gap between our experience and what we say about it when we talk about causation.**[4]

To put this point another way, there is no mark on experience, that is, no regularly occurring feature of the experience itself, that tells us this cor-relation between events is coincidental (accidental) and that correlation between events is necessary (causal).[5] Consequently, we sometimes make mistakes and attribute causal connections where there are none (for example, "That teacher gave me a bad grade because she doesn't like me.") and some-times we fail to see causal connections where we ought to ("I don't know why I didn't see the red light. I've only had a few beers."). What is truly sur-prising—and fortunate—is that we make relatively few mistakes in this regard.

---

[4]Sometimes we fill in the gap with technological descriptions, so the gap seems to get filled in. This filling in, however, is never complete. What happens is the big gap gets divided into smaller sections with gaps within the sections. Gaps remain. For example, for the ordinary person, pushing on the brake pedal causes the car to stop. The mechanic can fill in this causal gap with a number of mechanical connections but each one of the causal connections in the mechanic's causal chain contains a gap. Similarly, to say that gravity causes the pencil to fall does not eliminate the gap between what we experience and what we say about it. In many ways introducing gravity makes the gap wider, for what is gravity but a name for a force, which, like a cause, is something else we do not observe but which is part of our description of the world.

[5]The situation is similar to the difference between dreaming and being awake. While these two states are certainly different, there is nothing in the dream itself, while you are hav-ing it, that tells you "You are only dreaming." Everything happens as if you were wide awake. You know you were dreaming only afterwards—when you wake up.

That is, our expectations of necessary connections between events are usually born out in practice so we are not generally disappointed and we are very good at using those expectations to control, to some extent at least, our environment.

Since there is no mark on our experience of causation, there is no way to confirm the distinctions we draw between necessary and accidental connections. The only experiential difference we have is that with connections we deem necessary connections we have a psychological process of expectation which we do not have with accidental connections (correlations). We cannot set down any rules to guarantee that we are always right in our expectations. The best we can do in this case is to suggest some guidelines for causal reasoning based on the logical concepts of necessary and sufficient conditions. In our ordinary usage of the term *cause* we sometimes mean a sufficient condition, sometimes a necessary condition, and sometimes the set of both necessary and sufficient conditions. Necessary and sufficient conditions are **logical patterns** we impose on our experience of constant conjunction and our psychological experience of expectation to give that experience more order.

X is a sufficient condition for Y if every time X occurs, Y occurs. X is always followed by Y (or is simultaneous with Y). For example, if you drop salt in water, it dissolves. The salt's being dropped in water is a sufficient condition for the salt's dissolving. Dropping salt in water causes it to dissolve. But we might also say that the water causes the salt to dissolve. Water, that is, ordinary water that is not already saturated, is a necessary condition for dissolving salt. **Y is a necessary condition for X if whenever X occurs, Y occurs, or X cannot occur without Y.** (See Chapter 5 for a discussion of these formal logical relations.) And in some contexts it is appropriate to list both the necessary and sufficient conditions of an event as its cause: Dropping salt in ordinary water causes it to dissolve.

To be clear about this point, consider another example. You strike a match and the match lights. What caused the match to light? Striking it caused it to light. Striking it was sufficient, in that context, to cause it to light. But striking is not a necessary condition of a match's lighting. It could have ignited by being touched by another flame or by the rays of the sun focused on it with a magnifying glass. Also, we know that other conditions are necessary for the match's lighting. The match must not be wet. There must be oxygen. There must be a scratch pad to create friction. If we state all the necessary and sufficient conditions for the match's lighting, we could have quite a long list. (In fact, the list could go on and on. Usually we just aren't interested in the whole causal chain.) Most commonly we speak of the cause as the last event (striking the match) to complete a set of conditions sufficient for bringing about the effect (the match's lighting). Background knowledge comes into play. It is our background knowledge and our knowledge of the context which enable us to select from among the set of necessary and suffi-cient conditions for an event, one condition which we speak of as *the cause* of that event.

The philosopher John Stuart Mill set out some guidelines for deter-mining the cause of an event in his *System of Logic,* published in 1843. These guidelines have become known as Mill's methods. These are the method of agreement, the method of difference, the joint method of agreement and dif-ference, the method of residues, and the method of concomitant variation. We will consider only variations of the first two here. These methods are sug-gested by common sense. You have probably used them yourself at times when trying to figure out the cause of an event in your experience. For exam-ple, you may have tried to figure out why your face broke out so badly before the big dance or why the computer lost the paper you were writing for your history course.

In the first case, you might try to determine the cause by thinking back to other times that your face broke out, looking for some common factor that was present in all the cases. Perhaps the common factor is stress, a new face

"Has it ever occurred to anyone that if we stopped wearing these damned skirts we wouldn't have to march off to defend our manhood every five minutes?"

Perhaps the relevant common factor is wearing a kilt. Drawing by Ziegler; © 1995, The New Yorker Magazine, Inc.

cream, or something you ate. The success of your search for the cause will depend on how many cases you examine and the thoroughness with which you look for a common element, discarding elements which only appear in some of the cases. (This is a common-sense version of Mill's method of agreement.)

In the second case, you would probably look for what went wrong. (Similar to Mill's method of difference.) You would try to determine what you did this time while you were using the computer that you had not done before when you used it successfully. That is, you would try to find some relevant difference between this occasion that went awry and the other past times you successfully used the computer to prepare your paper. You may have hit a wrong key and accidentally erased it, there may have been a power surge that wiped it out, or someone may have handed you a highly magnetized object that interfered with the electrical circuitry of the computer. For your determination of the cause to be successful in this case you must not jump to conclusions too quickly. There may be several apparent differences that you may have to eliminate as possibilities and you will have to be careful to consider only relevant differences. That you were wearing your blue sweater for the first time is not relevant. That you were wearing an awkward bangle bracelet that caught on the keyboard might be relevant.

Making causal statements is an awful lot like making generalizations. A lot of our success depends on our **background knowledge**. There is no way, for instance, that the word *relevant* can be eliminated from the discussion of the above example, nor can it be characterized in a noncircular way which would help us avoid every mistake. Our background knowledge is what keeps us from making a lot of mistakes. It enables us to be selective in our choices of causal factors. Our background knowledge tells us that the color of our clothing is irrelevant to the operation of a computer. It also tells us that computers are directly responsive to the key we hit on the keyboard. If we mistype, we get what we typed.

Background knowledge also gives us more sophisticated guidelines. For all of our background knowledge is not alike. Some of our background knowledge is more fundamental to our ways of looking at the world than others. In the words of the philosopher Nelson Goodman, some of our beliefs are more **entrenched** than others.[6] A common-sense understanding of what Goodman means is that these beliefs lie deeper and more centrally in our web of belief than do other beliefs and, therefore, if we try to change them or remove them from our web of belief, we disturb many other beliefs that are connected to them. Consequently, the more entrenched a belief is, the less willing we are

---

[6] *Fact, Fiction and Forecast*, Cambridge: Harvard University Press, 1988.

to give it up because giving it up means giving up a great many other beliefs as well. Some beliefs are easy to give up. For example, suppose you believe that it is cold outside. Then you go out and find that the day is balmy. Other beliefs are much harder to give up. Your beliefs about what happens to a pencil when someone lets go of it in midair are very entrenched. Just think how shocked you would be if you let go of a pencil and it just stayed there, somehow suspended in space! We are not conscious of the pattern of entrenchment of our beliefs until one of them gets challenged. But it is there all the same. This pattern is not the same for everyone, but similarities of pattern will tend to characterize different groups of people, for example, family members, Americans, Asians, Catholics, or Muslims.

Entrenchment is a very important factor in our ability to distinguish accidental correlations from necessary connections or causal connections. To see how entrenchment works in causal reasoning let's go back to the earlier example of pennies in your pocket. Although you might pull one hundred (or even two hundred!) pennies from your pocket, you would continue to believe that this correlation between being a penny and being in your pocket is an accidental one, not a necessary one. Although you are experiencing constant conjunction between these two events, nothing else in your past experience or background knowledge supports a causal connection between a coin's being in your pocket and its being a penny. It is a well-entrenched belief of yours that coins don't change their denomination by being in a certain place. And this belief is connected with other well-entrenched beliefs about metals, the nature of pockets, and so on, all of which would have to be altered to **fit** with a new belief in a causal connection between being in your pocket and being a penny.

On the other hand, if you let go of your pencil and it stayed suspended in midair, you would suspect some unanticipated causal factor. A magician's string, perhaps. Or a stream of air blowing up beneath it. Your belief that there is a necessary connection between the pencil's being let go of and the pencil's falling is so well entrenched that you were already expecting the sound of the pencil hitting the floor! So we can see that background knowledge and well-entrenched beliefs about causal connections enable us most of the time to distinguish between accidental correlations and necessary connections. **It is important to remember, however, that even our well-entrenched beliefs are still only based on the experience of constant conjunction.**

Not only does entrenchment help us to distinguish accidental correlations from causal connections, it also helps us avoid a common error of causal reasoning, namely, the fallacy of *post hoc, ergo propter hoc.* This is a fallacy of thinking that just because X is followed by Y, X caused Y. While it is true that causes always precede their effects, it does not follow that whatever precedes an event is the cause of that event. Just because the last thing you did before the computer lost your paper was eat a candy bar, it would be poor causal reasoning to attribute the loss of your paper to the eating of the candy bar. It does not fit in with other well-entrenched beliefs you have about the nature of computers—unless, of course, you happened to have dropped some candy on your floppy disk before trying to print out your paper. It is easy to fall into *post hoc* reasoning because, again, there is no mark or distinguishing feature of experience which distinguishes necessary connections from accidental ones. While preceding the effect is a necessary condition for being a cause, it is not a sufficient condition for being a cause.

The reading about the 49ers football team presents some interesting examples for causal reasoning. You will remember that the players of the 1964 49ers team have a much higher incidence of victims of Lou Gehrig's disease than the population in general. That is, there is a higher than normal correlation between being a member of the 1964 49ers football team and being a victim of Lou Gehrig's disease. The obvious question is whether this correlation is accidental or causal in nature. If this unusual correlation is not accidental, then something may be learned from it which could benefit future victims. It should be clear from the discussion in this chapter that there is no sure way to decide; and as might be expected, different people quoted in the article have different views on the matter.

The investigators in the story were, in effect, applying Mill's methods. They looked for some common element that the three victims experienced, such as the fertilizer on the practice field, the DMSO ointment the men used to combat soreness, or the anabolic steroids some of them took. The common element they turned up was the Milorganite fertilizer. The claim that there is a necessary connection between the fertilizer and ALS, however, does not fit well with the background knowledge of most of the people involved in the case. Notice that Patrick Marchese, the executive director of the sewerage district responsible for the fertilizer, has particularly well entrenched beliefs which would conflict with the claim of a necessary connection between the fertilizer and ALS. Since there are many causal factors involved in why some people get a disease like ALS and others do not, it is very hard to track down common elements among cases. Also, the physical body is such a complicated organism with many internal causal chains that it is difficult to determine what is different about these three men who contracted this fatal illness. The higher than normal correlation only gives us a clue that some unknown additional causal agent may be at work here and more research will have to be done.

It should be clear from this discussion that the guidelines for good causal reasoning are similar to those for the other forms of reasoning with probability. The importance of background information is again quite clear. We cannot be good critical thinkers without having knowledge of the world around us. This is why we must be open and willing to watch and listen to that world.

Guidelines for good causal reasoning:

1. Proceed with caution. Remember that experience is only of constant conjunction, not of necessary connection, so it is easy to make mistakes when reasoning about causes.

2. Since mistakes are likely, always be ready to revise your causal claims. (This is true even for scientific, laboratory-tested claims, as we will show in the next chapter.)

3. Evaluate your causal claims by how well they fit together with the background knowledge you bring to your experience. When you have conflicting causal beliefs or are uncertain, look to your most well entrenched beliefs and look for the best fit with those beliefs. Since there is no mark on experience which would enable you to distinguish necessary connections from accidental correlations, this fitting in with your well-entrenched beliefs is your best guide in causal reasoning.

4. Look for the common factor when you have a number of similar occurrences. When you have one unique case (or unusual correlation), look for the relevant specific difference in that case.

From these guidelines and the guidelines set out earlier for the other forms of reasoning with probability, we can see that our projections are warranted if our projections are effective. By the same token, our projections are effective if they are warranted. There is no noncircular warrant for our reasoning with probability. We can avoid a vicious circle here, however, if we continue to increase our background knowledge and adjust our projections in light of new experience. **That is, to make sense out of our own experience together with others' reports, we must continually test our reasoning against future experience and adjust our background knowledge and projections in light of the results of those testings.**

EXERCISES

7–1

1. What are the guidelines for good reasoning using analogies?

2. What are the guidelines for good causal reasoning?

3. List the analogies and disanalogies cited by the experts between Shakespeare's poetry and the poem "Shall I die? . . ." Which list do you think is the stronger? Why?

7–II

1. Explain what a phobia is using concepts you have learned in this chapter. How can a phobia be seen as a failure of reasoning with probability?

2. Why is a telephone book not a good source for a random sample?

3. You may have heard the generalization "Everyone always acts in her own self-interest." How would you argue for or against this generalization? Are there better or worse ways of arguing here?

7–III

1. Explain why a bigot is not a good critical thinker.

2. When would it be more appropriate to use a random sample as opposed to a representative sample? When would it be more appropriate to use a representative sample instead of a random sample?

3. Critically evaluate the warning found on cigarette packages.

4. *The Literary Digest* articles continually talk about the assumptions one could make in analyzing the straw ballot it conducted. Are there any assumptions they made or failed to make that could have saved them from embarrassment?

5. Suppose someone said that it couldn't be the fertilizer that caused three members of the 1964 San Francisco 49ers to develop ALS because, if it were, it should have affected everyone, not just three team members. What would you say to them in response?

chapter 8

Scientific Reasoning

Introduction

It is very important in trying to become better critical thinkers to take a close look at scientific reasoning because science is considered to be very successful at predicting and controlling the world around us, enabling us to survive and even prosper. Hence, it is often taken as *the* model of good reasoning. Other disciplines, in fact, have tried to copy what they perceive as the pattern of scientific reasoning, even going so far as to call themselves "sciences" (for example, "social science"). Scientific reasoning is supposed to be different somehow, yielding accurate descriptions of the world, where other forms of good reasoning are distorted by assumptions and human biases, thereby producing less accurate results.

In this chapter you will see that scientific reasoning is not different from other forms of good reasoning. The scientist makes decisions about theories much the same way the person out shopping decides what to buy. You will also see that the method of science is not "the scientific method" most of you were taught. Science, in fact, is like other forms of reasoning or other disciplines in its use of assumptions and its reliance on background information. After all, science is based on the general principle we discussed in Chapter

7, namely, the principle that the future will be like the past (the principle of induction) and, hence, is subject to all the uncertainties of reasoning with probability that we have already discussed.

The reading in this chapter is from a book by Morris Kline, *Mathematics and the Search for Knowledge*. It discusses an event very familiar to you, the formulation of the hypothesis put forward by Copernicus that the sun is in the center of the universe and that Earth goes around the sun. What's different about Kline's discussion is that he approaches this discovery from the point of view of history. Like other disciplines, science has a history. Science courses tend to overlook this fact, which is unfortunate because it is a very fascinating history and one which reveals a great deal about the nature of scientific reasoning. We think you will have a renewed interest in science after reading this piece on a classic episode in the history of science.

The Heliocentric Theory of Copernicus and Kepler

MORRIS KLINE

Nevertheless it moves.

Galileo

The subject of this chapter is an oft-told tale concerning the adoption of a heliocentric theory of our planetary system, which replaced the Ptolemaic geocentric theory. Of course, the heliocentric theory seems now to be the correct one—but why should we accept it? It is contrary to our basic sensations. Does mathematics have anything to do with the acceptance of such a radical change in our conception of the physical world?

According to the heliocentric theory, the Earth rotates on its axis and completes a rotation every twenty-four hours of our measurement of time. What this means is that a person on the equator rotates through 25,000 miles in twenty-four hours or roughly at the rate of 1000 miles per hour. We may judge the incredible magnitude of this speed by our experience with speeds of 100 miles per hour in an automobile. Moreover, the Earth revolves

---

From *Mathematics and the Search for Knowledge.*

around the sun at the rate of 18 miles per second or 64,800 miles per hour, another incredible speed. Yet here on Earth we do not feel either the rotational or the revolving motion. Moreover, if we are rotating at a speed of even 100 miles an hour, why are we not thrown off into space? Most of us have ridden on a merry-go-round, which rotates at about 100 feet per second, and felt the force that would eject us into space if we did not hold on to some fixed object on the merry-go-round.

Yet today we accept the heliocentric theory as factual, although traces of the older geocentric theory are still in our everyday language. We still say that the sun rises in the East and sets in the West. Accordingly, the sun moves, not we on a rotating Earth.

Why did mathematicians and astronomers make the drastic change to a heliocentric theory? As we shall see, the role of mathematics was decisive in this revolution. We have already seen . . . that the Europeans learned about the Greek works, which emphasized the mathematical design of nature. This belief was reinforced by the Catholic doctrine, which dominated in the Middle Ages, that God had designed the universe. Presumably mathematics was the essence of this design.

During the Italian Renaissance the Greek mathematical works were recovered from numerous sources and bought by the literate. Perhaps the enterprising merchants of the Italian towns received more than they bargained for when they aided the revival of Greek culture. They sought merely to promote a freer atmosphere; they reaped a whirlwind. Instead of continuing to dwell and prosper on firm ground, the terra firma of an immovable Earth, they found themselves clinging precariously to a rapidly spinning globe that was speeding about the sun at an inconceivable rate. It was probably sorry recompense to these merchants that the very same theory that shook the Earth free and set it spinning and revolving also freed the human mind.

The reviving Italian universities were the fertile soil for these new blossoms of thought. There, Nicolaus Copernicus became imbued with the Greek conviction that nature's behavior can be described by a harmonious medley of mathematical laws, and there, too, he became acquainted with the hypothesis—also Hellenic in origin—of planetary motion about a stationary sun. In Copernicus's mind these two ideas coalesced. Harmony in the universe demanded a heliocentric theory, and he became willing to move heaven and earth to establish it.

Copernicus was born in Poland in 1473. After studying mathematics and science at the University of Krakow, he decided to go to Bologna, where learning was more widespread. There he studied astronomy under the influential teacher Domenico Maria Novara, a foremost Pythagorean. In 1512 he assumed the position of canon of the cathedral of Frauenburg in East Prussia, his duties being that of steward of church properties and justice of the peace. During the remaining thirty-one years of his life he spent much time in a little tower of the cathedral closely observing the planets with the naked eye and making untold measurements with crude homemade instruments. The rest of his spare time he devoted to improving his new theory of the motions of heavenly bodies.

Copernicus's published works gave unmistakable, if indirect, indications of his reasons for devoting himself to astronomy. Judging by these, his intellectual and religious interests were dominant. He valued his theory of planetary motion, not because it improved navigational procedures but because it revealed the true harmony, symmetry, and design in the divine workshop. It was wonderful and overpowering evidence of God's presence. Writing of his achievement, which was thirty years in the making, Copernicus could not restrain his gratification: "We find, therefore, under this orderly arrangement a wonderful symmetry in the universe, and a definite relation of harmony in the motion and magnitude of the orbs, of a kind that is not possible to obtain in any other way." He does mention in the preface to his major work *On the Revolution of the Heavenly Spheres* (1543), that he was asked by the Lateran Council to help in reforming the calendar, which had become deranged over a period of many centuries. He writes that he kept this problem in mind, but it is quite clear that it never dominated his thinking.

By the time Copernicus tackled the problem of the motions of the planets, the Arabs, in their efforts to improve the accuracy of Ptolemaic theory, had added more epicycles, and their theory required a total of seventy-seven circles to describe the motion of the sun, moon, and the five planets then known. To many astronomers, including Copernicus, this theory was scandalously complex.

Harmony demanded a more pleasing theory than the complicated extension of Ptolemaic theory. Copernicus, having read that some Greek authors, notably Aristarchus, had suggested the possibility that the Earth revolved about a stationary sun and rotated on its axis at the same time, decided to explore this possibility. He was in a sense overimpressed with Greek thought, for he also believed that the motions of heavenly bodies must be circular or, at worst, a combination of circular motions, because circular motion was "natural" motion. Moreover, he also accepted the belief that each planet must move at a constant speed on its epicycle, and that the center of each epicycle must move at a constant speed on the circle that carried it. Such principles were axiomatic for him. Copernicus even added an argument that shows the somewhat mystical character of sixteenth-century thinking. He found that a variable speed could be caused only by a variable power; but God, the cause of all motions, is constant.

The upshot of his reasoning was that he used the scheme of deferent and epicycle to describe the motions of the heavenly bodies; however, the all-important difference in his version was that the sun was at the center of each deferent, while the Earth itself became a planet moving about the sun and rotating on its axis. Thus, he achieved considerable simplification.

To understand the changes Copernicus introduced, we shall confine ourselves to a simplified example. Copernicus observed that by having the planet P revolve about the sun S (Figure 22), and by having the Earth E also revolve about the sun, the positions of P as observed from E would still be the same. Hence the motion of the planet P is described by one circle, whereas the geocentric view calls for two circles. Of course, the motion of a planet around the sun is not strictly circular, and Copernicus added epicycles to the circles shown in Figure 22 to describe the motions of P and E more accurately. Nevertheless, he was able to reduce the number of circles required from seventy-seven to thirty-four to "explain the whole dance of the planets." Thus, the heliocentric view permitted a considerable simplification in the description of the planetary motions.

It is of interest to note that about 1530 Copernicus circulated a short account of his new ideas in a little tract called the *Commentariolus* and that Cardinal Nicolaus von Schönberg, the archbishop of Capua, wrote to Copernicus urging him to make the full work known and begging him for a copy to be made at the cardinal's expense. However, Copernicus dreaded the furor he knew his work would generate and for years shrank from publication. He entrusted his manuscript on the revolutions to Tiedemann Giese, bishop of Kulm, who, with the aid of Georg Joachim Rheticus, a professor at the University of Wittenberg, got the book published. A Lutheran theologian, Andreas Osiander, who assisted in the printing and feared trouble, added an unsigned preface of his own. Osiander stated that the new work was a hypothesis that allowed computations of the heavenly motions on geometrical principles, adding that this hypothesis was not the real situation. Whoever takes for truth what was designed for different purposes, he added, will leave the science of astronomy a greater fool than when he approached it. Of course, Osiander did not reflect Copernicus's views, for Copernicus

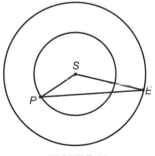

FIGURE 22

believed that the motion of the Earth was a physical reality. While lying paralyzed from a stroke, Copernicus received a copy of his book. It is unlikely that he was able to read it, for he never recovered. He died shortly afterward, in the year 1543.

The Copernican hypothesis of a stationary sun considerably simplified astronomical theory and calculations, but otherwise it was not impressively accurate. Copernicus fell far short of even 10 degrees of accuracy in predicting the angular positions of planets. He therefore tried variations on the basic plan of deferent and epicycle, with the sun, of course, always stationary and either at or near the center of the deferent. Although these variations were not much more successful, the failures did not diminish his enthusiasm for the heliocentric view.

When Copernicus surveyed the extraordinary mathematical simplification that the heliocentric hypothesis afforded, his satisfaction and enthusiasm were unbounded. He had found a simpler mathematical account of the motions of the heavens and hence one that must be preferred, for Copernicus, like all scientists of the Renaissance, was convinced that "Nature is pleased with simplicity, and affects not the pomp of superfluous causes." Copernicus could pride himself, too, on the fact that he had dared to think through what others, including Archimedes, had rejected as absurd.

As far as the mathematics of Copernican astronomy is concerned, it is purely a geometrical account involving no more than a reduction of a complex geometrical description to a simpler one. However, the religious and metaphysical principles affected by the change in theory were numerous and fundamental. On this account it is easy to see why a mathematician thinking only in terms of mathematics and unencumbered by nonmathematical principles would not hesitate to accept at once the Copernican simplification, while those who were guided chiefly or entirely by religious or metaphysical principles would not even venture to think in terms of a heliocentric theory. In fact, for a long time only mathematicians supported Copernicus.

As one would expect, a heliocentric theory that downgraded humanity's importance in the universe met severe condemnation. Martin Luther called Copernicus an "upstart astrologer" and "a fool who wishes to reverse the entire science of astronomy." John Calvin thundered, "Who will venture to place the authority of Copernicus above that of the Holy Spirit?" Do not the Scriptures say that Joshua commanded the sun and not the Earth to stand still? That the sun runs from one end of the heavens to the other? That the foundations of the Earth are fixed and cannot be moved?

The Inquisition condemned the new theory as "that false Pythagorean doctrine utterly contrary to the Holy Scriptures." The Catholic Church, in an official statement, called Copernicanism a heresy "more scandalous, more detestable, and more pernicious to Christianity than any contained in the books of Calvin, of Luther, and of all other heretics put together."

To these attacks Copernicus replied in a letter to Pope Paul III:

> If perhaps there are babblers who, although completely ignorant of mathematics, nevertheless take it upon themselves to pass judgment on mathematical questions and, improperly distorting some passages of the Scriptures to their purpose, dare to find fault with my system and censure it, I disregard them even to the extent of despising their judgment as uninformed.

Moreover, Copernicus added, the Bible may teach us how to go to heaven but not how the heavens go.

Although the hypothesis of a stationary sun simplified considerably astronomical theory and calculations, the epicyclic paths of the planets, as noted, did not quite fit observations. The definitive improvement was made some fifty years later by that almost incredible mystic, rationalist, and empiricist, Johann Kepler (1571–1630), a German who combined wonderful imaginative power and emotional exuberance with infinite patience in acquiring data and with meticulous adherence to the dictates of facts. The personal life of Kepler contrasts sharply with that of Copernicus. The latter had obtained an excellent education as a youth and lived a retired and secure life, which he was able to devote almost solely to his theorizing. Kepler, born in 1571 with delicate health, was neglected by his parents and received a rather poor education. Like most boys of his time who showed some interest in learning, he was expected to study for the ministry. In 1589 he enrolled at the German University of Tübingen where he learned astronomy from an enthusiastic Copernican, Michael Mästlin. Kepler was impressed by the new theory, but the superiors of the Lutheran Church were not and questioned Kepler's devoutness. Kepler's objections to the narrowness of the current Lutheran thought led him to abandon a ministerial career and accept the position of professor of mathematics and morals at the University of Graz in Styria, Austria, where he lectured on mathematics, astronomy, rhetoric, and Virgil. He was also called on to make astrological predictions, which at the time he seems to have believed in. He set out to master the art and practiced by checking predictions of his own fortunes. Later in life he became less credulous and used to warn his clients, "What I say will or will not come to pass."

At Graz, Kepler introduced the new calendar advocated by Pope Gregory XIII. The Protestants rejected it, because they preferred to be at variance with the sun rather than in accordance with the Pope. Unfortunately, the liberal Catholic ruler of Styria was succeeded by an intolerant one, and Kepler found life uncomfortable. Although he was protected by the Jesuits for a while, and could have stayed by professing Catholicism, he refused to do so and finally left Graz.

In 1600 he secured a position as assistant to the famous astronomical observer Tycho Brahe (1546–1601), who had been making the first large revision of astronomical data since Greek times. On Brahe's death in 1601 Kepler succeeded him as "Imperial Mathematician" to Emperor Rudolph II of Bohemia. This employer, too, expected Kepler to cast horoscopes for members of the court. Kepler resigned himself to this duty with the philosophical view that nature provided all animals with a means of existence. He was wont to refer to astrology as the daughter of astronomy who nursed her own mother.

About ten years after Kepler joined him in Prague, the Emperor Rudolph began to experience political troubles and could not afford to pay Kepler's salary; thus Kepler had to find another job. In 1612 he accepted the position of provincial mathematician at Linz, but other difficulties still plagued him. While he was at Prague Kepler's wife and one son had died. He remarried, but at Linz two more of his children died; in addition to personal tragedy, the Protestants did not accept him, and money was scarce, forcing him to struggle for existence. In 1620 Linz was conquered by the Catholic Duke Maximilian of Bavaria, and Kepler suffered still stronger persecution. Ill health began to weaken him. The last few years of his life were spent in trying to secure publication of more books, collecting salary owed to him, and searching for a new position.

Kepler's scientific reasoning is fascinating. Like Copernicus he was a mystic, and like Copernicus he believed that the world was designed by God in accordance with some simple and beautiful mathematical plan. "Thus God himself was too kind to remain idle, and began to play the game of signatures, signifying his likeness into the world; therefore I chance to think that all nature and the graceful sky are symbolized in the art of geometry." He says further in his *Mystery of the Cosmos* (1596), the mathematical harmonies in the mind of the Creator furnish the cause "why the number, the size, and the motion of the orbits are as they are and not otherwise." This belief dominated all his thinking.

Still, Kepler also had qualities that we now associate with scientists. He could be coldly rational. Although his fertile imagination triggered the conception of new theoretical systems, he knew that theories must fit observations and, in his later years, saw even more clearly that empirical data may indeed suggest the fundamental principles of science. He therefore sacrificed his most beloved mathematical hypotheses when he saw that they did not fit observational data, and it was precisely this incredible persistence in refusing to tolerate discrepancies, which any other scientist of his day would have disregarded, that led him to espouse radical ideas. He also had the humility, patience, and energy that enable great men to perform extraordinary labor.

During the years he spent as astronomer to the Emperor Rudolph, Kepler did his most serious work. Moved by the beauty and harmonious relations of the Copernican system, he decided to devote himself to the search for whatever additional geometrical harmonies the data supplied by Tycho Brahe's observations might suggest and, beyond that, to find the mathematical relations binding all the phenomena of nature to each other. His predilection for fitting the universe into a preconceived mathematical pattern, however, led him to spend years in following up false trails. In the preface to his _Mystery of the Cosmos_, we find him writing:

> I undertake to prove that God, in creating the universe and regulating the order of the cosmos, had in view the five regular bodies of geometry as known since the days of Pythagoras and Plato, and that he has fixed according to those dimensions, the number of heavens, their proportions, and the relations of their movements.

He therefore postulated that the radii of the orbits of the six planets were the radii of spheres related to the five regular solids in the following way. The largest radius was that of the orbit of Saturn. In a sphere of this radius he supposed a cube to be inscribed. In this cube a sphere was inscribed whose radius should be that of the orbit of Jupiter. In this sphere he supposed a tetrahedron to be inscribed and in this, in turn, another sphere whose radius was to be that of the orbit of Mars, and so on through the five regular solids. This allowed for six spheres, just enough for the number of planets known then. . . . Kepler soon realized that his beautiful theory was not accurate. Although his calculated interplanetary distances were very close to reality, they did not match exactly the spaces between the spheres separating the nested polyhedra.

Thus far, Kepler's work was subject to the same criticism that Aristotle used to attack the Pythagoreans: "They do not with regard to the phenomena seek for their reasons and cause but forcibly make the phenomena fit their opinions and preconceived notions and attempt to reconstruct the universe." However, the enlightened Kepler had too much regard for facts to persist with theories that failed to agree with observations and that could not yield accurate predictions.

It was after Kepler had acquired Brahe's data and had made additional observations of his own that he became convinced he must discard the astronomical patterns his predecessors, Ptolemy and Copernicus, and he himself had conceived. The search for laws that would fit these new data culminated in three famous results. The first two Kepler presented to the world in his book, _On the Motion of the Planet Mars_, published in 1609.

The first of these laws broke with all tradition and introduced the ellipse in astronomy. This curve had already been studied intensively by the

Greeks about two thousand years earlier, and therefore, its mathematical properties were known. Whereas the circle is defined as the set of all points that are at a constant distance (the radius) from a fixed point, the ellipse can be defined as the set of all points the *sum* of whose distances from two fixed points is constant. Thus, if F_1 and F_2 are the fixed points (Figure 24) [Figure 23 deleted.—Ed.], and P is a typical point on the ellipse, the sum $PF_1 + PF_2$ is the same no matter where P may be on the ellipse. The two fixed points F_1 and F_2 are called the foci. Kepler's first law states that each planet moves along an ellipse and that the sun is at one of the foci. The other focus is just a mathematical point at which nothing physical exists. Of course, each planet moves on its own ellipse, of which one focus, the one at which the sun exists, is the same for all the planets. Thus, the upshot of fifteen hundred years of attempts to use combinations of circles to represent the motion of each planet was the replacement of each combination by a simple ellipse.

Kepler's first law tells us the path pursued by a planet, but it does not tell us how fast the planet moves along this path; if we should observe a planet's position at any particular time, we would still not know when it will be at any other point on that course. One might expect that each planet would move at a constant velocity along its path, but observations, the final authority, convinced Kepler that this was not the case. Kepler's second discovery states that the area swept out by the line from the sun to the planet is constant. That is, if the planet moves from P to Q (Figure 25) in one month, say, and from P' to Q' in the same time, then the *areas* $F_1 PQ$ and $F_1 P'Q'$ are the same. Kepler was overjoyed to find that there was a simple way to state the mathematical law of planetary velocities. Apparently God preferred constant area to constant speed.

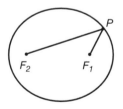

FIGURE 24

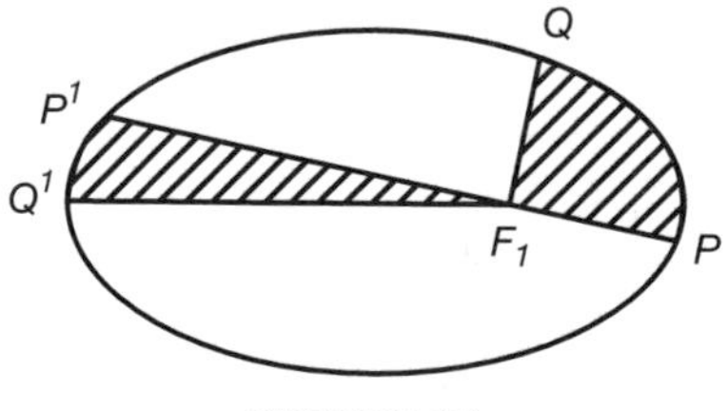

FIGURE 25

Another major problem remained unsolved. What law described the distances of the planets from the sun? The problem is complicated by the fact that a planet's distance from the sun is not constant, and Kepler searched for a new principle that would take this into account. He believed that nature was not only mathematically but harmoniously designed. Thus, he believed that there was a music of the spheres that produced a harmonious tonal effect, not one given off in actual sounds but discernible by some translation of the facts about planetary motions into musical notes. He followed this lead, and after an amazing combination of mathematical and musical arguments, arrived at the law that if T is the period of revolution of any planet and D is its mean (or average) distance from the sun then

$$T^2 = kD^3$$

where k is a constant that is the same for all the planets. (Note that the correct value for D is actually the semimajor axis of each elliptical path.) This statement is Kepler's third law of planetary motion and the one that he triumphantly announced in his book *The Harmony of the World* (1619).

Because the Earth's mean distance from the sun is 93 million miles and the time of revolution is one year, we can substitute these values of D and T in the law and determine k. Then the law can be used to compute a planet's mean distance from the sun if one knows its periods of revolution, or vice versa.

No doubt Kepler would have preferred to find some relationship among the distances themselves of the planets, but the result he did obtain overjoyed him so much that after stating it in his book he broke forth into a paean to God:

> The wisdom of the Lord is infinite; so also are His glory and His power. Ye heavens, sing His praises! Sun, moon, and planets glorify Him in your ineffable language! Celestial harmonies, all ye who comprehend His marvelous works, praise Him. And thou, my soul, praise thy Creator! It is by Him and in Him that all exists. That which we know best is comprised in Him, as well as in our vain science. To Him be praise, honor, and glory throughout eternity.

We should note parenthetically that Kepler was able to formulate simple laws only because the mutual gravitational attractions of the planets are relatively small and because the mass of the sun happens to be much larger than the masses of the planets. Nevertheless, Kepler's work was a major innovation and a great advance in the heliocentric theory.

Because we are today taught to accept the heliocentric theory and Kepler's laws, we no longer appreciate the full significance of Copernicus's and Kepler's achievements. It will profit us to go back for a moment to survey the setting in which these men worked and to see what their mathematics really accomplished.

We should recall that Copernicus and Kepler worked in the sixteenth and seventeenth centuries. The geocentric view had been in force since the days of Ptolemy and fitted in very neatly with the thoroughly entrenched religious doctrines. The Earth was at the center of the universe, and humans were the central characters in the universe. For us the sun, moon, and stars had been specially created. The heliocentric theory denied this basic dogma, implying instead that humanity was an insignificant speck of dust on one of many whirling globes. Was it likely then that humanity was the chief object of God's ministrations? The new astronomy also destroyed Heaven and Hell, which had very reasonable geographical locations in the geocentric view.

Copernicus and Kepler were highly religious, and yet both denied one of the central doctrines of Christianity. By displacing the Earth, Copernicus and Kepler removed a cornerstone of Catholic theology and imperiled the whole structure. Copernicus attacked the argument that the Earth is at the center of the universe by pointing out that the size of the universe is so immense compared to the Earth that to speak of a center is meaningless. However, this argument put him all the more into opposition with the Church.

There were also very reasonable scientific objections to a heliocentric theory. If the Earth is in motion, the directions of the stars, which seem to be fixed in the heavens, should be different at different points of the Earth's orbit. However, this difference was not observed in the sixteenth and seventeenth centuries. Copernicus disposed of this objection by stating that the distance of the stars is immense in comparison with the orbit of the Earth. However, his opponents argued that the distances necessary to make the change in direction insensible were inconsistent with the fact that the stars were clearly observable.

Copernicus's explanation proved to be the correct one, although even he would have been astonished to learn some of the modern figures for the distances of the stars from the Earth. The change in direction of the stars when viewed from one position on the Earth's orbit as opposed to another was first measured by the mathematician Friedrich Wilhelm Bessel (1784–1846) in 1838 and proved to be 0.76 seconds of arc (0.76") for the nearest star.

The above objection was taken seriously by only a few specialists, but there were other valid scientific objections to a moving Earth that every layperson appreciated. Neither Copernicus nor Kepler could explain how the heavy matter of the Earth could be put into and kept in motion. That the other planets were also in motion even under the geocentric view did not disturb people who believed the heavenly bodies were composed of light material and therefore could readily move. The best answer that Copernicus could offer was that it was natural for any sphere to move. Equally troublesome was the question: Why did not the Earth's rotation cause objects on it to fly off into space, just as an object on a rotating platform flies off? Indeed, Ptolemy had rejected the rotation of the Earth for this very reason. Furthermore, why did not the Earth itself fly apart? To the latter question Copernicus replied that because motion was natural it could not have the effect of destroying the body. He also countered by asking why the skies did not fall apart under the very rapid daily motion presumed by the geocentric hypothesis. Entirely unanswered was the objection that, if the Earth rotated from west to east, an object thrown up into the air should fall back to earth west of its original position. Again, if, as practically all scientists since Greek times believed, the motion of an object was proportional to its weight, why did not the Earth leave behind objects of lesser weights? Even the air surrounding the Earth should have been left behind. Although he could not account for the fact that all objects on the Earth moved with it, Copernicus "explained" the continued presence of the atmosphere by arguing that the air was earthy and so rotated in sympathy with the Earth. Kepler advanced the theory that an object thrown upward returns to its starting point while the Earth rotates under it, because magnetic invisible chains attach the object to the Earth.

Another and most reasonable argument against the new heliocentric theory was that nobody could *feel* either the rotation or the revolution of the Earth. On the other hand, everyone apparently did see the motion of the sun. To the famous astronomer Tycho Brahe, these and other arguments were conclusive proof that the Earth must be stationary.

The substance of all these arguments is that a rotating and revolving Earth did not fit in with Aristotle's physical theory of motion, which was commonly accepted in Copernicus's and Kepler's times. What was needed was a totally new theory of motion.

Against all these arguments, Copernicus and Kepler had one masterly retort. Each had achieved mathematical simplification and an overwhelmingly harmonious and aesthetically superior theory. If mathematical relationships are the goal of scientific work, and if a better mathematical account could be given, then this fact, reinforced by the belief that God had designed the world and would clearly have used the superior theory, was sufficient to outweigh all objections. Each believed and clearly stated that his work revealed the harmony, symmetry, and design of the divine workshop and overpowering evidence of God's presence.

In view of the variety of weighty objections to the heliocentric theory, Copernicus's and Kepler's willingness to pursue it is one of the enigmas of history. Almost every major intellectual creation is preceded by decades and even centuries of ground-breaking work that, in retrospect at least, makes the decisive step appear to be natural. Yet Copernicus had no immediate scientific predecessors, and his sudden adoption of the heliocentric view, despite the unquestioned acceptance for fifteen hundred years of the geocentric view, today seems decidedly unnatural. In the company of the astronomers of the sixteenth century Copernicus stands forth as a colossus.

It is true, as we have noted, that Copernicus had read the Greek works in which several astronomers had advanced the idea that the Earth was in motion, but none had attempted to work out a mathematical theory on this basis, whereas the geocentric theory had been intensively developed. Nor did Copernicus's observations suggest that something radically new was called for. His instruments were as crude as those of his predecessors and his observations no better. He was disturbed by the complexity of Ptolemaic theory, which by his time had become entangled in many more epicycles to make the theory fit Arabian and European observations. In the magnificent dedication of his book to Pope Paul III, Copernicus remarks that he was first induced to seek a new theory when he found that mathematicians were arguing among themselves as to the soundness of Ptolemaic theory. Nevertheless, historically, the appearance of his work is as surprising as a mountain suddenly rising from a calm sea.

Actually, religious convictions of a special sort account for the direction of the work of Copernicus and Kepler. The glimpse of a new possibility that might reveal the greater grandeur of God was sufficient to arouse them and to fire their thoughts. The results of their efforts satisfied their expectations of harmony, symmetry, and design in the divine workshop. The mathematical simplicity of the new theory was proof that God would have used it in preference to a more complicated design.

Ptolemy had asserted that in explaining phenomena it is necessary to adopt the simplest hypothesis that will fit the facts. Copernicus turned this very argument against Ptolemaic theory, and because he believed the universe to be the work of God, he interpreted the simplicity he had found to be the true design. Because Kepler's mathematics was even simpler, he had all the more reason to believe that he had found the very laws that God had incorporated in the construction of the universe. Kepler said of his theory, "I have attested it as true in my deepest soul and I contemplate its beauty with incredible and ravishing delight."

There was also a mystical element in their thinking that now seems anomalous in great scientists. The inspiration to conceive and carry out a heliocentric theory came from some vague and even primitive response to the power of the sun. Copernicus wrote: "The earth conceives from the sun and the sun rules the family of stars." He reinforced this argument by the statement, "For who could in this most beautiful temple place this lamp in another or better place than that from which at the same time it can illuminate the whole."

Despite the mystical and religious influences, however, Copernicus and Kepler were thoroughly rational in rejecting any speculations or conjectures that did not agree with observations. What distinguishes their work from medieval vaporizings is not only the mathematical framework of their theories but also their insistence on making the mathematics fit reality. In addition, the preference they showed for a simpler mathematical theory is a thoroughly modern scientific attitude.

Despite the weighty scientific arguments against a moving Earth, despite the religious and philosophical conservatism, and despite the affront to common sense, the new theory gradually won acceptance. Mathematicians and astronomers were impressed, especially after Kepler's work, with the simplicity of the new theory. Also, it was far more convenient for navigational computations and calendar reckoning, and hence many geographers and astronomers who were not convinced of its truth began to use it nevertheless.

It is not surprising that at first only mathematicians supported the new theory. Only a mathematician and only one convinced that the universe was mathematically and simply designed would have had the mental fortitude to disregard the prevailing philosophical, religious, and physical beliefs and to work out the mathematics of a revolutionary astronomy. Only one possessed of unshakable convictions as to the importance of mathematics in the design of the universe would have dared to affirm the new theory against the mass of powerful opposition it was sure to encounter.

The heliocentric theory found an extremely able defender in Galileo Galilei (1564–1642). Born in Florence, he entered the University of Pisa at the age of seventeen to study medicine. His reading of Euclid and Archimedes fired his interest in mathematics and science, and so he turned to these fields.

An offer of a professorship at the University of Padua prompted Galileo's move to northeastern Italy in 1592. Padua was then within the realm of the progressive Venetian Republic, and Galileo enjoyed total academic freedom. In 1610 the Grand Duke Cosimo de' Medici, his former pupil, engaged Galileo as court philosopher and mathematician. The move to Florence marked the end of his teaching duties and the beginning of his career as a full-time scientist.

In the summer of 1609 Galileo caught wind of a Dutch invention by means of which distant objects were distinctly seen as if nearby. Galileo wasted no time in constructing his own telescope and gradually improving the lenses until he reached a magnification of thirty-three times. In a dramatic demonstration to the Venetian Senate, Galileo showed the telescope's power to sight approaching hostile warships nearly two hours before their arrival.

But Galileo had grander plans for his instrument. Fixing his telescope on the moon, he observed vast craters and imposing mountains, thereby destroying the notion of a smooth lunar surface. By viewing the sun he discovered mysterious spots on its surface. He discovered also that Jupiter possesses four orbiting moons. (We can now observe sixteen.) This discovery showed that a planet, like the Earth, can have satellites. Galileo announced this discovery in *The Starry Messenger* (1610), describing the four moons of Jupiter that he observed in 1610 as "bodies that belong not to the inconspicuous multitude of fixed stars, but to the bright ranks of planets." In a rare act of political astuteness, he dubbed these moons the "Medici Planets," to honor his powerful Florentine patron.

Copernicus had predicted that if human sight could be enhanced, then we would be able to observe phases of Venus and Mercury, that is, to observe that more or less of each planet's hemisphere facing Earth is lit up by the sun, just as the naked eye can discern phases of the moon. Galileo did discover the phases of Venus. Here was further evidence that the planets were like Earth and certainly not perfect bodies composed of some special ethereal substance, as Greek and medieval thinkers had believed. The Milky Way, which had hitherto appeared to be just a broad band of light, could be seen with the telescope to be composed of thousands of stars, each of which gave off light. Thus, there were other suns and presumably other planetary systems suspended in the heavens; moreover, the heavens clearly contained more than seven moving bodies, a number that had been accepted as sacrosanct. His observations convinced him that the Copernican system was correct.

Annoyed by Galileo's defense of the heliocentric doctrine, the Roman Inquisition in 1616 declared the doctrine heretical and censored it, and in 1620 the Inquisition forbade all publications teaching this doctrine. Despite the earlier ecclesiastical prohibition of works on Copernicanism, Pope Urban VIII did give Galileo permission to publish a book on the subject, for the Pope believed there was no danger that anyone would ever prove the new theory necessarily true. Accordingly, in his *Dialogue on the Great World Systems* (1632) Galileo compared the geocentric and heliocentric doctrines. With the aim of pleasing the Church and so passing the censors, he incorporated a preface to the effect that the latter theory was only a product of the imagination. Galileo had been admonished to present the two theories, geocentric and heliocentric, as equally valid, but the bias in favor of the latter was evident. Unfortunately, Galileo wrote too well, and the Pope began to fear that the argument for heliocentrism, like a live bomb wrapped in silver foil, could still do a great deal of damage to the Catholic faith. Galileo was again called by the Roman Inquisition and compelled on the threat of torture to declare: "The falsity of the Copernican system cannot be doubted, especially by us Catholics." In 1633 Galileo's *Dialogue* was put on the Index of Prohibited Books, a ban that was not lifted until 1822.

We who live in an age of space exploration, with spaceships that can take people to the moon and travel to the farthest planets of our solar system, no longer can doubt the truth of the heliocentric theory. However, the people of the seventeenth and eighteenth centuries, even those able to understand the writings of Copernicus, Kepler, and Galileo, could with good reason be skeptical. The evidence of the senses went against the theory, and the mathematical arguments of Copernicus and Kepler, which apart from philosophical beliefs rested on the relative simplicity of the heliocentric theory, carried little weight.

There is one more implication that modern science has perceived in the work of Copernicus and Kepler. The same observational data that Hipparchus and Ptolemy organized in their geocentric theory of deferent and epicycle can also be organized under the heliocentric theory of Copernicus and Kepler. Despite the belief of the latter that the new theory was true, the modern view is that either theory will do and there is no need to adopt the heliocentric hypothesis except to gain mathematical simplicity. Reality seems far less knowable than Copernicus and Kepler believed, and today scientific theories are regarded as human inventions. Modern astronomers might agree with Kepler that the heavens declare the glory of God and the firmament showeth His handiwork; however, they now recognize that the mathematical interpretations of the works of God are their own creations, and mathematical simplicity wins out despite their sensations. How then do we determine what is real in our physical world?

Reflections on the Reading:

1. What surprised you most in learning how Copernicus made his "discovery"?

2. What differences do you see between the method of discovery of Copernicus and Kepler and "the scientific method" as it is usually taught?

3. Why did Kepler (and others before him) have such a hard time determining the ellipse as the orbit of planets around the sun?

4. Describe the role religious belief and mathematical insight played in the development of the heliocentric universe. Do you know of any other "discoveries" that rested on either religion or new mathematical insights?

5. The "Copernican Revolution" highlights the difference between the world described by science and the world of our experience.

Describe five other examples where our experience of the world is quite different from the description of the world given by science.

Copernicus and Kepler

You are familiar with our solar system and the revolution of the planets around the sun, so the accomplishment of Copernicus probably seems a bit old hat. Of course, the sun is the center of the solar system. That's the way it is. The Earth goes around the sun. Everybody knows that! And you have seen pictures or models of the solar system showing the planets and their proximity to the sun and to each other. What we tend not to realize, however, is that this picture does not exist—except as a drawing or representation in a book. That is, there is no correct point in space, if only we could get to it, from which we could take this "accurate" picture of our immediate solar system.

Think about this for a minute. Our naive view, encouraged by science teachers and science books, suggests that there is some privileged position in space where we could see, if we could get to it, our solar system with the sun in the center and the nine planets revolving around it. But how would we know it? What would tell us that *this* is the spot? There are no marks in space, no X saying "This is the spot." And why should any particular place be *the* place? What would make a view from one location in space any more "correct" than a view from some other place? Just as there is no privileged position on the Earth's surface, there are no privileged positions in space in general. We human beings see everything from our position on the Earth. From that position we see that the stars move. They change position over time. That could be because they are moving or that could be because we are moving. (Scientists believe we are both moving.)

What Copernicus did is realize that the picture of these motions that scientists in his day were using could be simplified. The picture, or **pattern**, would look less complicated and the calculations for plotting the positions of the planets would be easier by assuming that the sun, and not the Earth, was in the center of this system of moving bodies. The Ptolemaic theory was complex but not inaccurate. It required seventy-seven epicycles to account for the motions of the planets. An epicycle is a circle on a circle, or a loop. These epicycles were necessary because sometimes the motion of a planet or star would appear to be in a backwards direction and the epicycle captured this retrograde motion. Copernicus saw that by placing the sun in the center and the Earth in motion around this center he could reduce the number of epicycles to thirty-four. He still needed epicycles in his picture, however, because he assumed the planetary motions were circular motions.

It is important to see here that the Copernican picture is not more accurate than the Ptolemaic picture. They both at the time accurately predicted the past and future motions of the heavenly bodies. There was no observation of the heavenly bodies which distinguished between these two views. There were, however, plenty of observations of everyday phenomena that suggested that Copernicus's view was wrong, like the fact that everything happens as if the Earth is stationary! The sole reason that led Copernicus and others to prefer his view to the geocentric view was that it was **simpler**. The simplicity was in the mathematics. With fewer epicycles it was easier to calculate future (or past) positions of the heavenly bodies. Simplicity suggested the harmony and symmetry of a divine design to Copernicus and appealed to his strong religious convictions.

Kepler's reasoning is similar. He, too, firmly believed that there must be some pattern for describing the motions of the planets that was simple and elegant because God would only design a world of mathematical harmony. He discovered that if he took the sun as one of the two foci of an ellipse, he could describe the motions of the planets around the sun as ellipses. By doing this he eliminated the epicycles altogether and could also account for new observations that had been collected since the time of Copernicus. He also found that the planets do not move with constant velocity along their orbital paths but that they sweep out equal areas of the ellipse during equal times. He was led to this (second) law of planetary motion because of his firm belief that there must be an order and harmony in the pattern since it was created by God.

Clearly, Copernicus and Kepler made many assumptions in coming to their discoveries about our solar system. For both of them, the primary assumption was religious. They both believed in an all-powerful and all-rational God who would only create a world of rational design. They then set out to discover that design or pattern. They also made assumptions about what would constitute a rational design. Here they turned to the **values of simplicity, harmony, symmetry, and order**. We think of these as aesthetic values, values associated with our sense of **beauty**. Morris Kline, like the Pythagoreans and Copernicus and Kepler, associates these values also with mathematics. And, indeed, they are associated with mathematics. One of the things mathematics does for us is simplify and supply order to our experiences. To express a pattern in a formula is to give it a simplicity and order which otherwise may not be apparent.

We see these same aesthetic values of Copernicus and Kepler in the fundamental assumptions of contemporary scientists. For example, one of the heroes of modern biology, James Watson, who with Francis Crick won the Nobel prize for his discovery of the structure of DNA, in summing up the main points of his DNA model was said to have gazed at the model and remarked, "It's so beautiful, you see, so beautiful."[1] And Paul Dirac, Nobel prize-winning physicist, was well known for his strong belief in the connection between mathematical beauty and physical laws. "A theory with mathematical beauty," said Dirac, "is more likely to be correct than an ugly one that fits some experimental data."[2]

It is not hard to see why science is so intimately connected with values such as simplicity, harmony, symmetry and order. The scientist tries to make order out of experience. If there were no order in the universe, we would not be able to predict the course of future events and we would have little control over the world around us. (Just think what it would be like if everything happened by chance or accident.) Making order out of apparent disorder means making things simpler. It means construing events in **patterns** that can be remembered and used for future reference. In general, scientists have tried to describe these patterns in the language of mathematics. And mathematics is precisely that, a language. Mathematics is a very useful language because it allows us to use symbols to stand in for a range of individuals (numbers, people, things), so we don't have to write down all those individuals. That is, even by its very nature mathematics simplifies. So the scientist and the mathematician have similar values which are fundamental to their respective enterprises. These values are aesthetic. They include simplicity, harmony, symmetry, and order.

The scientist makes other assumptions as well. For instance, the scientist must assume he does not occupy a unique position in the universe. The laws of nature should be the same in China as they are in the United States. The same on Jupiter as in some distant solar system. The regularities discovered in one laboratory will be like the regularities discoverable in any other laboratory. Just to get started scientists must "take on faith" certain laws of nature which cannot be proven, such as the law that matter is always conserved. Scientists could never prove this law with certainty because they would be stuck in a vicious circle of assuming the conservation of the matter making up the instruments they were using to test the conservation of matter.

Science, then, is not "value-free," nor does it rest totally on observation. Scientists do make assumptions which they cannot prove by experiment. Some of these assumptions are necessary to the whole enterprise of collecting experimental data. The most fundamental assumptions of science are aesthetic in nature and represent the **values** that every scientist brings to his work.

---

[1] Quoted by Crick in *What Mad Pursuit: A Personal View of Scientific Discovery*, New York: Basic Books, 1988, p. 79.

[2] Quoted in "P.A.M. Dirac and the Beauty of Physics," R. Corby Hovis and Helge Kragh, *Scientific American*, May 1993.

Hypothetical-Deductive Reasoning

So far in _Thinking Socratically_ we have stressed the close relation between good reasoning and common sense. And, indeed, they are very close to being one and the same. When we turn to science, however, a few words of caution are necessary. For the world described by science is quite different from the world of our common-sense experience. We live in a world of rather medium-sized objects, while the world described by science is composed of microphysical particles and macrophysical systems. Much of the scientific description of the world doesn't seem very common-sensical, just as Copernicus's description of the solar system didn't seem very common-sensical to people in his day. We must be clear about the distinction between common sense, which can be thought of as the lowest theoretical level for making sense of experience, and the experience of the world through our senses. The latter often leads to very naive descriptions of our experience, which we then correct by using common-sense reasoning. For example, if you take a straight stick and immerse part of it in water, the stick will appear to be bent at the water's surface. If we were to describe this observation on the basis of sense experience alone, we would say that the stick was bent by the water. We know from our background knowledge, however, that water does not bend sticks and so we reason to the conclusion that this visual experience is a kind of optical illusion. That is, we use reason as well as sensory experience to arrive at our description of the world.

Similarly, the scientist also uses reason and sensory experience to arrive at a description of the world. This description is often quite different from our everyday description of events. We describe the sun as "coming up" in the morning while the scientist talks about the Earth turning on its axis. We talk about tables and chairs while the scientist may talk about atoms and molecules. It is important to see that the scientist's description of the world is just one description among many possible descriptions of the world. It is the appropriate description in some contexts but not in others. It is not better or more correct than others except in certain circumstances. For example, if someone asks you for a description of your significant other, he does not want a description of that person's physical chemistry. On the other hand, if a doctor asks for a description of a patient, he may want precisely that.

The scientific description of the world includes many entities which are not directly known through sense experience—like atoms, electrons, entropy, DNA, etc. How, you may ask, does the scientist get information about _this_ world of unobservable objects. This is a good question and one to which we will offer only a partial answer in this text. (Whole textbooks are devoted to answering this question.) The first point that should be noted is that scientists do not generally follow the method usually described as "the scientific method." According to this method, what scientists do is collect information about the world by observing it or by performing experiments and observing the results. They then organize this information into generalizations. These generalizations are considered lawlike if they are based on a large number of observations, the observations have been repeated under a variety of different circumstances, and the generalization—now a "law of nature"—does not conflict with any known observations. These generalizations are then used to predict future occurrences and to explain past events.

For example, the generalization that all metals conduct electricity is based on past observations of the behavior of metals. According to the scientific method, for this generalization to be considered lawlike, these observations must have been made in a variety of circumstances and under a variety of conditions, using a variety of different kinds of metals. Furthermore, there should be no observation of a metal that does not conduct electricity. Scientists then use this law to predict that in the future any specific piece of metal will conduct electricity.

There are several problems with this version of the method of science, some of which may be obvious to you already from your earlier reading. First, from the Copernican and Keplerian examples, we see that neither of these two famous astronomers could be said to have used this method. New observations were not the cause of their discoveries. If you were to review the history of science, you would find that the Copernican model is typical of scientific discovery. Second, in the discussion of forms of reasoning with probability in Chapter 7 it was clear how important **background knowledge** is in making warranted generalizations and warranted causal claims. Yet the "popular" version of the scientific method takes no account of its importance. Nor does it acknowledge the problem of induction.

Finally, this description of the method of science makes observation central to the scientific enterprise but it ignores the problematic character of observation which we saw in Chapter 1. There we pointed out that the same events can be described in different ways by different observers. Our **descriptions** of our experience are not neutral. In science, observation and experiment are guided by theory as much as the other way around. To see this, consider what would happen if they were not. What observations would the scientist gather? What experiments would he perform? He must already have an idea of what is important to know, what to pay attention to. As we said in the last chapter, there are too many **traces** and too many **patterns** of traces for us to pay attention to all of them. So we use theory (or a story) to guide us in our collection of information. (We should not be surprised, then, when our theory fits the information!) Consequently, "the scientific method" is rather limited in its usefulness to scientists.

A pattern of reasoning that scientists *do* use frequently, which is rather interesting, and useful in everyday affairs as well, is the **hypothetical-deductive pattern**. This reasoning pattern enables scientists to find evidence for

"There goes one strange cow."

Even cows cannot avoid the problem of induction. Drawing by P. Steiner; © 1995, The New Yorker Magazine, Inc.

claims that they cannot support by direct observation, claims about electrons, forces, chemical composition, psychological complexes, and so on. When a scientist has a hypothesis that cannot be tested directly (there is no direct observation evidence), he deduces (using reasoning with necessity) an observable consequence from the hypothesis which is very specific and therefore testable. If the observable result is as anticipated, then the scientist has evidence for the hypothesis. If the observable result is not as anticipated, then there is not evidence for the hypothesis. It is important to note that in neither case is the hypothesis proven or disproven. Let's look at some examples.

In the late eighteenth century Edward Jenner, an English country doctor working in the dairy region, discovered the first effective inoculation against the scourge of the English countryside, smallpox. It was a well-known fact that milkmaids got cowpox but not smallpox, cowpox being a milder, much weaker form of the disease. Jenner formulated the hypothesis that exposure to cowpox gives immunity to smallpox. Assuming this hypothesis is true, Jenner reasoned, if I take some pus from the cowpox sore of an infected milkmaid and expose another individual to cowpox by scratching the cowpox germs into his skin, then that individual will not get smallpox even if exposed to it. In 1796 he persuaded the parents of a small boy (by paying them money) to allow him to scratch pus from a cowpox sore of a milkmaid into his arm. Two months later the boy was injected with smallpox but did not develop the disease.

Jenner's result confirmed his hypothesis as do all the ensuing smallpox vaccinations. Today all American children must be vaccinated for smallpox before they can attend school and smallpox has been eradicated throughout the United States. These are observable results which provide evidence for a hypothesis which cannot itself be directly verified. At this point we would say that the hypothesis is well confirmed and, consequently, well entrenched in the set of beliefs of American pediatricians. In Jenner's day, however, his claim to have discovered a method for preventing smallpox was scoffed at and he had to postpone publishing his results for two years to avoid being thought a quack.

The hypothetical-deductive method of reasoning also played a role in the confirmation and eventual acceptance of the Copernican worldview. Astronomers reasoned that if the sun is in the center of the universe (a hypothesis whose truth is not directly observable), then Venus should appear to change size during the year as it is closer to and farther from the Earth. Also, Venus should exhibit phases. Like the moon, it should wax and wane. (Both of these are observable consequences of the theory.) But in this case, observations at the time could confirm neither of these! This inability to confirm his hypothesis did not lead Copernicus to change his mind, however; nor did it deter Galileo from adopting the Copernican worldview. Rather, as Kline points out, Galileo was spurred on to find and develop an instrument—the telescope—that could observe the change in size and the phases of Venus, thereby confirming Copernicus's hypothesis.

This last historical example is interesting because it points out the role that background knowledge and entrenchment play in science, both of which are ignored by "the scientific method." Copernicus and Galileo were steadfast in their belief in a solar system. Others of their contemporaries, such as Andreas Osiander and Tycho Brahe, were just as adamant in their support of the Ptolemaic view. Although it is not possible to give a rigorous comparison of the background knowledge of these scientists, it is possible to see that for Copernicus and Galileo what weighed most heavily with them was the mathematical attractiveness of the heliocentric theory. On the other hand, what was more important to Osiander and Brahe were the physical observations they made, namely, that Venus continued to look the same no matter what time of year they viewed it. There was *no* observational evidence they could point to that confirmed the heliocentric hypothesis and there were many observations that disconfirmed it.

That is, for Copernicus and Galileo the belief that the universe is simple, harmonious, and capable of being described by elegant mathematical formulas led them to discount the failure of observation to confirm the Copernican hypothesis. This belief was more entrenched than their belief in the information given by their senses. (After all, the senses often mislead us.) Osiander and Brahe, on the other hand, were more committed to observation and its dictates. Eventually, we know, the Copernican hypothesis acquired a large body of confirming evidence so that today it is firmly entrenched in the worldview of contemporary scientists.

The hypothetical-deductive method is clearly a method used by scientists to gather support for hypotheses which are not directly verifiable, that is, when no direct observations are possible. A person using this method uses deductive reasoning to derive a consequence from the hypothesis that can be observed. The scientist then sets up the proper conditions for making this observation and tests to see if he gets the predicted results.

It should be clear from these two examples that the hypothetical-deductive method does not prove or disprove a hypothesis. What it does is provide **evidence** for or against that hypothesis. Consequently, scientists may differ on whether to accept a hypothesis. Whether or not a scientist accepts an observation as evidence (either for or against) depends, in part, on his background knowledge and which of his beliefs are more fundamental than others—or, in the language of Chapter 7, which beliefs are better entrenched. Scientists, like the rest of us, find hypotheses acceptable which fit in well with the beliefs they already hold which are well entrenched. They tend to reject hypotheses that would upset or require them to change any well-entrenched belief. So how well a hypothesis fits into the scientist's web of belief is also a factor in accepting a hypothesis. Since, as we have already seen, scientists (at least most of them) tend to admire simplicity and order, they prefer hypotheses which are powerful but also economical. By this we mean that the hypothesis can explain a large number of observations but is itself rather simple. For example, Newton's second law of motion was thought to be very powerful, because it could explain all motion that results from the action of an external force, and at the same time it is very simple: $F=ma$ (force equals the mass multiplied by the acceleration).

A scientific hypothesis may become so well accepted that it is called a law of nature, but even so-called laws of nature are only part of our description of the world and are, therefore, only confirmed, not proven. The history of science is littered with "laws of nature" which have been discarded or altered. The Ptolemaic universe is one such discard. As Kline says in the reading, ". . . they [modern astronomers] now recognize that the mathematical interpretations of the works of God are their own creations. . . ."

But, wait a minute, you might say. There's a world out there that is fixed, that is not our creation. Isn't our description getting closer and closer to that fixed world, that "real" world? Unfortunately neither we nor the scientists can answer that question because there is no way of knowing. We have only our experience and our description of that experience. Like Sherlock Holmes, the scientist examines the **traces** and tells us a **story** about those traces. The scientist tries to include more and more detail in the story while at the same time keeping it neat and economical. The scientist tests the story by the hypothetical-deductive method (much as Holmes tests his hypotheses) and confirms or disconfirms it and adjusts the story accordingly. The story has no end and no proof. The story of modern science is an exciting and useful story, but, in the end, it is only a story! The scientific description of our world that we have today will not be the scientific description of the world tomorrow.

In sum, modern science presents us with one way, among many, of describing our experience. This way of describing the world has been very helpful to us, enabling us to predict and sometimes control events in our lives, generally making life more pleasant and fruitful. It is important to remember that this mode of description rests on implicit assumptions, not often acknowledged, and on unarticulated values, particularly the aesthetic values of simplicity and order and the rational values of coherence and consistency.

EXERCISES

8–I

1. What was Kepler's contribution to the heliocentric hypothesis of Copernicus?

2. What is hypothetical-deductive reasoning?

3. What was Edward Jenner's hypothesis?

4. List some of the aesthetic values generally found in science.

8–II

1. What role does the hypothetical-deductive method play in science?

2. Why is the hypothetical-deductive method a kind of reasoning with probability rather than a form of reasoning with necessity?

3. Describe a recent case of scientific discovery or controversy. Examine it for its implicit assumptions.

8–III

1. Formulate a hypothesis which cannot be directly verified and test it by deducing a consequence which can be directly observed. Collect your evidence. Was your hypothesis confirmed or disconfirmed? Describe in detail what you did.

2. List five of your most well entrenched beliefs. What kind of evidence would lead you to give up one of them?

3. "The scientific method" as it is usually taught could be said to be naive. How would you critique this method, given the insights you have gained from this chapter?

4. Observation is said to be "theory-laden." What do you think this means? What insights for thinking critically do you see as a consequence of this claim? (Hint: You might want to review Chapter 1.)

5. How has your view of science changed from reading about the history of science? What consequences for good reasoning do you see?

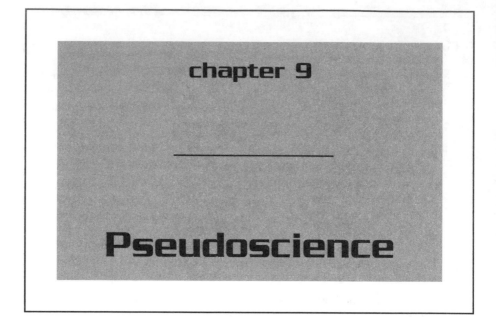

chapter 9

Pseudoscience

Introduction

Scientific reasoning is a very important part of critical thinking. The hypothetical-deductive method, which is a primary reasoning tool of science, is a
model of good reasoning that we all use at times. It is also good critical thinking to realize the limits of scientific reasoning and to see that science is one
way, among many, of describing our experience.

Pseudoscience is a way of reasoning that sometimes competes for our
attention as an alternative description of the world. Pseudoscience does not
use the skills of critical thinking. If anything, it asks that we suspend common sense and abandon our critical thinking skills. Pseudoscientists purport
to be scientists. That is why it is very important that we distinguish between
science and pseudoscience. We don't want to be misled and disappointed by
pseudoscience. We want to continue to use good common sense and our critical thinking skills.

You are familiar with pseudosciences. Astrology is a common pseudoscience. The astrologer who provides the newspaper with the daily horoscopes claims to have good reasons for the predictions she makes (she claims
that the predictions are warranted) and urges us to make decisions on the

basis of those predictions. Most people, however, take the astrologer's predictions with a grain of salt. Some people, however, are very committed to their favorite astrologer (former First Lady Nancy Reagan was a well-known devotee) and consult their horoscopes before making decisions. It is important to understand why this is not good critical thinking so you can avoid falling prey to a pseudoscience.

The reading in this chapter is by Martin Gardner, long-time editor of *Scientific American*'s mathematical puzzle page. In this article he debunks a very popular pseudoscience, biorhythm. This article shows why biorhythm is a pseudoscience.

Fliess, Freud, and Biorhythm

MARTIN GARDNER

At Aussee I know a wonderful wood full of ferns and mushrooms, where you shall reveal to me the secrets of the world of the lower animals and the world of children. I am agape as never before for what you have to say—and I hope that the world will not hear it before me, and that instead of a short article you will give us within a year a small book which will reveal organic secrets in periods of 28 and 23.

Sigmund Freud, in a letter to Wilhelm Fliess, 1897

One of the most extraordinary and absurd episodes in the history of numerological pseudoscience concerns the work of a Berlin surgeon named Wilhelm Fliess. Fliess was obsessed by the numbers 23 and 28. He convinced himself and others that behind all living phenomena and perhaps inorganic nature as well there are two fundamental cycles: a male cycle of 23 days and a female cycle of 28 days. By working with multiples of those two numbers—sometimes adding, sometimes subtracting—he was able to impose his number patterns on virtually everything. The work made a considerable stir in Germany during the early years of this century. Several disciples took up the system, elaborating and modifying it in books, pamphlets, and articles. In recent years the movement has taken root in the United States.

From *Mathematical Carnival*, by Martin Gardner

Although Fliess's numerology is of interest to recreational mathematicians and students of pathological science, it would probably be unremembered today were it not for one almost unbelievable fact: For a decade Fliess was Sigmund Freud's best friend and confidant. Roughly from 1890 to 1900, in the period of Freud's greatest creativity, which culminated with the publication of *The Interpretation of Dreams* in 1900, he and Fliess were linked in a strange neurotic relationship that had—as Freud himself was well aware—strong homosexual undercurrents. The story was known, of course, to the early leaders of psychoanalysis, but few laymen had even heard of it until the publication in 1950 of a selection of 168 letters from Freud to Fliess, out of a total of 284 that Fliess had carefully preserved. (The letters were first published in German. An English translation entitled *The Origins of Psycho-Analysis* was issued by Basic Books in 1954.) Freud was staggered by the news that these letters had been preserved, and he begged the owner (the analyst Marie Bonaparte) not to permit their publication. In reply to her question about Fliess's side of the correspondence Freud said: "Whether I destroyed them [Fliess's letters] or cleverly hid them away I still do not know." It is assumed that he destroyed them. The full story of the Fliess-Freud friendship has been told by Ernest Jones in his biography of Freud.

When the two men first met in Vienna in 1877, Freud was thirty-one, relatively unknown, happily married, and with a modest practice in psychiatry. Fliess had a much more successful practice as a nose and throat surgeon in Berlin. He was two years younger than Freud, a bachelor (later he married a wealthy Viennese woman), handsome, vain, brilliant, witty, and well informed on medical and scientific topics.

Freud opened their correspondence with a flattering letter. Fliess responded with a gift; then Freud sent a photograph of himself that Fliess had requested. By 1892 they had dropped the formal *Sie* (you) for the intimate *du* (thou). Freud wrote more often than Fliess and was in torment when Fliess was slow in answering. When his wife was expecting their fifth child, Freud declared it would be named Wilhelm. Indeed, he would have named either of his two youngest children Wilhelm but, as Jones put it, "fortunately they were both girls."

The foundations of Fliess's numerology were first revealed to the world in 1897 when he published his monograph *Die Beziehungen zwischen Nase und Weibliche Geschlechtsorganen in ihrer biologischen Bedeutungen dargestellt* (*The Relations between the Nose and the Female Sex Organs from the Biological Aspects*). Every person, Fliess maintained, is really bisexual. The male component is keyed to the rhythmic cycle of 23 days, the female to a cycle of 28 days. (The female cycle must not be confused with the menstrual cycle, although the two are related in evolutionary origin.) In normal males the male cycle is dominant, the female cycle repressed. In normal females it is the other way around.

The two cycles are present in every living cell and consequently play their dialectic roles in all living things. Among animals and humans both cycles start at birth, the sex of the child being determined by the cycle that is transmitted first. The periods continue throughout life, manifesting themselves in the ups and downs of one's physical and mental vitality, and eventually determine the day of one's death. Moreover, both cycles are intimately connected with the mucous lining of the nose. Fliess thought he had found a relation between nasal irritations and all kinds of neurotic symptoms and sexual irregularities. He diagnosed these ills by inspecting the nose and treated them by applying cocaine to "genital spots" on the nose's interior. He reported cases in which miscarriages were produced by anesthetizing the nose, and he said that he could control painful menstruation by treating the nose. On two occasions he operated on Freud's nose. In a later book he argued that all left-handed people are dominated by the cycle of the opposite sex, and when Freud expressed doubts, he accused Freud of being left-handed without knowing it.

Fliess's theory of cycles was at first regarded by Freud as a major breakthrough in biology. He sent Fliess information on 23- and 28-day periods in his own life and the lives of those in his family, and he viewed the ups and downs of his health as fluctuations of the two periods. He believed a distinction he had found between neurasthenia and anxiety neurosis could be explained by the two cycles. In 1898 he severed editorial connections with a journal because it refused to retract a harsh review of one of Fliess's books.

There was a time when Freud suspected that sexual pleasure was a release of 23-cycle energy and sexual unpleasure a release of 28-cycle energy. For years he expected to die at the age of 51 because it was the sum of 23 and 28, and Fliess had told him this would be his most critical year. "Fifty-one is the age which seems to be a particularly dangerous one to men," Freud wrote in his book on dreams. "I have known colleagues who have died suddenly at that age, and amongst them one who, after long delays, had been appointed to a professorship only a few days before his death."

Freud's acceptance of Fliess's cycle theory was not, however, enthusiastic enough for Fliess. Abnormally sensitive to even the lightest criticism, he thought he detected in one of Freud's 1896 letters some faint suspicions about his system. This marked the beginning of the slow emergence of latent hostility on both sides. Freud's earlier attitude toward Fliess had been one of almost adolescent dependence on a mentor and father figure. Now he was developing theories of his own about the origins of neuroses and methods of treating them. Fliess would have little of this. He argued that Freud's imagined cures were no more than the fluctuations of mental illness, in obedience to the male and female rhythms. The two men were on an obvious collision course.

As one could have predicted from the earlier letters, it was Fliess who first began to pull away. The growing rift plunged Freud into a severe neurosis, from which he emerged only after painful years of self-analysis. The two men had been in the habit of meeting frequently in Vienna, Berlin, Rome, and elsewhere, for what Freud playfully called their "congresses." As late as 1900, when the rift was beyond repair, we find Freud writing: "There has never been a six months' period where I have longed more to be united with you and your family. . . . Your suggestion of a meeting at Easter greatly stirred me. . . . It is not merely my almost childlike yearning for the spring and for more beautiful scenery; that I would willingly sacrifice for the satisfaction of having you near me for three days. . . . We should talk reasonably and scientifically, and your beautiful and sure biological discoveries would awaken my deepest—though impersonal—envy."

Freud nevertheless turned down the invitation, and the two men did not meet until later that summer. It was their final meeting. Fliess later wrote that Freud had made a violent and unprovoked verbal attack on him. For the next two years Freud tried to heal the breach. He proposed that they collaborate on a book on bisexuality. He suggested that they meet again in 1902. Fliess turned down both suggestions. In 1904 Fliess published angry accusations that Freud had leaked some of his ideas to Hermann Swoboda, one of Freud's young patients, who in turn had published them as his own.

The final quarrel seems to have taken place in a dining room of the Park Hotel in Munich. On two later occasions, when Freud was in this room in connection with meetings of the analytical movement, he experienced a severe attack of anxiety. Jones recalls an occasion in 1912, when he and a group that included Freud and Jung were lunching in this same room. A break between Freud and Jung was brewing. When the two men got into a mild argument, Freud suddenly fainted. Jung carried him to a sofa. "How sweet it must be to die," Freud said as he was coming to. Later he confided to Jones the reason for his attack.

Fliess wrote many books and articles about his cycle theory, but his magnum opus was a 584-page volume, *Der Ablauf des Lebens: Grundlegung zur Exakten Biologie* (*The Rhythm of Life: Foundations of an Exact Biology*), published in Leipzig in 1906 (second edition, Vienna, 1923). The book is a masterpiece of Teutonic crackpottery. Fliess's basic formula can be written $23x + 28y$, where x and y are positive or negative integers. On almost every page Fliess fits this formula to natural phenomena, ranging from the cell to the solar system. The moon, for example, goes around the earth in about 28 days; a complete sun-spot cycle is almost 23 years.

The book's appendix is filled with such tables as multiples of 365 (days in the year), multiples of 23, multiples of 28, multiples of 23^2, multiples of

28^2, multiples of 644 (which is 23×28). In boldface are certain important constants such as 12,167 [23×23^2], 24,334 [$2 \times 23 \times 23^2$], 36,501 [$3 \times 23 \times 23^2$], 21,952 [28×28^2], 43,904 [$2 \times 28 \times 28^2$], and so on. A table lists the numbers 1 through 28, each expressed as a difference between multiples of 28 and 23 [for example, $13 = (21 \times 28) - (25 \times 23)$]. Another table expresses numbers 1 through 51 [$23 + 28$] as sums and differences of multiples of 23 and 28 [for example, $1 = (\frac{1}{2} \times 28) + (2 \times 28) - (3 \times 23)$].

Freud admitted on many occasions that he was hopelessly deficient in all mathematical abilities. Fliess understood elementary arithmetic, but little more. He did not realize that if any two positive integers that have no common divisor are substituted for 23 and 28 in his basic formula, it is possible to express _any positive integer whatever_. Little wonder that the formula could be so readily fitted to natural phenomena! This is easily seen by working with 23 and 28 as an example. First determine what values of x and y can give the formula a value of 1. They are $x = 11$, $y = -9$:

$$(23 \times 11) + (28 \times -9) = 1$$

It is now a simple matter to produce any desired positive integer by the following method:

$$[23 \times (11 \times 2)] + [28 \times (-9 \times 2)] = 2$$
$$[23 \times (11 \times 3)] + [28 \times (-9 \times 3)] = 3$$
$$[23 \times (11 \times 4)] + [28 \times (-9 \times 4)] = 4$$
$$\cdots$$

As Roland Sprague recently pointed out in problem 26 of his _Recreation in Mathematics_, 1963, even if negative values of x and y are excluded, it is still possible to express all positive integers greater than a certain integer. In the finite set of positive integers that _cannot_ be expressed by this formula, asks Sprague, what is the largest number? In other words, what is the largest number that cannot be expressed by substituting nonnegative integers for x and y in the formula $23x + 28y$? The answer: $xy - x - y$.

Freud eventually realized that Fliess's superficially surprising results were no more than numerological juggling. After Fliess's death in 1928 (note that obliging 28), a German physician, J. Aelby, published a book that constituted a thorough refutation of Fliess's absurdities. By then, however, the 23–28 cult was firmly established in Germany. Swoboda, who lived until 1963, was the cult's second most important figure. As a psychologist at the University of Vienna he devoted much time to investigating, defending, and writing about Fliess's cycle theory. In his own rival masterwork, the 576-page _Das Siebenjahr_ (_The Year of Seven_), he reported on his studies of hundreds of family trees to prove that such events as heart attacks, deaths, and the onset of major ills tend to fall on certain critical days that can be computed on the basis of one's male and female cycles. He applied the cycle theory to dream analysis, an application that Freud criticizes in a 1911 footnote to his book on dreams. Swoboda also designed the first slide rule for determining critical days. Without the aid of such a device or the assistance of elaborate charts, calculations of critical days are tedious and tricky.

Incredible though it may seem, as late as the 1960s the Fliess system still had a small but devoted band of disciples in Germany and Switzerland. There were doctors in several Swiss hospitals who determined propitious days for surgery on the basis of Fliess's cycles. (This practice goes back to Fliess. In 1925, when Karl Abraham, one of the pioneers of analysis, had a gallbladder operation, he insisted that it take place on the favorable day calculated by Fliess.) To the male and female cycles modern Fliessians have added a third cycle, called the intellectual cycle, which has a length of 33 days.

Two books on the Swiss system have been published here by Crown: *Biorhythm*, 1961, by Hans J. Wernli, and *Is This Your Day?*, 1964, by George Thommen. Thommen is the president of a firm that supplies calculators and charting kits with which to plot one's own cycles.

The three cycles start at birth and continue with absolute regularity throughout life, although their amplitudes decrease with old age. The male cycle governs such masculine traits as physical strength, confidence, aggressiveness, and endurance. The female cycle controls such feminine traits as feelings, intuition, creativity, love, cooperation, cheerfulness. The newly discovered intellectual cycle governs mental powers common to both sexes: intelligence, memory, concentration, quickness of mind.

On days when a cycle is above the horizontal zero line of the chart, the energy controlled by that cycle is being discharged. These are the days of highest vitality and efficiency. On days when the cycle is below the line, energy is being recharged. These are the days of reduced vitality. When your male cycle is high and your other cycles are low, you can perform physical tasks admirably but are low in sensitivity and mental alertness. If your female cycle is high and your male cycle low, it is a fine day, say, to visit an art museum but a day on which you are likely to tire quickly. The reader can easily guess the applications of other cycle patterns to other common events of life. I omit details about methods of predicting the sex of unborn children or computing the rhythmic "compatibility" between two individuals.

The most dangerous days are those on which a cycle, particularly the 23- or 28-day cycle, crosses the horizontal line. Those days when a cycle is making a transition from one phase to another are called "switch-point days." It is a pleasant fact that switch points for the 28-cycle always occur on the same day of the week for any given individual, since this cycle is exactly four weeks long. If your switch point for the 28-cycle is on Tuesday, for instance, every other Tuesday will be your critical day for female energy throughout your entire life.

As one might expect, if the switch points of two cycles coincide, the day is "doubly critical," and it is "triply critical" if all three coincide. The Thommen and Wernli books contain many rhythmograms showing that the days on which various family people died were days on which two or more cycles were at switch points. On two days on which Clark Gable had heart attacks, the second fatal, two cycles were at switch points. The Aga Kahn died on a triply critical day. Arnold Palmer won the British Open Golf Tournament during a high period in July, 1962, and lost the Professional Golf Association Tourney during a triple low two weeks later. The boxer Benny (Kid) Paret died after a knockout in a match on a triply critical day. Clearly it behooves the Fliessian to prepare a chart of his future cycle patterns so that he can exercise especial care on critical days; since other factors come into play, however, no ironclad predictions can be made.

Because each cycle has an integral length in days, it follows that every person's rhythmogram will repeat its pattern after an interval of 23 × 28 × 33 = 21,252 days, or a little more than 58 years. This interval will be the same for everybody. For example, 21,252 days after every person's birth all three of his cycles will cross the zero line simultaneously on their upswing and his entire pattern will start over again. Two people whose ages are exactly 21,252 days apart will be running on perfectly synchronized cycle patterns. Since Fliess's system did not include the 33-day cycle, his cycle patterns repeat after a lapse of 23 × 28 = 644 days. Swiss Fliessians call this the "biorhythmic year." It is important in computing the "biorhythmic compatibility" between two individuals, since any two persons born 644 days apart are synchronized with respect to their two most important cycles.

POSTSCRIPT

George S. Thommen, president of Biorhythm Computers, Inc., 298 Fifth Avenue, New York, is still going strong, appearing occasionally on radio and television talk-shows to promote his products. James Randi, the magician, was moderator of an all-night radio talk-show in the mid-sixties. Thommen was twice his guest. After one of the shows, Randi tells me, a lady in New Jersey sent him her birth date and asked for a biorhythm chart covering the next two years of her life. After sending her an actual chart, but based on a *different* birth date, Randi received an effusive letter from the lady saying that the chart exactly matched all her critical up and down days. Randi wrote back, apologized for having made a mistake on her birth date, and enclosed a "correct" chart, actually as wrongly dated as the first one.

He soon received a letter telling him that the new chart was even *more* accurate than the first one.

Speaking in March, 1966, at the 36th annual convention of the Greater New York Safety Council, Thommen reported that biorhythm research projects were under way at the University of Nebraska and the University of Minnesota, and that Dr. Tatai, medical chief of Tokyo's public health department, had published a book, *Biorhythm and Human Life*, using the Thommen system. When a Boeing 727 jetliner crashed in Tokyo in February, 1966, Dr. Tatai quickly drew up the pilot's chart, Thommen said, and found that the crash occurred on one of the pilot's low days.

Biorhythm seems to have been more favorably received in Japan than in the United States. According to *Time*, January 10, 1972, page 48, the Ohmi Railway Co., in Japan, computed the biorhythms of each of its 500 bus drivers. Whenever a driver was scheduled for a "bad" day, he was given a notice to be extra careful. The Ohmi company reported a fifty percent drop in accidents.

Fate magazine, February, 1975, pages 109–110, reported on a conference on "Biorhythm, Healing and Kirlian Photography," held in Evanston, Ill., October, 1974. Michael Zaeske, who sponsored the conference, revealed that the traditional biorhythm curves are actually "first derivatives" of the true curves, and that all the traditional charts are "in error by several days." Guests at the meeting also heard evidence from California that a fourth cycle exists, and that all four cycles "may be related to Jung's four personality types."

Science News, January 18, 1975, page 45, carried a large ad by Edmund Scientific Company for their newly introduced Biorhythm Kit ($11.50), containing the precision-made Dialgraf Calculator. The ad also offered an "accurate computerized, personalized" biorhythm chart report for 12 months to any reader who sent his birthdate and $15.95. One wonders if Edmund is using the traditional charts (possibly off three days) or Zaeske's refined procedures.

A ridiculous book, *Biorhythm: A Personal Science*, by Bernard Gittelson, was published in 1975 by Arco, and later by Werner books as a paperback. Pocket Books jumped into the action with Arbie Dale's *Biorhythm* (1976). *Reader's Digest* (September 1977) gave the "science" a major boost with Jennifer Bolch's shameless article, "Biorhythm: A Key to Your Ups and Downs."

By 1980 biorhythm had become so popular among the gullible that half a dozen firms were manufacturing mechanical devices, electronic computers, and even clocks that told true believers what to expect each day. See *Fate* for advertisements. *Science 80*, in its January/February 1980 issue, ran an article by Russell Schoch called "The Myth of Sigmund Freud," which included a good photograph of Freud and Fliess together as young men.

Reflections on the Reading:

1. Why do you think people are drawn to a pseudoscience?
2. What differences do you see at this point between science and pseudoscience?
3. What gives biorhythm its credibility; that is, what makes it seem believable?
4. What other pseudosciences can you name?

Distinguishing Science from Pseudoscience

Clearly Gardner has no patience with biorhythm. His attack on the spurious scientific nature of biorhythm discredits the reasonableness of the theory, so we do not need to critically evaluate biorhythm here. We do need to be clear about the general characteristics of pseudosciences and what distinguishes them from genuine sciences so we are not led to unfulfilled expectations and disappointments by other false "sciences." After all, pseudosciences resemble sciences well enough that some people are misled into believing that they have the same authority that sciences do.

One of the characteristics of a pseudoscience is that it cannot be refuted. Not only do the adherents of a pseudoscience refuse to admit any evidence as refuting their position, the hypotheses of a pseudoscience are such that they cannot be refuted. The hypotheses are compatible with every outcome and every observation! Horoscopes are a familiar example of this. Most horoscopes are written in such broad terms that no matter what happens to you that day, it would be compatible with what is predicted for you. When it appears that the horoscope was inaccurate—for instance, it foretold that something was going to happen to you which didn't—adherents will dismiss the contrary evidence by saying that because you were forewarned, you changed your behavior and avoided the negative outcome that had been predicted. The prediction wasn't wrong, they say. Rather your behavior altered the circumstances. It turns out, then, that it is impossible to refute astrology. There are no consequences of the hypotheses of astrology that can be observed which would be considered by its adherents as disconfirming evidence. Other pseudosciences similarly rest on irrefutable hypotheses.

A scientific hypothesis, on the other hand, to be considered scientific must be capable of refutation. That is, although we can never prove a scientific theory, we can refute (or "falsify") it. A theory is capable of refutation if is possible to derive an observational consequence from the theory which would refute or contradict the theory if it were actually observed. For instance, "all substances expand when heated" is falsifiable. "The planets move in elliptical orbits because God prefers ellipses" is not.

Moreover, scientists are expected to regard scientific hypotheses with a certain amount of skepticism and to be always willing to change their assumptions in light of new evidence. If we look at the history of science we see that it is a history of the replacement of one theory by another, just as the Copernician theory replaced the Ptolemaic.

We saw in the last chapter, however, that Copernicus and Galileo did not accept the observational evidence of the constancy of the appearance of Venus as refuting Copernicus's hypothesis of a heliocentric universe. They continued to believe in the heliocentric universe despite the fact that they could not observe any change in the size of Venus or its waxing and waning. You might ask, then, how is this situation different from the situation of astrologers who refuse to accept evidence against their hypotheses? That is a good question.

The difference is that the observations of Venus as unchanging in size and neither waxing nor waning *did* count as evidence against the Copernican hypothesis. These were certainly disconfirming observations. It was only that other considerations in the background knowledge of Copernicus and Galileo weighed more heavily than the observational evidence. If future refinements of the telescope had not revealed the phases of Venus, and so on, other scientists would have eventually put the Copernican theory where scientists put other discredited scientific hypotheses—into the dustheap of the history of science.

Astronomers, unlike astrologers, are always ready to revise their hypotheses in the light of new information. This process of revision is sometimes slow but is always a possibility. **Scientific theories are always refutable**. Pseudoscientific theories are not refutable. (This probably sounds like a strange thing to say. We generally think of science as those theories which are not refutable. What we mean by science, however, are those theories which are refutable but have not been refuted.) We can see this when we look at what happened to the Copernican hypothesis. It was first revised by Kepler who changed the shapes of the orbits of the planets around the sun. Then in the twentieth century it was revised by Einstein and his theory of general relativity. Today scientists describe the planets as following straight-line paths in curved space which they call geodesics.

Another important difference between science and pseudoscience is that a scientific hypothesis must **fit in** with other scientific hypotheses. There is a **connectedness** in the story that science tells. One piece fits in with another piece so the connecting pieces get larger and larger over time, like a big jigsaw puzzle. Pseudosciences do not connect with one another or with other beliefs which we hold. The story the pseudoscientist tells is unique. Although she may use the language of modern science, the story doesn't really fit into a larger picture. Again, consider astrology. Your horoscope depends on the position of the planets, moon, and stars on the day you were born. How does that causal mechanism—whatever it is—fit in with what we

"Hobart, this is Merlin, my science adviser."

Many people have their "Merlins," even a recent President's wife. Drawing by Dana Fradon; © 1994, The New Yorker Magazine, Inc.

believe about gravity or human biology and psychology? What are the connections?

This leads us to a third major difference between science and pseudoscience and that is there is always an appeal to mystery or mysterious forces in pseudoscience. Of course, there are forces in science, too, and these are somewhat mysterious in that we can only describe their effects. But the scientist does not really want to stop at that point. She wants to learn more and eliminate mystery whenever possible. The pseudoscientist, on the other hand, is happy with mystery. She may even be said to glory in it! "That's just the way it is," she says. For example, the astrologer doesn't know and doesn't care to know why the positions of the stars and planets exert such power in our earthly lives. She is content with the story as is.

Before leaving this topic we should draw one more distinction that is helpful in understanding the difference between science and pseudoscience and that is the distinction between a would-be science and a pseudoscience. A would-be science is a new story that is beginning to be told that may not fit well with the current story told by scientists. The difference between a would-be science and a pseudoscience is their differences in methodology. The scientist of the potential new science uses the methods of critical thinking and is willing to test her hypotheses in the same way the established scientist is. Sometimes it is not clear whether an enterprise is a potential science or a spurious pseudoscience. An example here is parapsychology. Some parapsychologists have used the critical thinking techniques of science to examine the possibilities of extrasensory ways of communicating. Some parapsychologists, on the other hand, refuse to admit possible refutations of their hypotheses. Currently, to use the language of Gardner, there are more quacks in parapsychology than scientists.

To summarize: Scientists and pseudoscientists both tell stories, but the methods they use to arrive at their stories are different and consequently the value of the stories to us is different. The scientist uses the methods of critical thinking. She tests her story and changes her story in light of the evidence she finds. She is open-minded and in constant dialogue with other scientists, listening to their stories, and trying to make her hypothesis or story fit in with theirs. The pseudoscientist is locked into her story. Contrary evidence is ignored. The story is never revised. No effort is made to connect the story to a larger world picture. The dialogue is only among adherents or disciples. And the story always ends with a mystery which precludes further dialogue and discussion. The story told by the scientist helps us to predict and control events in our lives. The story told by the pseudoscientist suggests that we are at the mercy of forces which we cannot understand and can only accept.

Exercises

9–I

1. What are the hallmarks of a pseudoscience?

2. Why is astrology a pseudoscience?

3. Bring in a recent horoscope.

   a. Are these predictions refutable?

   b. Suppose you were to take these predictions seriously. What view of the universe would you have to hold to accept these predictions?

4. What does the biorhythm theorist claim?

9–II

1. Describe the marks of pseudoscience you see in biorhythm.

2. Choose another pseudoscience (the paperback book shelf can give you ideas here) and use its own examples to show why it is a pseudoscience.

3. Can you think of any other would-be sciences besides parapsychology?

9–III

1. What differences do you see between the unproven assumptions of Copernicus and the unproven assumptions of Fliess?

2. Why is it next to impossible to convince a firm believer in astrology that the astrologer's predictions are not warranted?

3. **a.** Develop an argument to show that the study of UFO sightings is a pseudoscience.

   b. Develop an argument to show that the study of UFO sightings is a scientific enterprise.

chapter 10

Common Mistakes in Reasoning

Introduction

Errors in reasoning occur with more frequency than we would like. These errors hinder our daily activities and often prevent us from enjoying life. Sometimes they even threaten life itself. One way to avoid errors in reasoning is to know what good reasoning is and to practice using good reasoning skills in our daily activities. Another way to avoid reasoning errors is to become familiar with some of the errors that reasoning people commonly make.

Erroneous reasoning is usually called fallacious reasoning. Fallacious reasoning often occurs in patterns. These fallacious reasoning patterns are referred to simply as **fallacies**. Some critical thinking textbooks focus exclusively on recognizing fallacies and being able to name them and distinguish one from another. Good critical thinking does not require that you should be able to recognize and name every pattern of fallacious reasoning you come across. It is helpful, however, to be familiar with some common patterns so you can spot them in your own and in other people's reasoning and can avoid being misled.

The first reading in this chapter comes from the book *The Many Loves of Dobie Gillis* by Max Shulman. Shulman is a bright and clever writer whose work you will enjoy. "Love Is a Fallacy" is a painless introduction to the topic of fallacies. The second reading is a political editorial from a community newspaper and is rather typical of that genre. As you read it, focus your attention on the author's thesis. What point is he trying to make? Later we will discuss how he goes about trying to make that point.

Love Is a Fallacy

MAX SHULMAN

Cool was I and logical. Keen, calculating, perspicacious, acute and astute—I was all of these. My brain was as powerful as a dynamo, as precise as a chemist's scales, as penetrating as a scalpel. And—think of it!—I was only eighteen.

It is not often that one so young has such a giant intellect. Take, for example, Petey Bellows, my roommate at the university. Same age, same background, but dumb as an ox. A nice enough fellow, you understand, but nothing upstairs. Emotional type. Unstable. Impressionable. Worst of all, a faddist. Fads, I submit, are the very negation of reason. To be swept up in every new craze that comes along, to surrender yourself to idiocy just because everybody else is doing it—this, to me, is the acme of mindlessness. Not, however, to Petey.

One afternoon I found Petey lying on his bed with an expression of such distress on his face that I immediately diagnosed appendicitis. "Don't move," I said. "Don't take a laxative. I'll get a doctor."

"Raccoon," he mumbled thickly.

"Raccoon?" I said, pausing in my flight.

"I want a raccoon coat," he wailed.

I perceived that his trouble was not physical, but mental. "Why do you want a raccoon coat?"

"I should have known it," he cried, pounding his temples. "I should have known they'd come back when the Charleston came back. Like a fool I spent all my money for textbooks, and now I can't get a raccoon coat."

"Can you mean," I said incredulously, "that people are actually wearing raccoon coats again?"

From _The Many Loves of Dobie Gillis_

"All the Big Men on Campus are wearing them. Where've you been?"

"In the library," I said, naming a place not frequented by Big Men on Campus.

He leaped from the bed and paced the room. "I've got to have a raccoon coat," he said passionately. "I've got to!"

"Petey, why? Look at it rationally. Raccoon coats are unsanitary. They shed. They smell bad. They weigh too much. They're unsightly. They——"

"You don't understand," he interrupted impatiently. "It's the thing to do. Don't you want to be in the swim?"

"No," I said truthfully.

"Well, I do," he declared. "I'd give anything for a raccoon coat. Anything!"

My brain, that precision instrument, slipped into high gear. "Anything?" I asked, looking at him narrowly.

"Anything," he affirmed in ringing tones.

I stroked my chin thoughtfully. It so happened that I knew where to get my hands on a raccoon coat. My father had had one in his undergraduate days; it lay now in a trunk in the attic back home. It also happened that Petey had something I wanted. He didn't *have* it exactly, but at least he had first rights on it. I refer to his girl, Polly Espy.

I had long coveted Polly Espy. Let me emphasize that my desire for this young woman was not emotional in nature. She was, to be sure, a girl who excited the emotions, but I was not one to let my heart rule my head. I wanted Polly for a shrewdly calculated, entirely cerebral reason.

I was a freshman in law school. In a few years I would be out in practice. I was well aware of the importance of the right kind of wife in furthering a lawyer's career. The successful lawyers I had observed were, almost without exception, married to beautiful, gracious, intelligent women. With one omission, Polly fitted these specifications perfectly.

Beautiful she was. She was not yet of pin-up proportions, but I felt sure that time would supply the lack. She already had the makings.

Gracious she was. By gracious I mean full of graces. She had an erectness of carriage, an ease of bearing, a poise that clearly indicated the best of breeding. At table her manners were exquisite. I had seen her at the Kozy Kampus Korner eating the specialty of the house—a sandwich that contained scraps of pot roast, gravy, chopped nuts, and a dipper of sauerkraut—without even getting her fingers moist.

Intelligent she was not. In fact, she veered in the opposite direction. But I believed that under my guidance she would smarten up. At any rate, it was worth a try. It is, after all, easier to make a beautiful dumb girl smart than to make an ugly smart girl beautiful.

"Petey," I said, "are you in love with Polly Espy?"

"I think she's a keen kid," he replied, "but I don't know if you'd call it love. Why?"

"Do you," I asked, "have any kind of formal arrangement with her? I mean are you going steady or anything like that?"

"No. We see each other quite a bit, but we both have other dates. Why?"

"Is there," I asked, "any other man for whom she has a particular fondness?"

"Not that I know of. Why?"

I nodded with satisfaction. "In other words, if you were out of the picture, the field would be open. Is that right?"

"I guess so. What are you getting at?"

"Nothing, nothing," I said innocently, and took my suitcase out of the closet.

"Where you going?" asked Petey.

"Home for the week end." I threw a few things into the bag.

"Listen," he said, clutching my arm eagerly, "while you're home, you couldn't get some money from your old man, could you, and lend it to me so I can buy a raccoon coat?"

"I may do better than that," I said with a mysterious wink and closed my bag and left.

"Look," I said to Petey when I got back Monday morning. I threw open the suitcase and revealed the huge, hairy, gamy object that my father had worn in his Stutz Bearcat in 1925.

"Holy Toledo!" said Petey reverently. He plunged his hands into the raccoon coat and then his face. "Holy Toledo!" he repeated fifteen or twenty times.

"Would you like it?" I asked.

"Oh yes!" he cried, clutching the greasy pelt to him. Then a canny look came into his eyes. "What do you want for it?"

"Your girl," I said, mincing no words.

"Polly?" he said in a horrified whisper. "You want Polly?"

"That's right."

He flung the coat from him. "Never," he said stoutly.

I shrugged. "Okay. If you don't want to be in the swim, I guess it's your business."

I sat down in a chair and pretended to read a book, but out of the corner of my eye I kept watching Petey. He was a torn man. First he looked at the coat with the expression of a waif at a bakery window. Then he turned away and set his jaw resolutely. Then he looked back at the coat, with even more longing in his face. Then he turned away, but with not so much resolution this time. Back and forth his head swiveled, desire waxing, resolution waning. Finally he didn't turn away at all; he just stood and stared with mad lust at the coat.

"It isn't as though I was in love with Polly," he said thickly. "Or going steady or anything like that."

"That's right," I murmured.

"What's Polly to me, or me to Polly?"

"Not a thing," said I.

"It's just been a casual kick—just a few laughs, that's all."

"Try on the coat," said I.

He complied. The coat bunched high over his ears and dropped all the way down to his shoe tops. He looked like a mound of dead raccoons. "Fits fine," he said happily.

I rose from my chair. "Is it a deal?" I asked, extending my hand.

He swallowed. "It's a deal," he said and shook my hand.

I had my first date with Polly the following evening. This was in the nature of a survey; I wanted to find out just how much work I had to do to get her mind up to the standard I required. I took her first to dinner. "Gee, that was a delish dinner," she said as left the restaurant. Then I took her to a movie. "Gee, that was a marvy movie," she said as we left the theater. And then I took her home. "Gee, I had a sensaysh time," she said as she bade me good night.

I went back to my room with a heavy heart. I had gravely underestimated the size of my task. This girl's lack of information was terrifying. Nor would it be enough merely to supply her with information. First she had to be taught to *think*. This loomed as a project of no small dimensions, and at first I was tempted to give her back to Petey. But then I got to thinking about her abundant physical charms and about the way she entered a room and the way she handled a knife and fork, and I decided to make an effort.

I went about it, as in all things, systematically. I gave her a course in logic. It happened that I, as a law student, was taking a course in logic myself, so I had all the facts at my finger tips. "Polly," I said to her when I picked her up on our next date, "tonight we are going over to the Knoll and talk."

"Oo, terrif," she replied. One thing I will say for this girl: you would go far to find another so agreeable.

We went to the Knoll, the campus trysting place, and we sat down under an old oak, and she looked at me expectantly. "What are we going to talk about?" she asked.

"Logic."

She thought this over for a minute and decided she liked it. "Magnif," she said.

"Logic," I said, clearing my throat, "is the science of thinking. Before we can think correctly, we must first learn to recognize the common fallacies of logic. These we will take up tonight."

"Wow-dow!" she cried, clapping her hands delightedly.

I winced, but went bravely on. "First let us examine the fallacy called Dicto Simpliciter."

"By all means," she urged, batting her lashes eagerly.

"Dicto Simpliciter means an argument based on an unqualified generalization. For example: Exercise is good. Therefore everybody should exercise."

"I agree," said Polly earnestly. "I mean exercise is wonderful. I mean it builds the body and everything."

"Polly," I said gently, "the argument is a fallacy. *Exercise is good* is an unqualified generalization. For instance, if you have heart disease, exercise is bad, not good. Many people are ordered by their doctors *not* to exercise. You must *qualify* the generalization. You must say exercise is *usually* good, or exercise is good *for most people*. Otherwise you have committed a Dicto Simpliciter. Do you see?"

"No," she confessed. "But this is marvy. Do more! Do more!"

"It will be better if you stop tugging at my sleeve," I told her, and when she desisted, I continued. "Next we take up a fallacy called Hasty Generalization. Listen carefully: You can't speak French. I can't speak French. Petey Bellows can't speak French. I must therefore conclude that nobody at the University of Minnesota can speak French."

"Really?" said Polly, amazed. "*Nobody?*"

I hid my exasperation. "Polly, it's a fallacy. The generalization is reached too hastily. There are too few instances to support such a conclusion."

"Know any more fallacies?" she asked breathlessly. "This is more fun than dancing even."

I fought off a wave of despair. I was getting nowhere with this girl, absolutely nowhere. Still, I am nothing if not persistent. I continued. "Next comes Post Hoc. Listen to this: Let's not take Bill on our picnic. Every time we take him out with us, it rains."

"I know somebody just like that," she exclaimed. "A girl back home—Eula Becker, her name is. It never fails. Every single time we take her on a picnic——"

"Polly," I said sharply, "it's a fallacy. Eula Becker doesn't *cause* the rain. She has no connection with the rain. You are guilty of Post Hoc if you blame Eula Becker."

"I'll never do it again," she promised contritely. "Are you mad at me?"

I sighed. "No, Polly, I'm not mad."

"Then tell me some more fallacies."

"All right. Let's try Contradictory Premises."

"Yes, let's," she chirped, blinking her eyes happily.

I frowned, but plunged ahead. "Here's an example of Contradictory Premises: If God can do anything, can He make a stone so heavy that He won't be able to lift it?"

"Of course," she replied promptly.

"But if He can do anything, He can lift the stone," I pointed out.

"Yeah," she said thoughtfully. "Well, then I guess He can't make the stone."

"But He can do anything," I reminded her.

She scratched her pretty, empty head. "I'm all confused," she admitted.

"Of course you are. Because when the premises of an argument contradict each other, there can be no argument. If there is an irresistible force, there can be no immovable object. If there is an immovable object, there can be no irresistible force. Get it?"

"Tell me some more of this keen stuff," she said eagerly.

I consulted my watch. "I think we'd better call it a night. I'll take you home now, and you go over all the things you've learned. We'll have another session tomorrow night."

I deposited her at the girls' dormitory, where she assured me that she had had a perfectly terrif evening, and I went glumly home to my room. Petey lay snoring in his bed, the raccoon coat huddled like a great hairy beast at his feet. For a moment I considered waking him and telling him that he could have his girl back. It seemed clear that my project was doomed to failure. The girl simply had a logic-proof head.

But then I reconsidered. I had wasted one evening; I might as well waste another. Who knew? Maybe somewhere in the extinct crater of her mind a few embers still smoldered. Maybe somehow I could fan them into flame. Admittedly it was not a prospect fraught with hope, but I decided to give it one more try.

Seated under the oak the next evening I said, "Our first fallacy tonight is called Ad Misericordiam."

She quivered with delight.

"Listen closely," I said. "A man applies for a job. When the boss asks him what his qualifications are, he replies that he has a wife and six children at home, the wife is a helpless cripple, the children have nothing to eat, no clothes to wear, no shoes on their feet, there are no beds in the house, no coal in the cellar, and winter is coming."

A tear rolled down each of Polly's pink cheeks. "Oh, this is awful, awful," she sobbed.

"Yes, it's awful," I agreed, "but it's no argument. The man never answered the boss's question about his qualifications. Instead he appealed to the boss's sympathy. He committed the fallacy of Ad Misericordiam. Do you understand?"

"Have you got a handkerchief?" she blubbered.

I handed her a handkerchief and tried to keep from screaming while she wiped her eyes. "Next," I said in a carefully controlled tone, "we will discuss False Analogy. Here is an example: Students should be allowed to look at their textbooks during examinations. After all, surgeons have X rays to guide them during an operation, lawyers have briefs to guide them during a trial, carpenters have blueprints to guide them when they are building a house. Why, then, shouldn't students be allowed to look at their textbooks during an examination?"

"There now," she said enthusiastically, "is the most marvy idea I've heard in years."

"Polly," I said testily, "the argument is all wrong. Doctors, lawyers, and carpenters aren't taking a test to see how much they have learned, but students are. The situations are altogether different, and you can't make an analogy between them."

"I still think it's a good idea," said Polly.

"Nuts," I muttered. Doggedly I pressed on. "Next we'll try Hypothesis Contrary to Fact."

"Sounds yummy," was Polly's reaction.

"Listen: If Madame Curie had not happened to leave a photographic plate in a drawer with a chunk of pitchblende, the world today would not know about radium."

"True, true," said Polly, nodding her head. "Did you see the movie? Oh, it just knocked me out. That Walter Pidgeon is so dreamy. I mean he fractures me."

"If you can forget Mr. Pidgeon for a moment," I said coldly, "I would like to point out that the statement is a fallacy. Maybe Madame Curie would have discovered radium at some later date. Maybe somebody else would have discovered it. Maybe any number of things would have happened. You can't start with a hypothesis that is not true and then draw any supportable conclusions from it."

"They ought to put Walter Pidgeon in more pictures," said Polly. "I hardly ever see him any more."

One more chance, I decided. But just one more. There is a limit to what flesh and blood can bear. "The next fallacy is called Poisoning the Well."

"How cute!" she gurgled.

"Two men are having a debate. The first one gets up and says, 'My opponent is a notorious liar. You can't believe a word that he is going to say.' . . . Now, Polly, think. Think hard. What's wrong?"

I watched her closely as she knit her creamy brow in concentration. Suddenly a glimmer of intelligence—the first I had seen—came into her eyes. "It's not fair," she said with indignation. "It's not a bit fair. What chance has the second man got if the first man calls him a liar before he even begins talking?"

"Right!" I cried exultantly. "One hundred per cent right. It's not fair. The first man has *poisoned the well* before anybody could drink from it. He has hamstrung his opponent before he could even start. . . . Polly, I'm proud of you."

"Pshaw," she murmured, blushing with pleasure.

"You see, my dear, these things aren't so hard. All you have to do is concentrate. Think—examine—evaluate. Come now, let's review everything we have learned."

"Fire away," she said with an airy wave of her hand.

Heartened by the knowledge that Polly was not altogether a cretin, I began a long, patient review of all I had told her. Over and over and over again I cited instances, pointed out flaws, kept hammering away without letup. It was like digging a tunnel. At first everything was work, sweat, and darkness. I had no idea when I would reach the light, or even *if* I would. But I persisted. I pounded and clawed and scraped, and finally I was rewarded. I saw a chink of light. And then the chink got bigger and the sun came pouring in and all was bright.

Five grueling nights this took, but it was worth it. I had made a logician out of Polly; I had taught her to think. My job was done. She was worthy of me at last. She was a fit wife for me, a proper hostess for my many mansions, a suitable mother for my well-heeled children.

It must not be thought that I was without love for this girl. Quite the contrary. Just as Pygmalion loved the perfect woman he had fashioned, so I loved mine. I decided to acquaint her with my feelings at our very next meeting. The time had come to change our relationship from academic to romantic.

"Polly," I said when next we sat beneath our oak, "tonight we will not discuss fallacies."

"Aw, gee," she said, disappointed.

"My dear," I said, favoring her with a smile. "we have now spent five evenings together. We have gotten along splendidly. It is clear that we are well matched."

"Hasty Generalization," said Polly brightly.

"I beg your pardon," said I.

"Hasty Generalization," she repeated. "How can you say that we are well matched on the basis of only five dates?"

I chuckled with amusement. The dear child had learned her lessons well. "My dear," I said, patting her hand in a tolerant manner, "five dates is plenty. After all, you don't have to eat a whole cake to know that it's good."

"False Analogy," said Polly promptly. "I'm not a cake. I'm a girl."

I chuckled with somewhat less amusement. The dear child had learned her lessons perhaps too well. I decided to change tactics. Obviously the best approach was a simple, strong, direct declaration of love. I paused for a moment while my massive brain chose the proper words. Then I began:

"Polly, I love you. You are the whole world to me, and the moon and the stars and the constellations of outer space. Please, my darling, say that you will go steady with me, for if you will not, life will be meaningless. I will languish. I will refuse my meals. I will wander the face of the earth, a shambling, hollow-eyed hulk."

There, I thought, folding my arms, that ought to do it.

"Ad Misericordiam," said Polly.

I ground my teeth. I was not Pygmalion; I was Frankenstein, and my monster had me by the throat. Frantically I fought back the tide of panic surging through me. At all costs I had to keep cool.

"Well, Polly," I said, forcing a smile, "you certainly have learned your fallacies."

"You're darn right," she said with a vigorous nod.

"And who taught them to you, Polly?"

"You did."

"That's right. So you do owe me something, don't you, my dear? If I hadn't come along you never would have learned about fallacies."

"Hypothesis Contrary to Fact," she said instantly.

I dashed perspiration from my brow. "Polly," I croaked, "you mustn't take all these things so literally. I mean this is just classroom stuff. You know that the things you learn in school don't have anything to do with life."

"Dicto Simpliciter," she said, wagging her finger at me playfully.

That did it. I leaped to my feet, bellowing like a bull. "Will you or will you not go steady with me?"

"I will not," she replied.

"Why not?" I demanded.

"Because this afternoon I promised Petey Bellows that I would go steady with him."

I reeled back, overcome with the infamy of it. After he promised, after he made a deal, after he shook my hand! "The rat!" I shrieked, kicking up great chunks of turf. "You can't go with him, Polly. He's a liar. He's a cheat. He's a rat."

"Poisoning the Well," said Polly, "and stop shouting. I think shouting must be a fallacy too."

With an immense effort of will, I modulated my voice. "All right," I said. "You're a logician. Let's look at this thing logically. How could you choose Petey Bellows over me? Look at me—a brilliant student, a tremendous intellectual, a man with an assured future. Look at Petey—a knothead, a jitterbug, a guy who'll never know where his next meal is coming from. Can you give me one logical reason why you should go steady with Petey Bellows?"

"I certainly can," declared Polly. "He's got a raccoon coat."

The Sleaze Merchants Attack

In recent days there has been an outpouring of hate, ridicule and oh-so-pious defense of the First Amendment in connection with the report of the Meese Commission on Pornography.* That report urged action against porn and its obvious negative effects on our society. The predictable and immediate reaction was to challenge the findings that porn results in violence in women.

Anyone with the slightest sense of history must admit that there has been an immense increase in pornographic material flooding this nation since Playboy's philosophy was hagiographed back in the mid-60's. And only the willfully ignorant will deny the tremendous increase in sexual crimes of all types during those two decades. Not *post hoc, propter hoc?* Let the critics of the Meese Commission prove their case because the burden is on them.

On March 18, 1985, *Newsweek*—no friend of the Meese Commission findings or recommendations—stated that the standard categories of the $8 billion a year porn industry in the U.S. "include films and magazines devoted to group sex, sex with pregnant women, sex with crippled women, bestiality, child porn and sadomasochism. S&M in turn has its own peculiar racial sub-categories, including black women bound and struggling against their tormentors; Asian women bound and hung from various objects, and white men bound and masked. . . . And spread across these categories is the eroticization of violence. A substantial percentage of the population is more aroused by themes that involve domination and conquest than by equally explicit but non-violent material."

Violence is the fastest growing part of the industry, netting some $2 billion dollars annually. As *Newsweek* notes: "The violence takes many forms: rape, beatings, whippings, dismemberment and, as best can be determined, simulated murder. In the highly specialized subgenre of Nazi porn, sexual torture and rape are presented with the Holocaust as background."

Does the Meese Commission need any more damning indictment of the traffic in porn than the *Newsweek* report?

(an editorial)

*The Meese Commission on Pornography was commissioned under President Reagan. Its conclusion was that pornography contributed to violence against women. This conclusion has been challenged by various groups including professional sociologists and feminists who find the data inconclusive.–Ed.

What we have, in the porn culture, is men—and women—being seduced by a civilization of death. One of the strangest aspects about sex is that, if it doesn't worship life, it will invariably worship death.

The porn trade ties in with the contraceptive self-genocide of the West. In recent weeks we have once again been regaled with "the five billionth human being born," and with the threat of over-population. It's a giant hoax against Western survival. Not so? Then consider the following:

It takes a reproduction rate of 2.1 children per woman to maintain a society. Yet, as Ben Wattenberg pointed out recently, "the important, modern, free, powerful nations of the world are not having the number necessary (for reproduction). Not even close. In the U.S., the rate is 1.8 children per woman; in England, 1.8; in France, 1.9; in Japan, 1.7; in Italy, 1.6; in West Germany, 1.4. This is the first time in history that a collection of nations, without the stress of war, famine or disease, have opted not to reproduce themselves."

What has happened is that the secular state has pronounced itself unworthy of being sustained in the future. Its chief spokesmen push national suicide, through contraception, abortion and unbridled hedonism, of which porn is a major part. It doesn't take the Meese Commission to figure it out.

At the present rates of reproduction in the first and third worlds, the Europeans will be serving mint tea to their Moslem conquerors, as Jean Raspail predicted nearly 15 years ago. In 1960, the European population—which includes the U.S.—constituted 25% of the world's population. If present trends continue they will represent only 5% of the world population in just 70 years. There is no way the West can survive such a reversal of population roles.

We are, indeed, coming to the end of an age, one in which European culture, art, religion were dominant. The torch is passing to the Third World, whose peoples instinctively react against the imposition of population control from without, from International Planned Parenthood and from population imperialism emanating from the money makers in the U.S.A. Ed Meese is wrong? Look at the facts and you can conclude that his commission didn't say the half of it! It touched only on today's increasing degeneracy without gauging the long-term depopulation of the West that it will cause.

Reflections on the Readings:

1. Were you surprised by any of the examples of fallacies in "Love Is a Fallacy"; that is, were there any arguments that you thought were good that turned out to be examples of poor reasoning?

2. Describe an instance when you deliberately used poor reasoning or a fallacy to try to convince someone of your point of view. Be specific.

3. List some situations where fallacies often occur.

4. Does the editorial writer have a powerful argument? What is his point? What is the evidence? Is there a difference between the substance of the argument and its appearance?

The Nature of Fallacies

Fallacies are bits of poor reasoning that appear in recurrent patterns. Most of these patterns were identified by philosophers of the Middle Ages called Scholastics and have Latin names. Fallacies give us trouble, not because they have Latin names that are hard to remember, but because they seem like pieces of good reasoning so we tend to accept the reasoning and to give more warrant to the conclusion drawn than we should.

Philosophers usually distinguish between two kinds of fallacies, the formal fallacies and the informal fallacies. The formal fallacies are mistakes in reasoning with necessity or deductive reasoning. Several of these have already been pointed out in Chapter 5 and will not concern us here. The informal fallacies are mistakes in reasoning with probability or inductive reasoning. We will look at a few of the more commonly committed informal fallacies in this chapter so you can recognize them when they occur around you.

A fallacy, for our purposes in this chapter, is a piece of reasoning with probability which gives the mistaken impression of conferring greater probability on the conclusion than is warranted by the evidence. Or to put it another way, the information offered as evidence only seems to increase the likelihood of the conclusion. When we take a closer look at the evidence offered, the apparent probability of the conclusion melts away.

Fallacies are tricky because they give the appearance of being good reasoning and supplying information (**traces**) we should count as sufficient evidence for the conclusion. If we use our **background knowledge**, however, we soon find that there is not enough **story** connecting the information to the conclusion. Consequently, we should not consider the information as sufficient evidence, or support, for the conclusion. For example, consider the case in the reading of the man who applies for a job and when asked about his qualifications, offers his wife and six needy children. From our background knowledge we know that these are not what the employer means by *job* qualifications. As much as we might want to help the poor man out by

Calvin and Hobbes

by Bill Watterson

As we all do when we commit a fallacy. CALVIN AND HOBBES © 1988 Watterson. Reprinted with permission of UNIVERSAL PRESS SYNDICATE. All Rights reserved.

giving him a job, there still remains the question about whether he is qualified for the job.

Fortunately, most fallacies fall into three primary categories so it is not necessary to learn all of them by name. Nor is it necessary to distinguish between fallacies that closely resemble one another in order to be a good critical thinker. It is important to know these three main groupings and to keep in mind some basic models or patterns of reasoning that are fallacious.

Some Common Fallacies to Recognize

One common form of fallacious reasoning is offering irrelevant material as evidence for a conclusion. We already saw in Chapter 6 that not all information or traces provide evidence for a conclusion. In Chapter 6 we stressed the point that Sherlock Holmes's success as a detective comes from his ability to see a **trace** as a trace. He can do this because of his large store of background knowledge which enables him to see connections where others do not. **Fallacies of irrelevance** present just the opposite situation. They imply connections where there are none. They draw us into believing a conclusion is warranted by suggesting considerations which seem to be evidence for the conclusion but which are not. It is always possible to weigh these considerations against our background knowledge to see that the information is irrelevant to the conclusion at hand.[1] This critical thinking skill can be aided, however, by learning some common patterns of using irrelevant evidence.

---

[1]While we have kept the commonly used designation of "fallacies of irrelevance" for this group of fallacies, it should be noted that they might better be called "fallacies of suppressed insupportable premises." Careful examination of these arguments reveals that the information in the premises is not irrelevant to the conclusion but rather is connected to the conclusion by an implicit premise which most people would not accept as factual if it were explicitly expressed.

One common pattern has already been introduced, namely, the pattern the Scholastics called **ad misericordiam** or **appeal to sympathy or pity**. Although a person may have need for a job, a good grade, or mercy, need is not the proper criterion for judgment in these situations. It is not a relevant quality for hiring, grading, or making legal decisions. So, when someone appeals to your sympathy in a particular situation, a little red flag should go up warning you that you should question carefully the relevance of that appeal to the question at hand.

At hominem is another common pattern of offering irrelevant information as evidence for a conclusion. A person who commits the *ad hominem* fallacy offers information about another's character as evidence against the content of that other person's ideas or point of view. For instance, if a politician is making a case for a particular stance on an issue, and his opponent in the discussion offers an irrelevant comment about the speaker's family life, then the opponent has committed the *ad hominem* fallacy. This pattern occurs frequently in politics. Of course, sometimes character is important. Character is important in leaders like presidents and teachers and police. In an *ad hominem* argument, however, character is irrelevant as evidence to the topic under discussion or dispute. It's like the baseball umpire saying, "You're out," and when you ask why he says, "Because I don't like your face" or "I don't like your grandmother." (In the Peanuts comic strip, Lucy often argues this way when she is losing an argument to Charlie Brown!)

The character of a witness on the witness stand is relevant to whether the jury takes the words of the witness as evidence. But the statement that his grandmother wore combat boots is not relevant. If you are arguing with a friend about whether God exists or not, and your friend is offering reasons for his position, it is *ad hominem* to respond with an attack on his character or ancestry or appearance, for example, "You're just the believing (doubting) type."

You probably can remember when you heard or read an *ad hominem* argument. You probably can remember when you uttered one yourself. ("You won't vote for Joe for student body president? You're just a creep.") *Ad hominem* arguments are very common but they are not very helpful. They shift the focus of a discussion from reasons which are evidence for a conclusion to information which is not relevant, thereby avoiding or subverting the critical thinking that the topic deserves. They also often play to biases and prejudices. Consequently, they should be avoided in discussion or dialogue and you should be on guard not to be pulled in by them. If you are arguing with someone who offers an *ad hominem* argument, it is usually a good idea to point out that this is not a good form of reasoning and that the information is irrelevant as evidence for the conclusion. An easy model of *ad hominem* to keep in mind here is the umpire who says, "You're out because I don't like your face."

Advertisements are a good source of fallacies of irrelevance. The most common fallacy exploited by advertisers is the **appeal to false authority**. The authority often cited by advertisers is a sports figure who is held up as an expert on underwear or cereal or automobiles. Appeals to false authority occur in other situations as well. Two little children on the playground arguing might try to settle their argument by appealing to the authority of one of their parents. For example, one child might claim that Willy Mays is the best baseball player ever. The other might claim that that honor belongs to Ty Cobb. "Oh, yeah? Who says?" "My father says, that's who!" In general an appeal to false authority occurs when we attribute to someone who does have expertise in one area, expertise in another area for which there is no reason to think that person has expertise.

Another fallacy of irrelevance that you surely have encountered is the fallacy called **slippery slope**. Political arguments often take this form; for example, "Some politicians want to ban cigarettes. Will alcohol be next? Will caffeine be next? Will high-fat foods be next?" The slippery slope argument generally comes in two varieties. According to one variety, once you take one step down the slope, whatever it is, you might as well keep on going until you reach the end of it. There's no obvious resting place or way to stop along the way once you have started so you might as well just enjoy the journey. The other variation of this argument is that since there's no obvious stopping place until you reach the bottom, you should not even take one step down the slope. Dieters are fond of slippery slope arguments. The loose-diet version: "Since I ate one piece of cake, I might as well ruin my diet some more and have a second." The strict-diet variation on this theme: "I won't even eat one peanut because if I do, I'll eat the whole bowl." (Once we start down that slope, there's no place to stop.) The person who commits the slippery slope fallacy uses the fact that there is no fixed place to draw a line between two conditions or properties to claim that no line can be drawn.

Many words have no obvious dividing line or point between themselves and their opposite, but this does not mean that there is no difference between the two extremes. For instance, it is certainly not clear when a person becomes bald. Will two more lost hairs be the deciding factor? Three? Although we cannot say just how many more hairs John will have to lose before we consider him bald, we do know the difference and can usually distinguish between bald and nonbald. Many opposites have no fixed line between them. When, for example, does a person become rich, or poor, or white-haired, or old, or tall?

In many cases we have to make a decision and say this person is rich and that one poor. That this distinction always contains an element of arbitrariness does not mean that the line cannot be drawn reasonably. The open dialogue is the best way to determine the best place to draw the line. There is still a difference between being rich and being poor and we all know which one we would rather be. Borderline cases will always be troublesome, especially when other goods or benefits are determined by where the line is drawn. For example, if people below a certain income level are entitled to a governmental support program, then where the line is drawn between poverty and nonpoverty takes on considerable importance. Because the line is arbitrary, it is open to rational discussion and possible adjustment. It does not mean, however, that no line can be drawn or that once it is drawn it has no significance.

The abortion debate is an area where slippery slope arguments are common—from partisans on both sides of this issue. The pro-life proponent often argues that since there is no way of saying when a fetus becomes a person, that is, no nonarbitrary line between being a fetus and being a person, we must accept the view that life begins at conception. (The argument sometimes takes the form, "If you are willing to abort impaired fetuses, then what is to stop you from killing impaired infants?") The pro-choice advocate sometimes argues the same way, namely, since there is no point before birth when a fetus becomes a person, the mother should always have freedom of choice and may choose abortion at any time during her pregnancy. Both of these arguments are guilty of the slippery slope fallacy. The dialogue about the moral legitimacy of abortion suffers because of this poor reasoning pattern and often becomes a stalemate, leading sometimes even to the use of force to express beliefs.

Although slippery slope arguments are tempting, we should avoid them in our discussions with others and with ourselves. That there is no nonarbitrary way of drawing a line does not mean that there is no line or difference between two opposite properties. Keep in mind the model of the dieter who will never lose weight thinking that there is no difference between eating and overeating, between one piece of cake or two!

There are many other fallacies of irrelevance. The four we have discussed here are very common and, in their own way, rather fun to know. It is good to keep the general category of irrelevance in mind as well as these specific named fallacies.

Another category of frequently committed fallacies is the category of **fallacies of faulty generalization**. We have already seen that generalization is one of the common forms of reasoning with probability so it is not surprising that there are some common patterns of poor reasoning associated with this type of reasoning. Several of these were exemplified in the first reading. **Hasty generalization** is one of them. A person who commits this fallacy draws a generalization from too small a sample. We saw in Chapter 7 that appropriate sample size is not something that can be specified without reference to background knowledge. There is no general rule that can be stated as to when a generalization is made too hastily. Consequently, the error of hasty generalization occurs frequently.

It is rather commonplace, for example, to decide on the basis of one bad meal in a restaurant not to go back to that restaurant or from owning a lemon of an automobile not to buy that make again. We human beings are often "jumping to conclusions." A good model of hasty generalization to keep in mind is, "I don't like people who go to State University. I met someone from there once and he was very stuck on himself." But how many times have you met someone that you reacted to negatively on the first meeting only to find on future encounters that you genuinely like that person!

Hasty generalizations can be rather sophisticated errors as we saw in _The Literary Digest_ misprediction of the 1936 presidential election. _The Digest_ thought long and hard about how to generalize from its sample results to the nationwide election. Since four previous predictions had been accurate, it assumed that the 1936 prediction would also be accurate. Unfortunately we sometimes cannot know that our generalization has been hasty until it has been tested and found to be so.

The mistake _The Literary Digest_ made could also be called the fallacy of **unrepresentative sample**. One can get into drawing finer distinctions between fallacies and their labels than we choose to do here but this does not help one become a better critical thinker. The discrimination between a sample that is too small, unrepresentative, or nonrandom can sometimes be a difficult matter of judgment, one best left to the experts. What is important is that you realize that sampling errors can be made despite the best of intentions not to be hasty.

Sometimes we even use hasty generalization on purpose, knowing that our reasoning is weak but hoping to convince someone of our point of view. Advertisements are notorious in this regard. "Try it, you'll like it," or "Doctors recommend. . . ." The best way to avoid committing the fallacy of hasty generalization or to avoid being taken in by it is to build up a good storehouse of background knowledge. The generalizations you draw and the generalizations you accept should fit in well with other beliefs that you hold, especially the beliefs which are more fundamental or well entrenched.

A variation of hasty generalization that deserves special mention is the fallacy called **anecdotal evidence** or **vivid data**. We commit this fallacy when we allow the last or most vivid of our experiences to outweigh all the previous experiences we have had. We cease looking at all the evidence and focus on a small part of it. Consequently we project the wrong conclusions into the future. A common example of this kind of reasoning is the person who has a bad experience flying and insists, therefore, on driving by car to every destination or on staying home. While we may sympathize with that person's fear, the overall safety record for long-distance traveling is much better for flying than it is for riding in a car. The person has given too much weight to his vivid experience and not enough weight to the less vivid but, nevertheless, overwhelming evidence that flying a long distance is safer than driving it.

This is not to suggest that being wary of something after one has had a bad experience is unreasonable. Unfortunately, there are many things to be afraid of in our world. But a fear that is based on one isolated personal experience needs to be put in perspective with the fuller picture so that reasonable judgments can be made in the future. Similarly, one should not let the most recent or most vivid experience override all previous experience, either his own or the collective experience of the larger group.

Another important area of overzealous generalization is that of causal fallacies; that is, the fallacies of attributing causal relations where the relationship is simply coincidental. The most common of these fallacies is the one mentioned in Chapter 7, namely, ***post hoc, ergo propter hoc*** or ***post hoc***, for short. This is the fallacy of thinking that just because X is followed by Y, X causes Y. A good example of this fallacy is found in your reading. It is an easy model to keep in mind when being on the look out for *post hoc* reasoning. This is the example of Eula Becker, who, according to Polly, always caused it to rain on the picnic.

We are all guilty of *post hoc* reasoning at times. Like reasoning about generalizations, the only way we can protect ourselves from *post hoc* reasoning is by using our background knowledge and relying on those beliefs which are well entrenched to guide us in distinguishing causal connections from accidental connections. This entrenchment is usually more reliable if it characterizes the web of belief of people who are recognized experts on the subject who have used Mill's methods to test for the constancy of the conjunction. For instance, there are many well-entrenched old wives' tales about what causes the common cold. Doctors tell us, however, that colds, like many other diseases, are caused by a virus and not by getting caught in the rain without a raincoat or going barefoot too early in the spring.

The third important category of fallacies for which you should be on guard are the **fallacies of emotional manipulation**. These fallacies provoke emotions through language and encourage us to substitute these emotional reactions for reason. It's not that emotions are illegitimate or unimportant to critical thinking. It is perfectly all right to indicate that you feel strongly about something. What is not all right, however, is to use emotional language to manipulate others—to inhibit them from using their powers of reason—or to preclude rational discussion altogether. It is only a small step between emotionally manipulating a discussion so that reason is precluded and getting one's way by threatening someone with a punch in the jaw. As Polly says in the reading, ". . . stop shouting. I think shouting must be a fallacy too."

The fallacy of **poisoning the well** is a common method of emotional manipulation. There were several examples of this in the Shulman reading. Someone who poisons the well says something derogatory before the discussion has even started. This has the effect of precluding further discussion, discussion being the most important ingredient in critical thinking. Calling your opponent in a discussion a liar before the discussion has even started, for instance, has the effect of casting suspicion on whatever he might say thereafter, no matter how cogent and well argued. Name calling, ethnic and racial slurs, and derogatory comments all have the effect of limiting or even precluding discussion of the actual merits of what a person has said or is about to say. They influence how we think about what is being said but without proper warrant.

In general, **emotionally loaded language** precludes discussion. "The Sleaze Merchants Attack" is a prime example here. Even the title is loaded. Who would give any merit to the point of view of a "sleaze merchant"? Nobody could like a sleaze merchant. The editorial continues in that same tone, using language that is both attention-grabbing and obfuscating at the same time. By the time you have finished reading the editorial, you are stirred up but not sure what the point is or what evidence has been offered in support of that point. No one is for "increasing degeneracy" and "depopulation of the West," but how do these two evils figure in our evaluation of the report of the Meese Commission on Pornography?

How would one discuss the findings of the Meese Commission with the author of this editorial? What room has been left for discussion? What kind of evidence would the author consider? A close examination of the editorial reveals that the author has tried to persuade—without presenting any evidence in support of his position. All the persuasion rests on the effect of its emotionally loaded language. No evidence is provided to support the claim that pornography results in the abuse of women or that it does not.

The most serious problem with this piece is that the author doesn't really want you to discuss with him. He only wants you to believe him. He only wants you to accept what he says. This is the problem with emotionally charged language and why it is a form of fallacious reasoning. It carries the pretense of rational dialogue but its primary goal is to preclude rational dialogue. And rational dialogue is the essence of good critical thinking. It is not that people should not be allowed to use emotional language or to express strong feelings—as long as that expression is not dangerous to others. But such emotionally charged language should not be passed off as rational dialogue or presented as a substitute for thinking critically about difficult controversial issues. When carried to extreme it becomes dogmatism which is the charade of reason. We shall have more to say about dogmatism in the chapters that follow.

The fallacies discussed in this chapter are only a sampling of the many fallacies that have been singled out and given names by philosophers as examples of faulty reasoning. Recognizing fallacies can be helpful in improving your reasoning skills. To make it easier to recognize fallacies we have grouped them into three categories which can be more easily remembered. These categories are **fallacies of irrelevance, fallacies of faulty generalization**, and **fallac-**

ies of emotional manipulation. If you have trouble remembering the specific fallacies, remember these general categories so you can examine the reasoning in question to see whether the evidence is relevant, the generalization sound, and the language not emotionally manipulative.

Ten specific fallacies have been discussed in this chapter. They are *ad misericordiam, ad hominem*, appeal to false authority, slippery slope, hasty generalization, unrepresentative sample, anecdotal evidence, *post hoc*, poisoning the well, and emotionally loaded language. The best way to remember these fallacies is to keep a model for each one in mind. Then, when you come across a piece of reasoning that resembles that model, a little red flag should go up telling you that the reasoning looks suspicious and that you should examine it carefully to make sure no fallacy is being committed.

Exercises

10–1

Name the fallacy in each of the following. Note: Where there are several possible choices, pick the one you consider to be the *best* one.

1. I'm not going to vote for Clinton. He's such a lousy saxophone player.

2. Did you know Elvis is still alive? It's true. There's a brand new picture of him on the front of the latest issue of the *National Star*. I saw it at the supermarket while I was checking out.

3. Don't buy that car. We had that same make once. It was always breaking down. The company really builds poor cars.

4. If we let 18-year-olds drink, then we might as well let 16-year-olds drink. And if we let 16-year-olds drink, then, before you know it, 14-year-olds are going to be drinking. And that will make 12-year-olds want to drink, too. But it's crazy for 12-year-olds to be drinking. So we might as well leave the drinking age at 21.

5. It's just not right that I'm going to be laid off. I just bought a new house and spent the rest of my savings on a vacation. I won't be able to survive two weeks without a job.

6. Let's decide together which movie to see tonight. Of course, you'll probably want to go see that stupid new Batman movie at the Ritz.

7. This was my first week in French I. All the teacher does is speak French. I haven't understood a single word in three classes. I'll never understand French.

8. Most college students drink too much. A recent survey reported in the Psi Psi Psi fraternity journal found that 80 percent of the respondents get drunk every weekend at college.

9. I bowled a perfect game last week! I was wearing my new purple socks. I'm going to wear them again this week for the big tournament!

10. The assault weapons ban is just one more example of the government's efforts to disarm and ultimately enslave the American people.

10–II

1. Collect five examples of fallacies from hard copy media (newspapers, journals, magazines, printed advertisements, etc.) There are ten fallacies discussed in the chapter and several more in the reading that you can use as models.

2. A common argument offered in the abortion debate is, "Abortion is murder." Why is this not an argument which promotes critical thinking?

3. You have probably heard someone argue in the following fashion, "I never wear my seat belt. A friend of mine was in an accident and luckily was thrown from the car before it rolled down a cliff. If he'd been wearing his seat belt, he'd have been killed." What's wrong with this bit of reasoning?

4. Suppose your friend is training for the marathon. He's becoming a fanatic about running twelve miles every day even though his knees are aching and his times are getting slower. What would you suggest he do? How would you argue your case?

10–III

1. If you were the opposing lawyer how would you argue with the man on the witness stand who is suing his employer for damages, including pain and suffering, because a piece of ceiling tile fell on his head at work after which he developed appendicitis?

2. You have been asked to serve as consultant to _The Literary Digest_ for its pre-election prediction for the 1940 presidential election to help it avoid the errors of its 1936 predictions. Reread the selections from _The Literary Digest_ in Chapter 7. Your job is to explain to _The Digest_ what it did wrong in 1936 and to make recommendations for developing a better pre-election poll. Your instructions must be spe-

cific. "Use good reasoning" and "Take a bigger sample" are *not* helpful. Remember that you are writing to a pollster, not a candidate. Make specific reference to the errors of 1936. Address your letter to the owner of *The Literary Digest*, Mr. Citizen Kane.

3. In the confirmation hearings for Justice Clarence Thomas, Thomas was accused by at least one witness of sexual harassment. Is this an instance of *ad hominem*? Defend your answer.

chapter 11

The Nature of Morality

Introduction

It is a common view—one that we think is fundamentally mistaken—that reasoning about values, especially about moral values, is different from reasoning about the nonmoral features of the world. Some people who hold this view claim that talk about values doesn't use reasoning at all. They think that when we talk about values we are only expressing our emotions. On this view, reason enters into talk about nonmoral features of the world, but values are irrational so there isn't much to say about them. They believe about morality what many people believe about beauty—that it is in the eye of the beholder. What is important in moral matters, they say, is simply the sincerity of one's belief or the degree of commitment one holds.

Sometimes people who hold this view support it with an argument about the logic of moral arguments. The philosopher David Hume is often cited as the source of this argument. Hume argued in a now very famous passage in his *Treatise of Human Nature* that one cannot reason (he meant reason with necessity) from statements about the way a thing *is* to statements about the way it *ought* to be without committing a jump that has no logical justification. Some people have thought, on the basis of Hume's argument, that critical thinking has no place in discussions of moral values. Since the topic of Chapters 11–14 is the use of critical thinking skills in moral discourse, it is important to take a closer look at Hume's argument:

> In every system of morality which I have hitherto met with, I have always remark'd, that the author proceeds for some time in the ordinary way of reasoning, and establishes the being of a God, or makes observations concerning human affairs; when of a sudden I am supriz'd to find, that instead of the usual copulations of propositions, *is*, and *is not*, I meet with no proposition that is not connected with an *ought* or an *ought not*. This change is imperceptible; but is, however, of the last consequence. For as this *ought* or *ought not*, expresses some new relation or affirmation, 'tis necessary that it should be observ'd and explain'd; and at the same time that a reason should be given, for what seems altogether inconceivable, how this new relation can be a deduction from others, which are entirely different from it. But as authors do not commonly use this precaution, I shall presume to recommend it to the readers; and am persuaded that this small attention wou'd subvert all the vulgar systems of morality, and let us see, that the distinction of vice and virtue is not founded merely on the relations of objects, nor is perceiv'd by reason.[1]

In this passage Hume makes a very good point, namely, that value statements ("ought" statements) cannot be logically derived from factual statements ("is" statements). It follows from this that there is no logical or deductive necessity when we use statements about the nonmoral features of the world to support moral claims. But this should not be surprising or disheartening. We have already seen there is no logical or deductive necessity in our reasoning about matters of fact or matters of scientific thought either.

Most of our everyday reasoning is reasoning with probability. Does Hume also mean (as he is sometimes interpreted to mean) that reasoning with probability (or inductive reasoning) is also irrelevant to moral discourse? If we look closely at the passage we see that Hume does not say that claims about what is the case are irrelevant to claims about what ought to be the case. He simply says that the latter do not logically follow (with necessity) from the former. This does not mean that statements about nonmoral features of the world cannot be used to give **rational support** to claims about values.

We will see that critical thinking is very important in discussions of value, perhaps more important than in discussions of nonmoral matters because we tend to have more disagreement when we deal with values and

---

[1]Book III, Part *i*, section *i*.

less evidence that we can offer to support our moral beliefs. **Our moral dialogues can profit from the same critical thinking skills that we would use in discussions of matters of fact: being open to discussion and being a good listener, having a large storehouse of background knowledge, being able to recognize patterns of traces and see a story that weaves those patterns in ever larger patterns, recognizing the limits of evidence and proof, and so on.** Let's face it, the alternatives to rational dialogue about moral beliefs are not attractive or helpful: seeing who can outshout the other, giving the other person a sock in the jaw, or as happens between nation states, waging war![2]

You probably hold a set of moral beliefs to which you are quite committed. But chances are you are unsure about how to justify them. As a consequence, you probably have avoided some moral discussion not to anger someone else or because you were not sure how to argue successfully for what you believe. These chapters on reasoning about values do not argue for any particular moral point of view. They are intended to help you sort out some of your confusions about how moral beliefs connect with beliefs about the world and help you support the beliefs you hold. We all need to learn how we can better support our point of view in a moral argument, whether toddlers in the sandbox or professional diplomats. Fisticuffs and war are not attractive alternatives.

Moral statements do appear to be different from statements about matters of fact. Moral statements have words in them like _ought, good, right, duty, should._ Something different is being said when we talk about what ought to be the case from when we talk about what is the case. This apparent difference makes us think that we have to support these two types of statements differently. Most of the time we think we know how to support nonmoral claims and how to dispute them. We give evidence from experience. We cite other nonmoral claims. We have already discussed a variety of ways we use to reason about matters of fact, including those which go beyond the evidence available and project into the future. Although we generally know how to support factual claims, we often do make claims which we later have to revise.

When it comes to supporting or disputing moral claims, however, we are often not so sure about how to go about it. Either we argue for or against moral statements with nonmoral statements—which do not convey or confer moral value—or we argue about them using other moral statements—which suggests that the reasoning is circular. An example of the first alternative is "You ought not to steal because you might get arrested." Here the moral force of _ought_ seems to get lost. It makes stealing sound like just a matter of prudence, something with unpleasant consequences like eating too much or get-

---

[2]A classical ethics that takes a similar view of the role of reason in ethics is Aristotle's model of the man of practical reason who is Aristotle's analogue to our critical thinker.

ting caught in the rain. An example of the second alternative is "You ought not to steal because stealing is wrong." This is like saying you ought not to steal because you ought not to steal, which is clearly circular reasoning.

This puzzle of justifying moral claims is not new. It has bothered philosophers for over two thousand years! We saw it already in the dialogue *Euthyphro* where Socrates asks Euthyphro why the gods love piety. ("Do the gods love piety because it is pious, or is it pious because they love it?")

The reading in this chapter is a small selection from *The Brothers Karamazov* by Fyodor Dostoevsky. The justification of moral values is one of the main themes of this very rich and rewarding novel. As part of the exploration of this theme, Dostoevsky tells a story, within the larger story of the Karamazov family, about a general and a serf boy. This story is very short and will make you think long and hard about the nature of morality.

The Brothers Karamazov

FYODOR DOSTOEVSKY

There was in those days a general of aristocratic connections, the owner of great estates, one of those men—somewhat exceptional, I believe, even then—who, retiring from the service into a life of leisure, are convinced that they've earned the power of life and death over their subjects. There were such men then. So our general, settled on his property of two thousand souls, lives in pomp, and domineers over his poor neighbors as though they were dependents and buffoons. He has kennels of hundreds of hounds and nearly a hundred dog-boys—all mounted, and in uniform. One day a serf boy, a little child of eight, threw a stone in play and hurt the paw of the general's favorite hound. 'Why is my favorite dog lame?' He is told that the boy threw a stone that hurt the dog's paw. 'So you did it.' The general looked the child up and down. 'Take him.' He was taken—taken from his mother and kept shut up all night. Early that morning the general comes out in full pomp, mounts his horse with the hounds, his dependents, dog-boys, and the huntsmen, all mounted around him. The servants are summoned for their edification, and in front of them all stands the mother of the child. The child is brought from the lockup. It's a gloomy cold, foggy

---

(a short excerpt)

autumn day, a capital day for hunting. The general orders the child to be undressed; the child is stripped naked. He shivers, numb with terror, not daring to cry. . . . 'Make him run,' commands the general. 'Run! run!' shout the dog-boys. The boy runs. . . . 'At him!' yells the general, and he sets the whole pack of hounds on the child. The hounds catch him, and tear him to pieces before his mother's eyes!

Reflections on the Reading:

1. The general believes he has done a morally correct act. Do you agree or disagree? How would you argue with him?

2. As the general, how would you argue for the moral correctness of your action?

3. Is the general's action morally correct in nineteenth-century Russia but not in twentieth-century United States? Focus on the moral value of the act, not the legality of it.

4. Are moral values in the eye of the beholder?

5. When we argue about moral values, why can we not just "agree to disagree"?

Objectivism/Subjectivism

Most people who read about the general's choice of punishment for harming his favorite hound believe this choice is morally wrong. While all punishments involve harming another person, here the punishment seems too severe for the nature of the crime. A child's life has more moral worth than a hound's injured paw. The general, of course, does not see it this way. From the general's point of view good hounds are hard to come by. The children of serfs are plentiful and so without much value. Besides, all assembled will learn an important moral lesson which will help to avoid harm in the future to both hounds and serf boys. So, he thinks, the sacrifice of one serf boy is outweighed by the future good that his punishment will bring about. The general does not think himself an evil person. He believes he is doing the morally correct thing.

What are we to say to this general? Or should we just keep silent? Some people would argue that the general's behavior is morally all right (at least not evil), given that it happened in Russia in the nineteenth century, but claim that times have changed and such behavior is no longer morally acceptable but rather today is morally blameworthy. Morality, on this view, would be a function of social values or cultural norms and would vary over times and places. This response is unsatisfing for two reasons. First, the general's action offends our moral sensibilities so much that it is hard to accept any claim about its being a morally acceptable act. Second, the view that behavior is morally blameless as long as it is acceptable within the cultural community in which it occurs allows the possibility of all sorts of atrocities and removes them from moral criticism as long as the relevant social community accepts them. This would put headhunting, terrorism, torture, slavery, gas chambers, etc., outside the realm of moral criticism which, again, offends our ordinary moral sentiments.

What we would like are some objective features of the world that we could point to, which we could use as evidence to support our belief that the general's behavior is morally incorrect. Such objective features would enable us to decide who is right, the general or we. We could settle moral disputes the same way we settle disputes about the height of the flag pole or the color of the neighbor's new car. Let's look back at the story for examples of objective features.

For instance, the day of the punishment is described as a "gloomy cold, foggy autumn day." *Cold* and *foggy* are usually taken as describing objective features of the world. We generally know when to use them correctly. We know that we know how to use them correctly because there is consensus about when to use them. We say the day is cold when the thermometer reads minus 10 degrees. We describe the day as foggy when there are tiny little water droplets in the air and it is hard to see far into the distance. There are publicly observable criteria for the proper usage of these words.

Of course, sometimes there is ambiguity about the use of these words. We are not sure if the day is cold or if it just feels cold to us or if it is fog or a haze that we're looking at. To avoid ambiguity we sometimes convert qualitative features of the world into quantitative features as, for example, when we agree to determine temperature by a scale measuring the height of a liquid in a sealed glass tube. Even the ambiguity about the proper usage of *cold* or *foggy*, however, is guided by consensus. That is, there is general agreement that it is difficult sometimes to distinguish fog from haze or smog. Note that the general consensus of language users guides us in describing the "objective features" of experience.

Similarly, many philosophers have established objective criteria for the proper use of moral terms (or for the appropriate moral evaluation of an act or agent) based on what they claim is the general consensus of moral language users. In the nineteenth century, for instance, philosopher Jeremy Bentham thought that what people mean when they call an act right is that it promotes the greatest amount of happiness for the greatest number of people. Perhaps you have heard of this view, called utilitarianism. Bentham tried to make this criterion for right very clear by making it quantitative—in the same way that the thermometer makes *cold* quantitative. He said that *happiness* means pleasure and pleasures are measurable by their intensity, duration, and so on. Hence, one can determine which acts should be performed and which acts should not, just by calculating the amount of pleasure which can be derived from them.

People frequently use Bentham's criteria—or some modification of them—in reasoning about values. It is not uncommon to hear, for instance, a legislator argue that a particular bill will promote more happiness for more people than an alternative, or that the severe punishment of a few individuals for a crime will have a deterrent effect in the future, thereby promoting the happiness of more people. Probably all of us have used utilitarian reasoning at some time. There is not the same kind of consensus, however, about these criteria as about the criteria for a cold day. Both philosophers and nonphilosophers have proposed different objective criteria for the rightness of an act which are at times inconsistent with the criteria of utility.

One of these alternatives was proposed by the philosopher Immanuel Kant. Kant claimed that the key objective criterion of a moral imperative is that it is noncontradictory. (This would be an objective feature of the world although it is not one directly experienced. Rather, it is a logical feature, a feature which all rational people are capable of recognizing.) Kant examined the way people use moral language and then determined that our common usage presupposes that beings who are rational and moral must act from rationally consistent principles. He interpreted this to mean that a person performs a right act when she acts on the basis of a principle that she can universalize without contradiction. That is, according to Kant, all of us must do what we think every other rational being should do in similar circumstances. We cannot make exceptions for ourselves. That would be logically inconsistent and not living up to our potential as rational human beings. What is important, then, on Kant's account, is the principle from which one acts, not the consequences and the good (or lack thereof) the act produces, and that principle must apply to everyone in like circumstances.

You can see from these brief accounts of utilitarianism and Kantian ethics that each uses different objective criteria for the rightness of an action. Consequently, they do not always agree on which acts are right. Let's look at one more effort to establish objective criteria for making moral claims, namely, the view often proposed by religious believers (although not usually by theologians) that an act is good if God wills it. There are many versions of this account of morality. We already saw one in *Euthyphro*. They refer to some divine being who approves, wills, is pleased by the act in question. You may not have thought of these views as proposing objective criteria for making moral judgments but they do. That is, it is an objective feature of the world whether God wills an act or does not will an act just as it is an objective feature of the world whether you will an act or not. You will that the car turns to the right when you turn the steering wheel to the right. You do not will that the car turns to the right when you hit a slick patch in the road and skid toward the right. Of course, we may have a harder time knowing what God wills than what our neighbor wills but not always. Historically religious groups have offered diverse ways of determining the will of God, ranging from reliance on the utterances of inspired individuals to reliance on the natural reason of the believer.

These three objectivist views—the utilitarian, the Kantian, and the religious—about the nature of morality have been enormously successful in that they generally make it much easier to make moral judgments. When in doubt one can find objective answers by calculating the total amount of pleasure, determining whether the moral principle is universalizable, or consulting the religious minister, priest, rabbi, or text. As a consequence, all three views have many adherents. There are several problems, however, that these objectivist views face. One obvious one is that they all do not pick out the same features of reality as the important criteria for making moral judgments. One has focused on features of human experience, one has focused on the nature of human rationality, and one has focused on the viewpoint of some divine being. This leads to conflicting moral judgments and sometimes fisticuffs and war. It also suggests that maybe the right objective features of experience are not being singled out since there is sometimes so little agreement.

There is a more fundamental problem here as well, one which we have already encountered and which makes the objective account of moral reasoning less attractive than it initially appears. This is the problem encountered with many of our statements about experience, even nonmoral ones, namely, that our statements of the "objective criteria" do not always agree. It is not just that people pick different objective criteria—like Bentham and Kant and Euthyphro did—but that they do not always experience the same "objective features" of the world. Where one person sees fog, another sees a fine mist. Where one person sees the houses of New York as "palaces," another sees them as intolerably ugly. (Remember the two quotations describing New York in Chapter 1.) The objectivist account seems to assume that we have certainty about the features of our experience and that this certainty can be used as the basis for certainty with regard to moral beliefs. We have already seen, however, that our descriptions of our experiences often vary and we can have disagreements about the "objective features" of experience. Even scientific descriptions of our experience are simply part of an unprovable story which rests on unproven assumptions. Thus, grounding moral judgments on the objective features of our experience does not provide moral judgments with such a firm base, certainly not as firm a base as many of the adherents of these views would like. Consequently, objectivist views of the nature of moral judgments cannot settle the issue of who is right.

These weaknesses of objectivism have led many people to think that moral judgments are subjective. According to the subjectivist account, moral judgments are the product of each individual subject's conscious deliberation and they are morally correct for that subject provided the judgment is a result of a process which is rational, impartial, and deliberate—and not simply a casual decision. There are no objective features of the world which serve as criteria for moral judgments unless a particular subject decides to rely on some feature as a criterion.

A number of philosophers have argued for a subjectivist view of moral statements. The seventeenth-century philosopher Spinoza is a good example of someone with a subjectivist view of morality. According to Spinoza, the world and God are identical so that everything that happens happens necessarily as a product, or function, of God's nature. Consequently, the world is neither good nor bad. It just is as it has to be. *Good* and *bad*, then, can only be terms used by human beings to reflect their own reactions to events in the world. They are not descriptive of objective features of the world. People like Spinoza who see events in the world as happening of necessity through the unfolding of a fixed nature, for example, or as governed by fixed mechanical laws generally hold subjectivist views of moral statements.

More contemporary subjectivist accounts of morality come from philosophical viewpoints that see the world as having no order or fixed nature at all. On these accounts, the world just is and human beings give it shape and form by describing it and by valuing certain aspects of it. Existentialists like Jean-Paul Sartre are subjectivists of this type. They hold that morality is an individual matter since there is no "human nature" that is fixed which would determine how human beings should behave.

The subjectivist viewpoint has much to recommend it. For one thing, it helps to explain why we have such differences of opinion and why we find it so hard to agree when it comes to making moral judgments. Since each of us is a separate subject, we are likely to have different views of the same events, and because the factors which enter into the judgment are particular to each of us as subjects, it is hard to have much agreement. The subjectivist viewpoint is also appealing in that it suggests a way to resolve moral disagreements: When the argument reaches a stalemate, we should just agree to disagree. We should avoid unpleasantness and not keep arguing—or fighting—because continued argument is useless. If the two arguers are arguing from considered judgments (judgments which are rational, impartial, and deliberate), then each disputant holds a view which is morally correct for her.

On the other hand, subjectivism seems counterintuitive to our ordinary moral sentiments in several important ways. We can see this by going back to the example of the general and the serf boy. Most people find the general's behavior morally unjustifiable if not morally blameworthy. It seems overbearing, vindictive, cruel, and selfish. On the subjectivist view, however, it makes no sense to argue with the general or to criticize his behavior. The general's decision must be construed as a considered judgment. It is not hasty. He has even slept on it. His behavior is very deliberate and thought out. In his own eyes his decision is just and right. On the subjectivist view, it makes sense for us to tell the general that we think his punishment is too harsh (because we seek to influence his opinion), but it does not make sense to say it is morally wrong or hold him responsible for a morally blameworthy act. The subjectivist view leads to the counterintuitive view that both the general and the serf boy's mother are morally correct, even though they judge the same act very differently.

Supporting Moral Claims

Both objectivism and subjectivism have some attractive features. Both make claims about the nature of moral judgments that fit well with our ordinary experiences in dealing with moral issues. Both, however, also lead to consequences which conflict with our ordinary moral sentiments, and neither appears able to resolve these differences. In this section we will present an alternative way of approaching moral judgments, showing how the ideas of good reasoning that we have already developed in preceding chapters can help us to support our moral judgments and become better moral reasoners.

Part of the difficulty in understanding the nature of moral judgments comes from a mistaken belief, encouraged by a misunderstanding of the Hume passage with which this chapter began, that there are two different kinds of statements which are always distinguishable from one another, statements about matters of fact and statements about values. This distinction, if we examine it closely, collapses under scrutiny and cannot be maintained.

Factual statements, as we pointed out in Chapter 1, **are simply those statements which have been found to be the most warranted**. Factual statements are statements that are rarely questioned, statements for which support is rarely demanded. The usage, "statements about matters of fact," tends to imply, however, that "matters of fact" are somehow separate from our statements about them. While the world itself is not identical with our statements about it or even with our perceptions of it, we have seen that the world is describable in a variety of ways, no one of which can be said to be the single correct description. What we can say is that some descriptions are more **warranted** than others and that some descriptions are **better** than others. We warrant a statement or show that it is a better description than another statement by supporting it with **other** statements.

For example, to call an apple "red" (usually called "fact") is much the same as calling an apple "good" (usually considered "value"). Either statement could be warranted or unwarranted and the warranting takes place in much the same way. We warrant "This apple is red" generally by comparing it with other red things. We warrant "This apple is good" by comparing it with other tasty things or perhaps with other nutritious things. Like detectives in the courtroom, we offer evidence to support our description and this is the only proof we can offer. Whether others accept our description depends sometimes on how well we have supported it with other statements, other times on how well it is seen to work, and most of the time on both.

It is important to remember that even scientific statements do not rest on neutral descriptions of experience. The scientist, like the rest of us, uses a theory or story to organize the myriad of traces in the world into a pattern that can be described and tested. Hence, the statements she chooses to describe the objective features of the world rest on certain assumptions. Some of these assumptions are about the efficacy of inductive reasoning and making casual claims, some are about the warrant for the theoretical framework from which the scientist works, and some are "value-loaded," like the assumption that simple theories and beautiful formulas are better than complex and untidy ones. Thus even in science, the human enterprise thought to be the most value-neutral, we are often faced with alternative descriptions of the objective features of the world.

A distinction which can be drawn, although not in every case, is the distinction between moral and nonmoral statements. Some statements are clearly nonmoral; for example, "The cat is on the mat." Some statements are clearly moral; for example, "It is wrong to steal." Some statements, however, do not fall neatly into one category or the other. Consider the statement, "John is anemic." Most people would think that it is not good to be anemic. Most people would not choose to be anemic. Although _anemic_ refers to a nonmoral feature of the world, namely, a quantitatively low hemoglobin level in the blood, it also carries evaluative content. It is not a value-neutral word. Many putatively descriptive words are like _anemic._ They are both descriptive and evaluative. Statements about the nonmoral features of the world and statements about values, then, are best thought of as being on a continuum. Some statements are clearly at one end of the continuum and some are clearly at the other. But there is also a gray area between the two ends where many statements about the world belong.

What this means is that the fact/value distinction which has bothered many people, including many philosophers, is not a distinction which can be clearly drawn. It certainly cannot be drawn in every case. Some statements about the world have both descriptive and evaluative content. Even scientific statements, while usually on the descriptive end of the continuum, rest in part on assumptions of value, namely the aesthetic values of beauty and simplicity and the rational values of coherence and consistency. While there is a difference between "is" statements and "ought" statements, when seen as a continuum the difference between them seems much more a difference of degree, not a difference of kind. Hence, it is reasonable to support moral statements in the same way that statements about the nonmoral features of the world are supported—by warranting them with other statements. Moreover, just as there are facts about the nonmoral features of the world (that is, statements that have been found to be the most warranted and for which support is rarely demanded) so, too, there are moral facts, that is, moral statements that are rarely questioned.

Calvin and Hobbes by Bill Watterson

Statements about moral matters are often clearly warranted (even if we would *want* to deny them). CALVIN AND HOBBES © 1988 Watterson. Reprinted with permission of UNIVERSAL PRESS SYNDICATE. All rights reserved.

    To support moral statements, then, we need to offer evidence for them in the same way we support nonmoral statements with evidence. We use reason and descriptions of our experience. We use a story (a theory) to guide our selection of evidence and give it a pattern that makes sense in relation to our background knowledge and the background knowledge of the people with whom we are reasoning. Some of the statements we offer in support of our moral claims will be statements about nonmoral features of the world and some will be statements with moral content.

    If we are reasoning with probability, and not formally or with necessity, there is no logical problem in offering (only) nonmoral statements in support of moral ones. If we are using reasoning with necessity, however, we must have at least one moral statement among our premises to derive a moral statement as our conclusion. That is what Hume means in the passage that introduces this chapter. From a formal logic point of view, we cannot draw an "ought" statement as the conclusion of an argument with only "is" premises. There is no logical error, however, in drawing a moral statement as the conclusion of a formal argument with a combination of moral and nonmoral premises. For example, "People ought not to take other people's property. Mary is taking Paul's book. Therefore, Mary's act is wrong." Of course, the first premise of this argument is a moral prescription with which everyone may not agree. A Marxist might disagree, for instance. A strict Marxist believes that no one should own private property or that only small items should be privately held.

It is harder to have moral facts than it is to have nonmoral facts because there is less agreement about prescriptive statements like these. There are no obvious nonmoral features of the world that one can point to to support them, no scientific instruments to provide quantitative results that can be used as evidence. But we must be careful not to overstate the difference between statements about the nonmoral features of the world and moral statements. **The vocabulary we use in both moral and nonmoral statements depends upon the consensus of language users for its efficacy.** For example, to know the meaning of the word *foggy* is to be able to use it in the appropriate circumstances, that is, at the times when other English speakers would choose to use the word *foggy*. The situation is the same when using moral words like *good* and *right*. To know the meaning of these words is to be able to use them in circumstances in which other language users would use them. If someone told you that *right* refers to all acts done east of the Mississippi and *wrong* refers to all acts performed west of the Mississippi, you would say that that person does not know the language, that the person does not know the meaning of *right* and *wrong*.[3]

Note, this does not mean that the consensus of the language speakers is the *defining* characteristic of *good* and *bad* or *right* and *wrong*. Just as it is possible for a group of language users to make a mistake about the nonmoral features of the world, it is also possible for them to be mistaken in a particular moral judgment. For example, we have already seen how people in the fifteenth century thought the sun went around the Earth. Today we believe that the Earth goes around the sun and call their belief a mistake. Similarly, until the Civil War it was the consensus in the American South that one person could own another person as private property. Today Americans, north and south, see slavery as immoral and call this earlier view a mistake. (We will have more to say about what it is for a moral view to be mistaken in Chapter 13.)

Let's look at how the consensus of language users functions in the example of the general and the serf boy. There are obviously more serfs than generals in the assembled group, so one might think that the consensus of the language users present would support the mother's belief that the punishment is too harsh and, therefore, conclude that the general's action is morally wrong. What is right or wrong in a particular case, however, is not something that can be determined in isolation. Rather, our judgments of right and wrong—just like our judgments of cold and foggy—must fit in with other

---

[3]This excellent example comes from Sam Gorovitz (*Doctors Dilemmas*, Macmillan, 1982).

beliefs we hold about the world. Each of our moral pronouncements entails a wide-ranging set of beliefs about the world, including nonmoral and moral beliefs. In the example above about Mary's taking Paul's book, for instance, the belief that Mary's action is wrong entails, among other things, that there is such a thing as private property and that books are appropriate kinds of private property. We could imagine a world where this is not the case. In a world where books are scarce, for instance, all books might be considered communal property to be held in libraries for the benefit of the few scholars able to read them—as in the Middle Ages.

In the example of the general and the serfs there is an interesting ambiguity about what is property. Moreover, it is not clear whether the general and his serfs form a community of language users or not. It is highly likely that the general regards "his" serfs as private property, much like his hunting dogs, and believes that he has command over them, including the right to do with them as he sees fit. The serfs, given their upbringing and experience, may not disagree with him. That is, they may see their fate as being at the mercy and whim of famous old generals whose land they work. After all, they watch without remonstrance as the boy is pursued and torn apart. We readers, on the other hand, are a different community of language users and do not see the serf boy as the general's property. We have such a different worldview from that of the general that we would probably have a hard time trying to convince him that his act is wrong. But surely we would have to try. The only way we could convince him would be by using language, trying to connect our worldview with his. Of course, we could use fists or a weapon, but using these tools of persuasion is inconsistent with our own worldview. Among contemporary American language users it would probably be fairly easy to warrant the view that the general's action is unjust, so much so that this judgment might be regarded as a moral fact.

It is important to note that all language, moral and nonmoral, has borderline cases. A borderline case is one where it is not clear which description is the most appropriate and people well versed in the language may disagree about the proper use of the language. The word *foggy* is a good example of a word that readily admits of borderline cases. Whether the day is foggy, misty, smoggy, or cloudy may not always be decidable. Similarly, there are borderline cases in the use of moral language. People who know the language, who are morally normal (not perverse), and who share similar worldviews may still disagree about the morally best course of action in some circumstances. Capital punishment is a moral issue of this sort. On the other hand, that it is morally wrong to boil babies for bouillon is a moral statement for which support is rarely demanded.[4] It can be regarded as a moral fact.

---

[4]Another good Sam Gorovitz example!

Reasoning about moral values, then, is like reasoning about the non-moral features of the world. These are not two different types of reasoning or reasoning about two different types of statements. While some statements are clearly about nonmoral features of experience, many of the statements which describe our experience presuppose implicit value assumptions (as in the fundamental assumptions of science) and many statements which describe nonmoral features of the world are not value-neutral (for example, "anemic"). It is a matter of degree, not a difference in kind. Some statements belong on one end of the descriptive evaluative continuum, for example, "The cat is on the mat"; and some statements belong on the other end of the continuum, for example, "Stealing is wrong." What we have seen is that the so-called fact/value distinction is a distinction which does not reflect our actual language usage and which, consequently, does not change the nature of good critical thinking and reasoning whether we are reasoning about moral matters or about the nonmoral features of the world.

Most statements, either about the nonmoral features of the world or about moral values, are not self-warranting nor are they warranted individually. Each statement is part of a larger worldview and is warranted by offering other statements from reason or experience. Some statements, moral and nonmoral, have come to be accepted as facts. These are statements for which warrant is rarely sought. These are statements which are rarely questioned. All statements, moral and nonmoral, are uttered within a community of language users who are the arbiters of that language. Sometimes the community will not agree about a particular usage. Perhaps there is no community or the case is a borderline case where knowledgeable, well-meaning people will differ. Sometimes the community makes a mistake which it later admits and corrects. Like beliefs about the nonmoral features of the world–which are usually the product of reasoning with probability, not with necessity–beliefs about values are not fixed but change over time both on the community level and on the individual level. Some beliefs are more fundamental than others and thus are changed, if at all, more slowly and with reluctance. Some beliefs are very peripheral and are readily changed. In the United States, for example, it would take the equivalent of a Copernican Revolution to change our fundamental beliefs about the inviolability of private property, while beliefs about the immoral or amoral nature of alcohol consumption have fluctuated over time.

Thus, the skills we need to critically evaluate statements about the nonmoral features of the world and moral statements are the same. These are the skills that enable us to reason together so that we can enjoy life with friends and have pleasant experiences and avoid intractable differences of opinion about moral matters. To reason together we need to be open to the world around us so that we are aware of traces, see patterns, and continually increase the storehouse of background knowledge we bring to experience.

We need to be aware of the limits of the evidence for our beliefs, both moral and nonmoral, so we are willing continually to test those beliefs against present and future experience. **Most of all, we need to make the effort that reasoning together requires. Moral arguments try our patience even more than arguments about the nature of experience, but they also lead to more hostile consequences if the participants are unwilling to make the effort to reason together.**

Exercises

11–I

1. Why is Kant a moral objectivist?

2. Why is existentialism an example of moral subjectivism?

3. Why is there no sharp line of demarcation between moral matters and nonmoral matters?

11–II

1. List ten (or more) words like *anemia* that describe nonmoral features of the world which also would generally be considered value-loaded.

2. Can you think of any historical examples of Copernican-like changes in moral beliefs?

3. What arguments could you present to the general in Dostoevsky's story to try to persuade him not to kill the serf boy? Hint: Are there potential beliefs in his worldview that might be in conflict with his choice of punishment?

4. What kinds of nonmoral features of the world do *you* think are most important in making moral judgments or in reasoning about moral values?

11–III

1. Islamic extremists were directed by their leader the Ayatollah Khomeini to kill the author Salman Rushdie for what the Ayatollah considered blasphemous passages in Rushdie's book *Satanic Verses*. Most Americans and other believers in liberal democracy believe that authors ought to enjoy freedom of speech. Explain how such a

difference in moral opinion could come about. Are there any possibilities for resolving it?

2. What are the fundamental beliefs and differences in worldview that make the abortion issue such an intractable one in the United States?

3. Why can *right* not be defined as "an act performed east of the Mississippi" and *wrong* defined as "an act performed west of the Mississippi"?

4. How much open-mindedness, when it comes to moral arguments, can one allow?

chapter 12

Reasoning About Good and Bad

Introduction

The passage from Dostoevsky in the last chapter has probably left you with some confusion about how moral beliefs can be supported. You would like to argue with the general about the morality of his actions. To help you get started in developing your own moral arguments, we will look at two examples of successful moral reasoning, one from Immanuel Kant and one from Jean-Paul Sartre. Both of these readings are classic examples of moral reasoning. They clearly set out their assumptions, or premises, and then show how, if one accepts those assumptions, certain conclusions follow. They have been very influential in our collective understanding of our moral experiences. You will see as you read the selections that the reasoning is not different in kind from reasoning about nonmoral issues.

It is important to realize that when we reason about values, we do not reason about them in isolation from other beliefs. Our moral beliefs, like our nonmoral beliefs, are part of a larger worldview which each of us brings to experience. Within this worldview there are beliefs which we consider to be factual—that is, we rarely question them—and there are beliefs for which we would like more evidence. There are also beliefs which we cannot clearly classify as moral or nonmoral. They have both descriptive and evaluative content. **None of our beliefs stands alone**. Even the belief you have that you are presently reading this text at a certain time, on a certain day of the week, in a certain place is part of a larger web of beliefs—about the nature of reading, of what it is for something to be a text, and even who, or what, you think you are.

Similarly, what we think is good, bad, right, wrong, beautiful, ugly is dependent on other beliefs we hold about what there is in the world, about human nature, and about what we can know about these things. For instance, if you believed that flowers when picked feel excruciating pain—pain of the same sort you would feel if someone cut off your arm—you would probably have strong moral beliefs about the immorality of picking flowers. Since people generally don't have such beliefs about flowers, picking a flower is not considered to present a moral problem. There is less agreement, however, when it comes to the sentience of animals, especially what are called the higher-order animals. Many people feel that these animals do feel pain (and other humanlike emotions) and, think, therefore, that it is immoral to kill such animals for human consumption. People who choose vegetarianism on moral grounds do so because they have a worldview that includes the sentience of higher-order animals as a fact.

In Chapter 11 we emphasized the importance of reasoning together about values. When we reason about values, however, we must look at the larger worldview that those moral values are part of. Some of the most heated and violent moral disagreements rest on differences of belief about the nonmoral features of the world rather than on differences of values. Our moral dialogues must include this larger world picture if we are to be able to reason together about moral values.

The two readings in this chapter were chosen, in part, to illustrate the interconnectedness of moral and nonmoral beliefs in a larger worldview. The first reading is a selection from Kant's famous work on ethics, *Grounding for the Metaphysics of Morals*. This short excerpt can only give you a small piece of the very powerful reasoning that Kant uses to support his moral beliefs. You may find the style of reasoning a little different from what you are used to. Kant is trying to develop a moral theory which can be used in all moral situations much as a mathematical formula might be used. Try to follow his reasoning, not just his conclusions. You will find it amply rewarding and you will probably find yourself agreeing with him.

The second reading, from the French philosopher Sartre, is part of a lecture that he gave in 1946. Clearly Sartre has a very different worldview from Kant's. The vocabulary and the issues of concern are very different. Sartre, who lived through the Nazi invasion of France, who spent time as a POW and later was a member of the French Resistance, is concerned primarily with human actions and not with deliberations about what is right. As you read this very powerful piece about human responsibility, think about Sartre's view of moral decision making and the very different concerns he has from those of Kant.

Grounding for the Metaphysics of Morals

IMMANUEL KANT

There is no possibility of thinking of anything at all in the world, or even out of it, which can be regarded as good without qualification, except a *good will*. Intelligence, wit, judgment, and whatever talents of the mind one might want to name are doubtless in many respects good and desirable, as are such qualities of temperament as courage, resolution, perseverance. But they can also become extremely bad and harmful if the will, which is to make use of these gifts of nature and which in its special constitution is called character, is not good. The same holds with gifts of fortune; power, riches, honor, even health, and that complete well-being and contentment with one's condition which is called happiness make for pride and often hereby even arrogance, unless there is a good will to correct their influence on the mind and herewith also to rectify the whole principle of action and make it universally comfortable to its end. The sight of a being who is not graced by any touch of a pure and good will but who yet enjoys an uninterrupted prosperity can never delight a rational and impartial spectator. Thus a good will seems to constitute the indispensable condition of being even worthy of happiness.

Some qualities are even conducive to this good will itself and can facilitate its work. Nevertheless, they have no intrinsic unconditional worth; but they always presuppose, rather, a good will, which restricts the high esteem in which they are otherwise rightly held, and does not permit them to be regarded as absolutely good. Moderation in emotions and passions, self-control, and calm deliberation are not only good in many respects but even seem to constitute part of the intrinsic worth of a person. But they are far from being rightly called good without qualification (however unconditionally they were commended by the ancients). For without the principles of a good will, they can become extremely bad; the coolness of a villain makes him not only

---

(an excerpt)

much more dangerous but also immediately more abominable in our eyes than he would have been regarded by us without it.

A good will is good not because of what it effects or accomplishes, nor because of its fitness to attain some proposed end; it is good only through its willing, i.e., it is good in itself.

The concept of a will estimable in itself and good without regard to any further end must now be developed. This concept already dwells in the natural sound understanding and needs not so much to be taught as merely to be elucidated. It always holds first place in estimating the total worth of our actions and constitutes the condition of all the rest. Therefore, we shall take up the concept of _duty_, which includes that of a good will, though with certain subjective restrictions and hindrances, which far from hiding a good will or rendering it unrecognizable, rather bring it out by contrast and make it shine forth more brightly.

I here omit all actions already recognized as contrary to duty, even though they may be useful for this or that end; for in the case of these the question does not arise at all as to whether they might be done from duty, since they even conflict with duty. I also set aside those actions which are really in accordance with duty, yet to which men have no immediate inclination, but perform them because they are impelled thereto by some other inclination. For in this [second] case to decide whether the action which is in accord with duty has been done from duty or from some selfish purpose is easy. This difference is far more difficult to note in the [third] case where the action accords with duty and the subject has in addition an immediate inclination to do the action. For example, that a dealer should not overcharge an inexperienced purchaser certainly accords with duty; and where there is much commerce, the prudent merchant does not overcharge but keeps to a fixed price for everyone in general, so that a child may buy from him just as well as everyone else may. Thus customers are honestly served, but this is not nearly enough for making us believe that the merchant has acted this way from duty and from principles of honesty; his own advantage required him to do it. He cannot, however, be assumed to have in addition [as in the third case] an immediate inclination toward his buyers, causing him, as it were, out of love to give no one as far as price is concerned any advantage over another. Hence the action was done neither from duty nor from immediate inclination, but merely for a selfish purpose.

On the other hand, to preserve one's life is a duty; and, furthermore, everyone has also an immediate inclination to do so. But on this account the often anxious care taken by most men for it has no intrinsic worth, and the maxim of their action has no moral content. They preserve their lives, to be sure, in accordance with duty, but not from duty. On the other hand, if adversity and hopeless sorrow have completely taken away the taste for life, if an unfortunate man, strong in soul and more indignant at his fate than despondent or dejected, wishes for death and yet preserves his life without loving it—not from inclination or fear, but from duty—then his maxim indeed has a moral content.

To be beneficent where one can is a duty; and besides this, there are many persons who are so sympathetically constituted that, without any further motive of vanity or self-interest, they find an inner pleasure in spreading joy around them and can rejoice in the satisfaction of others as their own work. But I maintain that in such a case an action of this kind, however dutiful and amiable it may be, has nevertheless no true moral worth. It is on a level with such actions as arise from other inclinations, e.g., the inclination for honor, which if fortunately directed to what is in fact beneficial and accords with duty and is thus honorable, deserves praise and encouragement, but not esteem; for its maxim lacks the moral content of an action done not from inclination but from duty. . . .

Thus the moral worth of an action does not lie in the effect expected from it nor in any principle of action that needs to borrow its motive from this expected effect. For all these effects (agreeableness of one's condition and even the furtherance of other people's happiness) could have been brought about also through other causes and would not have required the will of a rational being, in which the highest and unconditioned good can alone be found. Therefore, the pre-eminent good which is called moral can consist in nothing but the representation of the law in itself, and such a representation can admittedly be found only in a rational being insofar as this representation, and not some expected effect, is the determining ground of the will. This good is already present in the person who acts according to this representation, and such good need not be awaited merely from the effect.

But what sort of law can that be the thought of which must determine the will without reference to any expected effect, so that the will can be called absolutely good without qualification? Since I have deprived the will of every impulse that might arise for it from obeying any particular law, there is nothing left to serve the will as principle except the universal conformity of its actions to law as such, i.e., I should never act except in such a way that I can also will that my maxim should become a universal law. Here mere conformity to law as such (without having as its basis any law determining particular actions) serves the will as principle and must so serve it if duty is not to be a vain delusion and a chimerical concept. The ordinary reason of mankind in its practical judgments agrees completely with this, and always has in view the aforementioned principle.

For example, take this question. When I am in distress, may I make a promise with the intention of not keeping it? I readily distinguish here the two meanings which the question may have; whether making a false promise conforms with prudence or with duty. Doubtless the former can often be the case. Indeed I clearly see that escape from some present difficulty by means of such a promise is not enough. In addition I must carefully consider whether from this lie there may later arise far greater inconvenience for me than from what I now try to escape. Furthermore, the consequences of my false promise are not easy to foresee, even with all my supposed cunning; loss of confidence in me might prove to be far more disadvantageous than the misfortune which I now try to avoid. The more prudent way might be to act according to a universal maxim and to make it a habit not to promise anything without intending to keep it. But that such a maxim is, nevertheless, always based on nothing but a fear of consequences becomes clear to me at once. To be truthful from duty is, however, quite different from being truthful from fear of disadvantageous consequences; in the first case the concept of the action itself contains a law for me, while in the second I must first look around elsewhere to see what are the results for me that might be connected with the action. For to deviate from the principle of duty is quite certainly bad; but to abandon my maxim of prudence can often be very advantageous for me, though to abide by it is certainly safer. The most direct and infallible way, however, to answer the question as to whether a lying promise accords with duty is to ask myself whether I would really be content if my maxim (of extricating myself from difficulty by means of a false promise) were to hold as a universal law for myself as well as for others, and could I really say to myself that everyone may promise falsely when he finds himself in a difficulty from which he can find no other way to extricate himself. Then I immediately become aware that I can indeed will the lie but can not at all will a universal law to lie. For by such a law there would really be no promises at all, since in vain would my willing future actions be professed to other people who would not believe what I professed, or if they over-hastily did believe, then they would pay me back in like coin. Therefore, my maxim would necessarily destroy itself just as soon as it was made a universal law.

Therefore, I need no far-reaching acuteness to discern what I have to do in order that my will may be morally good. Inexperienced in the course of the world and incapable of being prepared for all its contingencies, I only ask myself whether I can also will that my maxim should become a universal law. If not, then the maxim must be rejected, not because of any disadvantage accruing to me or even to others, but because it cannot be fitting as a principle in a possible legislation of universal law, and reason exacts from me immediate respect for such legislation.

Existentialism Is a Humanism

JEAN-PAUL SARTRE

As an example by which you may the better understand . . . [human responsibility], I will refer to the case of a pupil of mine, who sought me out in the following circumstances. His father was quarreling with his mother and was also inclined to be a "collaborator"; his elder brother had been killed in the German offensive of 1940 and this young man, with a sentiment somewhat primitive but generous, burned to avenge him. His mother was living alone with him, deeply afflicted by the semi-treason of his father and by the death of her eldest son, and her one consolation was in this young man. But he, at this moment, had the choice between going to England to join the Free French Forces or of staying near his mother and helping her to live. He fully realized that this woman lived only for him and that his disappearance—or perhaps his death—would plunge her into despair. He also realized that, concretely and in fact, every action he performed on his mother's behalf would be sure of effect in the sense of aiding her to live, whereas anything he did in order to go and fight would be an ambiguous action which might vanish like water into sand and serve no purpose. For instance, to set out for England he would have to wait indefinitely in a Spanish camp on the way through Spain; or, on arriving in England or in Algiers he might be put into an office to fill up forms. Consequently, he found himself confronted by two very different modes of action; the one concrete, immediate, but directed towards only one individual; and the other an action addressed to an end infinitely greater, a national collectivity, but for that very reason ambiguous—and it might be frustrated on the way. At the same time, he was hesitating between two kinds of morality; on the one side the morality of sympathy, of personal devotion and, on the other side, a morality of wider scope but of more debatable validity. He had to choose between those two. What could help him to choose? Could the Christian doctrine? No. Christian doctrine says: Act with charity, love your neighbour, deny yourself for others, choose the way which is hardest, and so forth. But which is the harder road? To whom does one owe the more brotherly love, the patriot or the mother? Which is the more useful aim, the general one of fighting in and for the whole community, or the precise aim of helping one particular person to live? Who can give an

(an excerpt)

answer to that *à priori?* No one. Nor is it given in any ethical scripture. The Kantian ethic says, Never regard another as a means, but always as an end. Very well; if I remain with my mother, I shall be regarding her as the end and not as a means: but by the same token I am in danger of treating as means those who are fighting on my behalf; and the converse is also true, that if I go to the aid of the combatants I shall be treating them as the end at the risk of treating my mother as a means.

If values are uncertain, if they are still too abstract to determine the particular, concrete case under consideration, nothing remains but to trust in our instincts. That is what this young man tried to do; and when I saw him he said, "In the end, it is feeling that counts; the direction in which it is really pushing me is the one I ought to choose. If I feel that I love my mother enough to sacrifice everything else for her—my will to be avenged, all my longings for action and adventure—then I stay with her. If, on the contrary, I feel that my love for her is not enough, I go." But how does one estimate the strength of a feeling? The value of his feeling for his mother was determined precisely by the fact that he was standing by her. I may say that I love a certain friend enough to sacrifice such or such a sum of money for him, but I cannot prove that unless I have done it. I may say, "I love my mother enough to remain with her," if actually I have remained with her. I can only estimate the strength of this affection if I have performed an action by which it is defined and ratified. But if I then appeal to this affection to justify my action, I find myself drawn into a vicious circle.

Moreover, as Gide has very well said, a sentiment which is play-acting and one which is vital are two things that are hardly distinguishable one from another. To decide that I love my mother by staying beside her, and to play a comedy the upshot of which is that I do so—these are nearly the same thing. In other words, feeling is formed by the deeds that one does; therefore I cannot consult it as a guide to action. And that is to say that I can neither seek within myself for an authentic impulse to action, nor can I expect, from some ethic, formulae that will enable me to act. You may say that the youth did, at least, go to a professor to ask for advice. But if you seek counsel—from a priest, for example—you have selected that priest; and at bottom you already knew, more or less, what he would advise. In other words, to choose an adviser is nevertheless to commit oneself by that choice. If you are a Christian, you will say, Consult a priest; but there are collaborationists, priests who are resisters and priests who wait for the tide to turn: which will you choose? Had this young man chosen a priest of the resistance, or one of the collaboration, he would have decided beforehand the kind of advice he was to receive. Similarly, in coming to me, he knew what advice I should give him, and I had but one reply to make. You are free, therefore choose—that is to say, invent. No rule of general morality can show you what you ought to do: no signs are vouchsafed in this world. The

Catholics will reply, "Oh, but they are!" Very well; still, it is I myself, in every case, who have to interpret the signs. While I was imprisoned, I made the acquaintance of a somewhat remarkable man, a Jesuit, who had become a member of that order in the following manner. In his life he had suffered a succession of rather severe setbacks. His father had died when he was a child, leaving him in poverty, and he had been awarded a free scholarship in a religious institution, where he had been made continually to feel that he was accepted for charity's sake, and, in consequence, he had been denied several of those distinctions and honours which gratify children. Later, about the age of eighteen, he came to grief in a sentimental affair; and finally, at twenty-two—this was a trifle in itself, but it was the last drop that overflowed his cup—he failed in his military examination. This young man, then, could regard himself as a total failure: it was a sign—but a sign of what? He might have taken refuge in bitterness or despair. But he took it— very cleverly for him—as a sign that he was not intended for secular successes, and that only the attainments of religion, those of sanctity and of faith, were accessible to him. He interpreted his record as a message from God, and became a member of the Order. Who can doubt but that this decision as to the meaning of the sign was his, and his alone? One could have drawn quite different conclusions from such a series of reverses—as, for example, that he had better become a carpenter or a revolutionary. For the decipherment of the sign, however, he bears the entire responsibility. That is what "abandonment" implies, that we ourselves decide our being. And with this abandonment goes anguish.

As for "despair," the meaning of this expression is extremely simple. It merely means that we limit ourselves to a reliance upon that which is within our walls, or within the sum of the probabilities which render our action feasible. Whenever one wills anything, there are always these elements of probability. If I am counting upon a visit from a friend, who may be coming by train or by tram, I presuppose that the train will arrive at the appointed time, or that the tram will not be derailed. I remain in the realm of possibilities; but one does not rely upon any possibilities beyond those that are strictly concerned in one's action. Beyond the point at which the possibilities under consideration cease to affect my action, I ought to disinterest myself. For there is no God and no prevenient design, which can adapt the world and all its possibilities to my will. When Descartes said, "Conquer yourself rather than the world," what he meant was, at bottom, the same—that we should act without hope.

Reflections on the Readings:

1. Are you surprised by Kant's claim that the only thing good in itself is a good will? Why? Why not?

2. What does it mean to say that something is good in itself?

3. How would you explain the difference Kant draws between doing an act _from_ duty and doing an act _in accordance with_ duty?

4. Why does Sartre refuse to give advice to his former student?

5. Human beings, according to Sartre, are given to anguish and despair. Can you see a brighter side to this human condition? Explain.

6. What moral assumptions do you see Kant making? What moral assumptions do you see Sartre making?

Kant

The selection from Kant which you have just read begins with one of the most well known claims in the history of ethical thought, namely, that nothing " . . . can be regarded as good without qualification, except a _good will._" While not everyone agrees with this statement, it is still a very powerful claim because of the boldness with which it is stated and because as human beings, our ears perk up when we hear that something is an unqualified good. We would like to have or be, or at least be thought to have or be, that good. What could Kant possibly mean by a good will?

As the reading makes clear, Kant has something very specific in mind by "a good will." A will is good, according to Kant, if it acts _from_ duty and not just _in accordance with_ duty. We begin to see that the kind of _good_ that Kant is talking about is moral good, not other goods like pleasant surroundings, love of friends, or personal contentment. All of these other "goods" are worth having, says Kant, but as rational beings we would have to admit that even if a person has all these other goods, without a good will something is missing. A murderer who is intelligent, brave, and wealthy is just a more formidable murderer. We do not, and cannot, grant him our highest esteem.

And, indeed, this is familiar to all of us. We all know people who seem "to have it all" but whom we are not willing to call good, because they lack moral good. Similarly, probably all of us have asked ourselves at least once after someone has done something nice for us, "Did he really mean it or did he expect to get something out of it for himself?" Somehow, if the person does an act which accomplishes a desirable end but does the act for personal gain, that doesn't seem as worthy to us as the same act done because it was the right thing to do and for no other reason. Acts done because they are the right things to do are what Kant means by acts done from duty. Kant, then, believes that he is making clear what all of us intend when we say an act is good or that a person is good, that is, that the act was done from duty or the person acted from duty.

The next step of Kant's reasoning is just as you might guess. If to be good is to act from duty, then we need to know what it is to act from duty. When we act from duty, says Kant, we do not act from inclination or from selfishness. Sometimes inclination (or desire) and selfishness may lead us to do the same act that duty demands of us (that is, we act in accordance with duty)—but not always, so they are not possible guides in moral action. Moral action is too important to leave to chance. A good will chooses what it chooses primarily because it believes the act to be good.

This means, according to Kant, that the will must be determined by a rule or "law" which expresses the duty of any rational being. The most general law—which serves as the basic principle of duty—is that "I should never act except in such a way that I can also will that my maxim should become a universal law." (This is the famous categorical imperative of Kant.) By a "maxim" Kant means the specific principle that applies to the case at hand such as "I ought to preserve my life" or "I ought not to make a promise I do not intend to keep."

What Kant is saying is that moral acts are acts done from duty and acts done from duty are acts which are done on the basis of maxims that rational beings could will to be universal laws. It would be inconsistent for a rational being to will that he do something he would not will every other rational being to do. For example, he could not will that everyone lie or make false promises because what would happen to the whole institution of talking to other people or contracting in some way about future acts if everyone lied! Kant's point is not that a person's lying could lead to bad consequences like destroying the institution of promising (Kant thinks the morality of an act should not rest on the consequences of the act), but rather that the person is putting his will in conflict with itself. That is, he is both willing that promising be a universal law and not willing that promising be a universal law, namely, in this case. Such self-contradiction is inconsistent with his rational nature as a human being.

Let us review Kant's reasoning. A good person is a person who wills an action primarily because he believes that action to be his duty. His duty comes from the nature of human beings as rational creatures and is that he should act in conformity with a maxim which can be universalized for all other rational beings without contradiction. This categorical imperative is like a mathematical formula which can be used to determine one's duty in a particular situation. Kant does not simply claim that certain acts are right and others wrong, but rather gives us careful and clear arguments to support his thesis about the nature of a good will.

Although much has been written about how to interpret this moral reasoning of Kant, this short synopsis is sufficient for us to see that Kant can be considered a moral objectivist, although perhaps an unusual one, who believes there are factual moral statements. He believes that there is a procedure for discovering the right answer about what to do in a moral situation and this procedure is an objective feature of a world inhabited by rational beings. This does not mean, however, that we will not make moral mistakes or have misunderstandings and disagreements about how to apply this procedure or formula. Even though there are right answers, we may not always be able to uncover them. Again, morality is similar to mathematics. Just because we have a mathematical formula to resolve a particular puzzle does not mean that we will not make mistakes or have disagreements about the proper use of that formula.

Kant's account of what it is for an act to be morally good, then, gives us a way to reason together about what acts are morally good. Could such reasoning be used to persuade Dostoevsky's wealthy landowner not to kill the offending serf boy? Certainly. Would it be successful in persuading him? Perhaps—but perhaps not.

Kant's reasoning later in the *Grounding* goes on to show that "man and, in general, every rational being exists as an end in himself and not merely as a means to be arbitrarily used by this or that will." Kant reasons that since each of us regards himself or herself as an end, we would put our wills in contradiction with themselves if we failed to recognize that all other rational beings should likewise be treated as ends. Clearly bad actions follow, for Kant, when we make exceptions of ourselves. Then we are acting on the basis of an unjustifiable double standard.

One might use this reasoning and its conclusion to try to persuade the general that the boy is an end in himself who has "absolute worth" (Kant's terminology) and therefore should not be killed as a means to some end like setting an example for others or giving vent to (the general's) anger. We can guess that the general might respond that the boy, being merely a serf, is less than a rational being. One might try to reason further with the general, showing him that he is being inconsistent, on the one hand arguing that the boy is morally responsible for his act, and therefore a rational human being, and, on the other, that the boy is not a rational being and therefore can be used as a means to an end.

Of course, whether or not the general is persuaded by this argument depends on many factors. Most of all, it depends on whether he is willing to listen to any moral argument at all. Some people will not. They are called dogmatists. We will have more to say about dogmatists in the next chapter.

The main point we want to make here is that there are good reasons which can be offered in support of a moral point of view. Reasoning—good reasoning—can be used to support our moral beliefs. We should treat moral disagreements the same way we treat disagreements about who is going to win the next presidential election or whether Shakespeare is the author of a poem. We gather evidence from our experience and we present it in as cogent a form as we can.

We sometimes fail to persuade other people in moral arguments because they begin from very different assumptions. They have such different worldviews from ours. For instance, you yourself may or may not be convinced by Kant's argument that moral acts are acts done primarily because a person believes they are the right things to do. Kant does have a particular worldview which allows him to make certain assumptions in developing his ethical theory. You may not share that worldview. Let's take a look at some of those assumptions.

One of Kant's important assumptions is about what it is to be a human being. We have seen that, according to Kant, humans are rational beings (if not abnormal) and have a will which chooses a course of action. Our rationality is our essential feature. It is what makes us different from other things in the world. Our reason gives us our special worth and our dignity (as ends) and it also gives us freedom to act from reason and not from inclination or desire. Notice that we cannot act from duty, which is to act from the universal law given by reason, if we are beings whose wills can only act from inclination. Although these ideas probably have some familiarity to us, certainly not everyone shares Kant's worldview that human beings have a special nature because of their rationality and that their wills are free to determine themselves according to laws given by reason alone.

This is not to diminish Kant's powerful argument for his moral point of view but only to point out that disagreements about specific moral issues may have their roots in an individual's larger worldview and the assumptions which are part of that worldview. The situation is not unlike what we saw earlier when we talked about differences of background knowledge and how those differences influence what we experience. Our worldview includes our background knowledge but it also includes assumptions which most people do not consider knowledge. These assumptions are sometimes so fundamental that we would not even think of offering evidence to support them. For instance, whether a person sees human beings as creatures with individual souls (a traditional Western view) or as parts of a common world soul (a traditional Eastern view) or as machines without souls (a modern Western view) would be an important assumption within a person's worldview. Background knowledge, on the other hand, is much more specific and is generally supported with evidence and argument. The various schools of Western psychology (Freudian, Skinnerian, Gestalt, etc.) might be part of a person's background knowledge.

Most of us assume that the people with whom we are having a dialogue share much the same worldview that we do. If they are our friends and neighbors, this is not a bad assumption to make. We are less likely to assume that our friends have the same background knowledge as we do. We know that our friends have not had all the same experiences that we have had. They may have studied economics while we studied chemistry, for example. When we disagree with someone, we need to find out where the differences lie. We have a better chance of working out our differences and coming to an agreement if we do. However, it is not always so important to distinguish worldview from background knowledge. What is important is that you realize that there is a difference between them and are aware of the important role each one plays in both our moral and nonmoral discourse.

Kant is very helpful as a philosopher because he tells us a lot about his worldview. This makes it easier for us to decide whether we agree with him or not. Probably many people agree with him that human beings have an essential nature which is their rationality. This agreement makes Kant's claims about acting from duty very persuasive. Our next philosopher, however, has quite a different worldview, as you have already noticed from your reading.

Sartre

According to Sartre, most moral decisions are like the one faced by the student in the passage you read. Seldom are moral choices between some obvious good and some obvious bad. Indeed, it is often the case that by choosing one good, we are prevented from doing something else good. We are forced to choose between two goods—or two evils. The student wants to be a loving son. He also wants to be a patriot and to avenge his brother's death. How to choose—that is the question!

Surely you have faced similar situations even if not so life-determining. For example, Grandpa loves chocolate-covered pretzels and asks you to bring him some. You know that they are bad for his high blood pressure. Do you bring him some anyway, making him happy but less healthy—or do you arrive without them, leaving him sad but healthier? Life is full of such choices, some more agonizing than others, but all of them determinative of who we are as individuals.

Although Sartre like Kant is concerned with choosing a course of action and with being free to choose, unlike Kant he denies that there is any law which will tell us the right way to choose in particular circumstances. Laws and guidelines become laws and guidelines **for us**, says Sartre, because we

choose to follow or be guided by them. We choose how to interpret them. Similarly, we choose someone as an advisor. We decide to adopt that advisor's guidance. Each of us is free to choose a course of action and therefore bears full responsibility for that act. No formula, no ethic, no other person can take that responsibility from us. As Sartre says, ". . . we ourselves decide our being."

Clearly, then, freedom has a very different significance for Sartre than it does for Kant. For Kant, freedom means that we are free not to act from inclination and can, therefore, follow a rule given by reason which tells us how we ought to act in a given situation. For Sartre, on the other hand, our human freedom means that we have to make choices ourselves—without benefit of guidelines and without any way of sharing responsibility for our moral (and nonmoral) choices. The individual, and only the individual, can make the considered judgment that is an authentic moral choice. It cannot be any other way, so one must accept it and bear responsibility for the choice. There is no directive for the choice.

How, then, are we to choose? You choose, says Sartre, and in choosing you confer value on that choice—not the other way around! When you choose, you are saying by your choice, "This is good." Therefore you must choose what you can endorse. Your choice says that you are the kind of person who values this. When you make a choice, you are choosing your identity, the person you want to be. To go back to the story of the young man again, in choosing he is deciding whether he is a person whose life is directed by the needs of one individual or a person who serves the needs of the collective society. In choosing, he chooses which person he will be.

The key moral problem for Sartre is accepting responsibility. We are responsible for our choices. There are no excuses. The young man cannot put the responsibility for his decision on his mother and her needs. If he stays with her it is because he has decided that that is the kind of son he wants to be. If he joins the Free French Forces, it is because he has decided that he must serve his country. He cannot claim to have been overwhelmed by a need to avenge his brother's death. If he acts on that need, he is responsible for choosing to act on that need.

Since you are the person who is choosing, says Sartre, you are what you do. There is no "self" that is somehow different from the agent acting in the world. If you act in a selfish way, then you are a selfish person. The pose that many people adopt that they are not "really" the person who is acting so selfishly is just a very common way of avoiding responsibility for one's actions. For example, you have probably heard someone say, "I don't know why I said that mean remark. It just came out. I'm not that kind of person." Sartre would say such a person is kidding himself. Of course, he is that kind of person who says mean things. He just did. Such a person is guilty of self-deception. So is Sue who claims to be generous and loving but who never

Calvin and Hobbes

by Bill Watterson

seems to have time to show generosity and love. And so is Dave, the bank robber, who believes that only dire financial straights caused him to choose to rob the bank while the real Dave is not a bank robber at all.

When we recognize our responsibility for our actions, says Sartre, we feel *abandonment, anguish, and despair.* We feel abandonment (*forlornness* is perhaps a better translation) because we feel so alone. There is no one, no group, no fellow citizens on whom we can blame our faults and weaknesses. We feel anguish because only we can choose and the choices are so difficult— often between two goods or two evils. There is no right way to choose that dictates itself to us which avoids having to choose between a rock and hard place. And we feel despair because there is no moral order outside ourselves. We are forced to give meaning to our own lives through our own choices.

All is not negative, however. Because we are free to choose, we can choose differently today from the way we chose yesterday. We are constantly making our identity with our choices. Our identity is not something that is fixed. One is not a success or failure, a hero or a coward, except by how one chooses—the next time. The person who has acted shyly in the past, for instance, need not choose to act shyly in the future. And, says Sartre, that person cannot excuse his future shy behavior by saying that he is a shy person. He can always choose to act otherwise. In the reading Sartre gives an example of this freedom for the future to be what one chooses when he describes the case of the young man who had failed at business and at the military. Instead of seeing himself as a failure, he sees that the future holds other possibilities for him and chooses to become a priest. So while there is despair there is also hope. One can be what one chooses to be.[1]

---

[1]Obviously there are some limitations on our choices. Our physical bodies limit us in some ways. Our time and place of birth limit our options as well. Sartre calls this our facticity and we deceive ourselves if we ignore it. But, in general, says Sartre, we tend to see limitations where there are none. Being six feet tall is part of one's facticity. Being shy or a coward is not.

Sartre's view of morality is an extreme subjectivist view. Clearly for Sartre there are no objective features of the world which can be used for discovering the right choice in a moral situation. Not only must each person decide for himself what to do but there are no guidelines or procedures for making that decision. There is only the choice and the chooser, who places value in the world by choosing. Could Sartre's view of morality have anything to say to Dostoevsky's wealthy landowner? Again, the answer is yes and no.

Certainly on such an extreme subjectivist position, one cannot argue with the landowner that he is violating a law or rule by killing the serf boy. This does not mean, however, that one cannot argue with him. Whether he chooses to be influenced by the argument, however, is something only he can decide. One might try to persuade him to choose a different alternative by making clear to him that he is choosing to kill the boy and that he has sole responsibility for this act. He cannot claim that he is forced to do it because of the boy's behavior or because of his position as landowner. Those would be excuses and would constitute a failure to recognize the freedom he has in choosing a course of action.

If you were to argue with the landowner and fail to persuade him to choose another course of action, then *you* would be the one facing a choice. You could stand by and watch the serf boy meet his fate or you could try to intervene in the punishment. Of course your intervention may come to naught (it may even cost you your life) but you would have the choice! And not to choose is to choose.

Like Kant, Sartre also has a worldview which informs his beliefs about morality. Since his moral theory is quite different from Kant's we would expect his worldview to differ and it does. For one thing, Sartre is an existentialist. This is a term that is familiar to most people but, surprisingly, the philosophers who are most often referred to as "existentialists" have been rather uncomfortable with the term and what it might mean. Sartre himself sums up existentialism in an earlier portion of the essay excerpted here as the belief that "*existence* comes before *essence*" [italics in the original]. Although this phrase and his elucidation of it in the essay do not do justice to the rich philosophical meaning of existentialism, it does give us a starting point for understanding the existential worldview.

"We must begin from the subjective," says Sartre. That is, we begin from our subjective experience of the world and its objects. We first experience ourselves as beings in the world and only later come to define ourselves—by what we do. We have no essence which is the "real" human being or "real" person. "Man simply is. . . . Man is nothing else but that which he makes of himself." What this means for Sartre (and other existentialists) is that there is no human nature. A person is what he wills and, consequently, does. There is no human nature to provide a standard or guideline for how one should will. Sartre disagrees with Kant and other philosophers who believe that the essence of "man" is to be rational and that this essence can be seen as a standard by which to measure one's success or failure as a human being or to establish a rule of moral law. This worldview, that there is no human nature, underlies Sartre's view of human freedom which is so different from Kant's and leads him to a wholly different view about human choice and moral decision making.

Both these worldviews and their different views of human nature have much to recommend them. They both present well-reasoned accounts of our human experience. Yet they result in quite different ethical perspectives. Kant's ethical theory is an objectivist view, although a rather unusual one, in that he argues that right answers to moral questions can be discovered if one follows the right procedure and that this procedure is an objective feature of a world inhabited by rational beings. Sartre's moral point of view, on the other hand, is strongly subjectivist. But his subjectivism is very demanding. We cannot simply follow our feelings or desires. Each time we act we bring value into the world so that each of us bears the moral weight of the world on our shoulders.

Making Moral Decisions

Our own common-sense view of moral decision making probably includes some of the features of morality emphasized by Kant and Sartre. Somehow morality implies consistency, for example, as Kant suggests. To be a morally good person is to exhibit consistency in one's moral behavior. One generous act does not make someone a generous person. Universality also seems to characterize our ordinary moral thinking. It does not seem fair for a person to expect everyone else to keep their promises while he does not. Similarly, Sartre's emphasis on personal commitment and responsibility for our choices fits in well with our ordinary beliefs about morality. Society, for example, did not accept the claims of the Nazi war criminals that they were "just following orders" and therefore were not responsible for the atrocities they committed.

Whether either of these two ethical views is persuasive for you depends, as we have seen, on other beliefs you hold about the world and about human nature. This does not mean that morality is simply "in the eye of the beholder"—any more than most of our nonmoral beliefs can be said to be in the eye of the beholder. What these two views do show is that our moral judgments are capable of being supported by good reasoning, reasoning that makes sense if we are willing to listen to it. They also show that, like the theories of modern science which rest on fundamental claims which are assumed and not proven, ethical beliefs and theories are also part of a larger worldview that includes fundamental assumptions for which no proof is offered. When we have ethical disagreements it is helpful to keep in mind that we may be dealing with differences that originate in differences of world-views or background knowledge, rather than in differences of values. We will have more to say about resolving moral disagreements in the next chapter.

What can we say about resolving the moral problems or puzzles we all face as individuals? Are there any insights to be gained from the description of moral reasoning offered here? First, it should be clear that not all moral decisions fall into the category of moral dilemma. Many of our moral beliefs are beliefs which we rarely if ever question. We consider the statements of such a belief to be factual. That it is wrong to kill another person other than in self-defense, for example, would be such a belief. Moral beliefs that we consider factual are beliefs that fit in well with other things we believe, notably with our worldview and our background knowledge. They are part of a larger story that we tell about what it is to be a human being and the place of human beings in the universe. If questioned, we could give some reasons or an argument why one should not kill except in self-defense, but this belief is so fundamental in our worldview that it is rarely questioned. It is like the Copernican view of the Earth's rotation around the sun. We consider it factual and needing no further warrant. It is important, however, to remember what we learned from our study of scientific reasoning earlier, namely, no matter how well entrenched a scientific belief is, it can only be confirmed and not "proven." We are continually testing that belief against experience. The same is true for moral beliefs.

You may have noticed, for instance, that our well-entrenched belief that it is wrong to kill another person except in self-defense is beginning to be questioned because of recent advances in medicine. Because modern medicine has found so many ways to keep the human body functioning at least at a minimal level, people are beginning to ask whether mercy killing might also be an exception to the prohibition against killing. In this case changes in technology have brought about changes in the background knowledge we bring to our experience. They make us reconsider the meaning of what death is and when death comes to a person. They may even lead to changes in fundamental beliefs about what it is to be person.

Moral beliefs that are considered factual can also be troublesome when we seek to apply them to specific cases. We are often not so sure whether this or that instance of killing is in self-defense. For example, if an intruder enters your house or apartment in the middle of the night and is discovered putting your possessions into a bag, are you justified in shooting that intruder? How big does the threat to your life have to be to justify shooting and possibly killing the intruder?

Still more troublesome, and unfortunately quite common in our lives, is the kind of moral dilemma Sartre emphasizes, the kind where we must choose between two evident goods or two obvious bads ("the lesser of two evils"). Many people believe, or at least hope, that if they wait long enough and think "harder" about a moral dilemma that a *perfect* solution to the problem will arise. This is rarely the case. Life does not present us with perfect solutions. Nor does it present us with only one right solution. There may be several morally justifiable solutions to a moral dilemma. Also, life does not allow us to wait. Not to choose is to choose, because not choosing is a choice for the status quo. As in the case of Sartre's student, by choosing one good, the student gives up the opportunity to realize another good, but his inability to achieve both goods does not mean that his choice is wrong or bad. **One choice, however, could be better than another.**

To resolve these problems of moral reasoning we need good reasoning skills, the same good reasoning skills we use when dealing with nonmoral matters. Like all good reasoning, moral reasoning is best when conducted as an **open dialogue.** This dialogue is often just with yourself because ethical issues are personal and individual, but it can also include others. (As Sartre pointed out, however, others are not responsible for our moral decisions. Only we are. We decide how much to count their guidance.) This open dialogue needs to be continual and not confined to situations of moral deliberation. In a moral emergency (when the intruder is on your doorstep) there may be no time for discussion. Also, it should be noted that too much talk can be a way of not deciding, of choosing not to choose. It is important to think and talk about possible moral dilemmas before being faced with them.

Background knowledge is also important in making moral decisions. We have already seen the importance of background knowledge in good reasoning. The larger our store of background knowledge, the better judgments we will be able to make. Background knowledge will be particularly helpful in determining the right course of action in a specific situation. This is because part of the success of our decision will rest on the strengths of our generalizations, analogies, and causal inferences. Our background knowledge is our biggest help in anticipating the possible consequences of our actions. This is not to suggest, however, that resolving a moral dilemma is simply a function of knowledge. Knowing more does not make the *moral* issue go away. One still has to choose between two goods (evils). For example, knowledge of the risk factors in a situation does not determine how much risk is morally acceptable.

We also need to be **open to the world**. Our moral beliefs, like our nonmoral beliefs, cannot be proven, only warranted or disconfirmed; we need to be aware of the limitations of the evidence we have for our beliefs and the unproven assumptions of our worldview. Therefore, we need to be ready to revise our moral beliefs in light of new information, such as the changes in modern medicine. And we need to be ready to change our behavior in light of the successes and failures of past decisions. Like the young man

Sartre tells about who finds his calling as a priest, we are not bound by our past moral mistakes. Moral reasoning, like nonmoral reasoning, is open-ended. We test our expectations against future experiences and adjust our background knowledge and our moral reasoning accordingly.

Good reasoning of the kind we have described here is important for ethical decisions from both the objectivist and the subjectivist viewpoints. From the objectivist point of view, good reasoning helps us to *discover* the right moral behavior and avoid mistakes. When we do make mistakes, it helps us to recognize them and to correct them. While a staunch subjectivist holds that every choice we make is the right choice as long as it results from a considered judgment, good reasoning is important for the subjectivist because it helps us to *coordinate* our goals and develop a *consistent* self. It enables us to avoid choices which would thwart us from the things we as individuals think are important for us. On both accounts, the objectivist and subjectivist, reason helps us to continue the **story** of who we are and what we think is valuable. Ethical decisions are difficult because they are complex and because in deciding, we are deciding who we are. We are making ourselves. It's a daunting task and no one can do it for us. **It takes a lot of effort.**

Exercises

12-I

1. What does Kant mean by a good will?

2. Why for Sartre are there no excuses in morality?

3. What does *freedom* mean for Kant? What does *freedom* mean for Sartre?

12-II

1. What does Kant mean when he says that all rational beings ought to be treated as "ends in themselves"?

2. Kant and Sartre end up in such different places morally, Kant being a staunch objectivist and Sartre being a strong subjectivist. Yet in many ways their ethical views are more alike than different. Describe some of the similarities you see between the ethical views of Kant and Sartre.

3. The factual statement that one should not kill except in self-defense has begun to be questioned because of changes in modern medicine.

Describe other factual moral statements which are currently undergoing the same sort of questioning.

4. Explain how Sartre's subjectivism in ethics follows from his belief that there is no human nature.

5. Describe a moral belief which you once took to be factual but no longer consider factual. How did your change of belief come about?

12–III

1. Do you think ethical disagreements are more common than scientific disagreements? If so, why? If not, why not?

2. Kant describes someone who is good as someone who acts from duty. Is there a difference between Kant's good person and what is commonly known as a "goody-goody"? Defend your answer.

3. What are some of the most important features of your worldview? Where do they come from? How would you defend them against someone who does not share the same worldview?

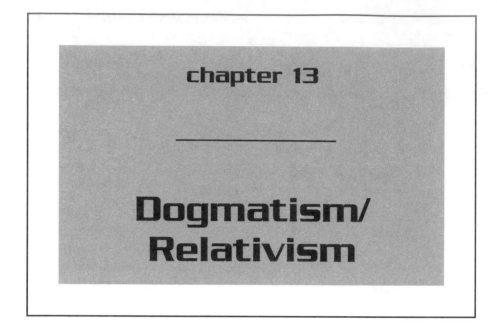

chapter 13

Dogmatism/ Relativism

Introduction

Moral disagreements are often painful, sometimes are downright nasty, and may have dire consequences for some or all of the participants. We try to avoid them. We walk away from them. We "agree to disagree." Moral disagreements, however, are too important to ignore. They are about how we ought to live. Nothing could be more important for an individual than answering the question, "How ought I to live my life?" While we cannot answer that question for you, we can take another look at moral disagreements to discover ways they can be more profitable to us as individuals—and sometimes to us as members of a group or nation.

    One of the problems with moral disagreements is that they often seem to be dominated by two types of arguers: people who are absolutely certain about the right course of action and who, therefore, want everyone else to agree to it and people who argue that there is no certainty in moral matters and, therefore, whatever an individual says is right is right for her, regardless of what others believe. Those who are sure they are right are called **dogmatists**. Those who insist that morality varies from individual to individual and that moral differences of opinion are arbitrary and cannot be bridged by reason are called **relativists**. There is a tendency to believe that people are either dogmatists or relativists. If you are not a dogmatist, you must be a relativist, and vice versa. This either/or kind of thinking gets people confused and even more eager to stay away from moral arguments. In this chapter we will show that neither dogmatism nor relativism is an appropriate stance to take in moral arguments and that there is a middle ground between these two poles of moral reasoning.

The reading for this chapter is one you have already read. It is Plato's _Euthyphro_, which was one of the readings in the Introduction. As you reread this dialogue, think about what the dialogue is trying to say about moral reasoning. Remember that Euthyphro is on his way into court to bring charges against his own father for murder and Socrates is going there because he has been charged with corrupting the morals of the youth of Athens. So morality is a primary theme in the dialogue. One of the surprising things about a Platonic dialogue is that each time you read it, you discover new insights that you did not notice before, and the _Euthyphro_ is no exception. The critical thinking skills you have already acquired will help you as you reread. You should reread this dialogue now as preparation for understanding the critical thinking concepts in this chapter.

Reflections on the Reading:

1. Why do people take offense when they are called dogmatic?

2. Many people feel threatened by relativism. Why might someone who advocates a relativist position in ethics make ordinary moral people upset?

3. Who is more dogmatic, Euthyphro or Socrates?

4. Socrates is generally considered to be Plato's hero. Why might someone consider Socrates a hero? What makes him heroic? What makes him unheroic?

5. Euthyphro is bringing his own father to trial for murder, a murder that is inadvertent at best. What kind of person would do something like this? Do you know people like Euthyphro?

Dogmatism/Relativism

We all know people who are dogmatic about what they believe. All of us are dogmatic about some beliefs we hold or as least have argued dogmatically at times. We become so excited about something that we consider factual that we want everyone else to consider it factual also. We cannot imagine anyone's questioning it. We also all know people who are relativists in their beliefs. They couldn't care less what other people believe and only want to be left alone with their own beliefs. They generally shrink from defending their beliefs, except their belief that beliefs are personal and that each person has "a right" to his or her beliefs. You probably have argued this way sometimes—perhaps when you thought a belief was warranted but felt at a loss to defend it.

Neither the dogmatist nor the relativist is willing to participate in dialogue about moral disagreement because they both see such dialogue as fruitless. The dogmatist does not want to discuss morality because she sees most moral issues as settled, with no further discussion necessary. The relativist does not want to discuss morality because she believes moral beliefs are arbitrary and cannot be rationally warranted. Moral dialogue is only an exchange of rationalizations and, therefore, pointless.

This dichotomy between dogmatists and relativists ignores a whole range of alternative moral stances between them. It rests on a misunderstanding of certainty and of what can or cannot be warranted. Before we take a look at some alternative moral stances it will be helpful first to explore some of the reasons for this misunderstanding that has led so many people to focus on the dogmatist/relativist dichotomy as the model of moral argument.

While there are certainly dogmatists and relativists in science[1] and other areas, dogmatism and relativism are less associated with scientific discourse, for example, than they are with moral discourse. One possible explanation for this is that there is a higher degree of consensus in the use of scientific vocabulary than there is in the use of our ethical vocabulary. The criteria for use of our scientific vocabulary are fairly clear, which means it is easier to get other people (scientists) to accept claims as warranted. There is less need for taking a dogmatic stand and less appearance of taking a dogmatic stand.

The question then becomes why there is an apparent greater consensus of usage for the vocabulary of scientific discourse than for the vocabulary of moral discourse. One explanation for this apparent consensus is that the scientific community is not nearly as large as the ethical community. To be admitted to the community of scientists one must learn to speak the language of physics or chemistry, for example. These languages are difficult, not everyone can learn them, and not everyone needs to learn them. Moreover, their

---

[1]See, for example, Paul Feyerabend, *Against Method*, New York: Verso, 1988, or some of the criticisms of Thomas Kuhn's *The Structure of Scientific Revolutions* (Chicago: University of Chicago Press, 1962) such as Imre Lakatos, "Falsification and the Methodology of Scientific Research Programmes," in I. Lakatos and A. Musgrave, eds., *Criticism and the Growth of Knowledge*, Cambridge: Cambridge University Press, 1970.

difficulty generally precludes nonscientists from entering into the scientific dialogue so that experts are left to carry on the dialogue alone.

On the other hand, all of us must make ethical decisions. We do not and cannot leave ethical decisions to the experts the same way we leave scientific decisions to the scientists. We all must speak the language of ethics. Moreover, because we all have had ethical experiences, we like to believe that we have some expertise ourselves. We are not as willing to listen to others or to allow someone to act as an "expert" in moral matters as we are in scientific matters. Consequently, there is less consensus in the use of our ethical vocabulary than in the use of the vocabulary of science and less consensus in our ethical discourse.

Given that we are all "experts" in morality, it is surprising that there is as much consensus in moral matters as there is. We have this consensus because we are all part of an ethical community and a community of ethical language speakers. As members of that community we share in its traditions, laws, and customs. They are part of our background knowledge. They inform our ethical beliefs. Consequently, we do have consensus about much of our moral life. We have already seen that there are factual statements about moral matters, that is, statements with moral content that are rarely questioned and are considered warranted in the same way that statements with nonmoral content are. Of course, sometimes there is no consensus in the community and sometimes the consensus is "soft" as, for example, when the old consensus is weak but no new consensus has emerged. The belief that killing another human being is wrong except in cases of self-defense is a possible example of a moral belief for which the consensus is soft. There is as yet, however, no new consensus about the rightness or wrongness of mercy killing.

This consensus, while less than the consensus of science, means that we _can_ discuss moral issues. Moral discussion need not deteriorate into a standoff between the dogmatists, on one hand, and the relativists, on the other. We do not use the moral vocabulary so differently that we do not understand each other. It is just that we do not always agree and a lot of us are in on the disagreement.

Both dogmatism and relativism rest on mistaken understandings of certainty. The dogmatist is certain of her belief. Her certainty, she believes, entitles her to forgo any further dialogue either with herself (as in thought) or with others. She wants only that others believe the same way. Hence, she presents her views dogmatically—with little room for further thought or discussion. The relativist, on the other hand, believes that because no moral argument is ever conclusive, in the sense of resting on premises that are entirely free of assumption, that moral conclusions are always arbitrary and without rational warrant. The relativist thinks moral dialogue is pointless because in the end there is only rationalization—merely the appearance of rational support for moral beliefs. The dogmatist errs in thinking that we human beings can be so certain that no further dialogue is necessary and the relativist errs in demanding the possibility of that same kind of certainty and in giving up the discussion because it is not possible.

This kind of certainty that the dogmatist thinks she possesses and the relativist thinks is impossible does not characterize science or any of our reasoning about nonmoral matters. We, therefore, should not expect it to characterize our moral discourse. It is helpful here to review the idea of science as a story and to look at the similarities between that story and the story which is moral discourse. The scientists tells a story which weaves the traces we note in our experience into a pattern that helps us to explain the past and predict the future. Moral discourse is similar. We weave together a story from our experiences which helps us to evaluate the past and make choices about the future. Each discourse has its appropriate style. The style of science generally is quantitative. The style of moral discourse is generally qualitative. Consequently, these two stories look different from each other. They tend to look different in kind. If we call the underlying structure, however, we see that they are much more alike than different.

For example, we have seen that scientific discourse rests on assumptions that cannot be proven, which are taken as fundamental. We have also seen that science rests in part on unarticulated values, particularly aesthetic values like simplicity and beauty. Also, scientific discourse is open-ended. The scientist is continually testing her hypotheses to see if they work, often adjusting her story to accord with her results. Moral discourse is similar. Like science, it rests on assumptions—usually about human nature—which are fundamental and unproven. Moral discourse also contains value assumptions, both moral and aesthetic. And it is open-ended. It is subject to revision in light of new insights and changes in background knowledge. Of course, moral discourse is not quantitative (except for versions of utilitarianism which adopt the quantitative methods of science) but quantitative discourse is just a different way of talking. It is just a different way of telling a story.

In many ways there is *less* certainty in science than in moral discourse. There have been more changes in the story told by scientists in the last two thousand years than in the story of moral discourse. Aristotle's *Nicomachean Ethics* still tells a helpful story about how to live a good life. Aristotle's *Physics*, on the other hand, describes the physical world in terms that we would find very out of date and not at all helpful. Even today science textbooks are very quickly obsolete. An old ethics textbook is much more likely to be useful than an old science textbook of the same vintage. The story told by the former tends to change much more slowly than the story told by the latter.[2]

---

[2]It is interesting to note that despite this uncertainty and the rapid pace of change, science teaching and science textbooks tend to be characterized by dogmatism. They both treat their subject matter as unquestionable and highly warranted.

Moderation As Key

Dogmatism and relativism are related to, but not identical with, the moral viewpoints of objectivism and subjectivism that we discussed earlier. As we saw in Chapter 11, the moral objectivist is someone who believes that there are objective criteria, that is features of the world, that can be used as evidence for the use of moral terms. One would expect a dogmatist also to be an objectivist and, indeed, most dogmatists are objectivists. They believe that they have evidence from experience which justifies their claims of certainty in moral matters. For example, a Benthamite who uses Bentham's pleasure calculus to determine the total amount of happiness derived from one action as compared to another has a high level of certainty about which act ought to be performed and is likely not to wish to discuss the issue further. A dogmatist, we can say, is a **certain objectivist** who believes there are objective criteria for moral statements and she knows them.

Not every objectivist, however, need be a dogmatist. Someone could believe, for instance, that there are objective criteria for the proper use of moral terms but also believe that she is uncertain about their particular application. This **modest objectivist** allows for moral dialogue and discussion by acknowledging that evidence, even if considered an objective feature of the world, is a matter of judgment and that, consequently, moral discourse must be open-ended in the same way that scientific discourse is open-ended. Some people might consider Kant a modest objectivist, that is, someone who thinks there are factual moral statements which can be known but who does not claim to know what they all are.

Relativists are subjectivists. The subjectivist view, as you will recall, holds that there are no objective features of the world which serve as criteria for moral judgments and that, therefore, moral judgments are the product of each individual subject, or person. The relativist is someone who adds to this the belief that this product is arbitrary, there being no possible deliberation sufficient for moral certainty. Hence, one moral conclusion cannot be said to be more reasonable than another. We might say that the relativist is a **cynical subjectivist**, someone who pushes subjectivism to its limit, believing that moral decisions are so subjective that deliberation is useless. We could imagine, however, someone who is a deliberate subjectivist. A **deliberate subjectivist** would be the person who believes that while there are no objective criteria for making moral judgments, that does not preclude moral judgments from being the products of conscious deliberation which is rational and impartial. For the deliberate subjectivist moral judgments are subjective but can be warranted.

We can think of these moral viewpoints, then, as being on a continuum with the dogmatist as the certain objectivist on one end and the relativist as the cynical subjectivist on the other. In the middle between them are the modest objectivist and the deliberating subjectivist. Dogmatism and relativism are not attractive stances in moral discourse and we have seen that they rest on a mistaken understanding of certainty; hence, the end points on this continuum are not very interesting moral viewpoints. Certain objectivism and cynical subjectivism do not accord with our ordinary moral sentiments and our moral discourse and they do not accord with our understanding of factual statements and warranted beliefs. We have already seen that our best thinking comes from the open dialogue—with ourselves and with others—and both dogmatism and relativism resist dialogue altogether. Fortunately, there are alternative moral stances.

Moral views, like Kant's and others, which fall on the continuum in the range of modest objectivism and deliberating subjectivism are potentially attractive moral views from the standpoint of rationality and the use of good reasoning skills. They allow for dialogue and even encourage it. They acknowledge the existence of factual statements about moral matters but do not claim or require absolute certainty. They encourage the gathering of a consensus among the members of the moral community. They allow that one moral judgment can be better or worse than another and suggest ways of determining the better and the worse. They are moral views which encourage moderation in moral matters.

Moderation in moral arguments means continuing the moral dialogue as long as possible, neither jumping to fisticuffs nor walking away, "agreeing to disagree." As we have said from the beginning, **the willingness to keep the dialogue open is the hallmark of the rational person**. In moral matters this is particularly important. Look, for example, at what happened to Socrates not long after the episode recorded in the dialogue you read. He and the people of Athens had a moral disagreement and, like Euthyphro, the Athenians got tired of continuing the moral dialogue and executed him. **The alternative to continuing the dialogue is usually harm to someone**. Even "agreeing to disagree" can be harmful because the disagreement is still there and can fester and become violent. It can also lead to the cynical point

◄─── **SUBJECTIVISM**   **OBJECTIVISM**───►

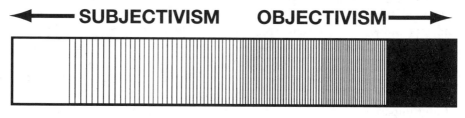

Relativist   **Deliberative Subjectivist**   **Modest Objectivist**   **Dogmatist**

While there is no hard and fast dividing line where one becomes clearly either a dogmatist or a relativist, the extreme forms of both are clear and shade toward more moderate views in the center of the continuum.

of view that moral disagreements are irrelevant and that nothing is ever worth fighting for, even verbally. While people are talking, they cannot be harming each other. (Note: Shouting and screaming at someone is *not* having a dialogue with someone.)

There must, of course, be more to morality than moral dialogue. Moral dialogues do not always end in consensus. People refuse to listen. Sometimes there is no time for dialogue. The baby is drowning and the house is on fire. And we did say in the previous chapter that not to act is to act! How do we know when to stop talking and to start acting? Where do we draw the line between tolerating what we think is a mistaken moral view and interfering in someone else's behavior to prevent her from doing something we think is immoral? Indeed, these are tough questions that we all have worried about– and should worry about.

There certainly are times when we must act, even against the will and moral beliefs of another. There are times when the dialogue must stop because to continue the dialogue would allow immoral behavior to continue and harm to be done. Making these decisions is not easy. It would be a relief to have a rule which we could plug into a situation to determine whether we should act, but such a rule would be most unusual. After all, no such rule exists for making decisions in nonmoral matters. This lack of a rule (or rules) in the nonmoral aspects of our lives does not stop us, however, from making decisions and taking action. We have factual statements about nonmoral matters and warranted beliefs and we use these to make rational decisions on which we then act, following the guidelines of rational decision making.

Let's consider an example to review decision making in the nonmoral sphere. You are about to board an airplane for a distant city. You believe, as you board, that you will arrive safely at your destination at the end of your flight. Surely this belief is warranted and your behavior based on that belief is justified. Are you absolutely certain that you and your plane will arrive safely? No, of course not. We all know there is a risk involved in flying and that a small, very small, percentage of air travel passengers do not arrive safely. No one, however, would think your choice of a means of travel unjustified, irrational, or foolish. Indeed, we look down on the John Maddens[3] of the world who refuse to fly as people who have "irrational" fears. The decision to fly is justified by the warranted belief that flying is a safe way to travel. Your behavior is based on good reasoning with probability.

The situation is analogous for moral reasoning. We can never be absolutely certain that our decisions are morally correct. We can be justified in taking moral action, however, on the same kinds of evidence we would use in nonmoral situations, using guidelines similar to the guidelines of ratio

---

[3]John Madden,, former pro-football coach and television football commentator, who refuses to travel by airplane.

nal decision making for nonmoral decisions. Just as in nonmoral decision making, there is always a certain amount of uncertainty and risk, but it is not irrational or immoral to proceed without absolute certainty if we have followed the guidelines.

Good moral reasoning, then, is like good reasoning about nonmoral matters. We have factual moral statements and warranted moral beliefs. We recognize that our moral actions are based on moral beliefs which are warranted but not absolutely certain and that acting is not without risk. The certainty that the dogmatist thinks she has does not characterize either our nonmoral or our moral decision making. This does not mean, however, that relativism is our only alternative. Both dogmatism and relativism get their credibility by claiming or by demanding, respectively, a kind of certainty that is not possible when reasoning about the world of our experience. Therefore, they have no place in our decision making.

The guidelines for moral decision making are similar to those for reasoning with probability:

1. We should proceed with toleration and moderation rather than haste or caprice, knowing that our moral community is large and diverse.

2. Our moral decisions should be the product of open dialogue—with ourselves and with others—since open dialogue is the best guarantee that our decisions will be the product of rational deliberation.

3. We should bring as large a store of background knowledge to the decision-making process as we can to avoid limited, uninformed judgments and possible future disappointment and regret.

4. In times of moral conflict and uncertainty we need to know what is important to us and for us. That means we must know which of our beliefs, especially our moral beliefs, are most entrenched and look to decisions which fit in better with those beliefs which are well entrenched.

5. As in all reasoning about experience, when we make a moral decision we are always at risk of being wrong. Consequently, we must always be testing our moral reasoning against future moral experiences and be ready to revise our background knowledge and our future decisions in light of those tests.

If our goal is to maintain and improve our relationships with those around us so that we have more friends and fewer enemies, to love and be loved, to have pleasant rather than unpleasant experiences, and to enjoy as much of our lives as we possibly can, then these guidelines of rational moral thinking increase the likelihood of successfully meeting those goals. No rule or guideline, however, guarantees success. **Good reasoning can and does make for better human relationships**. It takes effort but the rewards are great.

Exercises

13–1

1. Describe the deliberate subjectivist.

2. Describe the modest objectivist.

3. What are the differences between dogmatism and relativism?

4. What are the characteristics of a rational moral thinker?

5. Why are dogmatism and relativism not helpful positions to take in situations of moral disagreement?

13–II

1. We talk about making moral mistakes. How would a moral mistake be described by a dogmatist? A modest objectivist? A deliberate subjectivist? A relativist? Which account makes the most sense to you? Why?

2. Explain why this text is called _Thinking Socratically_.

3. Why is bumper-sticker morality potentially harmful?

13–III

1. Explain how someone can avoid relativism without being a dogmatist.

2. Why is it that violence begets violence? Give some examples from history and literature to support your position.

3. We live in a culturally diverse world. Students of this cultural diversity (anthropologists, for example) often believe that, given this diversity, relativism is the only possible moral stance. How would you explain to them that respect for other cultures does not mean that one must be a moral relativist?

chapter 14

Reason and Commitment

Introduction

Sometimes it is best to make a point, especially a moral point, by giving an example. As children we learn many of our moral beliefs and acquire much of our moral behavior from the examples of grown-ups whom we respect. We also learn from stories and literature. Even as adults we are still shaping the person we want to be, taking our cues from novels, biographies, newspapers, magazines, and even television sitcoms.

This final reading introduces the story of Pastor André Trocmé who, we think, exemplifies the highest standard of moral decision making and moral action of the sort we have been describing. Trocmé finds himself in a situation where dialogue is not possible and where inaction will allow harm to be done. He knows that violence begets violence but that he must take a stand against injustice–and he does. His commitment to what he believes is right leads others to commit themselves as well and, as a consequence, he and his fellow villagers of Le Chambon save hundreds of Jews from Nazi concentration camps.

While few of us can attain the moral heroism of Trocmé, his example can inspire us to raise our moral aspirations just as it enabled Philip Hallie, the author, to put aside his moral cynicism. We need not despair in moral matters. Although the moral need in the world seems overwhelming, our acts as individuals can be both noble and ennobling. Our behavior does make a difference. The question, is what kind of example will you set?

Prelude

PHILIP HALLIE

There was once an art critic, I have been told, who had a sure way of identifying ancient Maltese art objects: he found himself crying before them. John Keats had a similar reaction to excellence: the thought of his beloved Fanny Brawen, or of anything he associated with her, "goes through me like a spear," he said.

Of course, these are symptoms of an awareness of excellence. They are mere reactions, not rules that we ordinary people can use to separate excellent things from dross. But any doctor will tell you that symptoms are important, and just as pain can be a symptom of disease, painful joy can be a reliable reaction to excellence.

One afternoon I was reading some documents relating to Adolf Hitler's twelve-year empire. It was not the politics of these years that was at the center of my concern; it was the cruelty perpetrated in the death camps of Central Europe. For years I had been studying cruelty, the slow crushing and grinding of a human being by other human beings. I had studied the tortures white men inflicted upon native Indians and then upon blacks in the Americas, and now I was reading mainly about the torture experiments the Nazis conducted upon the bodies of small children in those death camps.

Across all these studies, the pattern of the strong crushing the weak kept repeating itself and repeating itself, so that when I was not bitterly angry, I was bored at the repetition of the patterns of persecution. When I was not desiring to be cruel with the cruel, I was a monster—like, perhaps, many others around me—who could look upon torture and death without a shudder, and who therefore looked upon life without a belief in its preciousness. My study of evil incarnate had become a prison whose bars were my bitterness toward the violent, and whose walls were my horrified indif-

From _Lest Innocent Blood Be Shed_

ference to slow murder. Between the bars and the walls I revolved like a madman. Reading about the damned I was damned myself, as damned as the murderers, and as damned as their victims. Somehow over the years I had dug myself into Hell, and I had forgotten redemption, had forgotten the possibility of escape.

On this particular day, I was reading in an anthology of documents from the Holocaust, and I came across a short article about a little village in the mountains of southern France. As usual, I was reading the pages with an effort at objectivity; I was trying to sort out the forms and elements of cruelty and of resistance to it in much the same way a veterinarian might sort out ill from healthy cattle. After all, I was doing this work not to torture myself but to understand the indignity and the dignity of man.

About halfway down the third page of the account of this village, I was annoyed by a strange sensation on my cheeks. The story was so simple and so factual that I had found it easy to concentrate upon *it*, not upon my own feelings. And so, still following the story, and thinking about how neatly some of it fit into the old patterns of persecution, I reached up to my cheek to wipe away a bit of dust, and I felt tears upon my fingertips. Not one or two drops; my whole cheek was wet.

"Oh," my sentinel mind told me, "you are losing your grasp on things again. Instead of learning about cruelty, you are becoming one more of its victims. You are doing it again." I was disgusted with myself for daring to intrude.

And so I closed the book and left my college office. When I came home, my operatic Italian wife and my turbulent children, as they have never failed to do, distracted me noisily. I hardly felt the spear that had gone through me. But that night when I lay on my back in bed with my eyes closed, I saw more clearly than ever the images that had made me weep. I saw the two clumsy khaki-colored buses of the Vichy French police pull into the village square. I saw the police captain facing the pastor of the village and warning him that if he did not give up the names of the Jews they had been sheltering in the village, he and his fellow pastor, as well as the families who had been caring for the Jews, would be arrested. I saw the pastor refuse to give up these people who had been strangers in his village, even at the risk of his own destruction.

Then I saw the only Jew the police could find, sitting in an otherwise empty bus. I saw a thirteen-year-old boy, the son of the pastor, pass a piece of his precious chocolate through the window to the prisoner, while twenty gendarmes who were guarding the lone prisoner watched. And then I saw the villagers passing their little gifts through the window until there were gifts all around him—most of them food in those hungry days during the German occupation of France.

Lying there in bed, I began to weep again. I thought, Why run away from what is excellent simply because it goes through you like a spear? Lying there, I knew that always a certain region of my mind contained an awareness of men and women in bloody white coats breaking and rebreaking the bones of six- or seven- or eight-year-old Jewish children in order, the Nazis said, to study the processes of natural healing in young bodies. All of this I knew. But why not know joy? Why not leave root room for comfort? Why add myself to the millions of victims? Why must life be for me that vision of those children lying there with their children's eyes looking up at the adults who were breaking a leg for the second time, a rib cage for the third time? Something had happened, had happened for years in that mountain village. Why should I be afraid of it?

To the dismay of my wife, I left the bed unable to say a word, dressed, crossed the dark campus on a starless night, and read again those few pages on the village of Le Chambon-sur-Lignon. And to my surprise, again the spear, again the tears, again the frantic, painful pleasure that spills into the mind when a deep, deep need is being satisfied, or when a deep wound is starting to heal.

That night, I decided to try to understand all this. I decided to understand it so that I could hold it more firmly than one can hold a tear, or an image. Since I was a student and a teacher of ethics, I would use what I had learned about man's standards of ethical excellence to help me understand the blessing—at least for me—of Le Chambon. Those involuntary tears had been an expression of moral praise, praise pressed out of my whole personality like the juice of a grape. And part of that personality had been the ideas of goodness and of evil that I had been learning and teaching for decades.

But I was not going to make Le Chambon an "example" of goodness or moral nobility; I was not going to use this story to explain some abstract idea of ethics. Ends are more valuable than means; understanding that story was my end, my goal, and I was going to use the words of philosophical ethics only as a means for achieving this goal. Or, to be more accurate, I was going to use the words of ethics to help me understand my deeply felt ethical praise for the deeds of the people of Le Chambon.

A year later, Pastor Édouard Theis was holding my arm to keep from slipping on an icy road in Le Chambon. The winter wind of the plateau, _la burle_, was blowing in its strange way: instead of pushing the snow away from us, off the plateau on which Le Chambon stands, it whirled the snow low and close around our feet. It hardly moved the tall pines on both sides of the road. It caught in its whorls the low, long-fingered evergreen bushes on the sides of the road. The bushes thrashed their green fingers around us, pointing in a thousand directions and in no direction at all. The people of the plateau used the long twigs to make their brooms in the old days, and so instead of calling the bushes by their proper names, *les genêts*, they called them *les balais* (brooms).

Night was almost at its darkest. The Protestant pastor and I were coming back from a day of interviews with some of the people of Le Chambon. Theis was miserable with influenza and still heavy with the sadness, two years old, of having lost his wife, Mildred. Everything—the wind, the slippery roads, the wild fingers of the broom—everything expressed loss, pointless loss, a whirling in deepening darkness. "Oh," Pastor Theis had said during one of our interviews, "I have been *unstable* since the death of Mildred Theis." And his heavy head, his big, curved nose that descended to a point, his wide shoulders—all seemed to be collapsing. This was the man who had helped another pastor, André Trocmé, make the village of Le Chambon one of the main forces in France for saving the lives of Jewish refugees during the four years of the Nazi occupation of France. In the last months of those years, when he was on the Gestapo's black list, he had guided refugees through the mountains of eastern France, through the French police and the German troops to the border of Switzerland and safety.

Though he reached for me to keep from falling on those icy mountain roads, he was helping me to keep from slipping as we walked together slowly. I had seen pictures of him in his thirties: the "rock of Le Chambon," the massive presence with a full, almost round face and big, heavy shoulders. But now Theis was seventy-five years old, and I felt under his coat (actually two thin, ragged raincoats) a thin, trembling man.

My God, I thought as we walked through *la burle*, we're losing everything. It's as if the broom were sweeping everything away, or inward and downward into darkness. At our last interview we had been talking with Madame Marion and her daughter, two of the strong women of Le Chambon during the Occupation. The precise, sixty-year-old daughter had told me her version of Theis's return to Le Chambon from a detention camp. She told me that when Theis and the other leader of Le Chambon stepped off the train, there were the villagers, waiting, with an open path through them. There was absolute silence at the railroad station. Not a word was said; there was not even a cry from a child and no shuffling of feet, she said. She told me that the two returning leaders had walked through the open path, and the villagers had silently closed behind them and followed them away from the station.

Theis, when he heard this, was surprised. "I remember no silence. Perhaps if Trocmé were here, he would remember it," he said.

"Why," the younger Marion insisted in her quick, factual way, "Monsieur Theis, they were silent, and silent for a very good reason. The Gestapo was there, and so were some collaborators from Vichy. They were looking for an excuse to arrest you again. Didn't you notice?"

"Oh, perhaps I did notice," Theis murmured, "and I have forgotten. But I am not sure. I am not sure at all. And André Trocmé is dead." The story of Le Chambon was being swept out of human memory.

The Baal Shem-Tov, the founder of Hasidism, the Jewish movement that finds God in good and evil—in everything—once said, "In remembrance resides the secret of redemption." This saying appears at the top of a citation from the state of Israel, a citation that attests to the fact that André Trocmé, the spiritual leader of the village of Le Chambon, "at peril of his life, saved Jews during the epoch of extermination." This citation accompanied the Medal of Righteousness that Israel awarded to Trocmé. If the secret of redemption lies in remembering, it is lost in forgetting. After more than thirty years, the story of Le Chambon lay in less than a dozen little-known pages, most of them rather vague and inaccurate. The whole story could be found only in the memories of a few people who were now old and sick.

Walking with Pastor Theis that evening in January of 1976, I was afraid that I did not have the gifts needed to uncover the "secret of redemption" that lies in the story of how Trocmé and the people of Le Chambon saved human lives at the peril of their own. I knew that I could not tell the story as thoroughly as a careful historian might tell it; I was neither trained nor inclined to report every detail I could find. Nor was I religious enough to be certain of exactly what the Baal Shem-Tov meant by "redemption." But I believed that here in Le Chambon goodness had happened, and I had come to this village on a high plateau in southern France in order to understand that goodness face-to-face.

Having lived the life I have, I have never doubted that evil, in the sense of grievous harm doing, is possible. It has happened, and it has happened to me. In New Lenox, Illinois, when I was seven years old, two blond, older boys smashed and bloodied my face because I was a Jew. As an artilleryman in World War II, I passed the bodies of human beings lying beside the road, chopped by our artillery into foot-long chunks, like fresh meat in a butcher shop. For more than six months I was in a gun crew that shot 155-millimeter shells into German troops, and since that time there has been a high-pitched humming in my head—every moment of my waking life—to remind me that I have killed human beings. If only such things were possible, then life was too heavy a burden for me. The lies I would have to tell my children in order to raise them in hope—which children need the way plants need sunlight—would make the burden unbearable.

I am a student and a teacher of good and evil, but for me ethics, like the rest of philosophy, is not a scientific, impersonal matter. It is by and about persons, much as it was for Socrates. Being personal, it must not be ashamed to express personal passions, the way a strict scientist might be ashamed to express them in a laboratory report. My own passion was a yearning for realistic hope. I wanted to believe that the examined life was more precious than this Hell I had dug for myself in studying evil.

But it was not easy to find out what had happened in this village. From the point of view of the history of nations, something very small had happened here. The story of Le Chambon lacked the glamour, the wingspread of other wartime events. Victories and defeats of nations are written large in men's minds because the lives and fortunes of so many human beings depend upon them. World War II, between the Axis and the Allies, was a public phenomenon; military, journalistic, and governmental reports made it abundantly available to the public. It impressed itself powerfully and deeply upon the minds of mankind, both during and after the war. The metaphors that describe it have a flamboyant cast: the war itself was a "world war," with many "heroes"; there were "theaters of war," and soldiers who participated in major "campaigns" received "battle stars."

No such language applies to what happened in Le Chambon. In fact, words like "war" are inappropriate to describe it, and so are words like "theater." While the story of Le Chambon was unfolding, it was being recorded nowhere. What was happening was clandestine because the people of Le Chambon had no military power comparable to that of the Nazis occupying France, or comparable to that of the Vichy government of France, which was collaborating with the Nazi conquerors. If they had tried to confront their opponents publicly, there would have been no contest, only immediate and total defeat. Secrecy, not military power, was their weapon.

The struggle in Le Chambon began and ended in the privacy of people's homes. Decisions that were turning points in that struggle took place in kitchens, and not with male leaders as the only decision-makers, but often with women centrally involved. A kitchen is a private, intimate place; in it there are no uniforms, no buttons or badges symbolizing public duty or public support. In the kitchen of a modest home only a few people are involved. In Le Chambon only the lives of a few thousand people were changed, compared to the scores of millions of human lives directly affected by the larger events of World War II.

The "kitchen struggle" of Le Chambon resembles rather closely a certain kind of conflict that grew more and more widespread as the years of the Occupation passed. Guerrilla action, clandestine, violent resistance to the German occupants, was as much a part of the history of that Occupation as the story of that little commune. Secrecy was as vital to guerrilla warfare as it was to the resistance of the people of Le Chambon, and so was a minimum of permanent records. In both cases military weakness dictated that there be few records and much secrecy.

But the kitchen struggles differed greatly from the bush battles (the *Maquis*, the name given to the wing of the armed resistance which had no direct connections with de Gaulle's Secret Army, refers to *le maquis*, the low, prickly bushes that grow on dry, hilly land). The guerrillas were fighting for the liberation of their country. Some of them received their orders from de Gaulle's exiled French government (Free France), and others owed their allegiance to the Soviet Union; still others had no particular political allegiance, but they were all parts of military units. Especially in time of war such units are primarily concerned with achieving by violent means a victory over the enemies of those units. Their primary duty is not to save lives but to save the life of some public entity; and especially in time of war they cherish heroism—living and dying gloriously for a public cause—more than they cherish compassion. The consciences of individuals in military units tend to be in lock-step with the self-interest of the units. In fact, for the bush warriors as for the uniformed warriors, public duty took precedence over personal conscience.

But the people of Le Chambon whom Pastor André Trocmé led into a quiet struggle against Vichy and the Nazis were not fighting for the liberation of their country or their village. They felt little loyalty to governments. Their actions did not serve the self-interest of the little commune of Le Chambon-sur-Lignon in the department of Haute-Loire, southern France. On the contrary, those actions flew in the face of that self-interest: by resisting a power far greater than their own they put their village in grave danger of massacre, especially in the last two years of the Occupation, when the Germans were growing desperate. Under the guidance of a spiritual leader they were trying to act in accord with their consciences in the very middle of a bloody, hate-filled war.

And what this meant for them was nonviolence. Following their consciences meant refusing to hate or kill any human being. And in this lies their deepest difference from the other aspects of World War II. Human life was too precious to them to be taken for any reason, glorious and vast though that reason might be. Their consciences told them to save as many lives as they could, even if doing this meant endangering the lives of all the villagers; and they obeyed their consciences.

But acts of conscience are not important news, especially while a war is going on. Only actions directly related to the national self-interest receive a measure of fame then. And this is why the Partisan Sharpshooters of the left and the Secret Army of General Charles de Gaulle were nationally though secretly revered during the Occupation, and were praised to the skies afterward. This is also why the armed resistance produced heroes like General de Gaulle himself, and the passionately beloved coordinator of the armed French Resistance, Jean Moulin.

There are no such nationally known names in the story of Le Chambon. When France was liberated, there were no triumphal marches for André Trocmé and his villagers through the streets of Paris or Marseilles. And this was as it should have been: they had not contributed directly to saving the life of the French nation. They were not so much French patriots as they were conscientious human beings.

In fact, as soon as the European war ended, the commune of Le Chambon went into a sharp decline. Almost all of those who had come to her for help left when the trouble ceased. The international, pacifist school that Trocmé and Theis had founded there before the war, the school that had sheltered so many refugees during the first four years of the decade, almost perished for lack of money and interest. Soon after the liberation of France, Trocmé had to go to America, hat in hand, in his only decent suit and his only pair of leather shoes, in hopes of finding money and workers to keep the school—and Le Chambon—alive. And of course what he found in America was complete ignorance of what his Chambonnais had done. There are many friends for the rescuers of nations, but there do not seem to be many sympathizers for the rescuers of a few thousand desperate human beings.

It is plain that the story of the struggle of Le Chambon is of no special political or military interest. But it is of ethical interest. The word *ethics* can be traced to the Greek word for character, an individual person's way of feeling, thinking, and acting. Ethics is concerned with praising some sorts of character and blaming other sorts. In that region of ethics concerned with matters of life and death (as against, for example, sexual or professional conduct), a person who destroys human life is blamed for doing this unless that destruction can be excused or justified in some way; and in life-and-death ethics a person who avoids or prevents the destruction of human life is praised for doing this unless his deed can be shown to be destructive of human life. In life-and-death ethics the person we blame is often called "evil," and the person we praise is often called "good," though we may use such milder terms of praise and blame as "bad" and "decent."

It is this important way of judging human character that helps us to understand what happened in Le Chambon in terms close to the story itself. In this village the characters of individuals were of immense importance, and most of these individuals were dedicated to protecting human lives instead of destroying them. It is as persons rather than as parts of some public entity that we shall find most of them praiseworthy according to a life-and-death ethic. In their conflict with those bent on diminishing or destroying human lives lies the story of Le Chambon.

What had brought me to this ice-covered village high in the mountains of France more than thirty years after the Liberation was the need to understand the story that connected these two kinds of individuals with each other and with their time. I needed this understanding in order to redeem myself—and possibly others—from the coercion of despair.

During the first few moments after Theis and I left the boardinghouse of the Marions, we walked separately through the snowy mountain wind. Two or three times Theis staggered and almost fell. Even I, with my younger reflexes, slipped once or twice. But when he reached out and intertwined his right arm with my left, suddenly the warmth of his thin body and the firmness of our intertwined arms created a new being moving upon four firm legs. Now we were stable, even though the icy road was still there, and even though the broom were still whirling their long evergreen fingers. The world was still cold, confusing, and dangerous. But we were close to each other, parts of a new whole, and we felt suddenly surefooted.

The day before this walk we had been in the home of the Chazots, who had kept a Jewish family in their home for most of the four years of the Occupation, even though their house is on a road that was much frequented by Vichy and German troops. During our conversation, Theis had said suddenly, *"Oh! Que c'est difficile d'être seul!"* At that moment his phrase, "Ah, but it is hard to be alone!" had only the pathos of bereavement in it: Mildred Theis was dead. But now, when I have thought long about our walk and have learned the story of Le Chambon, the phrase means, "Ah, but it is a joy to be together, always joyously good!"

Reflections on the Reading:

1. Why is Trocmé a hero?

2. Why is it important to have moral heroes?

3. Is the world a gloomy and evil place as Hallie once thought? What is your worldview here?

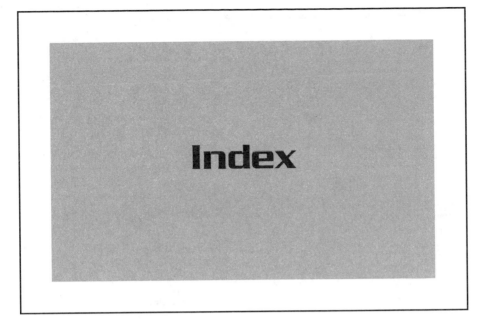

Index